Cognitive Behavioral Therapy for the Busy Child Psychiatrist and Other Mental Health Professionals

Cognitive Behavioral Therapy for the Busy Child Psychiatrist and Other Mental Health Professionals

RUBRICS AND RUDIMENTS

Robert D. Friedberg, Angela A. Gorman, Laura Hollar Wilt, Adam Biuckians, and Michael Murray

Illustrated by Jolene H. Garcia

Routledge
Taylor & Francis Group
New York   London

Routledge
Taylor & Francis Group
270 Madison Avenue
New York, NY 10016

Routledge
Taylor & Francis Group
27 Church Road
Hove, East Sussex BN3 2FA

© 2011 by Taylor and Francis Group, LLC
Routledge is an imprint of Taylor & Francis Group, an Informa business

Printed in the United States of America on acid-free paper
10 9 8 7 6 5 4 3 2 1

International Standard Book Number: 978-0-415-99127-8 (Hardback)

Library of Congress Cataloging-in-Publication Data

Cognitive behavioral therapy for the busy child psychiatrist and other mental health professionals : rubrics and rudiments / authored by Robert D. Friedberg ... [et al.] ; illustrations by Jolene H. Garcia.
    p. cm.
    Summary: "Teaching Child Psychiatrists Cognitive Behavioral Therapy is an essential resource for clinical child psychologists, psychiatrists, psychotherapists, and mental health professionals. Since 2001, psychiatry residency programs have required resident competency in five specific psychotherapies, including cognitive-behavioral therapy. This unique text is a guidebook for instructors and outlines fundamental principles, while offering creative applications of techniques to ensure that residency training programs are better equipped to train their staff"-- Provided by publisher.
    Includes bibliographical references and index.
    ISBN 978-0-415-99127-8 (hardback)
    1. Cognitive therapy for children. 2. Cognitive therapy for teenagers. 3. Child psychotherapy. 4. Adolescent psychotherapy. I. Friedberg, Robert D., 1955- II. Title.

RJ505.C63C648 2011
618.92'89142--dc22
                                               2010043260

Visit the Taylor & Francis Web site at
http://www.taylorandfrancis.com

and the Routledge Web site at
http://www.routledgementalhealth.com

Contents

Acknowledgments

As always, the love and inspiration of my life, Barbara, deserves opening credit for putting up with my moods, self-indulgences, and, at times, self-absorption during the completion of this project. My daughter, youth culture consultant extraordinaire and communications whiz, Rebecca, gets a heartfelt thank you and appreciation for her infectious sense of humor. I also appreciate the contributions of my parents, Mort and Rachelle Friedberg, and especially my grandparents Rose and Frank Derewitz who taught me the dual ethos of persistence and generosity. Most notably, I am gifted with the best in-laws imaginable, Harry and Helen Fabe. Their consistent support, interest, encouragement, and communication that I was a source of pride for them meant a tremendous amount and served as motivation to keep writing. Over the course of my career, I have been fortunate to sit at the knees of exceptional mentors and colleagues including Christine A. Padesky, Raymond A. Fidaleo, Aaron T. Beck, Judith S. Beck, Jessica McClure, Donald J. Viglione, Jr., Alan Kaufman, Susan Jasin, Mark Sherman, Julian Meltzoff, James Shenk, James Dobbins, Janeece Warfield, Victor McCarley, Brenda Mobley and Eric Minturn. To my coauthors, I say it has been a long ride but I am proud of the final product and hope they find satisfaction in their contributions. Finally, to the many patients I have had the pleasure to care for at the Cognitive Behavioral Clinic for Children and Adolescents at Penn State Milton S. Hershey Medical Center, thank you for entrusting your care to me.

Robert D. Friedberg

I would like to thank my husband Ben, and my son Mateo, for being my greatest loves and sources of support, for they make everything possible. A very special thanks goes to Bob Friedberg, my coauthor, for believing in me, always standing by me, and reminding me that handing out muffins is not necessary. I am forever grateful to my parents, José and Sylvia Alvarado, and my mother-in-law, Jean Rouleau, for their undying support, dedication, and wisdom. Also, a thank you goes out to my "sisters" Maria Coletta (and her family) and Claudia

Villarreal, for their love throughout the years and for showing me a world of compassion and loyalty. I appreciate my other coauthors for their collaboration and making this adventure a great one. Last, and important, thank you to all the youth and families I serve—I am fortunate to have the honor and pleasure of helping you.

Angela A. Gorman

I owe a debt of gratitude to the people who have contributed to this book in many ways. I want to thank my colleagues, R. Friedberg, C. Newman, M. Rapp, and J. Hegarty for their efforts to help me develop into the clinician I am. I want to thank my family for their loving support of my work, and my patients for providing the motivation and inspiration to undertake this task.

Laura Hollar-Wilt

I would like to thank my wife, April, for her support and my parents for all that they have done for me.

Adam Biuckians

Thanks to all of my colleagues and the trainees from whom I have learned so much over the years. And, as always, to Angie whose love and support make everything else possible.

Michael J. Murray

Thank you to my family for their love, support, and consistent example of faith, especially to my husband for his undying patience and continued encouragement to follow my calling. Thank you to my colleagues and friends for their humor and inspiration. I am grateful to my teachers and mentors for their knowledge and advice. Thank you to Robert Friedberg for inviting me along. And to my patients and their families, thank you for the honor of learning from you and the joy of caring for you.

Jolene Hillwig Garcia

Authors

Robert D. Friedberg, PhD, ABPP, is Associate Professor, Director of the Cognitive Behavioral Therapy Clinic for Children and Adolescents, and Director of Postdoctoral Fellowship Programs in Psychology in the Department of Psychiatry at the Penn State Milton S. Hershey Medical Center and College of Medicine. A clinical psychologist, Dr. Friedberg is the author of six other books and numerous scholarly publications. He has presented many national and international workshops on cognitive therapy with children. He is also on the training faculty of the Beck Institute for Cognitive Therapy and Research where he supervises extramural trainees. Dr. Friedberg is a board certified diplomate in cognitive behavioral therapy and a Founding Fellow of the Academy of Cognitive Therapy.

Angela A. Gorman, PhD, is a clinical psychologist and an Assistant Professor in the Department of Psychiatry at the Penn State Milton S. Hershey Medical Center and College of Medicine. She is also the Program Director of the Child and Adolescent Psychiatric Inpatient Unit at the Pennsylvania Psychiatric Institute (PPI), where she creates and directs cognitive behavioral therapy (CBT)–based programming for hospitalized youth. Additionally, she maintains an outpatient caseload at PPI, and teaches and supervises psychiatric residents and fellows, psychology students, and medical students. Her areas of child/adolescent-focused clinical and research interests include multiculturally sensitive models of CBT for inpatient youth, posttraumatic stress disorder (PTSD), attention deficit hyperactivity disorder (ADHD), and anxiety disorders.

Laura Hollar Wilt, MD, is an Assistant Professor of child and adolescent psychiatry at Penn State. She completed her residency and fellowship at Penn State as well as extensive extramural instruction with the Beck Institute. Dr. Hollar-Wilt's research and clinical interests include cognitive treatments in infant psychiatry and postpartum mental health, as well as CBT with child and adolescent patients. She also works as a consultation psychiatrist at the Penn State Milton S. Hershey Medical Center.

Adam Biuckians, MD, did his undergraduate work at Pennsylvania State University as part of an accelerated 6-year premedical–medical program in conjunction with Thomas Jefferson University. He graduated from Jefferson in 2003, and completed his adult psychiatry residency and child fellowship at the Penn State Milton S. Hershey Medical Center. Dr. Buickians has been in full-time practice in Lancaster County, in a busy hospital clinic setting since 2008. He lives in Lancaster, Pennsylvania, with his wife and three children.

Michael J. Murray, MD, is the Director of the Division of Autism Services at the Penn State College of Medicine. In this role, he educates medical students, psychiatry residents, child psychiatry fellows, and other medical professionals about the clinical aspects of autism spectrum disorders. Dr. Murray's clinical research addresses the social skills deficits experienced by individuals on the autism spectrum.

Jolene Hillwig Garcia, MD, completed her psychiatric residency training in the Department of Psychiatry at the Penn State Milton S. Hershey Medical Center and College of Medicine, and has completed a fellowship in child and adolescent psychiatry. She received her MD from Penn State University and a BS in biology and BA in art–commercial design from Lycoming College (Pennsylvania). Dr. Garcia has been involved in scholarly research and publications as well as professional presentations on topics of interest in child and adolescent psychiatry. In addition, she continues her work in graphics and fine art.

One

Introduction
The Whys and Wherefores of This Book

Cognitive behavioral psychotherapy (CBP) approaches with youth is steadily gaining empirical ground, clinical recognition, and widespread use (Brent & Birmaher, 2002; Graham, 2005; Kazdin & Weisz, 2003; Kendall, 2006; March, 2009). Cognitive behavioral spectrum approaches for depression (Brent & Birmaher, 2002; Brent et al., 1997, 2008; Treatment for Adolescents with Depression Study [TADS] Team, 2003, 2004, 2005, 2007; Weisz, Southam-Gerow, Gordis, & Connor-Smith, 2003), anxiety (Flannery-Schroeder & Kendall, 2000; Kendall et al., 1992, 1997; Kendall, Aschenbrand, & Hudson, 2003), obsessive-compulsive disorder (March & Franklin, 2006; March & Mulle, 1998; Piacentini, March, & Franklin, 2006; Pediatric OCD Treatment Study [POTS] Team, 2004), posttraumatic stress disorder (PTSD) (Cohen, Deblinger, Mannarino, & Steer, 2004), anger management (Lochman & Wells, 2002a, 2002b), and pervasive developmental disorders (Attwood, 2004; Myles, 2003) demonstrate empirical support. Finally, psychiatry has embraced CBP. In fact, March (2009) predicted that "psychiatry will move to a unified cognitive-behavioral intervention model that is housed within neurosciences medicine" (p. 174).

CBP includes social learning theory, classical conditioning, and operant conditioning paradigms (Hart & Morgan, 1993). Additionally, CBP blends various techniques into a coherent whole. There is quite a wide spectrum of CBP-based approaches to childhood problems. Indeed, many CBP techniques exist. Unfortunately, without an organizing theory and paradigm, the disparate tools float in a disembodied manner. This haunting phenomenon caused several authors (Ronen, 1997; Shirk, 1999) to lament the lack of theoretical coherence in child psychotherapy. Kendall, Chu, Gifford, Hayes, and Nauta (1998) argued that CBT with children is guided by its theoretical rationale rather than any specific technique. Accordingly, we adopt a theoretical focus point in this book. More specifically, Aaron T. Beck's cognitive therapy (CT) forms the theoretical core to the many different interventions outlined in this book. Due to the flexibility and theoretical robustness of Beck's CT, it has been referred to as *the* integrative psychotherapy (Alford & Beck, 1997).

While the empirical findings produced by the research on cognitive behavioral therapy with children are meritorious and exciting, community practitioners too commonly neglect them. The difficulty translating protocols to practice is problematic and is currently receiving a great deal of attention (Aarons, 2004; Addis, 2002; Chorpita, 2003; Flannery-Schroeder, 2005; Garland, Hurlburt, & Hawley, 2006; Kendall, 1998; Weisz, 2004; Weisz, Doss, & Hawley, 2005; Weisz & Jensen, 2001; Weisz, Jensen-Doss, & Hawley, 2006). The empirical literature base that supports cognitive behavioral therapy with children is methodologically rigorous and yields significant efficacy results. These promising results led to calls for empirically supported or at least empirically informed practice. However, many practitioners feel left out and alienated by this movement (Southam-Gerow, 2004; Weisz, 2004). They remain skeptical of translating research protocols to clinical practice. Indeed, efforts at disseminating effective treatment to the community have been well intentioned but largely unsuccessful (Addis, 2002; Carroll & Nauro, 2002; Chambless & Ollendick, 2001).

Indeed, perhaps researchers and clinicians are concerned with different questions (Weisz, 2004). In general, academic researchers are concerned with randomization, experimental design, grant funding, large numbers of patients, between group variance, and within group variance. On the other hand, clinicians represent local practitioner scientists who are doing a series of single case studies ($n = 1$) on a daily basis. They consume research but are primarily concerned with issues of direct patient care, patient satisfaction/attrition, time and cost efficiency, and reimbursement. Clinicians are often under burdensome productivity demands and are deluged by bureaucratic requirements, forms, and paperwork (Southam-Gerow, 2004; Weisz, 2004).

This text is tailored to helping real-world cognitive behavioral therapists meet their goals with a variety of patients. The sad reality suggests that few psychiatric practitioners feel competently equipped to deliver innovative cognitive behavioral approaches. Put quite simply, the circumstance is like developing a cancer treatment that few oncologists apply. Thus, the treatments need to be simply explained, engagingly presented, and effectively disseminated so child psychiatrists and other mental health clinicians can feel confident using them with children.

BREAKING THINGS DOWN TO PRACTICE ELEMENTS: MODULAR CBP

My (RDF) interest in teaching and helping others probably began when I was a boy in New Jersey living above my grandparents in a duplex. My grandmother, Rose, who had to leave school in the sixth grade to care for her brothers and sisters, would encourage me to teach her what I knew. She wanted to learn everything from chemistry (e.g., "H2O means water, Nana") to playing Scrabble and trying to ride a bike. When preparing her lessons, I tried to break things into simple and entertaining forms. I came to recognize that understanding and change propelled through learning is best realized through interactive dialogue. Consequently, the book provides complex information in a highly interactive format.

Most professionals who are familiar with cognitive behavioral therapy know about a manual-based approach to psychotherapy. Manuals are in fashion in randomized clinical trials where treatment efficacy is studied. Manuals specify the precise content and operationalize the procedures. Additionally, most manuals outline a specific sequence to the procedures and interventions. In randomized clinical trials, manuals often include adherence checks that ensure the interventions are properly employed. Finally, most manuals include a discrete and limited number of sessions.

Academic and clinical cognitive behavioral therapists generally agree that manuals are starting points rather than end points, should be flexibly applied and embedded within a case conceptualization (Persons, 1989, 2008). Additionally, it is incumbent on clinicians to breathe life into a manual by creatively adapting the procedures to the individual child (Kendall et al., 1998). This text partners with clinicians to deliver lively cognitive behavioral therapy.

Like many other recent CBP texts (Chorpita, 2006; Friedberg, McClure, & Garcia, 2009), this book adopts a modular approach

to treatment. A modular approach groups the many CBP techniques into meaningful interrelated conceptual categories such
as psychoeducation, self-monitoring, behavioral techniques,
cognitive restructuring, rational analysis, and experiment/
exposure procedures. For example, psychoeducation contains
instructional material that orients patients to CBP, teaches
them about their diagnosis/disorder, and provides self-help
resources. Self-monitoring provides a baseline assessment and
points the way toward self-directed change. Behavioral procedures focus on modifying the point-at-able actions as well as
their antecedents and consequences. Cognitive restructuring
involves self-talk intervention, which alter the content of maladaptive cognitions. Rational analysis is characterized by a set
of sophisticated logical reasoning techniques targeting the process or way children form conclusions. Experiments and exposures are based on experiential learning and encourage children
to put their acquired skills to use in real-life contexts.

The chapters are sequenced in the same order they should
be applied. Treatment begins with case conceptualization.
Second, you need to mindfully adopt a therapeutic stance
that boosts productive outcomes. Self-monitoring baseline
and assessment lights the way toward your desired goals.
Then, you orient the patient to the approach via psychoeducation and typically begin with simple behavioral techniques.
Interventions then progress from the cognitive intervention
pods to the experiments and exposure procedures.

Modules make use of practice elements (Chorpita, Daleiden,
& Weisz, 2005a). Chorpita et al. noted that practice elements
are identified by a particular content and different elements
may be sequentially or simultaneously administered. In this
scheme, a practice element can be used in a single session or in
repeated sessions.

A modular approach to cognitive behavioral therapy seems
to be nice bridge between manuals and typical care. Modular
CBT distills discrete techniques from the manuals and orga-
nizes these sundry techniques into conceptual categories (e.g.,
modules) based on shared elements (Chorpita, Daleiden, &
Weisz, 2005a; Curry & Wells, 2005; Rogers, Reinecke, & Curry,
2005). Chorpita, Daleiden, and Weisz (2005b) defined *modularity* as referring to "breaking complex activities into simpler parts that function independently" (p. 142). In a modular
approach, categories are conceptually related to one another
and connected by a shared theoretical rationale.

The title of this book, *Cognitive Behavioral Therapy for the Busy Child Psychiatrist and Other Mental Health Professionals: Rubrics and Rudiments*, is purposefully telling. In the following chapters CBP is broken down into its simplest practice-friendly elements. Care is taken to make the material clear, comprehensible, and engaging. Between chapters the material is presented sequentially beginning with case conceptualization and ending with experiments and exposure. Chapters 2 through 4 place the various procedures (Chapters 5 through 10) in context. Case conceptualization leads off emphasizing the pivotal role case formulation plays in treatment and delivery. Chapters on therapeutic stance and session structure teach you how to create productive ambient conditions for various interventions. Chapters 5 through 10 are stocked with both theoretical background information and clinical guidelines that shepherd you through psychoeducation, self-monitoring, behavioral techniques, cognitive restructuring, rational analysis, and experiments/exposure procedures. Chapter 11 applies CBP to medication checks. Your own performance worries are discussed in Chapter 12 and various techniques for managing anxiety are suggested.

Each chapter from Chapters 2 to 12 is separated into rudiments and rubrics. *Rudiment* is referenced as a first principle, element, or fundamental (*Webster's Ninth New Collegiate Dictionary*, 1991). *Rubric* is traditionally defined as "an established custom or procedure" (*Webster's Ninth New Collegiate Dictionary*, 1991). Accordingly, the rudiments or theoretical rationales of each chapter are presented initially to set the stage for the rubrics or procedural guidelines. After the basic theory is introduced, you learn the procedural guidelines for intervening.

WHAT IT TAKES TO BE A COMPETENT CBP THERAPIST

A certain aim for this text is to propel you toward becoming a more competent cognitive behavioral psychotherapist with children, adolescents, and their families. Sudak, Beck, and Wright (2003) identified crucial components central to obtaining competency in CBP including case formulation, developing collaborative therapeutic alliances, maintaining session structure, monitoring progress, identifying thoughts and feelings, using cognitive behavioral techniques as well as strengthening treatment generalization and relapse prevention.

Competence includes the acquisition and application of knowledge techniques, and clinical acumen coupled with a contextual understanding of people (Barber, Sharpless, Klosterman, & McCarthy, 2007). Barber et al. (2007) explained that "nested within the contextual nature of competence is an appreciation and comfort with issues of diversity at the surface (e.g., diversity of gender, ethnicity, or psychopathology) as well as deeper senses of the term (e.g., diversity of values or knowledge)" (p. 494).

A former colleague at Wright State University School of Professional Psychology (WSU SOPP), Dr. James Dobbins, taught me (RDF) that people's context is vitally important to understanding and proper intervention. Context shapes people's specific beliefs, feelings, and actions as well as their core worldviews, schemata, rules for living, and basic philosophies. Whenever you read a journal article or textbook, hear a lecture, view an educational video, and receive supervision, be mindful of the person's context. It will add valuable perspective.

Freeman (1990) addressed competency in CBT by distinguishing between technicians, magicians, and clinicians. Technicians rely on tools in a kit and have minimal interest in underlying theories or empirical findings. Technicians are similar to the cartoon character, Felix the cat, who relies on his wonderful bag of tricks. Magicians, on the other hand, are not keen about skill training and attribute therapeutic change to the personal qualities of the therapist. Clinicians integrate theory, research, and specific clinical skill training into their development. A good cognitive behavioral therapist is a clinician! Therefore, while we provide many rubrics, we are careful to embed the techniques in a theoretical understanding, cultural context, and empirical basis.

Learning CBP with children and adolescents requires declarative, procedural, and self-reflective knowledge (Bennett-Levy, 2006; Binder, 1999). Declarative knowledge involves the facts associated with theories, empirical findings, and technical procedures associated with CBP. Declarative knowledge also includes knowledge about how people work and operate in the world. Bennett-Levy (2006) refers to this as declarative interpersonal knowledge. This information helps you to predict and manage children's, adolescents', and families' interpersonal reactions to treatment. Moreover, this declarative knowledge facilitates empathic attunement to patients; it helps you know "where they are coming from."

Procedural knowledge puts declarative information into motion through clinical practice. Clinical plans, rules, and strategies are represented in procedural knowledge. For example, clinical algorithms that stipulate when and how to intervene are good examples of procedural knowledge. Procedural knowledge guides you toward decisions about what intervention to make for which children under certain circumstances at a particular time (Bennett-Levy, 2006).

Self-reflection is a third type of knowledge. Bennett-Levy (2006) defines *self-reflection* as a "metacognitive skill which accompanies the observation, interpretation, and evaluation of one's own thoughts, emotions, and actions and outcomes" (p. 60). Bennett-Levy claims self-reflection contributes to what is commonly referred to as clinical wisdom. The reflective system makes use of self-monitoring and self-observation. In order to reflect, Bennett-Levy states you have to focus on your experience, compare it to your declarative and procedural knowledge base, and decide on whether to continue your current course of action.

Declarative, procedural, and self-reflective knowledge are all addressed in the following chapters. Not surprisingly, the book, like any text, is heavy on the declarative knowledge. The empirical and theoretical basics form the foundation for each chapter. However, the treatment rubrics specifically provide you with how and when guidelines. Practicing the techniques with actual patients will cement your procedural understanding. Experiential application transfers learning from the page to the present (Bennett-Levy, 2006; Safran & Muran, 2001). In this way, the "fancy book learnin'" in the chapters get put into action rather than remaining inert (Binder, 1999).

Self-reflection is initially fostered in Chapter 3 and formally elaborated in Chapter 12. Self-reflection involves psychotherapists identifying, focusing on, and processing their own reactions during CBP (Milne, 2008). Not surprisingly, this self-reflection results in a "deeper sense of knowing of CT practices" (Bennett-Levy, Lee, Travers, Pohlman, & Hamernik, 2003). Accordingly, Chapter 12 identifies common beliefs and emotional reactions beginning therapists encounter during their work and multiple methods to manage these experiences.

Scientific-mindedness and the capacity for abstract reasoning are key ingredients in a recipe for a good cognitive behavioral psychotherapist (Dobson & Shaw, 1993; Padesky, 1996). Abstract thinking and inductive reasoning are pivotal in the case formulation process (Chapter 2). Scientific mindedness fuels a hypothesis testing approach that is marked by collaborative empiricism and guided discovery (Chapter 3).

Moreover, the thought testing procedures and behavioral experiments (Chapters 6 through 10) are highly dependent on well-developed critical reasoning skills.

Good cognitive behavioral therapists embrace immediacy in sessions and diligently work to make CBP real and relevant (Friedberg & Gorman, 2007; Friedberg, Gorman, & Beidel, 2009). Immediacy in session and an experiential focus in treatment bring CBP to life. Samoilov and Goldfried (2000) remarked that in-session arousal creates emotional, cognitive, and behavioral change. Accordingly, Chapter 3 teaches you how to add vitality to your sessions through a productive therapeutic stance.

Technical proficiency certainly defines cognitive behavioral competency (Dobson & Shaw, 1993). Teaching you to do the plain and fancy cognitive behavioral procedures is an important part of the book. Chapters 5 to 10 step you through learning the simple and sophisticated techniques.

New cognitive behavioral therapists begin their training with biases about CBP. A number of biases have been identified (Friedberg & Clark, 2006; Gluhoski, 1995; Pretorius, 2006). Freiheit and Overholser (1997) warned that these attitudinal biases shape the subsequent acquisition and application of cognitive behavioral principles and procedures. Sheikh, Milne, and MacGregor (2007) wrote that openness to change and improvement is directly related to the requisite professional commitment that characterizes a good cognitive behavioral therapist. This committed openness fuels an active transformative process where new information is internalized. Not surprisingly then, processing open and flexible attitudes is important in CBP training (Dobson & Shaw, 1993).

Ethnocultural responsiveness is another good clinical skill in CBP and is associated with open and flexible attitudes (Friedberg et al., 2009; Hays, 1995; Hays & Iwamasa, 2006). CBP is well suited to ethnocultural modifications (Hays, 1995, 2001). Cultural factors are explicitly addressed in the case formulation chapter (Chapter 2) as well as throughout the book.

Many new cognitive behavioral therapists may mistakenly believe that CBP neglects the treatment relationship (Friedberg & Clark, 2006; Gluhoski, 1995). However, the importance of a sound working alliance has long been a staple of CBP (A. T. Beck, Rush, Shaw, & Emery, 1979; Waddington, 2002). Southam-Gerow (2004) emphasized that CBP is "specifically designed to occur within interpersonal relationships" (p. 188). Friedberg and Gorman (2007) referred to the therapeutic alliance as a very important process (VIP). When problems arise in the working alliance, they must be addressed from a cognitive behavioral perspective. Chapter 3 provides several rubrics for this working through process.

A second frequent faulty assumption is that CBP is a sterile, emotionally distant, and mechanical approach (Friedberg & Clark, 2006; Gluhoski, 1995; Pretorius, 2006). Knell (1993) noted that beginning therapists are surprised by the fact that CBP with children and adolescents involves emotionally evocative here-and-now moments. Gosch, Flannery-Schroeder, Mauro, and Compton (2006) aptly noted, "A key ingredient to success-ful CBT is making the therapy content child focused and the process experiential" (p. 259). Kendall et al. (1998) reminded cognitive behavior therapists that experiential learning and emotional arousal brings manuals to life. Throughout this book, you will find rubrics and rudiments that help you remain faithful to the experiential roots of CBP.

Beginning cognitive behavioral therapists believe that treatment is all about disputation and refutation (Friedberg & Clark, 2006). They believe the therapeutic goal is to crush irrational thoughts into mush. Unfortunately, this does noth-ing but bring treatment to a grinding halt. Children's beliefs are not eggs like Humpty Dumpty who we have to make a great fall and crack into irreparable pieces. Rather, the beliefs are inaccurate assumptions about themselves, the world, other people, their experiences, and their future that render their lives distressing albeit understandable. These beliefs are strengthened by the hard knocks of their circumstances. Therefore, a gentle, collaborative approach is adopted. The crucial elements in this approach, guided discovery, and collaborative empiricism are explicated in Chapter 3 and emphasized throughout the text.

A WORD ABOUT THE CASE EXAMPLES AND TRANSCRIPTS

All the case examples are combinations of actual cases or dis-guised patients. Any identifying information has either been removed or altered to protect confidentiality.

CONCLUSION

When asked to explain what makes a joke funny, the come-dian Sarah Silverman replied, "If you have to break it down, it's not funny." While this idea works for humor, we believe the opposite is true for learning CBP with children and adolescents. Complex psychotherapeutic procedures and processes need to be taught through concrete rudiments and rubrics. Accordingly, in this book, we break down the complexities of CBP with children into its fundamentals.

Fundamentals can be dull. However, we devoted attention to putting the "fun" back into the fundamentals. Care was directed toward maintaining a conversational, easy-to-read format. Moreover, various metaphors and popular culture references are sprinkled throughout the text. By emphasizing the fun inherent in fundamentals we provide a model for intervening with children and adolescents. The importance of fun in CBP with children is elaborated in Chapter 3 concerning therapeutic stance.

Dr. Victor McCarley, another insightful colleague at WSU SOPP, often equated basic intervention skills to driving. For instance, he referred to the common practice of teaching beginner drivers to keep their hands at 10 and 2 o'clock. Indeed, this is a first rubric. Once drivers gain practice, comfort, and practice, they find their own locations for their hands. Similarly in this book, we teach 10 and 2 o'clock rubrics with the expectation that over time with experience and successful practice, you will develop flexibility as you internalize the rubric.

Two

Case Conceptualization

INTRODUCTION

Children and adolescents yearn for understanding. Genuine understanding propels accurate and impactful empathy. This chapter sets the table for the therapeutic practices and procedures that follow. Our approach emphasizes that techniques are never enough and illustrates the practicality of case conceptualization. The rubrics explain the "conceptual guts." Rudiments teach you how to construct case conceptualizations from an inferential process.

Techniques Are Never Enough

Case conceptualization is the handiest tool in your toolkit. In fact, Bieling and Kuyken (2003) argued that case formulation is at "the heart of evidence-based practice" (p. 53). To do cognitive behavioral therapy (CBT), you have to think like a cognitive behavioral therapist. Cognitive behavior therapy is more than a set of procedures and tricks. CBT is a way of seeing young patients' symptoms, development, and cultural context. The procedures need to be embedded in a case formulation or else they will fall flat. It is important to breathe life into CBT (Kendall, Chu, Gifford, Hayes, & Nauta, 1998) and the case conceptualization provides the oxygen that keeps the techniques from suffocating.

Case formulation acts as a clinical compass (Kuyken, Padesky, & Dudley, 2008b). The compass is a quite brilliant metaphor. As Kuyken et al. (2008b) asserted, a compass orients you to the proper direction regardless of winding twists and wrong turns. It keeps you pointed toward desired goals. In psychotherapy, patients' problems can present in a dizzying flurry causing treatment to spin without direction. The clinical compass provided by the formulation prevents psychotherapeutic vertigo and drifting off course.

Case conceptualization focuses on the patient rather than on his or her disorder or condition. Although our current diagnostic manuals are useful, they are nonetheless limited in their explanatory value due to their generic nature. Nezu and Nezu (1989) knowingly stated that excellent cognitive behavioral practice is marked by the "idiographic application of nomothetic principles" (p. 86). Case formulation allows you to personalize the treatment and fit the approach to the patient. For instance, if we read that a patient has a *Diagnostic and Statistical Manual of Mental Disorders (DSM)-IV* diagnosis of 313.81 (oppositional defiant disorder [ODD]), what do we really know? We know that he or she meets a frequency count of symptoms but we may not even immediately know the specific symptoms. Diagnosis is simply a summary term. Additionally, it is important to remember that diagnosis is atheoretical whereas case formulation is firmly rooted in theoretical premises.

Why Is a Case Formulation Handy? Value-Added Benefits

There are many benefits of case conceptualization that add value to your cognitive behavioral psychotherapy (CBP) practice. Case conceptualization is very practical. First, case conceptualization guides therapy (Kuyken et al., 2008a, 2008b; Persons, 1989). Case formulations allow you to select a particular tool from the wide array of available procedures. Additionally, case formulations help you choose among several compelling intervention points discerning relevant from irrelevant foci. It permits you to predict behavior, manage noncompliance, address alliance problems, and evaluate therapy.

Developing a case formulation involves constructing a set of theory-based hypotheses about the patient (Kuyken et al., 2008b). Rather than being cemented in stone, they are sculpted in clay and continually remolded to dynamically account for new information. In addition to assessing for presenting problems, cognitive behavioral therapists collect information about a patient's learning history, development, cultural context, cognitive structures, and behavioral antecedents. Although we present many procedures and techniques, we do not want you to take a cookbook approach to your psychotherapeutic work. Therefore, while techniques and procedures are important, they are never enough. In order to put the techniques

together, you need a template. Case conceptualization provides you with this necessary guide.

RUDIMENTS: THE CONCEPTUAL GUTS

The following section describes the salient elements in case
conceptualization. We refer to them as the "conceptual guts."
These core features include cultural context, developmental
history, the hierarchical organizational model, cognitive model
of presenting problems, physiological functioning, behavioral
consequences/antecedents, and emotional functioning.

Cultural Context

Patients' cultural contexts set the frame for case conceptualization. Disregard of ethnocultural complexities creates invisibility and the negative impact of cultural invisibility is well
documented (Ellison, 1952; Franklin & Boyd-Franklin, 2000).
Wright, Basco, and Thase (2006) wrote, "Sensitivity to sociocultural issues is an essential component of forming authentic
and highly functional working alliances" (p. 36). Ridley, Chih,
and Olivera (2000) wrote that minority patients are more likely
to receive a misdiagnosis from less experienced professionals,
suffer premature termination, and experience greater dissatisfaction with treatment. Ethnocultural context variables shape
symptom presentation, help-seeking behavior, and treatment
response (Carter, Sbrocco, & Carter, 1996; Cartledge & Feng,
1996a, 1996b; Sue, 1998). Cartledge and Feng (1996b) parsimo-
niously described cultural complexities by stating "Culture is
like a webbed system in which various aspects of life are inter-
connected. The various components of culture are not discrete
but interactive. Kinship, economic, and religious subsystems,
for example, all affect one another and cannot be understood
in isolation" (p. 14). Expressive and receptive language is also
mediated by cultural factors (Tharp, 1991). Unfortunately,
demographic characteristics are often confused with genuinely powerful cultural variations (Beutler, Brown, Crothers,
Booker, & Seabrook, 1996).

Lack of attention to cultural factors truncates treatment validity (Chorpita, Barlow, Albano, & Daleiden, 1998; Pinderhughes,
1989). Cultural responsiveness is identified as a core clinical
skill to cognitive behavioral therapists (Friedberg, McClure,
& Garcia, 2009). Finally, in an increasingly multicultural
world, neglect of cultural vicissitudes is unethical (American

Psychological Association, 1993). Shapiro, Friedberg, and Bardenstein (2005) rightly cautioned that "we want to strike a balance that combines valid generalizations about cultural tendencies with attention to individual differences and exceptions" (p. 279).

There are a number of culturally salient psychological variables to incorporate in your case conceptualization. Determining how patients' self-identify is a key first step. This type of understanding contributes to an appreciation of their level of acculturation and assimilation. You will also want to consider how patients' experiences with power and privilege influence their symptoms. Useful questions to ask include:

What languages are spoken in your home?
What cultural barriers have you and your family encountered?
What is the level of acculturation in the family?
How does your cultural identity shape your symptom presentation?

When getting to know your patient, it is important to inquire about experiences of oppression, marginalization, and prejudice. This may be uncomfortable to assess, but it is crucial nonetheless. Dobbins and Skillings (2000) remind us that minority youth are targets of race-based teasing and bullying, social isolation as well as psychological and physical violence. Engaging in this difficult but necessary dialogue promotes trust and understanding (Cardemil & Battle, 2003). Definitions of *oppression*, *marginalization*, *stereotyping*, and *prejudice* are given in Box 2.1.

Developmental History and Background

Developmental history gives you clues about predisposing and precipitating factors. Obtaining a developmental history is a familiar task for child psychiatrists and other mental health professionals. The familiar areas of a developmental history include developmental milestones, school functioning, social history, past abuse and trauma (including vicarious traumatization such as witnessing domestic violence), family relationships, medical conditions, legal history, substance use, and prior treatment experiences. Your training prepares you well in gathering comprehensive information. However, you may have gaps in how to integrate this information into a cognitive behavioral case formulation. Disembodied developmental data

BOX 2.1   IMPORTANT CULTURAL VARIABLES

Minority culture—While minority culture is often associated and confounded with "numbers," it is more properly defined by access to power (Hays, 2001; Pinderhughes, 1989).

Race—Frequently, race is seen as a categorical variable referring to skin, hair, and eye color. However, race is a murky socially constructed concept (McAuliffe, 2008). McAuliffe, Gomez, and Grothaus (2008) in reviewing genetic findings concluded that human beings share common genetic markers so it becomes nearly impossible to define biological groups.

Ethnicity—McAuliffe, Kim, and Park (2008) defined ethnicity as "the identity of groups of people who acknowledge their shared origins, geographic, and customs" (pp. 85–86). McAuliffe (2008) noted that ethnicity shapes peoples' standards, beliefs, and behaviors.

Ethnic identity—Marsella and Yamada (2000) defined ethnic identity as "the extent to which an individual endorses and manifests the cultural traditions and practices of a group" (p. 12). Identity includes feelings of belongingness, commitment, and shared sense of attitudes and values toward an identified group (Phinney, 1990).

Acculturation—Acculturation is the active process where people incorporate elements of a new culture into their already existing cultural makeup (Yamamoto, Silva, Ferrari, & Nukariya, 1997).

Assimilation—Assimilation is another active process where individuals primarily adopt the host culture and their original culture fades into the background (Phinney & Chavira, 1995).

Power—Power is the capacity to influence people and systems. Power creates an established order and elitism. This order maintains access to disproportionate resources and privileges (Overbeck, 2010). Oppression and marginalization may be used to keep power structures in place.

Privilege—Privilege refers to a set of unearned assets that gives people unfair advantages (Hays, 2001; McIntosh, 1998). Often, privilege creates insiders and outsiders. Insiders have access to hidden rules or opportunities that help maintain advantages over outsiders. Not surprisingly, privilege contributes to isolation (Hays, 2001).

Marginalization—McAuliffe, Kim, and Park (2008) defined marginalization as "the process where a nondominant group is made peripheral by the larger society. A marginalized individual or group is excluded, or devalued in the economy, in the daily social discourse and in the customs of the dominant group" (p. 93). McAuliffe, Gomez, and Grothaus (2008) noted that identification and connection with their indigenous culture helps individuals cope with marginalization.

Oppression—Sue and Sue (1999) explained that oppression is described as living in a world where dominant culture "demeans, disadvantages, and denies equal access and opportunity" (p. 31).

Prejudice—To Aronson, Wilson, and Akert (1997) "prejudice is a hostile or negative attitude toward people on a distinguishable group based solely on their membership in that group" (p. 478). Simply, prejudice reflects preferences for some individuals over others. Prejudices include all-or-none labels that are overgeneralized and passionately applied to all group members. When prejudice is combined with power, various "isms" emerge.

Stereotypes—Using Lipmann's (1922) notion of "the little pictures we carry around inside our head," Aronson et al. (1997) saw stereotyping as a cognitive/attitudinal variable. Stereotypes are the sturdy, generalized representations about groups of individuals that make them see like "they are all the same." More specifically, Aronson et al. (1997) explained that a stereotype is a "generalization about a group of people in which identical characteristics are assigned to virtually all members of the group regardless of the actual variation among the members" (p. 478).

> *Isms*—Racism, sexism, heterosexism, and so forth, occur when power is added to stereotypes, prejudice, and bias (Hays, 2001). Isms are practiced when behaviors and policies systematically restrict/deny access to opportunities and privileges to members of a group while promoting access to these same opportunities and privileges to another group (Ridley et al., 2000).

is not particularly helpful in conceptualization or treatment planning. Therefore, we offer a few rudiments for tethering disparate data points to the formulations.

1. *Developmental experiences inform learning history.* Developmental history allows you to track learning patterns of self-regulation and responsiveness to environmental demands. For example, examining the developmental trajectory of eating, sleeping, toileting habits, and responses to changes in routine gives you clues regarding children's characteristic ways of soothing and calming themselves, frustration, delay of gratification, and controlling impulses. Developmental delays expose children to more potential embarrassment, ridicule, criticism, and failure experiences. Moreover, developmental experiences inform you about parental caregiver responsiveness and children's negotiation of tasks such as separation. If the child has directly experienced trauma or victimization such as domestic violence, it may form the basis for their beliefs about emotional control, safety, and quality of relationships. Questions you may want to consider include:

   How did the child react to the toilet training process?
   How was any reluctance by the child to the toilet training process handled by parents?
   How did the child and parent respond to accidents?
   What are the child's academic difficulties? Learning problems? Developmental delays? How do the parents respond to these difficulties? What is the reaction of peers and teachers? How does the child interpret these learning experiences?

What trauma has the child experienced or wit-
nessed? How has this shaped his or her view of the
world, people, and the self?

What medical conditions has the child experienced? How do parents, caretakers, or families
react to it? How do peers react? How does it contribute to the view of the self?

What was the child's and parent's experience of
separation and transition to school? How does
this shape the child view of self, world, and their
experiences?

What is the child's friendship history? How does
this influence the view of self and others?

2. *Account for the quality of report.* Clinical experience
teaches that parents vary in approach as historians
and reporters. Some parents come to therapy equipped
with folders brimming with details about the child.
Others arrive at the appointment clueless and lacking
even the most basic information about the child's functioning or history. Most parents arrive at the session
somewhere in the middle of the spectrum. All circumstances provide fodder for the formulation. Use your
curiosity about these events to craft some hypotheses.
You might wonder:

How does this level of organization and detail play
out in the family?

What is going on with the parent that he or she is
so oblivious to child's development, history, and
functioning?

What does it say about the child–parent relationship that the parent is so attuned or misattuned to
the child's experience?

What contributes to the parents' excessive level of
attention to detail about their child's development?

What does it say about the parent–child relationship that the parent is so attuned to the minute
details about the child?

Rings of Fire: Cognitive Hierarchical Organizational Model

The hierarchical organizational model informs case conceptualization by sketching the patients' automatic thoughts,
underlying assumptions, and schemata. The model outlines

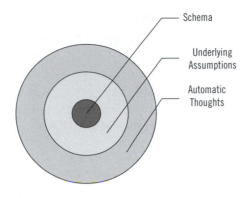

Figure 2.1 Hierarchical organizational model.

the basic components of personality. In cognitive therapy, people work according to three concentric layers of cognition (A. T. Beck & Clark, 1988; Ingram & Kendall, 1986; Padesky, 1988, 1994), which we refer to as the rings of fire (see Figure 2.1). Each layer is proportionally tied to levels of emotion with the centermost ring connected to the strongest level of emotional intensity. More specifically, the outermost circle represents automatic thoughts, the middle ring is underlying or intermediate assumptions, and the center ring reflects core schemata.

Automatic thoughts characterize individuals' internal dialogues and are marked by stream of consciousness thoughts, images, conclusions, interpretations, attributions, and judgments about oneself, others, ones' experiences, the world, and the future. They reflect any time period. That is, you can have automatic thoughts about the past ("All the bad decisions I made in the past make me stupid"), the present ("No one in my class likes me"), and the future ("Something horrible will happen to my mother and father"). Automatic thoughts are situationally specific. This is important to keep in mind because it makes them easier to identify and test.

The content-specificity hypothesis (Alford & Beck, 1997; A. T. Beck, 1976; Clark & Beck, 1988; Jolly, 1993; Jolly & Dyckman, 1994; Jolly & Kramer, 1994; Laurent & Stark, 1993) is one of the most clinically useful and applicable rudiments. *Simply, the content-specificity hypothesis emphasizes that different thought content characterizes different feeling states.* The thoughts that accompany depressed moods are not the same as the ones associated with anger. The content specificity hypothesis helps you identify meaningful thoughts and connect these thoughts to

Table 2.1 Content Specificity Hypothesis

Feeling State	Cognitive Content
Depression	Negative view of self
	Negative view of the experiences/others
	Negative view of the future
Anxiety	Overestimation of the probability of danger
	Overestimation of the likelihood of danger
	Neglect of rescue factors
	Ignoring coping resources
Social Anxiety	Fear of negative evaluation
Panic	Catastrophic misinterpretation of normal bodily symptoms
Anger	Hostile attributional bias
	Confusion between accidental and deliberate
	Labeling the other
	Others' violation of personal imperatives (should/must rules)
	Sense of unfairness

their appropriate feeling states. This practice is fundamental to the basic completion of a thought diary (Chapter 5). Table 2.1 summarizes the relationship between feeling states and cognitive content espoused by the content-specificity hypothesis.

Cognitive distortions (Burns, 1980) or *cognitive errors* (J. S. Beck, 1995) are well-known and popularized terms. Alcoholics Anonymous uses the term *stinkin' thinkin'* to refer to cognitive distortions. They refer to styles or patterns of inaccurate thinking. All-or-none thinking, overgeneralization, personalization, emotional reasoning, and mind reading are just some examples of cognitive distortions. Interested readers are referred to Burns (1980) and J. S. Beck (1995) for a complete listing and definitions. Friedberg, McClure, and Garcia (2009) presented a child-friendly list of cognitive distortions.

Cognitive distortions' role in the hierarchical model of organization is to serve the assimilation process. They work for the schema. Cognitive distortions bend disconfirming data to fit the schema content. They may discount discrepant information or twist it so the schema content does not need to change.

Common cognitive distortions include emotional reasoning, overgeneralization, catastrophic thinking, all-or-none thinking, shoulds, negative predictions, mind reading, labeling, personalization, selective abstraction, cognitive avoidance, and somatic misfocus (Thase & Beck, 1993). Emotional reasoning refers to predominantly basing conclusions, judgments, and

decisions on emotional states. Overgeneralization is inaccurately stretching information obtained in one circumstance
to other dissimilar situations. Catastrophic thinking reflects
an overestimation of the probability and magnitude of dangers. All-or-none thinking is exemplified by categorical rather
than dimensional thinking where shades of gray are ignored.
Personal rules and imperatives are included in these should
demands. Negative prediction is referred to as the "fortune
teller" error where doom and gloom is predicted for the future.
Mind reading is another derivation of the fortune teller error
where individuals believe their inferences about another person without checking them for accuracy. Labeling is a type of
all-or-none thinking where an absolute negative term is used to
define oneself or others. Personalization refers to misattribut-
ing too much personal responsibility for events and outcomes
that are beyond one's control. Selective abstraction is emphasizing or giving too much weight to negative aspects of oneself or situations while simultaneously minimizing positive
aspects. When negative thoughts are avoided or suppressed
because they are seen as overwhelming, this is called cognitive avoidance. Finally, somatic misfocus is characterized by
a catastrophic misinterpretation of normal bodily sensations.

Underlying assumptions are intermediate rules and beliefs
that are cross-situational, relatively less accessible to immediate awareness, and allow people to operate in the world as well
as keep the schemata intact. Frequently, they are conditional
imperatives that are couched in if–then terms (e.g., "If I reject
others before they reject me, then it doesn't hurt as much"). The
underlying assumptions allow for limited intimacy and connection (e.g., being in relationship for a circumscribed period
of time, then rejecting the other) without the risk associated
with deeper relationships.

Schemata are the ringmasters. They are core meaning
structures that power attention, encoding, retention, and
recall (Fiske & Taylor, 1991; Guidano & Liotti, 1983, 1985;
Hammen & Zupan, 1984). These cognitive emotional power
plants contain the most basic beliefs about oneself, others,
experiences, relationships, and the world that individuals
hold. Schemata seep into one's mental life over time with
repeated reinforced learning experiences and eventually
become entrenched in young adulthood (Guidano & Liotti,
1983; Hammen & Zupan, 1984; Young, 1990). Thus, schemata
tend to be more influential in adolescents' behavior than in
younger children's behavior.

Schemata operate through schema maintenance, schema avoidance, and schema compensation (Young, 1994). Schema maintenance accounts for apparent rigidity and intractability. The cognitive distortion process (Burns, 1980) and self-defeating behaviors work to keep maladaptive schemata in place. Cognitive distortions' mental filtering process maintain schemata by negating, discounting, minimizing, exaggerating, and otherwise twisting discrepant information so it consistently fits the schema. Self-defeating behavior patterns are schema-driven behaviors that create self-fulfilling prophecies. They form behavioral cycles that repeatedly conform to negative schemata. It's very similar to Einstein's maxim about the short-sided notion of continuing the same maladaptive things and expecting a different result.

Schemata are core beliefs that serve as organizing principles in people's lives (Mash & Dozois, 2003). These general views provide coherence and consistency to life. Core beliefs form the persistent and pervasive lenses from which people view themselves, others, and their experiences across circumstances over time.

Young (1994) conceptualized five domains for schemata (autonomy, worthiness, connectedness, reasonable expectations, and realistic limits). According to Young, when adverse environmental circumstances and poor relationships with parents, siblings, or peers compromise children's ability to satisfactorily complete developmental tasks, early maladaptive schemas (EMS) grow.

Several untoward circumstances may predispose children to develop schemata relating to vulnerability to illness, fears of loss of control, subjugation, and excessive dependency (Young, 1994). Families who continually constrict or punish self-expression, and communicate that their child is fragile and the world completely dangerous, limit chances for children to develop self-confidence and autonomy. Generally, these families are characterized by overprotection, overcontrol, and emotional constriction.

For Young (1994), connectedness includes a sense of intimacy and a recognition of social integration. In this model, intimacy is operationalized as a belief that one is loveable and others are trustworthy. Environments that are reliable, nurturing, and communicate caring without coercion protect against EMS related to connectedness. Environments that are bereft of warmth, love, respect, and marked by maltreatment and abuse promote EMS in this domain. Additionally, repeated peer rejection and loss or prolonged separation of caregivers contribute to a sense of disconnectedness.

Worthiness is a third schema dimension. According to Young (1994), *worthiness* is defined by the sense you are lovable, competent, and desirable. The main culprit in developing EMS in this domain is excessive parental criticism and punishment. Core beliefs associated with defectiveness, social undesirability, incompetence/failure, guilt, and shame result from these untoward circumstances.

The fourth and fifth domains involve reasonable expectations and realistic limits. Reasonable expectations require people's abilities to establish realistic standards for oneself and others. Rotter's (1982) notion of minimal goal level (MGL) is particularly useful here. MGL is the point of lowest value that children and adolescents find motivating and satisfying. Overachieving, perfectionistic children are often overburdened with too high an MGL. The child sets up an unattainable standard and then repeatedly fails further reinforcing self-criticism and doubt. Rotter simply states that the standard for reinforcement is too high. Consequently, over time, the children become resentful and frustrated about their performance and achievement pressures. Bandura (1977b) also wrote about this problem in dysfunctional standard setting where people set unrealistically high standards for themselves and then harshly criticize their perceived subpar performance. Bandura referred to this process as a sort of double whammy where people overaspire, underachieve, and discount their actual positive performances.

The unrelenting standards schema arises when whatever someone does is never enough. Parents inculcate the sense that achievement is more valued than happiness. Moreover, there is a core belief along the lines that "lovability absolutely depends on high achievement."

Schemata operate according to three components: cognitive avoidance, affective or emotional avoidance, and behavioral avoidance. According to Young (1994), cognitive avoidance includes depersonalization and compulsive behaviors. For example, compulsive exercise may be a way to avoid a schema such as "Happiness is achieved only through absolute control." Cognitive avoidance may rear its head in session when adolescents are asked, "What is going through your mind, right now?" and then respond blankly claiming "Nothing. My mind is empty."

Affective or emotional avoidance is a common subtype. When adolescents are engaged in emotional avoidance, they keep feelings associated with schemata at a far distance. This emotional remoteness is fueled by an intolerance for negative feelings such as anxiety, sadness, quiet, shame, embarrassment, and anger. Simply, adolescents who report no feelings and numbness are engaging in emotional avoidance. When we see self-mutilation (burning, cutting, etc.) and somatization, we think emotional avoidance. Finally, repeated presentation of complaints in vague, generalized, and diffuse ways are signs of emotional avoidance.

Behavioral avoidance is relatively easy to spot. In these circumstances, adolescents act in ways to escape situations that may activate dormant negative schemata. They stay away from people, places, and things that may wake up sleeping schemata. For example, they may withdraw from performance or evaluative situations, excessively limit their responsibilities or commitments, or self-handicap by feigning injury or illness.

Schema compensation is the third intriguing schema process. Young (1994) uses schema compensation to explain adolescents' overt behavior patterns that seem opposite or contrary to schema content. The powerless male who acts blustery or the teenage girl with a poignant sense of worthlessness who behaves in an entitled manner are examples of patients engaging in schema compensation.

The Cognitive Model

The cognitive model is outlined by A. T. Beck (1985). The model presents a dynamic interaction between physiology, mood, behavior, and cognition. It proposes that each element is causally linked to one another. Therefore, a change in one factor contributes to a change in the other three. No causal primacy is attributed to any one variable. Therefore, cognitive therapists do not believe thoughts cause feelings. Rather, we believe that physiology, mood, behavior, and thoughts, co-vary with each one another when symptoms erupt. These variables are in motion when patients present for therapy. For instance, an anxious child experiences physiological, biological, and chemical changes (changes in neurotransmitter substances, activation in the amygdala, sweating, heart rate changes, respiration changes, etc.). Youngsters also have concurrent mood or emotional changes (worry, anxiety, panic, sadness, etc.), behavioral/action reactions (avoidance, escape, etc.), and cognitive symptoms (e.g., "I am going to lose control. Something bad will happen to me or my family. Being away from home is dangerous").

Physiological and Biological Variables

Physiological and biological variables include the many brain and body processes associated with psychological disorders and emotional distress. They include elements such as cortisol levels, neurotransmitters, hormone levels, blood sugars, peptides, and amino acids (Oatley, Keltner, & Jenkins, 2006; Plizka, 2003; Siegel, 1999). Additionally, fatigue, excessive or impaired sleep patterns, and over- and undereating are physiological variables in the model. These variables are often detected by lab findings, vital signs readings, and self report. Less frequently, specialized MRI and PET scans may identify these processes in clinical practice.

Behavioral Antecedents and Consequences

Behavioral cues and consequences are implicated in the initiation, maintenance, and exacerbation of problematic behaviors. Cues or antecedents set the stage for the behavior and trigger the emergence of children's actions. Consequences determine whether the behavior is strengthened or weakened. Cues may be external (e.g., physical setting, time, people present, type of task, and so forth) or internal (physiological, hunger, fatigue, emotional state, cognitive, sugar level), which prompt or provoke the behavior. Consequences are the reinforcers (presentation of positive stimulus, removal of aversive stimulus) punishments (scolding, spanking), and response costs (time-out, loss of privileges) that make the behavior more or less likely. These cues and consequences are more fully elaborated in Chapter 7.

Emotional Functioning

Emotions are seen as biologically endowed processes (Hannesdottir & Ollendick, 2007). They may be unpleasant (pain, fear, anger, sadness, disgust, worry) or pleasant (happiness, pride). Oatley et al. (2006) noted that emotions are expressed in facial movements, posture, gesture, voice intonation, and bodily responses (sweating, tears). These emotional states include but are not limited to those feelings listed in Table 2.2. These emotional labels can also help you craft empathic statements.

RUBRICS

Case formulations are idiosyncratic (J. S. Beck, 1995; Drinkwater, 2004; Friedberg & McClure, 2002; Persons, 1989).

Table 2.2   Sample "Feeling" Words

Mad	Sad	Glad	Worried
Angry	Lonely	Happy	Shy
Furious	Depressed	Excited	Embarrassed
Disgusted	Down	Joyful	Frightened
Irritated	Blue	Cheery	Anxious
Annoyed	In the dumps	Tickled	Scared
Enraged	Shitty	Good	Nervous
Pissed off	Crappy	Great	Spooked
Ticked off	Bummed up	Fine	Tense
Grumpy	F----- up	On top of the world	Uptight
Bitter	Low	Light	Fearful
Steamed	Disappointed	Thrilled	Edgy
Outraged	Rotten	Content	Jittery
Cranky	Terrible	Carefree	Shaky
Frustrated	Awful	Cool	Stressed
Resentful	Gloomy	Chill	Jumpy
Offended	Drained	Lively	Unsettled
Jammed up	Troubled	Brave	Unsure
Fired up	Worn out	Content	Doubtful
Hot	Lousy	Bold	
On fire	Discouraged		

Although we provide rubrics, they need to be individually developed rather than constructed via boilerplates. Once the data is collected, the case formulation may be constructed. Like Persons (1995), we believe parsimony is preferable. There is nothing wrong with simple conceptualizations. We urge you to seek ordinary explanations for problems and avoid overreaching for the extraordinary. Like Kuyken et al. (2008a, 2008b), we advocate an integration of disorder specific and generic conceptualization models. Thus, the elements in a case conceptualization include synthesizing the existing cognitive behavioral theory and research, clinical observation and evaluation of the patients' experience, and the patients' reactions to the hypotheses.

Forming Conceptual Hypotheses: Writing in the Sand

Case conceptualizations are not marble statues of patients. They are not written in hardened stone with granite certainty rather they are hypotheses written in sand. Kuyken et al. (2008b) noted that case conceptualizations evolve over time via the natural process of obtaining both confirming and disconfirming information. We believe in a *bottom-up inferential process*. Bottom-up thinking makes use of inductive reasoning and is data driven. Inductive reasoning proceeds from the specific case to general principles (Trochim & Donnelly, 2006). Discrete observations are used to build broader theories by identifying and recognizing regularities within and between these patterns. Trochim and Donnelly (2006) noted that inductive reasoning is inherently open ended. You might even see case conceptualization as an exercise in pattern recognition.

Accordingly, you begin with collecting specific, discrete, and ostensibly disparate pieces of data. Then, you examine the presenting problems, cultural context, developmental history, behavioral antecedents and consequences, and automatic thoughts. Next, you search for common themes. Persons (1989) recommends asking yourself, "What do all these things have in common?" and "What general beliefs, rules, and assumptions would a child who had these experiences hold?" Additionally, ask yourself how the behavioral cues and consequences might shape the belief system. Sifting through collections of the patient's negative thoughts for evidence supporting or disconfirming the inference is a good next step. The process is summarized in Figure 2.2.

Since CBT is based on collaborative empiricism and employs a hypothesis testing approach, inferences are tested for accuracy (Kuyken et al., 2008b; Persons, 1989, 2008). It is important during this process to remain scientifically minded, which simply means staying open to being wrong. Nonetheless, the case conceptualization should be written.

Persons (1989) instructs us to determine how well the case hypotheses account for the presenting problems. Second, Persons concludes that a good formulation should explain why the precipitating factors triggered the presenting problems. Third, the case formulation should yield robust predictions about patients' responses to treatment, obstacles, impasses, and productive strategies. Finally, case formulations are collaborative activities and therefore the child's or family's reaction is a valuable source of information (Kuyken et al., 2008a). Further, Kuyken et al. (2008a) noted that collaboration provides a vital check on clinician's reasoning errors.

Supervisory experience with many psychiatric residents and fellows and psychology practicum, predoctoral, and postdoctoral trainees reveals that many beginning cognitive therapists have difficulty "finding the words" to construct an

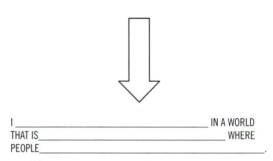

DEVELOPMENTAL HISTORY

X

CULTURAL CONTEXT

X

PRECIPITATING, MAINTAINING, AND EXACERBATING EVENTS

X

BEHAVIORAL ANTECEDENTS AND CONSEQUENCES

X

PHYSIOLOGICAL SYMPTOMS

X

MOOD SYMPTOMS

X

BEHAVIORS

X

AUTOMATIC THOUGHTS

I _____ IN A WORLD
THAT IS_____ WHERE
PEOPLE_____.

Figure 2.2   Case formulation rubric.

idiosyncratic case formulation. Consequently, we developed an aid contained in Table 2.3 to help you form individualized case conceptualizations.

As you can readily see, the thesaurus is organized according to various schema content domains described earlier in the chapter (e.g., abandonment, subjugation, autonomy). Each domain is connected to example "I" stems, "people/other" stems, and "world/experiences" stems. These stems ideally

Table 2.3 Schema Content Thesaurus

Schema Domain	Sample Self Stems (I ...)	Sample People Stems (People Are...; Others Are ...)	Sample World Stems (The World Is ...)
Autonomy	I'm directionless	People must help me	The world is too difficult
	I'm trapped	People must rescue me	The world is confusing
	I'm a prisoner	Others must guide me	The world is too demanding
	I'm a hostage	Others should hold my hand through all my troubles	The world requires too much of me
	I'm a slave	Others should tell me what to do, think, and feel	The world limits me
	I'm purposeless		The world binds me in chains
	I'm paralyzed		
	I'm stuck		
	I'm reliant on others for guidance		
	I must count on others for my total well-being		
	I'm too needy		
	I'm captive		
	I'm helpless		
	I'm powerless		
	I'm hooked on others for help		
Vulnerability to Harm	I'm crippled	Others are stronger than I am	The world is filled with threats

(Continued)

Table 2.3 Schema Content Thesaurus (Continued)

Schema Domain	Sample Self Stems (I ...)	Sample People Stems (People Are...; Others Are ...)	Sample World Stems (The World Is ...)
	I'm fragile	Others are immune to life's hardships	The world is dangerous
	I'm breakable	Others are more protected from harm	The world is menacing
	I am sick	Others are sheltered	The world is not survivable
	I'm deformed	Others are better fighters	The world should be defended against
	I'm scarred	Others are shielded	The world is full of hunters
	I'm deformed	Others are camouflaged	
	I'm defenseless	Others are watched over	
	I'm unprotected	Others attack me	
	I'm weak		
	I'm unable to cope		
	I'm abused		
	I'm victimized		
	I'm unguarded		
	I'm out in the open		
Abandonment	I'm all alone	People leave me	The world is cold
	I'm neglected	People disappear	The world is unforgiving
	I'm out in the cold	People come and go unexpectedly	The world is barren
	I'm left behind	People vanish	The world is emotionally sterile

Mistrust		
I'm forgotten	People desert me	The world has no one for me to turn to
I'm an afterthought	No one will ease my way	The world turns a deaf ear to me
I'm on my own	No one searches for me	The world is a dark abyss
I'm stranded	People leave me in the lurch	
I'm neglected	People leave me stranded	
I am without a home	My loved ones are emotionally AWOL	
I'm casted out		The world sucks
I can't count on anyone	Others are tormenters	The world rewards cheaters
I'm passed over	People will torture me	The world f----- me over
I'm duped	Others will mistreat me	The world encourages others to stab you in the back
I'm tricked	People will abuse me	Relationships cause only pain
I'm fooled	Others are violent	The world is at war
I must be always vigilant	Others are out of control	The world is full of strangers
I must watch out for others' motives	People are unreliable	The world lies
I get screwed by others' agendas	Others are assholes	The world is full of creeps
I must never let anyone get to know me	People are shitheads	The world is trying to screw me over
I'm an impenetrable fortress	Others are demeaning	
I must never put my faith in others	People are rejecting	
I must always doubt others' motives and intents	Others are mocking	
I must keep on high alert	People disrespect me	

(Continued)

Table 2.3 Schema Content Thesaurus (Continued)

Schema Domain	Sample Self Stems (I …)	Sample People Stems (People Are…; Others Are …)	Sample World Stems (The World Is …)
		Others are arrogant	
		People are stuck up	
		People are full of themselves	
		Others are selfish	
		Others are phony	
		Others are false	
		People are two-faced	
		People are sneaky	
		Others will exploit me	
		People will hook me into doing things I won't like	
		People will deceive me	
		Others will mislead me	
		Others will torment me	
		People will hurt me	
		Others will get over on me	
		Others are attackers	
		People betray me	
		People are better than me	The world has no place for rejects
Defectiveness	I'm bad		

	I'm flawed	People are flawless	The world must have winners
	I'm messed up	People are perfect	The world ignores those that are lost and confused
	I'm screwed up	People are stronger than me	The world is no place for defects like me
	I'm inept	People are more emotionally fit than me	The world works only for kings and queens
	I'm f----- up	People are sure of themselves	
	I'm incompetent	People are talented	
	I'm unable		
	I'm handicapped		
	I'm clueless		
	I'm ugly		
	I'm a piece of shit		
	I'm gruesome		
	I'm a reject		
	I'm a devil		
	I'm a loser		
	I'm a peasant		
Worthiness	I'm flawed	Others are better than me	The world devalues me
	I'm disfigured	Others are more prepared to deal with life than me	The world hides its prizes from me
	I'm unlovable	Others are more interesting than me	The world recognizes only the totally virtuous
	I'm defective	Others are more appealing than me	The world welcomes the righteous

(Continued)

Table 2.3 Schema Content Thesaurus (Continued)

Schema Domain	Sample Self Stems (I …)	Sample People Stems (People Are…; Others Are …)	Sample World Stems (The World Is …)
	I'm incompetent	Others are more attractive than me	The world is disgraced by me
	I'm corrupt	Others are more powerful than me	I am a zit on the world's face
	I'm bad	Others are smarter than me	The world spurns the lowly
	I'm dirty	Others are more deserving	
	I'm soiled	Others are more virtuous	
	I'm deserving punishment	Others are more upstanding	
	I'm ugly	Others are pure	
	I'm inadequate		
	I'm not whole		
	I'm invisible		
	I don't count		
	I don't matter		
	I'm unimportant		
	I'm meaningless		
	I don't measure up		
	I'm hideous		
	I'm wicked		
	I'm the scum of the earth		
	I'm lame		

Subjugation	I'm subhuman	People keep me under their thumb	In my world, safety is assured by being quiet and compliant
	I'm impure		
	I'm vile		
	I must sacrifice myself for others' well-being	Other people are leaders and I must follow	The world directs me to mind their business
	I should rarely be seen or heard	Other push me around	The world is blind to my wishes
	I must put others ahead of me	People know more than me	The world demands I hide myself
	I must be sure others' needs are taken care of before I am cared for		
	I am responsible for the emotional well-being of others	People are more powerful than me	The world discounts me
	I must never disagree with anyone	People boss me around	The world invalidates me
	I must remain defenseless	People pull me in directions I do not want to go in	The world places me in its margins
	I should let others shit on me		The world does not shine upon me
	I must allow others to abuse or mistreat me		
	I must always give in		
	My voice is silent		
	I must be an ass kisser		
Connectedness	I'm left out	People are strange	The world cuts me off
	I'm alienated	People are distant	The world is emotionally cold and reserved
	I'm isolated	People are unable to be connected with	The world is standoffish

(Continued)

Table 2.3 Schema Content Thesaurus (Continued)

Schema Domain	Sample Self Stems (I …)	Sample People Stems (People Are…; Others Are …)	Sample World Stems (The World Is …)
	I'm marooned	People are impossible to relate to	The world exiles me
	I'm excluded	People are hard to understand	The world is a barren, godforsaken place
	I'm a stranger	People are weird	The world is a place of solitary confinement
	I'm dissed	People are different than me	
	I'm mocked	People are aloof	
	I'm ridiculed		
	I'm a misfit		
	I'm out of place		
	I'm mismatched		
	I'm awkward		
	I'm different		
	I'm deviant		
	I'm odd		
	I'm weird		
	I'm emo		
	I'm a "psycho"		
	I'm a foreigner		
Entitlement	My wishes and wants are superior to others	Everyone must bow to me	Privileges must be given on demand

Self	Others	World
It is good to be king/queen	People must notice my specialness or uniqueness	The world is my kingdom
I should always get what I want	Others' attention toward me must never be diverted or distracted	The world owes me my dues
I am always owed good fortune	People should never deprive me	The world owes me happiness, success, and fairness
I am exceptional	Others should never put me down	The world must kiss my ass
I must never be inconvenienced	Others must never slight me	The world must never place demands on me
I am extraordinary	Others are prey	The world owes me favors
My demands and commands are law	Others have no rights	
I must hoard all of life's advantages		
I am understood only if I am indulged		

Unlovability

Self	Others	World
I'm unattractive	No one finds me appealing	Love escapes me
I'm unlovable	Others reject me	Love eludes me
I'm left out	Others dump me	Love is blind to me
I'm excluded	Others are disgusted by me	The world is where my heart beats to a lonely drummer
No one will want me	Others find me hideous	The world is a place I must travel on my own
I'll never have a shoulder to cry on	No one yearns for me	The world is filled with couples and pairs
I'll grow old alone	Others don't burn for me	Love escapes me
I'm untouchable	Others are cold	Love eludes me

(Continued)

Table 2.3 Schema Content Thesaurus (Continued)

Schema Domain	Sample Self Stems (I ...)	Sample People Stems (People Are...; Others Are ...)	Sample World Stems (The World Is ...)
	I'm gross	Others are empty-hearted	
	I'm odd		
	I'm a sock without a match		
	I'm without a mate		
	I am more trouble to others than I am worth		
	I'm an old maid		
	I'm not hot		
	I'm pathetic		
	I'll never be the one chosen by another		
Fears of Loss of Control	I must always be vigilant	Others are out of control	Strong emotions are dangerous
	I must always know what will happen next	Others are disorderly	The world is unpredictable
	I must never be out of balance	Others act too wild	Control determines competence
	I must never be perplexed	Others are deranged	Control equals power
	I must always be certain	Others are far crazier than me	Having control leads to approval
	I must always be disciplined	Others are too rowdy	Control equals safety
			Confusion is weak
			The world is divided along clear lines of right and wrong

Unrelenting Standards	I must always do right	People love a winner	Doubt is disastrous
			Negative emotions are terrifying
			Exceptional achievement is a requirement
	I can never lose my way	People are drawn to the exceptionally superb	Being the best means everything
	I must be perfect	People expect me to be an example who is always correct	Winning comes first
	I must be flawless	People love me only as an ideal	Love is achieved only through the pursuit of perfection
	I can never be second best		The world is made of winners and losers
	I must be exact		The world is divided into major leaguers and minor leaguers
	I must be pure		Precision is admired
	My needs will never be met	No one can fulfill me	Caring equals control and coercion
Emotional Deprivation	I am deprived	People are sour on me	The world denies me
	I never get what I want	People are emotionally stingy	The world withholds affection
	I am empty	People are cheap with their love	The world denies me warmth
	I am a bottomless pit	People are never tender	The world fills me with woe
	I am hollow	People are never charitable	The world lives in color and I feel in shades of black and white
	I am a robot		
	I'm passionless		

stimulate your thinking in various areas. While many stems will fit for your patients, you should take care not to use these statements as boilerplates. Rather, you should tweak them to fit the individual presentation of the child.

Figure 2.3 diagrams reflective bottom-up steps for forming conceptual hypotheses. The reflection is represented by the various questions embedded in each incremental step. As the figure indicates, revisions are expected. The reflective process yields the revisions based on analysis of the data and evaluation of patient feedback.

Case Example 1: Sean

Sean is an 11-year-old Asian American boy who lives at home with his mother, father, and 7-year-old brother. He presents with symptoms of separation anxiety and oppositional defiant disorder. More specifically, he becomes quite agitated when leaving for school in the morning exemplified by hyperventilating, pacing, and sweating. He will cling to his parents and literally needs to be dragged into the school building. Occasionally, he has left the school building after being dropped off in the morning. He requests and is granted absences from the classroom and goes to the nurse multiple times daily. At home, when his parents go to social events without him, he becomes anxious and angry. Frequently, he will steal and hide the car and house keys. He is known to chase the car down the driveway grabbing onto the door handles. When either parent places demands on Sean, he reacts angrily. He has a history of threatening his parents with a screwdriver and a spatula. He has also locked his parents out of the house after being grounded.

His developmental history reveals considerable problems in self-regulation. Sleeping schedules were extremely difficult to establish and maintain. Currently, he has difficulty initiating and maintaining his sleep throughout the night. Additionally, toilet training was established with great difficulty and marked by several accidents until 6 years of age. His parents explained this by saying, "He wanted to do this on his own terms."

At school he has a few friends. His school performance is average (C's) which is far below his standardized test scores. He often refuses to do school assignments and has earned several detentions due to frequent but minor disruptive behaviors (e.g., talking, leaving class, out-of-seat behavior, disrespectful speech to teachers). Educational testing reveals no learning disabilities.

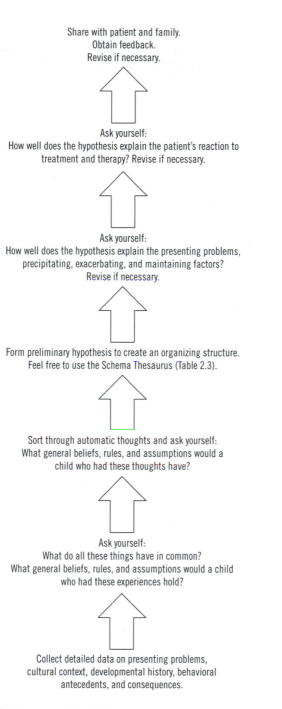

Share with patient and family.
Obtain feedback.
Revise if necessary.

Ask yourself:
How well does the hypothesis explain the patient's reaction to
treatment and therapy? Revise if necessary.

Ask yourself:
How well does the hypothesis explain the presenting problems,
precipitating, exacerbating, and maintaining factors?
Revise if necessary.

Form preliminary hypothesis to create an organizing structure.
Feel free to use the Schema Thesaurus (Table 2.3).

Sort through automatic thoughts and ask yourself:
What general beliefs, rules, and assumptions would a
child who had these thoughts have?

Ask yourself:
What do all these things have in common?
What general beliefs, rules, and assumptions would a child
who had these experiences hold?

Collect detailed data on presenting problems,
cultural context, developmental history, behavioral
antecedents, and consequences.

Figure 2.3   Bottom-up case formulation process.

His parents are both highly educated second-generation Asian American professionals. His father is an oncologist and his mother is an attorney. Father has a history of generalized anxiety disorder (GAD). The family values achievement, self-control, and respect. When Sean avoids school or reacts angrily to demands at home, his parents tend to indulge him by letting him stay at home and relieving the demands. His child psychiatrist has placed him on several trials of SSRIs.

Sean holds beliefs such as "School is boring," "I know more than my teachers," "Others should not make the rules," "Emotions make me feel out of control," "When I am anxious and panicking, the only people who can comfort me are my mom and dad," "Without my mom and dad, I'll go crazy," and "My mom and dad must make sure I am safe."

Using the rudiments and rubrics, Sean's problems were conceptualized along the lines of "I must remain in absolute control to maintain my sense of competence and safety in an overly demanding, unpredictable, and restrictive world where negative feelings signal being out of control and others must make sure I am comfortable."

Case Example 2: Ami

Ami is a 9-year-old first-generation American girl of Arabic descent who presents with significant depressive symptoms. She suffers from sad and anxious moods, fatigue, loss of appetite, disturbed sleep, anhedonia, social withdrawal, and lethargy. She isolates herself at recess and roams the playground aimlessly. Frequently, she kicks a soccer ball around the field by herself. Ami is reluctant to join group games, projects, or select partners at school instead preferring to play alone.

Her social history is punctuated by teasing, bullying, and racial slurs. She has been the target of bullying by peers who say she is not wanted because of "my brown skin" and "I am not a Christian." At lunch, Ami reported that several boys refer to her as a "terrorist." At recess, she is tagged so hard she falls down ("They hurt my back"). When she cries at these incidents, the teacher moves her desk away from the others in a corner to "protect" her.

Ami holds the following beliefs: "I'll never fit in," "I'm an outcast," "I'm a freak," "I'm ugly," "No one will be my friend," "I should stay quiet and still until I am safe," "There's something wrong with me," and "There's nothing I can do to make things work out."

All developmental milestones are within normal limits. Her medical history is unremarkable and no medicine is prescribed. Her Children's Depression Inventory raw score is 28 indicating presence of strong self-reported depressive symptoms. She is pessimistic but denies suicidal ideation. A recent Wechsler Intelligence Scale for Children (WISC)-IV IQ score is 140 indicating intellectual giftedness. She is also a talented soccer player.

Ami lives at home with her mother and father who own a grocery store. Her father was a professional soccer player in Iran. Her mother worked as an English translator. Her parents see her as "too sensitive" and worry she is a "trouble maker" at her school. Ami's emotions are dismissed with the parents stating, "There is no time for tears. She put her heart toward studying and soccer." They urge her to "hold your tears until they dry up inside you."

For Ami, the conceptual hypothesis was "I'm strange, peculiar, odd, and inadequate in a rejecting, hostile, critical, judgmental, and excluding world where people don't accept me or my feelings."

Case Example 3: Josef

Josef is a 14-year-old Caucasian child who lives in an ultraconservative, highly religious Christian home. He is an average student who goes to private Christian school. His biological mother died unexpectedly in a car crash when he was 7 years old. His father then had a brief affair with his deceased wife's married younger sister, which was discovered by his in-laws. Subsequently, his deceased wife's family disowned him as well as Josef. Josef's father then remarried a very religious and conservative woman when Josef was 9 years old. At her urging, father became "born again."

The stepmother and Josef have a very conflictual relationship. She bans music, pop culture (e.g., *People* magazine, lingerie inserts in the Sunday paper) and screens movies and television shows in strict accordance with the guidelines posted on the church's Web site.

Although Josef was described as somewhat withdrawn and mildly depressed after his mother's untimely death, there were no significant concerns until age 9. At that time, he began to exhibit rapidly escalating behavior problems such as fire setting, stealing, lying, searching the Internet for pornography, and bedwetting. At family gatherings, which occur at the stepmother's family, he steals and hoards female undergarments. He frequently writes his name on the under-garment with a red felt pen. His medical and developmental history is unremarkable. His family history is remarkable for cocaine abuse by father when he was in his 20s. History of child abuse, domestic abuse, or any trauma other than loss of mother was denied.

At school, he is very disruptive often refusing to do assign-ments and making rude comments to female teachers ("I don't take instructions from bitches like you"). Recently, he stole breath mints and makeup from a teacher's purse. At a school dance, he stole a bracelet from a female peer. In general, he does well with male teachers and has numerous strong friend-ships with male peers. When he is confronted with his misbe-haviors, he claims no knowledge of the incident.

Josef holds the following automatic thoughts: "My urges are too strong to control so why try?" "I am a bad seed and no one can help me," "I am following a life of no purpose and no one can correct me," "I am weird and have strange habits," "I must have the advantage in all relationships," "Weak peo-ple are asking to be taken advantage of. I feed off of them. It's kind of like the laws of nature," "If I don't get caught, who cares," "Girls are there to be taken advantage of," and "Self-control is BS."

For Josef, the case formulation was "I am unwanted, sinful, and deprived in a world filled with loss, lack of affection and pleasures I must have where people are rejecting, abandoning, overcontrolling, and more fortunate than me."

CONCLUSION

Ideally, the case examples illustrate the conceptualization process. Indeed, Betan and Binder (2010) adopt an interest-ing perspective on case conceptualization and encourage clinicians to metabolize theory. Specifically, they (p. 144) explained "making theory one's own involves what we refer to as a metabolizing theory—to be so familiar in the theory's key concepts, explanation of pathology, and mechanism of change that they become automatic in one's way of thinking about and approaching unique clinical contexts." We hope you are able to metabolize the rubrics of case conceptualization pre-sented in this chapter and become facile in your appreciation of patients' individual circumstances.

Three

Therapeutic Stance

INTRODUCTION

Embedding procedures and techniques into a robust therapeutic stance is a pivotal first clinical step. A therapeutic stance is the way you conduct your therapeutic business. It involves your approach, style, and manner with patients. The therapeutic stance shapes the therapeutic alliance and the application of techniques.

The stance is characterized by a collaborative approach, guided discovery, and flexible attitudes. Moreover, the stance facilitates tolerating negative emotional states and discomfort, and managing ambiguity. The stance enables you to maintain transparency, focus on creating doubt, and remain faithful to the experiential foundation of cognitive behavioral therapy (CBT).

RUDIMENTS

In this section, key rudiments are explained. You will learn to adopt a treatment stance that emphasizes collaborative empiricism and guided discovery. Additionally, the importance of harvesting flexible attitudes, tolerating ambiguity, and focusing on creating doubt is discussed. Finally, you learn to conduct cognitive behavioral psychotherapy (CBP) in a transparent way that brings the head and heart to consensus.

Collaborative Rather Than Prescriptive Approach

A core therapeutic value in cognitive behavioral therapy is *collaboration* (A. T. Beck, Rush, Shaw, & Emery, 1979; J. S. Beck, 1995). Collaboration means working together toward reaching the patients' and families' goals. Creed and Kendall (2005) found the perception of high levels of collaboration between child and therapist predicted a strong working alliance. This partnership agreement requires active engagement by patients and an authoritative but not authoritarian stance on the part of the therapist. There is less emphasis on the doctor's authority or prescriptive power. Accordingly, most interventions are built by consensus rather than unilaterally imposed.

Collaboration is a dimensional process and is measured by degrees rather than in all-or-none terms (Friedberg & Gorman, 2007; Friedberg & McClure, 2002). Several variables shape the appropriate degree of collaboration including level of acuity, emotional maturity, stage of treatment, and patient characteristics (Friedberg & McClure, 2002). Table 3.1 summarizes these variables and gives rules of thumb about therapeutic directiveness.

Table 3.1   Rules of Thumb Regarding Levels of Therapeutic Directiveness

Factor	Specific Dimension	Level of Directiveness
Age	Younger	Higher
	Older	Lower
Level of acuity	Higher	Higher
	Lower	Lower
Stage of treatment	Early	Higher
	Later	Lower
Patient motivation	Higher	Lower
	Lower	Higher
Patient hopelessness	Higher	Higher
	Lower	Lower
Patient fear of disclosure	Higher	Higher
	Lower	Lower
Patient controllingness	Higher	Lower
	Lower	Higher
Patient competitiveness	Higher	Lower
	Lower	Higher
Patient argumentativeness	Higher	Lower
	Lower	Higher
Patient frustration tolerance	Higher	Lower
	Lower	Higher
Patient tolerance for ambiguity	Higher	Lower
	Lower	Higher
Tolerance for negative affect	Higher	Lower
	Lower	Higher

Guided Discovery Rather Than Interpretation: Facilitating the Art of the Possible

The engine of CBT is *Socratic dialogue*. Socratic dialogue enables patients to create their own data platform upon which to base their conclusions. Guided dialogue prompts a discovery of new alternatives, perspectives, and possibilities.

Guided discovery is based on dialogue not debate (Rutter & Friedberg, 1999). Berman (1997) pointed out the differences between dialogue and debate. Debate requires opposition, whereas dialogue emphasizes collaboration. Debate narrows possibilities, whereas dialogue broadens perspectives. Debate drives people further into their own worldviews, whereas dialogue prompts sharing differing views. Dialogue encourages the view that there are many angles from which to view things, whereas debate communicates there is only one answer.

Guided discovery relies on the principle that data is generated by the patient. Interpretation tends to rely on data generated by the clinician. As cognitive therapists, we are concerned about how patients subjectively interpret their experiences rather than superimposing an interpretation on their experience. In our view, interpretations come from inside the therapist's head rather than from the patient. Interpretations almost create the pressure to read patients' minds. Guided discovery, on the other hand, eliminates the need for such mindreading and instead honors patients' reports.

Guided discovery involves asking questions and coaching patients to form their own conclusions. Interpretations involve the doctor making conclusions and judgments for the patients about their experience. Guided discovery also relies on hypothesis testing (Perris, 1989). Perris (1989) noted that hypotheses are forward-looking questions that offer tests based on data, whereas interpretations are backward-looking statements that apply an explanation to something that already happened. Interpretations also do not involve testable consequences.

Harvesting Open and Flexible Attitudes

In the wonderful movie *Dead Poets Society* (Haft, Witt, Thomas, & Weir, 1989), the creative teacher, played by Robin Williams, invites the students to leave their seats, stand on the teacher's desk, and scan the room. The idea is to teach the children to see the world from a new angle.

Similarly, cognitive therapists work diligently to help youngsters harvest open and flexible attitudes (Friedberg,

Gorman, & Beidel, 2009). In a very simple sense, through the course of cognitive therapy children learn there are always multiple ways to look at one situation. Openness in cognitive therapy is sparked by a curious attitude. As a therapist, your job is to stimulate children's curiosity and search for alternative explanations. Therefore, you need to avoid either directly or indirectly communicating that there is only one right way to think. The point is facilitating children's accurate thinking rather than encouraging them to parrot back what you think.

Finally, the goal of cognitive therapy is developing accurate appraisals rather than 100% positive thoughts (Padesky, 1988; Seligman, Reivich, Jaycox, & Gillham, 1995). Thus, some accurate appraisals may be tinged with negativity (e.g., "I screwed up but that doesn't mean I am an awful person"). Seligman et al. (1995) remarked that cognitive therapy relies on thought testing, data collection, and behavioral experiments, whereas positive thinking merely counts on affirmations and verbal persuasion. You should remember that verbal persuasion is the least effective form of behavior change (Bandura, 1977b).

Harvesting open and flexible attitudes promotes being attuned to cultural variables. Cornel West urged individuals to "interrogate their hidden assumptions." Further, Wright, Basco, and Thase (2006) recommended deliberate introspection and self-reflection to examine potential cultural biases. They suggested several specific guidelines for monitoring negative reactions to groups of diverse patients including asking yourself "Am I having difficulty expressing empathy with a particular type of patient?" "Do I feel stiff or unnatural in treatment sessions with specific patients?" and "Am I dreading appointments with particular patients of different groups?" (p. 36). As mentioned in Chapter 2, tuning into cultural vicissitudes also requires asking about and discussing experiences of oppression, marginalization, and prejudice. Cultural sensitivity and responsiveness requires self-acceptance of naïveté as well as an appreciation of individuals living in contexts (Ridley, Chih, & Olivera, 2000).

Tolerating Negative Emotional States and Discomfort

Cognitive behavioral psychotherapists learn about the tragedies of patients' lives on an hourly basis (Leahy, 2007). In psychotherapy, children, adolescents, and their families share their painful experiences in heartfelt and detailed ways. They express privately held secrets to therapists that they otherwise would tell no one (Brew & Kottler, 2008). Effective cognitive

behavioral psychotherapists are skilled at provoking emotionality in patients, tolerating their distress and applying coping
skills to modulate the emotional state. CBT is an emotionally
evocative approach and requires child psychiatrists to welcome, accept, and work with patients' high levels of expressed
emotion.

Tolerating Ambiguity

Like most people, child psychiatrists and other mental health
professionals seem to gravitate toward absolute certainty.
Certainty provides a perception of control and sometimes
safety. However, psychotherapy is an ambiguous task regardless of efforts toward clarity. Elements of doubt inevitably
creep into the therapeutic encounter. Schulte, Bochum, and
Eifert (2002) characterized psychotherapy as a time pressured,
complex and constantly changing experience "that presents
an overload of information of high uncertainty" (p. 321).
Accordingly, cognitive behavior therapists are advised to tolerate this ambiguity (Padesky, 2007).

Young people's lives are often complicated and messy circumstances that are multidetermined by an often undefined
interaction of systemic, environmental, biological, ethnocultural, developmental, contextual, and dispositional variables.
Waiting to intervene before clarity is achieved is commonly
impractical. Therefore, clinicians must be comfortable with
known unknowns (Friedberg, Gorman, & Beidel, 2009).

Focus on Creating Doubt Rather Than Refutation or Disputation

The noted CBT expert, Dr. Christine A. Padesky (1988), stated
that the goal of cognitive therapy is to create doubt where
there was once certainty of belief. The key is for patients to
develop balanced accurate appraisals rather than 100% positive beliefs. Simply, in your work, young people do not have to
convince themselves their negative beliefs are totally untrue.
Rather, they need to see them as not 100% accurate. Indeed,
this decreases the possibility of having to browbeat youngsters
until they submit to a Pollyannish conclusion.

CBT Is Transparent and Empirical

"What you see is what you get" is a common-sense way to
describe CBT's transparent nature. There is no mystery about
CBT. Because of this transparency, CBT is sometimes mistakenly seen as simplistic. CBT is common-sensical but far from

simplistic. CBT is committed to patients and doctors being on the same page. Therefore, case conceptualizations, treatment plans, therapeutic rationales, and specific procedures are shared and explained in everyday language with a minimum of jargon.

Bring the Head and Heart to Consensus

It is common for patients to say they believe new attributions on a logical or rational level but the thoughts do not feel right (J. S. Beck, 1995). Simply, they are complaining that the thoughts lack emotional resonance. There is a disconnect between the head and the heart. The job of a cognitive behavioral therapist is to help bring the patient's head and heart to consensus (Padesky, 2004).

Applying an experiential here and now focus in treatment unites the head and heart in cognitive therapy. Cognitive behavioral psychotherapy becomes a most exciting enterprise when children and adolescents restructure their thoughts and feelings in present tense and real time (Friedberg & Gorman, 2007). There should be a sense of the urgency of now in your sessions.

RUBRICS

The "Rudiments" section details the practical guidelines associated with establishing and maintaining a productive therapeutic stance in CBP. The section begins with recommendations for creating a productive working alliance and engaging avoidant children, adolescents, and families. Showing concern and keeping an alert ear are the next rubrics. Learning to rely on open-ended questions, eliminating why questions, unpacking generalities, working with intense emotions, and applying CBP in a fun way round out the "Rubrics" section.

Create a Productive Working Alliance

We agree with Shirk and Karver's (2006) definition of a working alliance: "the client's experience of the therapist as someone who can be counted on for help in overcoming problems or distress" (p. 480). The key is for the child to see you as an advocate rather than an adversary. Put another way, you want to work with rather than against the child. While this seems like a very simple rubric, it is sometimes difficult to maintain. At times, children and families may become anxious, angry, and hopeless during the course of psychotherapy. They may avoid or rebel against change. In these circumstances, we recommend aligning with patients against their distress. Toward this end, it is often helpful to make the clinical complaint the third-party enemy and steadfastly team up versus a common foe.

The following three tips give you a guide for developing a productive working alliance.

1. *Instilling hope* is a central element in facilitating a productive working alliance (Frank, 1961). Increased hopefulness propels motivation (Goldfried & Davila, 2005). Hope is not blind, false optimism but rather a sense of positive expectations. Dr. Christine Padesky (1988) operationalized this process by teaching patients that where their thinking is inaccurate, we'll teach them better questions to ask and where their thoughts accurately reflect negative realities, we'll teach them to problem solve.

2. *Tuning into patients' internal and external experiences* develops a productive alliance (Bennett-Levy, 2006). Greenberg and Elliott (1997) noted that empathic therapists are alert to the subtleties of meaning and emotion. Citing Adam Smith, Brew and Kottler (2008) concluded that empathy requires observation of another person's emotional arousal and the imagination necessary to share this experience.

3. *Setting limits* is a third essential feature in an impactful alliance. Limit setting is reassuring and reduces ambiguity. Without limits, children do not know what is acceptable or unacceptable. Therefore, in this vacuum, they may inhibit their behavior due to the fear that it is inappropriate or exhibit inappropriate behavior due to lack of information. Every therapist adopts a different set of limits, but regardless of the limit, follow-through is essential.

Engage Avoidant Children, Adolescents, and Families

When I (RDF) was an intern at the Naval Training Center–San Diego, my supervisor warned me, "The only person who likes change is a wet baby." Avoidance is the rule rather than the exception in clinical practice. In CBT, avoidance is a self-protective maneuver that is motivated by anxiety (Liotti, 1987). It is the patient's way to retain the status quo, the predictable, and the familiar. Avoidance is a natural, not a negative treatment phenomenon. Working with avoidance rather than against it is a necessary struggle (Chu, Suveg, Creed, & Kendall, 2010). Following we list six rubrics for these necessary struggles.

Provide choices and options. Newman (1994) recommended giving patients a set of options when stuck points in therapy are encountered (e.g., What would you like to do? What would you like to happen? Which things would you like to address: _____, _____, or _____? Do you think it would be helpful to talk about _____?). If options are provided, it is less likely that patients will see themselves as cornered and they will not be so ready to push back.

Ask permission. Newman (1994) suggested that therapists ask patients' permission to broach their avoided areas (May I ask you about _____? May I ask you a difficult question? May I ask you to do something difficult?). Asking for permission facilitates informed consent. Moreover, giving permission bolsters the patient's sense of control and active ownership in the therapeutic process.

Be empathic with the avoidance. Change is hard. Children and their families generally seek treatment after periods of struggle where unproductive thinking, feelings, and behavior patterns have become rigid and overlearned. Therefore, change requires them to think, feel, and act out of their familiar comfort zone. Therefore, avoidance is reduced and therapeutic approach behavior is reinforced when you become empathic with avoidance rather than blaming the patient.

Speak the patient's language but don't become a peer. CBT, like any psychotherapy, is language based. Therefore, productive therapeutic stances are marked by the ability to speak a child's or adolescent's language. You should pay particular attention to the vocabulary or words you use with patients. Be particularly cautious with big words (*defensive, provocation*), abstract concepts (*engaged in treatment, externalization*), and jargon (*diagnosis, prognosis, alliance*) with young patients and their families. Additionally, please be careful about talking down to youngsters and their parents.

Finally, while it is perfectly appropriate to sprinkle your language with child- and teen-friendly language, be wary about talking like a teenager. Teenagers are particularly sensitive to preserving their argot (Kail & Cavanaugh, 2009). If you trespass their boundary, they are likely to resent your intrusion and withdraw.

Use prefacing remarks. Preparing children and their families for potentially difficult and distressing issues reduces their avoidance. Prefacing remarks soften the blow (Newman, 1994).

Therefore, telling patients "I'm going to ask you a difficult question," "Some boys and girls find this issue upsetting," and "The next thing we are going to do may get you angry" allow children and their families to ready themselves and achieve a greater sense of control.

Keep your eye on the ball. Newman (1994) nicely teaches us to "gently persist when patients subtly avoid" (pp. 64–65). When emotionally evocative items are brought up in treatment, young patients may derail and distract. They may want to try to change the topic to red herrings or unimportant subjects. In these circumstances, use the case formulation to guide you and keep you on track toward treatment targets. Gently persist by prompting patients to return to the relevant issues. Empathize with the pressure to change course (e.g., "This is hard work. Talking about _____ makes it very real. Of course, you would want to change topics"). Process their continued avoidance by tying it to their presenting complaints (e.g., "I can really see how much you believe that avoiding strong feelings is better than dealing with them head on").

Show your concern rather than persuading the patient you can be trusted and take care of them: Talk is cheap.

Bandura (1977b) illustrated the notion that persuasion is the least efficacious form of behavior change. Nonetheless, many clinicians urge patients to trust them and try to convince them their office is a safe place. Not surprisingly then, these same therapists are disappointed when patients do not immediately trust them completely.

Trust is earned the hard way in the minute-to-minute transactions with the patient. Rather than persuading the patient or relying on your degree or authority, you must demonstrate your trustworthiness. As previously mentioned, setting limits is a great way to show trustworthiness and concern. Being on time and consistent with your appointments is another way to build trust. Lateness and repeated cancellations communicates disrespect. Following through on commitments is another way to communicate trust. In a general sense, this means if a letter needs to be sent, the letter is placed in the mail in a timely fashion. Following up on homework is another way to demonstrate trustworthiness and concern. If you do not follow up, it sends the message that you do not think the process is important. Another simple way to demonstrate concern is to remember what the patient says and does. Following up on their responses on any self-report communicates to the patient that you are consistent and concerned.

KEEP AN "ALERT" EAR

Television's fictional psychiatrist Frasier Crane famously began his radio show by declaring, "I'm listening …" Although his comments were comical and often wildly off base, the idea of alert listening is pivotal to conducting good CBT with children and adolescents. Alert therapeutic listening is intense, focused, and requires undivided attention that many believe resembles a meditative stance (Brew & Kottler, 2008). In this stance, you are undistracted by irrelevant internal (e.g., What's for lunch?) and external stimuli (noises in the hall or outside on the street). When you are fully "present" in this way, you genuinely hear your patient.

The curiosity associated with collaborative empiricism and guided discovery encourages alert listening. Active, alert listening works to decode subtle messages and make the implicit explicit (Brew & Kottler, 2008). Figure 3.1 provides some guidelines on keeping an alert ear.

Allowing yourself to stay dumb is a great way to keep alert. For example, Raymond A. Fidaleo, MD, a wonderful mentor, friend, and colleague, taught me (RDF) to see myself as Columbo the TV detective who seemed clueless but eventually grasped everything. Young, Grant, and DeRubeis (2003) noted that Columbo always seemed puzzled and asked questions that were aimed at gathering information rather than trapping someone. When you adopt a Columbo therapeutic stance, you pick up on nuances and subtleties then curiously ask what they mean rather than presuming you know what they imply. Figure 3.2 gives some examples of Columbo comments.

Rely on Open-Ended Questions

Open-ended questions facilitate a fuller exploration of children's experiences (Brew & Kottler, 2008). They tend to be more ambiguous and offer the freedom of an array of responses (e.g., What bothers you about your mother?). Moreover, they tend to be less directive and leading (How did you come to that conclusion?). Open-ended questions encourage more detailed and spontaneous responses. Finally, because they are ambiguous, not a yes or no type query, and the range of possible responses is wide, children and adolescents find it harder to give what they think is the right answer. Figure 3.3 lists some closed-ended questions and their open-ended alternatives.

Revealing Comment	Alert Ear Guided Discovery Question
I cry a river of tears.	A river of tears? Tell me more about what happens when this river of tears flows.
I'm torn between my wild and tame side.	Describe your wild and tame sides. What do you do when you are wild? Tame? How acceptable is your wild side? Tame side? When are you wild? Tame? With whom are you wild? Tame?
I build myself an island of fear.	An island? What are the ways to and from this island? In what ways is this island connected to the mainland?
I want the soundtrack of my life to have a hip-hop beat but it really sounds like an accordion.	What is it like for you to live with an accordion soundtrack? How would a hip-hop beat be better for you?

Figure 3.1 Keeping an alert ear.

Strike Why Questions From Your Vocabulary

Why questions have extremely limited usefulness in CBT with children. Why questions cause children to reflect rather than report their experience. Therefore, intellectualization is fostered and the experiential, phenomenological approach is compromised. Second, why questions prompt children to explain and defend their position possibly facilitating an adversarial rather than a collaborative approach (Padesky, 1988). Third, children and adolescents are likely to see why questions as implicit criticisms and accusations (e.g., Why would you do that?; Brew & Kottler, 2008).

Why questions seem to target patients' motivations. However, we believe relying on X-File questions instead of why questions is a better, more collaborative strategy. X-File questions are inspired by the TV show and movies. (For those unfamiliar, X-Files are unknown mysterious cases where events occur but no one knows why.) X-File questions help you determine the reasons things occur without relying on why questions.

"Forgive my ignorance but I don't know what went through your mind when _____ happened."

"Help me out, I don't know what your eye blinking is trying to say."

"I'm a little lost. You said you didn't care what your mother thinks about you, but you get really upset when she criticizes you."

"I'm trying to keep things straight. Can you break things down much more simply for me?"

"I'm an expert on children in general, but you're the expert on what is going on with you."

"I noticed you looked away when you said you thought Dad loved your sister more than you. What do you suppose your looking away means?"

"You keep saying 'I don't know' or 'nothing' but there's so much going on inside you. How can that be?"

Figure 3.2   Columbo comments.

Closed-Ended Questions	Open-Ended Alternatives
Are you sad?	How do you feel?
	What things make you cry?
	When do you feel sad?
	What makes you feel down?
Do you have any friends?	Who do you play with?
	Tell me who you hang out/chill with?
	Who do you sit with at lunch?
	Who do you play with at recess?
Do you like school?	What are your favorite things at school?
	What are your least favorite things?
	Tell me about your teacher? Your class?
Do you want to change?	What are the advantages of things staying the same?
	What are the disadvantages of things staying the same?
	What's in it for you if you change?
	What do you expect will happen if things change?
	How hard do you think it will be to change?

Figure 3.3   Open-ended questions.

Figure 3.4 lists several why questions and recommended
X-File alternatives.

Unpack Generalities Into Specifics

Vague generalities are difficult to translate into viable treatment targets. Thus, it makes designing interventions and
measuring the effectiveness of these interventions quite problematic. The more generally the complaint is described, the
more the demand for therapist mindreading and overreaching
becomes. You want to make diffuse problem descriptions into
discrete ones by unpacking generalities into specifics.

"Bobby doesn't feel good about himself," "Courtney does not
listen," "Sal has an attitude," and "Maya panics in school" are
all examples of diffuse complaints. We do not know enough

Why Question	**X-File Alternative**
Why did you skip school?	What problem were you trying to solve by skipping school?
	What's going on at school that you would prefer not having to deal with?
	What's hard about going to school?
Why don't you get along with your parents?	What bugs you about your parents?
	What does it seem they don't get about you?
	What do your parents do that annoys you?
	How would you like your parents to change?
Why are you so worried?	What is so scary for you?
	What dangers are you expecting?
	What is risky about _____?
Why don't you want to talk in therapy?	What do you guess might happen if you shared your thoughts and feelings with me?
	How do you suppose I will react if you shared your thoughts and feelings?
	What stops you from telling me about your thoughts and feelings?

Figure 3.4   X-File questions.

specifics to intervene. In what circumstances does Bobby not feel good about himself? When Courtney does not listen, what does she do? What does Sal have an attitude about? What runs through his head at that time? What does Maya's panic look like to others and feel like to her? Therefore, use open-ended questions to break these generalities into components.

Open-ended questions should help you discern the frequency (how often), intensity (how strong, severe, or impairing), and duration (how long) of the problem. Further, open-ended queries should identify the context of the problem (where, when, with whom, etc.). Finally, successful open-ended probes are aimed at pinpointing the observable elements of the problems (What does he do? What does the panic look like?). Figure 3.5 gives numerous examples.

Get Your Hands Dirty: Work With Strong Emotions

Goldfried (2003) emphasized the notion of "hot cognitions." Hot cognitions are the thoughts and images linked most closely to emotional intensity. To realize optimal therapeutic impact, you must assess, test, and modify these fired-up thoughts and images. In-session arousal is a simple way to work with hot cognitions (Friedberg & Gorman, 2007; Samoilov & Goldfried, 2000). When sessions are punctuated by emotional arousal and affective engagement, they become experiential and transparent. You are privileged to see and work with the youngsters' distress. Problems are dealt with in their raw, messy realities. In sum, this experiential process is seen as contributing to CBT's success with children (Gosch, Flannery-Schroeder, Mauro, & Compton, 2006).

Apply CBT in a Creative and Fun Way

You must remember that children are not just short adults. I (RDF) was also fortunate to have Eric Minturn, PhD, as a supervisor. Minturn used humor to remind us not to adultomorphize young children by using abstract and applying arcane concepts to them. I fondly recall him stating, "It is hard to contemplate the existential philosopher Binswanger when you are sitting in a child-size chair." CBT is not a sterile, mechanistic enterprise (Friedberg & Clark, 2006). Rather, creativity and fun is encouraged to enlist children in the treatment process (Kendall & Beidas, 2007; Kendall et al., 1992; Kendall, Gosch, Furr, & Sood, 2008; Knell, 1993; Nelson, Finch, & Ghee, 2006; Stallard, 2002, 2005; Wright et al., 2006). Fun and creativity fit nicely with the here and now experiential, nature of CBT with

General Description	Unpacking Questions
I'm panicking.	How do you panic?
	What do you do when you panic?
	What do you look like when you panic?
People think I am a dork.	Who thinks you are a dork?
	When do they think you are a dork?
	What do you mean when you say "dork?"
	How can you tell they think you are a dork?
I'm a freak.	What do you mean by "freak?"
	What are you referring to?
	What do you see as the signs that make you a freak?
I'm invisible.	What makes you say you are invisible?
	How do people treat you when you are invisible?
	If you were truly seen, how would things in your life be different?

Figure 3.5   Unpacking generalities.

children (Knell, 1993). Wright and colleagues (2006) stated that humor "normalizes and humanizes" (p. 34) treatment. Therefore, being animated and playful is vital in CBT with children. Borcherdt (2002) noted that humor decreases defensiveness, demandingness, and guardedness. Additionally, he stated humor increases transparency, emotional tolerance, energy, and therapeutic investment.

Artwork, storytelling, crafts, puppet play, improvisational theater games, board games, and toy play are all welcomed in CBT. The judicious use of humor is also a good therapeutic stance. All these elements make CBT more accessible and engaging to children. Indeed, "play is the medium by which inaccurate internal dialogues are elicited and more adaptive coping methods are taught" (Friedberg & McClure, 2002, pp. 150–151). Children and adolescents feel freer to express themselves in a creative and fun environment. In essence, you want children to feel comfortable being fully and genuinely themselves.

CONCLUSION

This chapter spelled out the rubrics and rudiments associated with a productive therapeutic stance. Practicing the guidelines for engaging avoidant patients will help you smooth out the rough spots in the therapy. Behaving in a concerned and genuinely interested manner propels a good working alliance. Listening alertly and intervening with open-ended and X-File questions helps you gain a fuller appreciation of children and adolescents' problems. Finally, remember to make sure you get your "hands dirty" when working creatively with strong emotions.

Four

Session Structure

INTRODUCTION

Session structure is a general rubric for conducting cognitive behavioral therapy (CBT) sessions. A template helps you organize and prioritize what you do in session. Templates assist you in making the session flow smoothly and logically. With experience, you will find that the structure of the session becomes second nature and you will gain flexibility. Flexibility allows you to tailor your sessions to each individual patient. However, to get to that point, it is important to have a solid grasp of the rudiments and rubrics of session structure. This chapter describes the rudiments associated with mood check-ins, homework review, agenda setting, session content, homework assignment, and eliciting feedback. The "Rubrics" section provides detailed information on implementing the components of session structure.

RUDIMENTS

Typically, cognitive therapy sessions are broken down into six distinctive components (J. S. Beck, 1995). Session structure's six components consist of a mood check-in; homework review; setting the agenda; the actual session content; homework assignments; and then feedback from the child, adolescent, or family regarding their perception of the session. Beginning therapists may feel lost and not know where to begin or how to proceed within a session. Adhering to the session structure offers you a guiding outline from which to structure sessions. It can also be helpful for patients because it reduces the anxiety associated with the therapeutic process. Session structure produces an organized flow and adds predictability to sessions. Simply, children and their parents learn what to expect from psychotherapy. Following a routine session structure often promotes a feeling of self-control that many clients lack and teaches them how to regulate and manage their thoughts and feelings.

Mood Check-In

Sessions begin with a check-in, which serves multiple purposes. It allows the therapist and the patient a chance to reflect on his or her current mood and symptoms as well as compare them to previous sessions. Mood check-in also provides practice in self-reflection. Detailed information on the children's reported moods prompts identification of various triggers.

Regular mood check-ins allow you to assess symptom relief or worsening. Using self-report measures, such as the Children's Depression Inventory (CDI), Multidimensional Anxiety Scale for Children (MASC), or Screen for Anxiety Related Emotional Disorders (SCARED) can give more objective data and are often used for this purpose. Children often find reporting symptoms on a scale much easier and less threatening than verbal expression therefore allowing you to get more accurate information. It also gives them the opportunity to be at a somewhat greater distance from their emotions psychologically, which may be important if they have difficulty sharing their painful feelings or if they are intimidated sharing their dysphoric feelings with an adult authority figure. In the following paragraphs we discuss recommendations for objective measures for mood check-ins. Additionally, the Web site operated by Massachusetts General Hospital school psychiatry program offers a very complete list of measures (www.schoolpsychiatry.org).

Depression and Anxiety

A variety of self-report inventories for depression and its accompanying features are available. The CDI (Kovacs, 1985, 1992) is easy for children to complete and clinicians to score. Although it should not be used as a diagnostic tool, the CDI is a valuable instrument for tracking symptoms and evaluating treatment effects (Brooks & Kutcher, 2001; Friedberg, McClure, & Garcia, 2009; Myers & Winters, 2002; Silverman & Rabian, 1999).

The Beck Depression Inventory (BDI)-II is another widely used tool for assessing depression (A. T. Beck, 1996; A. T. Beck, Steer, & Brown, 1996; Dozois & Covin, 2004; Dozois, Dobson, & Ahnberg, 1998). Like the CDI, the BDI-II is sensitive to treatment changes. We recommend the use of the BDI-II with adolescents. The Beck Youth Depression Inventory is a new generation instrument that taps depressed mood and depressogenic symptoms in children ages 7 to 14 years (J. S. Beck, Beck, &

Jolly, 2001; Bose-Deakins & Floyd, 2004; Steer, Kumar, Beck, & Beck, 2005). Due to its recent emergence, sensitivity to treatment effects is unclear (Bose-Deakins & Floyd, 2004).

Finally, there are a number of measures available for assessing suicidal ideation. Items 2 and 9 on both the CDI and BDI-II are useful screens. The Suicidal Ideation Questionnaire (SIQ) and its junior high school version (SIQ-JR; W. M. Reynolds, 1987, 1988) are more detailed instruments and offer a more molecular analysis of the suicidal ideation. The Hopelessness Scale for Children (Kazdin, Rodgers, & Colbus, 1986) and the Beck Hopelessness Scale (A. T. Beck, Weissman, Lester, & Trexler, 1974) provided an in-depth look at children's hopelessness.

Anxiety

In this section, we will briefly discuss a variety of self-report measures for anxiety. The Screen for Child Anxiety Related Emotional Disorders (SCARED; Birmaher et al., 1997) and its revision (SCARED-R; Muris, Merckelbach, Van Brakel, & Mayer, 1999) are solid psychometric tools that are easy to administer and score. The Multidimensional Anxiety Scale for Children (MASC; March, 1997a, 1997b; March, Parker, Sullivan, Stallings, & Connors, 1997; March, Sullivan, & James, 1999) is another new generation self-report measure for children. The measure is somewhat longer and more complicated to score than the SCARED. Nonetheless, its psychometrics and clinical value are strong. The Beck Youth Anxiety Scale (BYAS; J. S. Beck et al., 2001) assesses fearfulness, worry, and somatic symptoms of *Diagnostic and Statistical Manual of Mental Disorders (DSM)-IV* anxiety disorders.

Particular anxiety disorders can be monitored with specific self-report tools. The Fear Survey Schedule (FSS-R; Ollendick, 1983; Ollendick, King, & Frary, 1989) identifies specific fears in children 7 to 16 years old. Social anxiety is the focus of the Social Phobia and Anxiety Inventory for Children (SPAI-C; Beidel, Turner, & Morris, 1995) and the Social Anxiety Scale for Children-Revised (SASC-R; LaGreca & Stone, 1993). The School Refusal Assessment Scale (SRAS; Kearney & Silverman, 1993) provides a functional analysis of school refusal behavior.

Anger

The Children's Inventory of Anger (CHiA; Nelson & Finch, 2000) provides a self-report of anger intensity and the situations that elicit the emotion. Like the CHiA, the Novaco Anger Scale and Provocation Inventory (NAS-PI; Novaco, 2003) also assesses emotional intensity and triggering situations. The Beck Anger Inventory for Youth (BANI-Y; J. S. Beck et al., 2001; J. S. Beck, Beck, Jolly, & Steer, 2005) specifically taps cognitive, behavioral, and physiological symptoms of anger.

Homework Review

Homework review is the next part of the session. When reviewing homework, you examine whether the patient has actually completed the assignment, the content of the assignment, what the patient thought about the assignment, and the patient's reaction. Homework assignments allow the child to practice skills important for decreasing symptoms and improving mood. When you review homework in session, it emphasizes to the children or adolescents the importance you place on the assignment.

Agenda Setting

Agenda setting refers to the collaborative identification of items or topics that will be addressed during the session. Agenda setting sets the outline for what you and your patient are going to be discussing during the session. Typically, they are listed in order of importance or preference.

In our experience, psychotherapists who do not consistently set agendas frequently complain they end sessions with an unsettling sense of incompleteness, disorganization, confusion, and dissatisfaction. They feel like they are spinning in place trying to focus on an endless array of seemingly disjointed and numbingly competing issues. Freeman and Dattilio (1992) poignantly called this a Hansel and Gretel approach to therapy where

> the patient goes through session dropping crumbs behind him or her labeled, "when I was younger ...," or "My mother ...," the aimless therapist runs along behind the patient scooping up the crumbs and hoping the patient will get to be where he or she is supposed to be going. When time has run out, the therapist ends the session and the patient, like Hansel and Gretel, is lost in the forest. (p. 376)

Freeman and Dattilio also tell us that agenda setting is a way to ensure true informed consent in every session. When children, adolescents, families, and clinicians collaboratively agree on the content of therapy, there are fewer surprises and potential misunderstandings.

The hand on the door phenomenon is a crucible that tests many psychotherapists. The hand on the door phenomenon refers to patients' "sharing the most emotional intense information at the end of the hour" (Bender & Messner, 2003, p. 156). Simply, at the end of the session, the patient tells you a provocative secret or urgent issue (e.g., "By the way, my uncle is molesting me" or "Oh, I forgot to tell you I am cheeking my pills and I'm going to kill myself. Good-bye."). While agenda setting will not completely eliminate the hand on the door phenomenon, clinical experience shows it reduces its frequency and highlights critical ruptures in the treatment alliance.

Agenda setting is most effective and engaging when patients assume ownership for the content. Collaboration promotes adherence and motivates patients. However, most patients enter therapy naïve to the process. Therefore, agenda setting needs to be explained to the patient. Moreover, children are used to parents and teachers dictating their agendas. The process of agenda setting allows them the opportunity to set up their own goals and fosters a greater sense of control. When children's self-identified issues are explored and discussed in the therapy session, they begin to feel as if they are being listened to and understood.

Session Content

Agenda items are specifically addressed in the session content. The content of the session is processed using a variety of techniques including psychoeducation, self-monitoring, behavioral procedures, cognitive restructuring, rational analysis, and performance attainment. Goals for the session content might range from increasing understanding of symptoms or the rationale for treatment; recognizing thoughts, feelings, and behaviors; modifying these thoughts, feelings, and behaviors; symptom relief; and relapse prevention. The therapist guides the patient to focus on particular problem areas, help with problem solving, and elicit specific thoughts and feelings about specific issues (A. T. Beck, Rush, Shaw, & Emery, 1979). Many of the therapeutic stance variables in Chapter 3 are applied during the session content.

Meaningful Compounds in Session Content: Skill Acquisition, Skill Application, Therapeutic Structure, Content, and Process

Integrating therapeutic structure, content, and process is pivotal (Friedberg & Gorman, 2007; Friedberg & McClure, 2002). Therapeutic structure involves the 3 T's of therapy: tools, tasks, and techniques. These are the elements presented in Chapters 5 to 10. Therapeutic content represents the thoughts, feelings, and behaviors produced by the structure. Therapeutic process refers to the way children negotiate the 3 T's. The 3 T's are general, whereas therapeutic content and process are individualized. Indeed, balancing structure, process and content is a difficult calculus (Friedberg, 2006).

Therapeutic structure includes diverse tasks, tools, and techniques such as agenda setting, homework assignments, feedback, psychoeducation, assessment, self-monitoring, problem solving, cognitive restructuring, social skills training, and exposure. The therapist structures the specific elements of each session. These elements provide the platform for the content and process to emerge. Structure variables are the sine qua non (without which there is nothing) in CBT. It always has to be there in order for you to get to the process and content.

Therapeutic content and process are first-degree relatives in CBT. In ordinary circumstances with typically straightforward patients, content is central to your therapeutic work. You apply acquired skills to the reported problematic thoughts, feelings, situations, and behaviors. In the extraordinary circumstances, process trumps content. This is where manuals and mere descriptions of techniques are silent. Process issues emerge when patients are noncompliant, competitive, rebellious, passive, ashamed, flirtatious, avoidant, controlling, withholding, cryptic, and so on. Process markers include tearfulness, psychomotor agitation, sighs, postural changes, tremulous speech, and eye rolls. Process becomes important when these markers and manifestations overshadow the content.

The following is an example where process overshadows content. Lianna is a 10-year-old perfectionistic, approval-seeking girl who presents with eating disorder not otherwise specified and generalized anxiety disorder. She dutifully completes homework assignments, puts written work in colorful folders, and does her homework on a word processing program so that it looks perfect. In the following dialogue, she has just handed in a daily thought record (Chapter 6) complete with coping counter thoughts (Chapter 7) packaged in a beautiful spiral-bound notebook.

Lianna: What do you think of my homework?
Therapist: It looks like you put a lot of care into it just like all your other assignments.
Lianna: Thanks. I love to do work and make things nice.
Therapist: I am curious about one thing, though.

Lianna: What's that?
Therapist: What would happen if your work was not so perfect?
Lianna: What do you mean?
Therapist: You said you love to make things nice. What if what you made was not so nice?
Lianna: I don't know.
Therapist: What about if you made a really messy assignment and even had some negative automatic thoughts and you couldn't turn it around?
Lianna: I wouldn't ever do that (hesitantly).
Therapist: So, what do you guess I would do if you gave me something not so nice?
Lianna (pausing and tearing up): I guess you would think I was lazy, messy, and not making the most of my opportunities.
Therapist: Wow, that's a lot of pressure.
Lianna (nods and more tears): I feel like that a lot especially with my mom and dad. I have to measure up to my older sister.

In this example, the therapist alertly realized that Lianna's perfectionistic way of completing and presenting her homework overshadowed the actual homework material. When the therapist made the process foreground and the content background, Lianna let loose with the automatic thoughts, "You'll think I was messy, lazy, and not making the most of my opportunities." This led to more productive work with hotter cognitions in the session.

Skill acquisition and application combine in CBT to form a powerful union. Skill acquisition is characterized by educating and teaching patients skills such as identifying thoughts and feelings, relaxation, and self-instruction. Skill application puts these procedures into action. Skill acquisition is commonly a straightforward and clean process. You introduce the skill in a gradual, clear, concise, and systematic manner. Skill application is generally a messier practice. In this process, you coach children to call on their acquired skills in problematic situations (e.g., when angry, depressed, tearful, and so forth). Skill application builds children's confidence in their coping through repeated practice.

Teaching a child to complete a thought record in session is a good example of skill acquisition. You can coach the child to complete the diary by using a typical example. The following short dialogue with 13-year-old Jai shows you how.

Therapist: Jai, let me show you how to complete this diary. Remember when you were outside in the waiting room watching MTV.

Jai: Yeah, that was good. I love MTV. I never get to watch it at home.

Therapist: So, we'll put watching the show under this column called situation. Now when Mom told you it was time to come back to my office for your appointment, how did you feel?

Jai: Mad, I wanted to watch more.

Therapist: OK, let's write that down here. And what went through your mind then?

Jai: Why can't you be late for once? It's not fair.

Therapist: Great. We'll put that down under the column called thoughts. See how easy this is.

After the skill has been acquired, application and generalization to the child's real-life issues takes place. As previously stated, CBT is best applied in the white-hot context of emotional arousal and raw world circumstances. Thus, the best time to apply the skill is when it is genuinely needed. Continuing with the earlier example with Jai, the following example shows you how to apply the thought diary.

Jai (crying): I hate my life. My parents are so bossy. They treat me like a baby and smother me (gasps). They suck the air right out of me.

Therapist: You have so many thoughts and feelings about your mom and dad bouncing around inside you.

Jai: I don't know what to do about them.

Therapist: Let's try to sort them out with a thought diary. How does that sound?

Jai: I don't know if it will help.

Therapist: That's a good question. Let's keep a watch out for that and check in after we try it. Now, I'll get you started. The situation is mother and father not letting you call your friends and go to the movies with a mixed group of boys and girls.

Jai: That's right.

Therapist: And you felt?

Jai: Sad and mad.

Therapist: How sad on a 1 to 10 scale?

Jai: 8.

Therapist: And mad?

Jai: 9.

Therapist: Good write those two feelings and their ratings in the feelings column. What did you tell me went through your mind?

Jai: You mean I hate my life and my bossy parents treat me like a freaking baby and suck all the air from me?

Therapist (smiles): Yeah, that's it. Write that down. Which thoughts seem to go with the sad feelings?

Jai: I hate my life.

Therapist: And the angry feelings?

Jai: My parents are treating me like a freaking baby and they suck all the life out of things.

Therapist: Now for the check-in I promised. ... You look calmer. How much did the diary help?

Jai: It's weird. It kind of sorts things out. I'm not so confused. And you know what's really weird, I didn't think you were listening or taking me too seriously. But when we wrote it down, I really thought you were.

Jai experienced the usefulness of the daily thought record (DTR) in real time and with a relevant issue. Additionally, completing the DTR had the added benefit of increasing the therapeutic alliance.

Homework Assignments

Homework is fundamental to CBT. Homework is a task that facilitates learning and generalization to children's natural environment (Tompkins, 2004). Additionally, homework translates abstract concepts into concrete activities. Homework assignments should naturally flow from the session content. It is one thing for a child to practice and master a skill in the therapist's office, but a completely different thing to actually utilize that skill in real-life situations. By assigning and reviewing the homework you send the message to the child that it is very important to continue working on the various skills that they practice in the midst of a therapy session. Without practice in their home environment, the chances of them generalizing their newly developed skills are much less likely.

Eliciting Feedback

Eliciting feedback strengthens the therapeutic alliance tremendously and reinforces the partnership between therapist and child. Feedback allows the therapist to gauge what the client is thinking about and how the therapy session is unfolding, as well as giving the therapist a chance to uncover misperceptions, distortions, and dissatisfactions the client has regarding the treatment. Without this feedback, these feelings may go on for weeks unaddressed, thus stalling therapy and delaying the advancement of the therapeutic process. Typically, feedback is elicited near the end of the session, but it is worthwhile to obtain feedback even during the midst of a session.

This portion of the session structure can be difficult at times, particularly for the beginning therapist. You may have doubts about your skills and fear potential negative feedback from the client that may reinforce your ideas about your inadequacy. To help face your fear, it may be very helpful to anticipate worst-case scenarios with regards to feedback from the client and prepare in your mind how you will handle them. It also helps to remember that for each individual client, you will have no idea at the beginning what may or may not be helpful for them, so it is unreasonable to expect yourself to be able to know the best therapeutic path every step of the way. In fact, it is expected that some trial and error will occur with regard to what therapeutic techniques and structure may be helpful for any particular client. Finally, as you practice eliciting feedback, it gets easier and easier.

When eliciting feedback from children, one needs to keep in mind they likely have never, or very rarely, been encouraged to give feedback to an adult. They may be very reluctant to give feedback to you because the process is so unfamiliar to them. Children and adolescents may have been taught that giving feedback to adults is disrespectful and may have experienced rejection or reprimands for giving negative feedback. Other children may be very sensitive and fear hurting your feelings if they give negative feedback. These circumstances are more fully elaborated in the following "Rubrics" section.

RUBRICS

In this section, we elaborate the rubrics with specific guidelines. Five pointers for getting the most out of mood check-ins are recommended. Ways of working with 12 reasons for noncompliance are suggested. Methods for processing session content without cognition hopping, doing superlative work with superficial cognitions, colluding with patients' distortions, and being caught in maladaptive interaction patterns are described. Finally, navigating problems in eliciting feedback and assigning homework are also outlined.

Mood Check-In

Mood check-ins may be done informally (e.g. "How did your week go?" "How are you feeling this week?") or more formally with assessment measures (e.g., CDI; SCARED; MASC; BDI-II; Swanson, Nolan, and Pelham Questionnaire [SNAP-IV]). Cognitive behavioral therapists regularly administer these measures depending on the severity, acuity, and lability of the patient. In the typical case, we administer the measure every 4 weeks. However, in unusual and severe cases, we give the instruments every week. In the following section we offer a few guidelines for processing the objective measures suggested.

Review the measure at the beginning of the session. If the measures are used as mood check-ins, they should be discussed in the beginning of the session. The measures highlight important potential agenda items and consequently help you guide the session.

Always check on the critical items regardless of the total score. The BDI-II and CDI both contain two items you should always review (items 2 and 9). Item 2 is the pessimism and hopelessness item, and item 9 is the suicidal ideation item. As you can readily realize, the total score may be relatively low but the child's suicidal potential could be quite high.

Inquire about changes from last administration. When you regularly administer the formal measures, tracking changes becomes easier. When the scores improve or deteriorate, you are able to identify factors that may promote risk and resilience. After reviewing the scores you might ask:

Your score is much better than last time. What's changed? What's been helpful for you?
Your score is much worse than last time. What's been different? What's made things worse for you?

Explore discrepancies between child and parent reports. Discrepancies between parent and child report are quite common (De Los Reyes & Kazdin, 2005; Silverman & Ollendick, 2005). A parent may unwittingly misattribute the cause of behavioral problems because they are not attuned to a child's internal states. Conversely, children may minimize symptoms in their self-reports to avoid circumstances such as further treatment, scrutiny, negative evaluation, or punishment. Children are better reporters of their internal states (e.g., thoughts, feelings), whereas parents are better reporters of behavior problems (Bird, Gould, & Staghezza, 1992; Loeber,

Green, Lahey, & Stouthamer-Loeber, 1991; Pelham, Fabiano, & Massetti, 2005). Moreover, parental reports of children's problems are influenced by parental moods (Chi & Hinshaw, 2002; Najman et al., 2000; Youngstrom, Loeber, & Stouthamer-Loeber, 2000).

Discuss discrepancies or inconsistencies between verbal report, clinical presentation, and the measure. Occasionally, results from the formal measure may not jive with the indications from children's verbal report or clinical presentations. For instance, the measures may reveal few problems but the child presently is in a profoundly depressed state. On the other hand, the scores may be sky high but the child presents in a bright, carefree, and unburdened manner. This discrepancy should be addressed directly and respectfully. Helpful questions might be:

> How much do these scores reflect the way you genuinely feel?
>
> Your scores on the form say you are feeling pretty well but you look really down. Which should we rely on? The form or the way you look?
>
> You scores on the checklist tell me that you are feeling pretty badly but you are joking around. How can we make sense of that?

Agenda Setting

As stated in the "Rudiments" section, an introduction to agenda setting is merited. The introductions should be clear and concise. The following is an example of an introduction.

> One way I work with boys and girls your age is to decide at the start of the session what we are going to work on together. Most of the time what we do here is up to you. Some of the time I will have things I want to make sure we work on. So each time we meet I'll ask you what you want to talk about right at the beginning of our time together. How does this sound?

Figure 4.1 gives you a list of top 10 questions for agenda setting.

The hand on the door phenomenon was initially described in the "Rudiments" section. In this section, we give you some rubrics to deal with the hand on the door. If the hand on the door phenomenon occurs, you, of course, must manage the immediate crisis. When the dust clears at the next session, you then place the hand on the door phenomenon on your agenda. You want to address the issue directly and in a curious,

1. What is it that we should talk about today?
2. What is on your mind today?
3. What should we focus on today?
4. How do you want to spend or use our time today?
5. What is it that you want to make sure we talk about today?
6. What is it that you absolutely, positively want to make sure we talk about before we end today? (Fed Ex question)
7. What is it that you want to make sure we cover today?
8. What things do you think we should deal with today?
9. What is on your agenda today?
10. What problems and challenges do you want to take on today?

Figure 4.1   Top 10 sample questions to set agendas.

1. What is the reason you were silent about _____ until the very end of the session?
2. How come you left talking about _____ until you were just about out the door?
3. What were your expectations about what I would do when you told me about _____ at the very end of our session?
4. What were the reasons you did not mention _____ until we said good-bye?
5. What does it say about our partnership when you leave these important issues unsaid until the end of our work?
6. What does it say about the trust you have in our relationship when you leave _____ until the very end of the session?
7. How can we make sure that you don't leave these things until the very last parts of the session?
8. How can we improve our partnership so you put the important problems on the table when we set agendas?
9. What are some ways we can make sure we do not have any hidden agenda items?
10. How can we make better use of the agenda setting?

Figure 4.2   Top 10 questions for processing the hand on the door phenomenon.

problem-solving manner. Faithfully adhering to session structure promotes transparency. Since the agenda setting has been introduced and applied in previous sessions, the hand on the door phenomenon clearly reflects a rupture in the collaborative alliance. Accordingly, we present the top 10 questions for processing the hand on the door in Figure 4.2.

Although agenda setting is frequently a straightforward practice, several interesting and clinically revealing processes may erupt. The following items address some common processes that may challenge beginning cognitive therapists.

Passive avoidance of agenda setting. Passive avoidance is reflected by responses such as "I don't know," "You're the doctor, you decide," or "Whatever" when asked for agenda items. When this happens, dive right into addressing the beliefs mediating the passive avoidance. These beliefs are most likely connected to the problems that bring the patient into cognitive behavioral psychotherapy ("What if I don't choose the right thing?" "It's better to let others decide," "Being invisible makes me less of a target," "If I don't attend to my problems, they will go away," and "Avoidance is ideal"). Useful questions might include:

> What goes through your mind when I ask for agenda items?
> What is it like for you to decide what we focus on today?
> What do you guess might happen if you picked what we talked about today?

Active avoidance of agenda setting. Active avoidance is marked by overt opposition to this part of the session structure. Adolescents may respond to this task by dramatic outbursts and complain, "I am a spontaneous person. I don't know what I want to talk about until we are into it" or "I am a 'go with the flow' person." These patients may hold absolute beliefs about the value of disorganization, drama, and chaos (e.g., " I'm a drama queen. Drama defines me," "I love excitement. It's interesting," or "Creating chaos is fun"). Useful processing questions for active avoidance include:

> What goes through your mind when we set agendas?
> What is the bad thing about setting agendas?
> What things about agenda setting are you opposed to?
> What do you guess it would mean about you if we set an agenda?
> What might you lose if you set an agenda?

Too many items on the agenda. Having too many items on the agenda generally occurs in work with adolescents. Teens may not know where to begin and agenda setting helps them carve out a coping path so they are not so overwhelmed. When there is an overcrowded agenda, adopt a systematic problem-solving approach that prioritizes items and allocates time (Friedberg & McClure, 2002). Useful questions might include:

> What issues are most important?
> What makes them most important to you? Least important?
> What are the pros and cons of dealing with this issue first?
> What are the advantages and disadvantages?
> What things must we work on today? What things can we put off until next week?

What makes this a must for today?
What are the disadvantages of putting this off for a week?
How much time should we spend on _____?

Homework Review: Herding the 12 Elephants in the Room

Homework noncompliance is commonplace. Nonetheless, addressing the noncompliance in a curious, open, and non-judgmental manner is an important rubric. Homework non-compliance is a clinical issue and often reveals psychological data about the patient. Following are several rudiments or 12 elephants in the room to review when dealing with non-compliance (Friedberg & McClure, 2005; Hudson & Kendall, 2005; Lazarus & Fay, 1975; Liotti, 1987; Padesky, 1988).

Hopelessness and lack of motivation. Children, adolescents, and their families usually enter treatment with rigidified thoughts, feelings, behaviors, and interaction patterns hardened by the rough knocks of time, practice, and often adverse circumstances. Thus, they may be pessimistic about the potential for therapy to work and subsequently reluctant to invest the energy in an assignment they see as unpromising. Further, hopelessness is a fundamental symptom of depression. Thus, depressed children who enter treatment with accompanying hopelessness, pessimism, and lack of motivation are primed for noncompliance. In these circumstances, initial homework should specifically address hopelessness. Further, during the homework assignment, you should anticipate the disruptive influence of hopelessness/pessimism and ask:

How helpful do you guess this homework will be?
How optimistic are you about the homework?
How much do you think the homework will make you
   feel better?

Incomplete/inaccurate understanding of the task. Patients, like clinicians, are not mind readers. You need to explain the homework in a clear, organized, and concise way that minimizes linguistic, developmental, cultural, and educational barriers. Do not take anything for granted.

Inaccurate assignment. Like the incomplete understanding of the task, this reason is due to clinician error. Frequently, young patients and their families do not do the homework because it does not meet their treatment needs. In these circumstances, the best way to proceed is to use your error as data, model the experimental method, embrace making mistakes, and redesign a better assignment.

Lack of skill. Most, if not all, of the homework assignments you might collaboratively craft require some level of skill. The most basic skill is reading and writing. Children with undeveloped writing and reading skills may feel ashamed about their deficits. Therefore, they will avoid the task. Second, as mentioned in Chapter 3, any therapeutic task needs to be taught to children and families first. Completing a thought diary is an unfamiliar task at first so patients should be stepped through the process. Doing a sticker chart for parents who are naïve to the procedure is not easy for the beginner. By teaching the task first, you decrease the chances the patients will avoid the task due to lack of skill.

Context does not reinforce homework assignment. After therapy sessions are over, children and adolescents return to their unique circumstances. Most of the time therapists, families, and children are all on the same page regarding treatment. Regular collaboration and feedback help reinforce this necessary consensus. However, occasionally the homework assignment may not be reinforced in their natural environment. For instance, the family culture may encourage submission, lack of assertiveness, and restricted expressiveness. They may hold family rules like "Children should be seen and not heard" or "Children should carry out tasks without complaining and whining." Thus, homework assignments to an individual child to let his parents know his thoughts and feelings may be punished by the context. Additionally, a child who lives in a violent neighborhood and rides a school bus where others are taunted and bullied will not profit from "by the book" social skills training and conflict management (e.g., "I" messages) because that skill set does not fit the cultural circumstances. We want to make sure that the skills developed through homework transfer from the corner office to the street corner. Therefore, adopt a broad contextual perspective and collaborate as much as possible by asking children:

How does this homework fit into your life?
How do you expect your family to react to the assignment?
How will this assignment work back at home or school?
What do you guess might happen at home, school, or the neighborhood if you did this assignment?

Fear of failure and perfectionism. Some children who are overly eager to please may avoid homework because they do not want to mess it up. Homework then becomes an opportunity to reveal their incompetence and inadequacy. To test this hypothesis, you might ask:

How much do you worry about doing this wrong?
What do you worry might happen if you mess up the assignment?
How do you think I will react if the homework is not just right?

Fear of loss of control. Similar to fears about change, fears of loss of control also fuel homework avoidance. Many children who are homework noncompliant may believe that if they begin to work on their thoughts, feelings, and behaviors, they will lose control over them. For instance, Sasha, a 14-year-old depressed girl, believed that if she recorded her sad feelings, they would intensify. Questions to ask might be:

How much do you fear that if you write down your thoughts, they are no longer in your control?
How much do you worry that doing the homework will open a door to your feelings that you won't be able to close?

Fear of discomfort. Like hopelessness, emotional intolerance brings patients into treatment. Good homework assignments might provoke negative emotions. Therefore, some children and adolescents may avoid assigned homework due to fear of discomfort. For example, a socially anxious boy named Fred avoided his adventure to say hi to three new peers in school when he was changing classes. When his noncompliance was addressed, he said, "It was too scary to do that." Questions to check out this hypothesis are:

How much did this assignment make you uncomfortable?
How much did you worry that doing this would upset you?

Fear of loss of approval. Many children and adolescents enter therapy wanting to please the therapist and look good. They may dread completing a homework assignment for fear of losing the therapist's approval or appearing abnormal. Children and adolescents may worry the therapist will no longer like them if they learn what is going on inside of them or in the world surrounding them. To check out this hypothesis, ask:

> What did you imagine I would think of you if you wrote down what was bothering you?
> How much did you worry that I would think badly of you if you got angry with your friend during this experiment?
> How did you predict I would react when I saw that you had trouble coming up with coping thoughts this week?

Fear of change. As previously stated in Chapter 3, change is hard. Compliance with homework is an early step toward productive change. Therefore, worries about what change may mean or involve can compromise compliance. To explore this hypothesis, you might ask:

> How worried do you feel about changing the way you feel, think, or act?
> What is scary about changing for you?
> What do you guess might happen if you took the first few steps toward change?

Fear of disclosure. Children may not comply with homework due to fears about revealing themselves. Completing homework that makes their feelings, thoughts, and behavior more transparent may be very anxiety producing. In order to check out this hypothesis, you might ask:

> How comfortable are you letting me know what is going on with you?
> How much do you want to keep your thoughts, feelings, and behaviors to yourself?
> How much do you want to camouflage your thoughts, feelings, and behaviors?

Rebelliousness/opposition. A proportion of children and adolescents actively revolt against homework. They draw lines in the sand and dare you to cross them. These youngsters are far more interested in fighting rather than working with you. A collaborative stance is necessary to maintain an advocacy rather than adversarial stance. Questions to collaboratively process rebelliousness might include:

> What about homework are you opposed to?
> How does not completing the homework help you?
> In what ways does fighting homework serve your needs?

How might homework help you?

How can I help your rebellion work for you rather than
   on you?

Session Content

There are several rudiments to remember when processing
session content. They are avoiding cognition hopping, superlative work with superficial cognitions, and colluding with the
patient's maladaptive cognitions (Padesky, 1988). Additionally,
you want to be sure not to get caught in the patients' maladaptive interaction patterns (Persons, 1989).

Cognition hopping. According to Padesky (1988), cognition
hopping refers to the haphazard practice of jumping from
thought to thought without landing on a central hot belief.
Therefore, you and the patient spin in a directionless cycle in
session. The best way to avoid cognition hopping is to remain
mindful of the content specificity hypothesis and be guided
by your case formulation. You want to shed light on those hot
beliefs that are consistent with your conceptual hypotheses
and tied to youngsters' emotional experiences and problems.

Doing superlative work with superficial cognitions. This trap
is most likely to occur as you gain somewhat greater familiar-
ity with cognitive behavioral procedures. You become infatu-
ated with the powerful thought testing techniques (Chapters 7
and 8). You want to show them off. A child may immediately
call out something that sounds like a meaningful automatic
thought and you dive in with a cognitive restructuring or
rational analysis without considering the case conceptualization or content specificity hypotheses.

Colluding with the patient's distorted beliefs. This is a very
tricky and subtle error. Frequently, a clinician's frustration
and helplessness and overempathizing paves the way for
this trap. At times with difficult and complex cases that are
embedded in adverse circumstances, you may think you do
not have enough techniques in your repertoire. One super-
visee of mine (RDF) equated this to "not having arrows in
my quiver." Therefore, colluding with a patient's or family's
faulty belief, "This is hopeless, there is nothing I can do"
occurs.

Overempathizing also may occur when patients present
after an unfortunate circumstance and accompanying all-or-
none conclusions. For example, a loved one dying, parents
leaving, loss of a job, natural disasters (e.g., floods, hurricanes,

earthquakes), and the patient concludes, "My life will never be the same. Why do those things happen to me? I'm doomed and there is nothing I can do to make this better." Collusion is reflected in buying into the sense of doom and there is nothing that can be helpful and productive. This is different from empathizing and appreciating painful and difficult context of patients' lives. You can empathize with the patient yet also mobilize productive action. Ellis was fond of commenting that in most circumstances the worst outcome is 100% inconvenient. The best way to avoid collusion with distorted beliefs is to steadfastly maintain an objective problem-solving stance.

Getting caught in maladaptive interaction patterns. At times, clinicians may unwittingly become co-opted by a patient's or family's characteristic style of relating to others. For instance, a child who sees himself as helpless and needing constant protection from doting on others may expertly get the therapist to consistently rescue him from emotional discomfort. A teenager who believes he must dominate others in a world that is coercive may ensnare you into seemingly endless control battles. Further, an adolescent who predicts she is unfairly criticized in a harsh world where others do not accept her may prompt the therapist to reject her. Raymond A. Fidaleo, MD, is fond of calling this process "being hooked by the patient." The patient dangles something that appears shiny in front of you and you unwittingly bite!

Jake is a 17-year-old with disruptive behavior problems including aggression, truancy, and substance use. By his 17th birthday he had fathered two children from different high school females. He believed "Life is best lived on the edge and in chaos. Others only care for me when I am in desperate need." He regularly hooked others into his chaotic lifestyle. Consequently, each session was marked by putting out the fires in his life (e.g., arrests, suspensions, crisis calls). The therapist reflexively responded to each isolated crisis and helped him resolve them. Thus, she became co-opted by his maladaptive interpersonal patterns. Extracting yourself from this collusion requires relying on an old friend: The case conceptualization.

Eliciting Feedback

Capturing children's, adolescents', or families' session feedback is often straightforward. The top 10 questions contained in Figure 4.3 offers you some starting points. However, there can be some interesting clinical variations.

1. What was helpful/not helpful about our work today?
2. What did you like/not like about our work today?
3. What seemed right about today's session? What seemed wrong about today's session?
4. What was satisfying about our work today? What was not satisfying?
5. What rubbed you the wrong way? What seemed to make sense to you?
6. What title would you give to today's session?
7. What worked for you today? What did not work for you today?
8. What things did I seem to get? What things did I miss?
9. What things do you want to make sure we keep the same? What things should we change about how we work together?
10. What is the takeaway message from our session today?

Figure 4.3   Ten questions to elicit and process feedback/summaries.

Reluctance to give feedback. Providing feedback to adult authority figures can be difficult for young patients and their families. Nonetheless, obtaining feedback is pivotal since unexpressed concerns about content and conflict with the therapist undermines successful treatment (Persons, 1989). Reluctance to give feedback may be due to several factors. First, eager to please patients and patients who are highly invested in being a caretaker may worry they might hurt your feelings with their negative comments. They withhold their dissatisfactions in order to protect you. Some patients and their families may worry about disappointing you with their feedback. They are concerned that their feedback is wrong. Further, other patients may be uncomfortable or embarrassed about giving direct feedback to another person. They dread the discomfort associated with giving feedback. Finally, a few patients may be so invested in maintaining control that they do not want you to know what is helpful or unhelpful. They want to keep you in the dark and guessing about what works and what does not. These patients step back from genuine collaboration. Useful questions to process reluctance to provide feedback might include:

What is it like for you to give me feedback?
What do you guess will happen if you tell me your negative (positive) feedback?
How do you suppose I will see you if you give me feedback?
What are the advantages and disadvantages of giving feedback?

Giving overly positive feedback. Children, adolescents, and families may give you overly positive feedback (e.g., "I've seen many therapists and you are the best! Everything we do is helpful. You are wonderful"; "Can you come live in our house?"; etc.). While on a superficial level this may be heartening to hear, it is important to realize that receiving only positive feedback represents a problem in the feedback process and the working alliance. You need to process the feedback to address the beliefs that buttress the behavior. Questions you might ask may include:

> What do you guess would happen if you gave me negative feedback?
> What rules might you break if you gave me negative feedback?
> What would it mean about you if you gave me negative feedback?
> What would it mean about me if you gave me negative feedback?

Giving overly negative feedback. Getting blasted by negative feedback can be an icy introduction to the psychotherapy process (e.g., "I've seen many therapists and you are the absolute worst! You suck!" "I'm not sure you are smart enough to grasp the complexities of our son's problems," "You are far too inexperienced to help me," "You are a fool! Did you even graduate from high school?"). As painful as it might be you must process this harsh feedback in a collaborative, nondefensive, and accepting way so you can sift through what is accurate and inaccurate about the feedback.

> What's it like to give an adult this type of feedback?
> What's it like to give an authority this type of feedback?
> What is it that made you see me as stupid?
> What happened that made you sense I could not grasp the complexities?
> How did you expect I would react to this feedback? What do you make of my reaction?
> What surprises you about my reaction to your feedback?
> What do I do that a horrible therapist would never do?
> What does a horrible therapist do that I would never do?

Homework Assignment
Assigning homework may be tricky for the beginning therapist. Adolescents are at a developmental stage where they

struggle with issues of autonomy and sometimes can be quite oppositional to an authority figure. As previously stated, a collaborative approach should be fashioned. Remaining curious about avoidance and opposition is also a good strategy. Instead of saying to patients that they are wrong, you can simply ask them to test out their assumptions about homework. Then, have them come back the next week and review the results of their experiments. In the following we offer nine guidelines for effective homework assignments.

Dressing Homework to the Nines: Nine Guidelines for Assigning Homework

Collaborate. Homework tasks will likely be completed if they are mutually agreed upon. Spend time gaining patients' input rather than unilaterally prescribing them. Once assignments are crafted, children's feedback on them should be explored (e.g., "How does this assignment sound?" "How helpful did you expect this to be?").

Provide a rationale for any therapeutic assignment. To be on the same page with young patients, you need to communicate the reason for the homework. If they do not understand the purpose of the task, they are flying blind. For example, with an angry youngster who flies off the handle and seemingly has "meltdowns out of the blue," you might introduce self-monitoring (Chapter 6) by saying, "We are going to use this chart to see what makes you angry and how angry you get. In this way, you'll get a better sense of control. How does this sound?"

Link the homework to children and adolescents presenting complaints, problems, and/or the session agenda. This idea is directly related to the previous point. If patients recognize the connection between their problems and the homework, they are more likely to comply. For example, when introducing a contingency management contract, you might say,

> You and your mom don't seem to be on the same page with your behavior. You think you do what she asks pretty well, but she thinks you don't follow the rules much. You say your mom doesn't pay attention to the good things you do. Mom says she does. So, this chart should help clear that up. This column shows the things mom asks you to do. The next one lists what you did and the last column is mom's reaction. How does this seem as a way to clear things up?

Begin the assignment in session. Anyone who has stared fruitlessly at a blank sheet of paper and put off a term paper realizes the importance of this rubric. Getting started is usually the hardest step. Therefore, beginning an assignment in session provides momentum toward completion. It demonstrates the minimal time and effort necessary to accomplish the task. Finally, you are able to see whether the child understands the exercise and possesses the skill to complete it.

Simple assignments are preferable. There is no prize for constructing elaborate, complex incomprehensible assignments. The key is mobilizing children's motivation to attempt the task, ensuring their understanding, and matching the assignment to their skill level.

Apply a graduated approach. Breaking down the homework into accomplishable substeps is a fundamental rule in motivation (Bandura, 1977b). Accordingly, initial procedures should be subdivided into components. For instance, when first assigning a thought record (Chapter 6), we recommend doing the first two columns (situation and feeling) before having the child attempt to complete the entire three-column record.

Problem-solve obstacles and address avoidance. Obstacles are problems blocking homework compliance. A systematic objective problem-solving stance should be applied to obstacles. A plan should be collaboratively constructed that potentially enhances homework completion. Thoughts and feelings accompanying the homework assignment should be elicited and tested.

Consider calling homework something else. Therapeutic homework may be avoided because it conjures up images of schoolwork (Friedberg & McClure, 2002). Various alternatives are recommended such as Show That I Can (Hudson & Kendall, 2005; Kendall, Choudhury, Hudson, & Webb, 2002), self-help tools (Burns, 1980), and challenges/adventures (Friedberg, McClure, & Garcia, 2009).

Make homework fun. For children, it is usually helpful to assign homework that has some intrinsic reinforcing properties for the child. Take advantage of the things the child is naturally drawn to such as games, art, storytelling, or interesting activities. Assigning homework that takes advantage of their interests will help the child feel motivated to do it and buy into the therapeutic process of homework.

CONCLUSION

This basic session structure forms the basis of a sound therapeutic approach to each session. Implementing the structure may at first seem difficult and overwhelming, but as with any skill, practice will improve your ability to flow through a session more smoothly. With practice, you will also become more adept with being flexible in the session structure to meet individual patients' needs. Session structure gives a guiding outline for how to proceed through therapy. Simply, it helps you and the patient keep your eyes on the ball.

Five

Psychoeducation

INTRODUCTION

Goldman (1988) insisted that psychoeducation (PE) is essential in all forms of psychotherapy and that teaching is core to almost all forms of medical care. More specifically, psychoeducation plays an important role in cognitive behavioral psychotherapy (CBP). Psychoeducation facilitates genuine informed consent. In this chapter, you will find the definition of psychoeducation, its functions, and learn methods for making PE relevant. You will also find resources and tips for using these resources. Examples are often provided to illustrate how you might introduce and use some PE concepts and resources.

RUDIMENTS

The following rudiments include defining PE and its function. More important, guidelines for delivering PE are suggested. Reviewing the material, keeping it simple, enhancing relevance, maintaining cultural alertness, ensuring developmental sensitivity, *enactive* demonstrations, and multimedia applications are key guidelines.

Definition of Psychoeducation

Psychoeducation is typically defined as teaching patients and their families about the symptoms of their illness, treatment options, and the course of treatment (Ong & Caron, 2008). This provision of information is commonly referred to as prebriefing where patients are readied for treatment (Wessely et al., 2008). In psychoeducation, the clinician blends the role of psychotherapist and teacher (Cuijpers, Munoz, Clarke, & Lewinsohn, 2009). The instruction may be delivered through explanations, reading assignments, Internet, videotapes, and audiotapes. In this way, PE helps reduce anxiety and stigma as well as promoting informed consent.

Functions of Psychoeducation

Goldman (1988) insisted that PE should be integrated with broader approaches such as pharmacotherapy (Chapter 11) and psychotherapy (Chapters 6 through 10). Friedman, Thase, and Wright (2008) agreed that PE is best delivered within treatment sessions that rely on interactive dialogue.

Wessely et al. (2008) identified several core functions of PE. First, it *orients* patients to their symptoms. In his seminal text, Frank (1961) emphasized the importance of patients making sense of their distress. He wrote, "Naming something is the first step toward controlling it" (p. 65). PE is also *comforting* to patients (Wessely et al., 2008). Further, psychoeducation *demystifies* disorders and potentially reduces shame and their sense they are "weird" or "freaky" (Hannesdottir & Ollendick, 2007). PE works to demystify treatment and promote collaboration and active participation between youth and their parents by describing disorders and the therapeutic process (Curry & Reinecke, 2003). Patients and families gain a *sense of universality* rather than feeling isolated through PE.

Wessely et al. (2008) also noted that PE *facilitates help-seeking*. When patients understand and recognize the nature of their conditions, they are more likely to seek help. Moreover, PE typically informs patients about the sources for help with their problems. In this way, PE promotes necessary transparency in cognitive behavioral therapy (CBT).

Essentially, knowledge is power. Wills (2009) concluded that a goal of PE is to narrow the gap between patients' and clinicians' knowledge base. Consequently, PE *empowers* patients with greater information (Wessely et al., 2008). Therefore, it is entirely consistent with a self-control model of psychotherapy (Cuijpers et al., 2009). Rachman (1977) identified transmission of information as a pathway for learning fears and avoidance patterns. Accordingly, the provision of simple information may partially begin *modifying inaccurate beliefs*.

Ong and Caron (2008) noted that PE may *increase communication and support between family members*. More specifically, Fristad (2006) wrote that PE offers a "no fault conceptualization of the condition" (p. 1291). Accordingly, blaming is reduced (Himle & Franklin, 2009). Additionally, PE *objectifies the illness* and separates it from the individual or the family system (Fristad, 2006). This distancing, this enables the therapist to align with the family against a common enemy.

PE propels hopefulness (Goldfried & Davila, 2005). The powerful effects of hope are well documented (Frank, 1961). When expectations of hope are mobilized, inert coping resources may ignite. Additionally, hopefulness allows patients greater access to their previously hidden coping capacities.

Seven Guidelines for Delivering Good Psychoeducation

Seven guidelines for delivering good psychoeducation are listed and described next. First, clinicians are cautioned to review material carefully before offering the resource to parents and children. Second, simple information is preferred to complicated material marked by psychobabble. Next, the resources should be real and relevant so the information does not lie inert. Fourth, remain culturally alert when presenting psychoeducational material. Fifth, developmental sensitivity is a must. Sixth, psychoeducation should be delivered via an active process between patients and clinicians. Last, feel free to use multimedia when doing psychoeducation.

Review Material Carefully Before You Offer It to Parents and Children

This guideline seems like a no-brainer but in clinicians' busy realities, no-brainers can sometimes be forgotten. First, check to see if the material is free of bias and misinformation (Briere & Scott, 2006). Second, be sure the information is current and credible. Third, familiarize yourself with the content so you can review it with patients and thoughtfully answer questions.

Psychoeducation Should Be Presented in a Simple and Accessible Manner

Piacentini and Bergman (2001) urged clinicians to avoid jargon and psychobabble. We agree and let's face it many clinicians like to hear themselves talk. Concepts should be taught in a cogent and concise manner. Long-winded, obtuse explanations are to be diligently avoided. It may help to think about communicating educational material in a bullet-point format. Teach the material simply and check back with the family to assess their level of understanding to assess the need for clarification. When possible, printed material summarizing the material should be given to patients. If no material is available, you might write out the points or make a copy of them on a word processing program.

Psychoeducation Should Be Real and Relevant

Situations that resonate with patients will evoke their intense emotions. Waller et al. (2007) stated, "For psychoeducation to be effective, it needs to involve both a review of specific facts and an opportunity to reflect on how they impact on the individual" (p. 140).

Remember your patients' context. If you are working with a single mother of four children who works three jobs to make ends meet and who can barely find the time to bring your patient to sessions as it is, she likely won't have extra money to buy a text let alone read an entire text. Similarly, patients who struggle with anxiety and depression may feel overwhelmed and discouraged if you give them too many resources and materials to read (Bermudes, Wright, & Casey, 2009). Consequently, this may reinforce their assumptions and negative beliefs about themselves (e.g., the belief "I'm a failure" is reinforced if the patient is unable to complete six assigned readings before her next weekly session). Essentially, the dose of PE is too high. Therefore, the notion of graduated tasks should be applied.

Psychoeducation Should Be Culturally Alert

Cultural alertness also enhances relevance. There are several methods of achieving this goal during administration of the PE module. Culture and cultural values should be assessed for their influence on parenting skills and ultimately on patients' lives (Wells & Albano, 2005). Pay attention to particular cultural interests and preferences. Briere and Scott (2006) noted that materials written in the families' primary language increases relevance. Moreover, any psychoeducation material should be inclusive and reflect diverse concerns.

There is an increasing amount of information presented in non-English language formats. Most national institutes (e.g., National Institute of Mental Health [NIMH: www.nimh.nih. gov], National Institute on Drug Abuse [NIDA], Substance Abuse and Mental Health Agency [SAMSHA]) offer Spanish-language versions of materials. The Family Doctor Web site (www.familydoctor.org) also provides information on disorders in Spanish. The National Association for Mental Illness (NAMI) presents information on disorders in Spanish and English as well. The teens health site maintained by the Nemours Foundation (www.teenhealth.org) offer materials on conditions and coping in English and Spanish. The exceptional About Our Kids (www.aboutourkids.org) Web site maintained by the New York University Child Study Center offers materials for parents in English and Spanish. The University of Pittsburgh Medical Center Department of Psychiatry maintains a comprehensive Web site stocked with information in English and Spanish (www.upmc.edu). Autism Speaks (www.autismspeaks.org) includes resources in Spanish. The American Academy of Child and Adolescent Psychiatry (AACAP) offers Facts for Families in many different languages.

Language is an important issue in PE but not the only important variable. Hays (2009) rightly reminds us that materials should appreciate cultural groups' worldviews reflecting interdependence, subtle communication, and spiritual practices. The material should respect cultural notions of healers and mental health. Remember that socioeconomic status and educational levels are cultural variables. Therefore, for children and families with limited reading abilities, materials should be accordingly modified. Psychoeducational materials should be recommended in a financially responsible manner. Graphics, pictures, and metaphors also need to be culturally responsive.

Psychoeducation Should Be Conducted in a Developmentally Sensitive Manner

Children commonly face lectures. To reduce the possibility of a child becoming numb to psychoeducational efforts, using developmentally sensitive and engaging procedures and processes are recommended. Friedberg, McClure, and Garcia (2009) compiled a long list of storybooks and movies that could be used for psychoeducation. It is particularly important to make PE concrete and developmentally appropriate. You would not want to teach a 17-year-old female with a high level of cognitive ability social skills modeled after the Hannah Montana character. Similarly, you would not want to recommend an advanced self-help book for anxiety management to a 7-year-old boy with limited cognitive ability.

Psychoeducation Is an Active Process

Information that lies unapplied is inert. Friedberg et al. (1998) insisted "patients who understand the skills but remain unconvinced to use them are analogous to individuals who realize the benefits of seat belts but fail to buckle up when driving" (p. 54). Briere and Scott (2006) urged that any educational product should be processed with the family rather than just handed to the patient.

Part of being active involves attention to patient confusion and doubt about the material (Curry & Becker, 2009). Therefore, therapists should be certain to process any questions and reservations about the material. For instance, coaching patients and families to highlight parts they agree and disagree with is an active assignment. Referring back to educational points in materials over the course of treatment refreshes and reinforces basic concepts.

Psychoeducation Is Presented via Multimedia

Wessely et al. (2008) emphasized that PE assumes many forms. Books, leaflets, audios, videos, Internet, and even minilectures by the clinician represent psychoeducational procedures. The method of PE intervention delivery will vary based on your patient's needs, available resources, and the type of facility in which you work.

The use of movies and filmed vignettes is commonplace when working with children and adolescents. Movies provide visual, auditory, and contextual input as well as being ecologically valid (Golan, Baron-Cohen, & Golan, 2008). Listening to music lyrics, discussing the song's message, and applying their relevance to oneself normalizes patients' experiences (DeLucia-Waack, 2006). Moreover, universality is achieved which decreases youngsters' alienation and isolation. Activities and crafts are also useful interventions. Finally, teaching in PE may be enhanced with metaphors and exercises (Friedberg, McClure, & Garcia, 2009; Tolin, 2009).

RUBRICS

Resources

Resources power psychoeducation. Therefore, we recommend you stock your office with various pamphlets, self-help books, fact sheets, articles, and educational DVDs. Moreover, knowing where to direct patients and their families for accurate and reliable information when you do not have the materials on hand is key. Offering resources not only educates patients and their families, but also demonstrates your investment (strengthening your therapeutic alliance) and helps them to understand factors that potentially contribute to their child's maladaptive behaviors and thoughts. The computer is an invaluable PE resource for patients.

Information on Cognitive Behavioral Psychotherapy

Teaching children and families about the CBT model is typically an initial step in PE. When patients learn about the model, they are able to genuinely agree to informed consent. A simple analogy emphasizes the crucial nature of educated informed consent. Imagine if someone tried to sell you a $5,000 orange arguing that it will change your life if you take a bite out of it three times a day for three days, you would want to know how it works before investing. You are asking your patients and their families to make a rather large emotional, time, and monetary investment. Let's make sure they understand the value of their investment so that they *want* to invest. The Association of Behavioral and Cognitive Therapy (www.abct.org), Academy of Cognitive Therapy (www.academyofct.org), and the Beck Institute for Cognitive Therapy and Research are one-stop Web sites for consumer information on CBP.

Friedberg, McClure, and Garcia (2009) summarized six important aspects involved in PE about CBP. First, patients and families learn that physiological, emotional, cognitive, and behavioral symptoms are all causally related. Second, making conclusions, interpretations, and judgments is a normal human process. Third, unfortunately, not all judgments and interpretations are inaccurate. Fourth, when negative conclusions are accurate, problem solving is a helpful alternative. Fifth, in other circumstances where explanations are inaccurate, learning how to construct alternative explanations is a good strategy. Finally, behavioral experiments will be applied to test new judgments.

There are multiple ways to present the cognitive model to children. For instance, the balloon story (Friedberg & McClure, 2002), Diamond Connections (Friedberg, Friedberg, & Friedberg, 2001), and what the dog left behind (Kendall, 2006) are all entertaining ways to teach the model. Berg (1986, 1989, 1990a, 1990b, 1990c, 1992a, 1992b, 1992c) created a series of CBP games that are excellent teaching tools. Finally, books for children (Waters, 1979, 1980) and adolescents (Shaw & Barzvi, 2005) explain CBP to young patients.

Emotional Education

Suveg, Kendall, Comer, and Robin (2006) explained that children with emotional problems lack skills in emotional understanding. Psychoeducation addresses understanding emotions and uncomfortable affective experiences (Trosper, Buzzella,

Bennett, & Ehrenreich, 2009). Central aims of affective education are teaching children the functions of emotions, helping them recognize that emotions exist in various degrees, and that emotions have communicative value (Attwood, 2004; Huppert & Alley, 2004).

Trosper et al. (2009) recommended explaining the helpful, normal, and natural aspects of emotions. For example, they described anger as "a natural response to the belief that you have been hurt or mistreated. This includes ideas, objects, dreams, and values and people. Anger motivates us to take action to define ourselves and/or the things we care about and is often directed at the person or thing we find threatening" (p. 244).

Attwood (2004) recommended creating an emotional scrapbook one feeling state at a time. Children select an emotion (sad) and collect pictures as well as other items that make them feel sad. The pictures and items are pasted onto pages in the scrapbook. Then, children begin a subsequent "chapter" with a new emotion (worried). Movies, television shows, music, crafts, and storybooks can facilitate affective education.

Disorder Information

Major professional organizations and national mental health Web sites offer specific information in various childhood disorders. The American Psychiatric Association (www.psych. org), American Psychological Association (www.apa.org), and American Academy of Child and Adolescent Psychiatry (www.aacap.org) are a few examples.

Pervasive Developmental Disorder Spectrum

There are some excellent resources for patients who have a pervasive developmental disorder (PDD) spectrum diagnosis and their families. You might begin by visiting the aforementioned NIMH and AACAP Web sites. The National Institute of Child Health and Human Development (www.nichd.nih. gov/autism/) and the Centers for Disease Control (www.cdc. gov) offer up-to-date resource materials. The Autism Speaks Web site, found at www.autismspeaks.org, provides a wealth of information regarding epidemiology, diagnosis education, and parenting and management skill information offered in both Spanish and English languages. This site also provides information on resources within the community and ordering information for other resources (e.g., DVDs, books). The Autism Society of America (www.autism-society.org) and

Organization for Autism Research (www.researchautism.org)
are good psychoeducational resources. Lockshin, Gillis, and
Romanczyk (2005) wrote a very detailed workbook to help
parents whose child is diagnosed with a pervasive developmental disorder.

Anxiety Spectrum

There are many excellent resources for psychoeducation
on anxiety. The Anxiety Disorders Association of America
(www.adaa.org) is a robust source for materials on the nature
and treatment for anxiety spectrum disorders. Additionally,
Worry Wise Kids (www.worrywisekids.org) is a very friendly
consumer Web site. Parenting books for parents whose children are challenged with anxiety offer psychoeducational
materials and are listed in Table 5.1. The Oxford University
Press Adolescent Mental Health Initiative includes several
adolescents' personal accounts of coping with anxiety disorders (Kant, Franklin, & Andrews, 2008; Ford, Liebowitz, &
Andrews, 2007). Finally, there are a number of very engaging self-help storybooks and workbooks for younger children.
These resources are listed in Table 5.2.

PE teaches youth and their parents that anxiety is a naturally occurring, normal, and adaptive emotion, and the CBP
targets the management of anxiety rather than aiming to get
rid of it (Gosch, Flannery-Schroeder, Mauro, & Compton, 2006).
They also learn about the role of a "miswired" alarm response
to stimuli not actually dangerous or threatening in reality,
but that are perceived that way by the patient (Gosch et al.,
2006). Alarms are good metaphors for teaching about anxiety
(A. T. Beck, Emery, & Greenberg, 1985; Piacentini, Langley,

Table 5.1   Books for Parents of Anxious Children

Psychoeducational Resource	Application
Up and Down the Worry Hill (Wagner, 2000)	Obsessive-compulsive disorder (OCD)
What to Do When Your Brain Gets Stuck (Huebner, 2007b)	OCD
Worry Wart Wes (Thompson, 2003)	Worry
What to Do When You Worry Too Much (Huebner, 2006)	Worry
The Lion Who Lost His Roar (Nass, 2000)	Fearfulness
The Bear Who Lost His Sleep (Lamb-Shapiro, 2000)	Worry

Table 5.2   Parenting Books With Children Diagnosed With an Anxiety

Resource	Application
Help for Worried Kids (Last, 2006)	Wide spectrum of anxiety disorders
Freeing Your Child from Obsessive-Compulsive Disorder (Chansky, 2000)	Obsessive-compulsive disorder (OCD)
Talking Back to OCD (March, 2007)	OCD
Helping Your Child With Selective Mutism (McHolm, Cunningham, & Vanier, 2005)	Selective mutism
Helping Your Child Overcome Separation Anxiety or School Anxiety (Eisen & Engler, 2006)	Separation and school anxiety
Helping Your Socially Vulnerable Child (Eisen & Engler, 2007)	Social anxiety
Getting Your Child to Say "Yes" to School (Kearney, 2007)	School refusal
If Your Adolescent Has an Anxiety Disorder (Foa & Andrews, 2006)	Wide spectrum of anxiety disorders

& Roblek, 2007a, 2007b; Piacentini, March, & Franklin, 2006; Shenk, 1993).

Depression Spectrum

The Optimistic Child (Seligman, Reivich, Jaycox, & Gillham, 1995) is an excellent resource for parents whose children are highly self-critical and prone to helplessness. There are several useful books for teens on depression and suicide (Cobain, 2007; Irwin, Evans, & Andrews, 2007; Lezine & Brent, 2007). Hamil (2008) developed a self-help workbook for PE with depressed children. The National Organization for People of Color Against Suicide (www.nopcas.org) provides suicide prevention and support for racial and ethnic minorities. Additionally, the Trevor Project (www.thetrevorproject.org) emphasizes suicidal prevention information for gay and lesbian youth.

Bipolar Disorder Spectrum

Raising a Moody Child (Fristad & Goldberg-Arnold, 2004) and *If Your Adolescent Has Depression or Bipolar Disorder* (Evans & Andrews, 2005) are handy parent education aids. For adolescents themselves, *Mind Race* (Jamieson, 2006) is a teenager's personal account of coping with bipolar disorder (BPD). There are several Web sites containing useful information including the Child and Adolescent Bipolar Foundation (www.bpkids.org) and the Juvenile Bipolar Research Foundation (www.jbrf.org). The Depression and Bipolar Support Alliance (DBSA: www.dbsalliance.org) and the Depression and Related Affective Disorders Association (DRADA: www.drada.org) provide educational materials for parents.

Substance Dependence

Patterson and O'Connell (2003) emphasized the value of PE in substance abuse treatment. PE resources aim to alter the "perceptions, attitudes, and beliefs of chemically dependent patients" (p. 74). Patients also learn about the physiological and "spiritual" effects of substances, as well as effects on mental health. PE also teaches patients about the relationship between the chemical effects of substance, impairment, and impaired functioning. Additionally, the PE component strives to teach them about the negative effects that substances have on their own values and biases.

The Substance Abuse and Mental Health Services Administration (SAMHSA) offers a very engaging comic book for young children using superheroes, the Fantastic Four and Spider-Man, for drug education (www.samhsa.gov/choices). Additionally, there are numerous games, puzzles, and interactive quizzes contained in the Web site. National Institute for Drug Abuse (NIDA) offers online and printed resources (http://drugabuse.gov/nidahome.html). Keegan (2008) also penned a personal account of struggles with substance abuse.

Eating Disorders

The National Eating Disorders Association (www.nationaleatingdisorder.org) maintains a Web site that offers information in both English and Spanish. The site includes videos, toolkits, and resource material. Parenting information for parents whose children are diagnosed with eating disorders is contained in some excellent self-help books (Lock & LeGrange, 2005; Walsh & Cameron, 2005). Waller et al. (2007) contains rich educational resource material for a variety of eating disorders. Zeckhausen (2008) penned an engaging storybook for young children to teach them about food and feelings. *Next to Nothing* (Arnold & Walsh, 2007) is a personal account of an adolescent's struggles with anorexia.

Attention Deficit Hyperactivity Disorder and Externalizing Disorders

Thompson (2002, 2007) wrote some very entertaining story-books for children with attention deficit hyperactivity disorder (ADHD). These books are especially valuable because they include diverse main characters. Workbooks such as *The Putting on the Brakes Activity Book for Young People* (Quinn & Stern, 1993) and *50 Activities and Games for Kids With ADHD* (Quinn & Stern, 2000) contain good PE materials. Personal diaries are also quite effective PE materials. As demonstrated in the book *The Freedom Writers Diary* (The Freedom Writers, 1999) and movie *The Freedom Writers* (LaGravenese, 2007), adolescents' personal accounts of adverse circumstances are compelling psychoeducational materials. Additionally, *The Diary of a Young Girl* (Frank, 1953) was used with diverse inner-city youth with the Freedom Writers, and the French-language film *The Class* (Cantet, 2008) can facilitate a sense of universality.

Trauma Disorder Spectrum

The Medical University of South Carolina maintains a Web site that is easy to access and provides a wealth of resources in both English and Spanish (http://tfcbt.musc.edu/). The National Center for PTSD (www.ptsd.va.gov) and the National Child Traumatic Stress Network (www.nctsnet.org) are bountiful sources for information. There are several valuable sites for children who have experienced disasters (www.fema.gov/kids and www.disastereducation.org/guide.html).

Military Children

Recent estimates show 1.2 million school-age children have at least one parent serving in the military (Finkel, Kelley, & Ashby, 2003). Current missions in Iraq and Afghanistan require more deployments than in the past (Drummet, Coleman, & Cable, 2003). Children are especially vulnerable to their parents' deployment (Chartrand, Frank, White, & Shope, 2008; Cozza, Chun, & Polo, 2005; Friedberg & Brelsford, in press). Lincoln, Swift, and Shorteno-Fraser (2008) emphasized that "having a parent sent to an active combat zone with an undetermined return date may rank as one of the most stressful events of childhood" (p. 984). Moreover, when these missions inevitably end, families will need to cope with the enduring effects of the conflict. There are some extremely helpful Web sites devoted to psychoeducation that contain materials for coping with deployments. Table 5.3 lists and describes these Web sites.

Table 5.3   Resources for Military Children and Families

Resource	Application
American Academy of Pediatrics (www.aap.org/sections/unifserv/ deployment/index.htm)	Materials to foster child adjustment during deployment
U.S. Department of Veterans Affairs (www.va.gov)	Materials and resources for children of deployed parents
Surviving Deployment (www.survivingdeployment.com)	Interactive games, activities for coping with deployment
DeploymentKids.Com (www.deploymentkids.com)	Activities, games, and information
National Military Family Association (www.nmfa.org)	Facts on military life
Salute Our Services (www.saluteourservices.org)	Information and resources
Military OneSource (www.militaryonesource.com)	Information and resources for emotional support
Deployment Health Clinical Center (www.pdhealth.mil)	Practice guidelines and mental health resources
Center for Deployment Psychology (www.deploymentpsych.org)	Practice guidelines and mental health resources
Real Warriors (www. realwarriors.net)	Information and resources
Sesame Street Workshop (www.sesameworkshop.org)	Videos, information, and games

Parenting and Child Management Issues

Parent education is a prime target for psychoeducation. Parent education materials offer specific information about developmental issues, psychiatric/psychological disorders, and behavior management strategies. These resources promote realistic expectations and goal setting (Friedberg, McClure, & Garcia, 2009). The literature is replete with parenting books and the following resources are simply a sampling of our preferred resources. We recommend you begin creating a library of resources and regularly add to the collection throughout your career. The New York University Child Study Center Web site (www.aboutourkids.org) is a continuously updated source of valuable information for clinicians and parents. Its parent newsletter offers very accessible and practical information for parents.

There are several excellent behavior management books for parents. Kazdin's (2008) new parenting book is very detailed, easy to follow, and an engaging treasure trove of parenting strategies. Further, it comes with a DVD illustrating key principles. Classic parent handbooks by Barkley and colleagues (Barkley, 1995; Barkley & Benton, 1998; Barkley, Robin, & Benton, 2008), Greene (2001), Clark (2005), Patterson (1976), and Becker (1971) fit the psychoeducational bill nicely.

Several other parenting books detail normal developmental processes. What childhood is all about (Vernon & Al-Mabuk, 1995) gives parents specific information on developmental periods. Greenspan and colleagues (Greenspan, 1993; Greenspan & Greenspan, 1985, 1989) offer a series of excellent books geared at improving parent–child interpersonal relationships.

CONCLUSION

Psychoeducation flows through the heart of patient empowerment and informed consent. It decreases power differentials between clinicians and the children and families they serve. In this chapter, rubrics and rudiments for PE were explained. Numerous resources and guidelines for their use were outlined. As you apply the principles and processes included in Chapters 6 through 10, continue to return to this chapter to refresh your understanding.

Six

Self-Monitoring

INTRODUCTION

Self-monitoring is a keystone for self-directed change. Simply, a person cannot self-regulate unless they pay attention (Bandura, 1977b). Bandura noted that self-observation aids in developing realistic standards and increasing motivation. Self-monitoring works to increase self-awareness of thoughts, feelings, and behaviors as well as their impact on other people. Often, youngsters are clueless about their internal experiences and oblivious to the ways they affect others. Goldfried and Davila (2005) commented that "metaphorically speaking they are in the dark about these determinants/dynamics and the role of the therapist is to use various clinical interventions to focus a light on these factors" (p. 427).

Self-monitoring is the light that teaches children, adolescents, and their families to observe and record their behaviors, thoughts, and emotions (Spiegler & Guevremont, 1998). Self-observation may be completed rapidly, and patients may readily access their own internal and external processes (Spiegler & Guevremont, 1998). Self-monitoring is a widely used means of initiating the cognitive behavioral therapy process with children who have an array of symptoms and mental health problems.

Self-monitoring tools teach children to become alert objective observers of their external and internal states (Goldfried, 2003). Self-monitoring increases one's self-awareness and consequently serves as an impetus for change. Hayes, Strosahl, and Wilson (1999) observed that "a person who is not able to be aware of and utilize ongoing behavioral states cannot address the highly individualized and changing circumstances that daily life presents" (p. 183). In short, self-monitoring is a pivotal step on the road toward cultivating healthy coping strategies (Southam-Gerow & Kendall, 2000).

Self-monitoring is an acquired skill. Children learn to observe environmental events, physiological reactions, interpersonal patterns, thoughts, feelings, and behaviors. A self-monitoring record may help the child and clinician identify precipitants, activating events, and physiological cues and reactions. Tompkins (1999) defines *precipitants* as trigger events that give rise to cognitive, behavioral, and emotional reactions. He describes activating events as situations that happen repeatedly, which create dysphoric moods and distorted beliefs. Additionally, self-monitoring trains children to become more keen-eyed toward physical sensations linked to problem situations that may act as cues to the occurrence of distressing emotions and maladaptive thought patterns.

This chapter offers rudiments associated with behavioral, emotional, and cognitive self-monitoring. Additionally, rubrics enabling you to get accurate data from patients and their families are explained. Further, traditional and innovative ways to complete behavioral, emotional, and cognitive self-monitoring are described.

RUDIMENTS

This section provides tips for behavioral, emotional, and cognitive self-monitoring. Basic definitions and functions for each type of self-monitoring are included. The fundamental principles set the table for the subsequent "Rudiments" section.

Behavioral Self-Monitoring

Behavioral monitoring allows for a full appreciation of the ecology of children's behavior. Behavior never occurs in a vacuum and behavior logs set the contextual parameters for children's actions. Behavioral self-monitoring enables patients to identify and rank behavior problems as well as to evaluate the associations between problems (Haynes & O'Brien, 2000).

Behavioral self-monitoring involves teaching children to examine and record their actions. These methods collect information on the intensity, frequency, and duration of behaviors. Additionally, situational parameters of the behavior are distinguished by recording when, where, and around whom the behavior occurs. Finally, the consequences of behavior are also monitored. The methods might include rather traditional procedures such as frequency counts on paper to wearing a number of bracelets to using various counters (e.g., golf counters, ticket counters, and so on) representing how many times a patient executes a behavior.

Consider this example. A young patient's mother created a very clever way for her 9-year-old son who was quite reluctant to count the number of times he washed his hands to keep track of the handwashing. Her son loved marbles so she suggested he put a marble in his pocket every time he washed his hands. She placed bowls of marbles at each sink and cued her son to empty his pocket at regular intervals. Marbles collected at each interval were recorded on paper. The marbles were a particularly good idea because they were so appealing to the child. He enjoyed keeping them in his pocket and counting them regularly.

Emotional Self-Monitoring

Learning to regulate emotions is basic to the success of psychotherapy (Burum & Goldfried, 2007; Ehrenreich, Fairholme, Buzzella, Ellard, & Barlow, 2007). Emotional regulation is facilitated via the increased self-awareness that self-monitoring tools provide. Without understanding one's own emotions, acquiring and implementing adaptive responses to emotionally laden events is a thorny task (Zeman, Cassano, Perry-Parrish, & Stegall, 2006). Lack of emotional awareness creates negative interpersonal consequences (Burum & Goldfried, 2007). Poor emotional awareness contributes to anxiety, depression, and eating disorders (Sloan & Kring, 2007). Self-monitoring tools are direct methods of accessing crucial information regarding the child's emotional awareness.

Hannedottir and Ollendick (2007) advocated for the positive effects of emotional self-monitoring. They argued that emotional identification helps propel youngsters toward productive action and coping. Additionally, emotional identification increases a perceived sense of control. Naming and reporting distressing feelings is not easy for children. It is unfamiliar business. Therefore, detailed rubrics are recommended in later sections.

Cognitive Self-Monitoring

Cognitive self-monitoring enables children to observe, monitor, and record their automatic thoughts related to specific situations and emotions. Automatic thoughts are often discovered and recorded using thought diaries. Thought diaries come in a variety of forms, and may contain different amounts of information depending upon the form used. Simple thought diaries typically contain three columns and record children's problematic situations, related emotions and the intensity of those emotions, and associated automatic thoughts experienced in the situation. However, when using thought diaries with children, it is essential that the clinician keeps them as simple and entertaining as possible, and tailors them to children's specific needs.

RUBRICS

Now that you appreciate the underlying principles of self-monitoring, you are ready to learn the specific techniques. This section provides you with the detailed information and examples of behavioral, emotional, and cognitive tools for self-monitoring. The section begins with recommendations for getting good data. Next, various forms of behavioral self-monitoring are described including formal teacher and parent report measures, behavioral logs, and hierarchies. Rubrics for emotional self-monitoring including providing retrieval and report cues, minimizing blaming, varying questions, using a simple classification system, tying emotions to physical experiences, and applying multimedia are illustrated. The third part of the section addresses cognitive self-monitoring and teaches the necessary steps required to complete a daily thought record (DTR). Various examples of self-monitoring techniques punctuate the chapter.

Getting Good Data From the Patient:
Garbage In Creates Garbage Out

Self-monitoring requires getting good information from children and their families. Freeman, Pretzer, Fleming, and Simon (1990) offered a number of strategies for collecting useful self-report data. First, you need to motivate patients to be open and honest. Freeman et al. recommended giving patients a simple and understandable reason for wanting information (e.g., "By getting a clear sense of what happens before and after a meltdown, we can find ways to deal with the meltdowns and prevent them in the future"). Motivation is also enhanced if you show children, adolescents, and their families how self-monitoring is linked to their own identified treatment goals (e.g., "Catching your thoughts when you are freaked out in the cafeteria will help us decrease your worrying about throwing up in public"). Finally, once the patient has given you the information, use it.

Freeman et al. (1990) urged therapists to keep a lookout for factors that compromise self-monitoring. First, some patients withhold information due to fears that clinicians will be annoyed, embarrassed, disappointed, disapproving, or disgusted. It is like the Jack Nicholson character in *A Few Good Men* (Reiner, 1992) who proclaimed, "You cannot handle the truth." Patients are protecting you from their emotional and cognitive truths. In these instances, the therapeutic relationship becomes deformed and disfigured. Patients are taking care of you instead of you taking care of them. Therefore, you must demonstrate that you can handle the truth by modeling welcoming negative affect and discomfort in the session by assiduously adopting the therapeutic stance variables recommended in Chapter 3.

Freeman et al. (1990) reminded us that self-monitoring might be compromised if patients fear that the disclosed information will be used against them. They may predict others' coercion or control will be increased after receiving the information. In this way, the therapist usurps power. To minimize this obstacle, collaboration (Chapter 3) should be faithfully maintained.

Finally, self-monitoring may be avoided due to worries associated with discomfort, disaster, and out of control feelings (Freeman et al., 1990). Avoidant children and their families may predict that paying attention to their internal experiences is dangerous and avoidance is better than facing their distress. Others may fear that the more they deal with thoughts and feelings, the more likely they will get out of control. A graduated approach that includes a scaling component is a good way to manage these concerns.

Behavioral Self-Monitoring
Formal Parent and Teacher Report Rating Forms

Formal parent and teacher report forms are best suited to externalizing behavior disorders (Bird, Gould, & Staghezza, 1992; Loeber, Green, Lahey, & Stouthamer-Loeber, 1991). Nonetheless, parents' reports are subject to their own biases and mood states (De Los Reyes & Kazdin, 2005; Krain & Kendall, 2000; Silverman & Ollendick, 2005). Therefore, caution with parent and teacher rating forms is warranted.

There are several rater reports for attention deficit hyperactivity disorder (ADHD) symptoms. The Conners' Parent and Teacher Rating Scales-Revised (CRS-R; Conners, 2000) is a widely used and popular instrument (Reddy & De Thomas, 2007). The Conners' scales include seven primary factors: oppositionality, inattention, hyperactivity, anxious-shy, perfectionism, social problems, and psychosomatic issues. The norms for the Conners' scales are based on large samples. The scales come in long and short forms and are translated into multiple languages (Johnston & Mah, 2008).

The Swanson, Nolan, and Pelham Questionnaire (SNAP)-IV (Brock, Jimerson, & Hansen, 2009; Swanson, Sandman, Deutsch, & Baren, 1983) assesses both oppositional defiant and conduct disorders. The SNAP-IV is based on *Diagnostic and Statistical Manual of Mental Disorders (DSM)-IV* criteria. Items are rated on a 4-point scale (0 to 3) based on the frequency of the behavior. Items are then summed and averaged for each subscale. Finally, there are different cutoffs for each scale and respondent (e.g., teacher, parent).

The Vanderbilt ADHD Teacher Rating (VADTRS; Wolraich, Feurer, Hannah, Baumgaertel, & Pinnock, 1998) and the Vanderbilt ADHD Parent Rating Scale (VADPRS; Wolraich et al., 2003) are simple-to-use measures that also closely aligned with *DSM-IV* criteria. Both parent and teacher versions include the 18 principal symptoms of ADHD. The Parent Report Version is written at a third-grade reading level.

The Behavior Assessment Scale for Children-2 (BASC-2; Reynolds & Kamphaus, 2004) is a scale recommended for assessment of conduct disorders as well as broad childhood psychopathology (Kamphaus, VanDeventer, Brueggemann, & Barry, 2006; McMahon & Kotler, 2006; Murphy & Christner, 2006). The BASC-2 offers parent and teacher forms and takes approximately 20 minutes to complete. The clinical scales include aggression, anxiety, attention problems, atypicality, conduct problems, depression, hyperactivity, learning problems, and withdrawal. The BASC-2 offers the advantage of validity checks (Johnston & Mah, 2008).

The Achenbach Scales (ASEBA; Achenbach, 1991a, 1991b; Achenbach & Rescorla, 2001) are broadband measures assessing a spectrum of disorders. Achenbach (2007) noted that the ASEBA compares data from multiple informants and allows for interpretation of contextual variations. The Achenbach Scales take approximately 10 minutes to complete.

Behavior Charts and Hierarchies

In this section, we offer you suggestions for completing behavior charts and hierarchies. The essentials of each tool are spelled out. Traditional as well as innovative methods are presented. Several examples and applications are described. Finally, sample forms are included in the section.

Behavior Charts/Logs

Behavioral charts/logs classify the point-at-ables relevant to children's problems. Behavior logs are very easy to complete and tailor to individual patients. Generally, you target the behavior you want to monitor (e.g., arguing with sister). Then, you set the context (where, when, over what, who is present). Finally, you specify the outcome or consequences of the behavior.

A simple behavior log is presented in Form 6.1. Several online resources offer very child-friendly behavior charts. For instance, www.freeprintablebehaviorcharts.com offers charts separated by age (3 to 10 years, 11+ years) and by target behavior (e.g., chores, potty training, homework, practicing musical instruments, etc.). They also offer NFL logo charts, Arthur, Barney, Batman, Dora, Hannah Montana, Hello Kitty, Shrek, Spider-Man, and many other versions that are appealing to young patients.

Behavior charts often contain frequency counts, time blocks, and response duration. *Frequency counts* record the number of target behaviors during a standard interval such as one hour or a classroom period. This method is suitable for behaviors that occur consistently but not at a high frequency. They might be used to track property abuse (e.g., breaking pencils out of frustration) or the number of repetitive behaviors (e.g., number of times windows and doors were checked prior to going to bed). Frequency counts do not require a lot of effort on the observer's part, which makes them easy to implement. *Response duration* methods measure the amount of time an individual engages in a target behavior. This approach is designed for behaviors that have long durations such as tantrums or avoidance behaviors. *Time block* methods are useful for high frequency behaviors and for behaviors that are difficult to accurately record. The observer records the presence or absence of the target behavior within a predetermined interval for a set period of time. For instance, you might want to track tics. Tics can be difficult to accurately count as different observers may record the same observed behavior differently. For instance, a teen may have a vocal tic (throat clearing) followed immediately by two different motor tics (eye blinking twice and head turn). One observer might record this as one tic since the behaviors were continuous. Another observer might record this as two tics because there were vocal and motor tics. Still, a third observer might record this as three tics reflecting the different facial areas involved. These inconsistencies will produce data that is faulty and not useful for determining treatment efficacy. Time block recording

Form 6.1 Behavior Chart

Date	Target Behavior	Location	Frequency	Intensity	Duration	Who Was Present	Consequences

may resolve the discrepancy and simplify the task in a reliable way. For instance, adopting a time block method of 30-second intervals over a 20-minute observation time and instructing the raters to note any tic, it is likely all three observers would agree that a tic occurred in that 30-second interval leading to standardization of the data.

Hierarchies

Hierarchies are special instances of behavioral self-monitoring that make use of specific targeting of actions and circumstances as well as emotional scaling. Hierarchies are like ladders where each rung represents a step toward higher levels of distress. The key in constructing a useful hierarchy is defining terms in a realistic concrete manner. This is more difficult than it first seems and calls for similar skills discussed in Chapter 3 when you transformed obtuse vague complaints into more operationalized terms.

For most patients, 10 items in a hierarchy suffice (Masters, Burish, Hollon, & Rimm, 1987). You also enjoy several options when creating a hierarchy. A thematic hierarchy orders distressing items along a specific issue (e.g., fear of an object or situation such as giving an oral book report, being teased, dogs, spiders, and so forth). A spatial temporal hierarchy ranks the items along a space and time continuum. Higher items are closer in space and time or longer in duration (e.g., you are right next to a child who is vomiting and the child is throwing up right now). Examples of thematic and spatial–temporal hierarchies are presented in Figures 6.1 and 6.2.

SUDS	Item
10	Someone hitting, spitting, kicking me.
9	Someone threatening to hit, spit on, or kick me.
8	Someone telling me to f--- off.
7	A teacher telling me to shut up.
6	A teacher giving me extra work or spewing shit.
5	Another kid acting like he/she is better than me.
4	Someone cutting in line in front of me.
3	Someone acting like a fool or being stupid on the bus.
2	My brother going into my room and messing up my stuff.
1	My brother eating with his mouth open.

Figure 6.1   Thematic hierarchy. (SUDS—Subjective Units of Distress.)

SUDS	Item
10	Being in front of the classroom on the first day of school.
9	Riding in the car about a block from school on the first day of school.
8	Lying in bed the night before the first day of school thinking about the next day.
7	Getting a letter from school a month before school starts.
6	Being in Walmart getting supplies, seeing a classmate a week before school.
5	Seeing commercials for school supplies on TV during the summer.
4	Looking at my old papers over the summer.
3	Passing by school in a car over the summer.
2	Seeing next year's teachers in the hall at the end of the year.
1	Saying good-bye to my old teacher on the last day.

Figure 6.2   Spatial thematic hierarchy (anxiety). (SUDS—Subjective Units of Distress.)

There are a number of ways to make hierarchies fun for young people. Bubble-up (Friedberg, Friedberg, & Friedberg, 2001) is an entertaining way to teach children hierarchy construction. First, children specifically list their distressing situations on a line on the left side of the paper. A string of 10 bubbles lie on the right side of the written item. Children then color in the number of bubbles associated with each of their items. Friedberg et al. recommended following this activity with toy soap bubbles. Children are invited to blow bubbles while they explain their hierarchy. This creates an experiential exercise that facilitates greater recall and engagement.

Up, up, and away (Friedberg, McClure, & Garcia, 2009) is another way to teach the skill. Hierarchy items are drawn or written on index cards and each card is placed on the string. The string is then attached to a piece of construction paper cut in the shape of a kite. As the child moves up the hierarchy, a token or chip is placed on each item as it is encountered. When the child completes the item, it is removed from the tail of the kite. When items are removed, the kite becomes more aerodynamic facilitating the metaphor of being unburdened by distress (e.g., "You are ready to fly now!").

The lineup card is a method for hierarchy construction that speaks to children who enjoy baseball or softball. A lineup card is a good metaphor because batting orders are based on a scaling process (e.g., better hitters hit earlier than less able batters). Additionally, you can extend the metaphor by referring to the present item as being "up to bat," the next item as being "on deck," and completed items may be placed in the dugout. If you need to change or replace an item, you can call it a pinch hitter. The following dialogue shows how to use the lineup with Reese, a 12-year-old female who dreaded making mistakes.

Therapist: Reese, I know you like softball.
Reese: I love it.
Therapist: So, you know what a lineup is?
Reese: Sure, I hit second.
Therapist: Well, we're going to make a lineup or batting order with your worries about making a mistake. How does that sound?
Reese: Good!
Therapist: In our lineup, we are going to start with your weakest worry first and then work your way up to the biggest or number 9 worry. OK?
Reese: I think so.
Therapist: OK, let's try it. Let's lead off with a small worry about making a mistake. What would that be?
Reese: Maybe calling my relative by the wrong name at Thanksgiving dinner.
Therapist: OK, We'll give that a number 1 for the least worry and write it on the card. That's our lead off worry. I'll write it on the card. What's our number 2 worry?
Reese: Spilling on something new my mom bought me for church or school.
Therapist: Our lineup is taking shape! I'll write that one on a card, also.

Reese and the therapist gradually worked their way through the lineup card ending with her worst worry. In the dialogue, the therapist fostered collaboration and engagement (i.e., "How does that sound?"). Moreover, he wrote the worries on index cards for easy ordering and shuffling. Finally, the therapist reinforced Reese's efforts (i.e., "Our lineup is taking shape").

Emotional Self-Monitoring

Emotional self-monitoring is no easy chore. Negative feelings are avoided like the plague in most clinically referred children. Therefore, considerable gentility and creativity is required to obtain full and accurate emotional readings. Following are several rubrics we suggest for collecting data on children's emotional states.

Include retrieval and report cues. Retrieval and report are enhanced by specific probes that have concrete referents

(Brems, 1993; Freeman et al., 1990; Hughes, 1988), for example, "When you threw the block at your brother, how did you feel?" The use of names instead of pronouns also increases retrieval (e.g., "When he said you were a fart catcher how did you feel?" versus "When Johann said you were a fart catcher, how did you feel?"). Simple rather than abstract questions are preferable (e.g., "How does your face look when you are sad?"). You might want to attend to a specific situation in session to encourage a child's expression (e.g., "I noticed you had a tiny tear in your eye when you talked about being out in kickball").

Minimize blaming the child for problems in identifying emotions. If you find the child does not respond or understand the question or comment, rephrase rather than repeat it. Try a shorter question or comment. Be patient with children's reluctance or avoidance ("It can be a hard thing to talk about your feelings. Do you think it would OK to come back to it later?).

Vary how you ask about feelings. Children, especially younger ones, may withdraw if they believe they are on the spot. Therefore, peppering the children like a suspect is not a productive approach. Instead, change up the way you try to verbally identify feelings and add a mix of the following:

a. Declarative comments: I wonder how you feel when kids say you are a freak.
b. Reflective repetition: Your mom acted weird?

You feel like a breached fortress?
He let out his inner jerk?

c. Statements: Tell me about _____
Describe _____

Use a simple classification system. Although lists of feelings exist, keeping it simple for children and adolescents is recommended. As you recall from Chapter 2, emotions were grouped into four simple categories: mad, sad, worried, and happy. We suggest using this same rubric to help children and adolescents clarify their feelings.

Tie emotions to physical experiences. Children are sometimes better able to recognize the bodily sensations (e.g., bellyache, sweating, tension in their fists) that accompany emotions rather than the feelings themselves. Southam-Gerow and Kendall (2000) suggested teaching children to attend to their physical reactions via perceptual imagery such as "butterflies in the stomach," or "boiling mad." Therefore, physical sensations may be a window to discussing feelings. Their somatic experiences provide a concrete referent. You might then ask:

> When your fists get tight, what feeling do you have?
> When you find yourself sweating, what feeling word goes
>   along with that?

Use multiple media to identify feelings. Pictures, movies, cartoons, TV shows, and music facilitate emotional identification. Pictures showing different feeling states may be cut and pasted on a sheet of paper to make an individualized feeling chart. The children can add their own feeling labels beneath the picture. The magazine pictures provide a culturally rich alternative because the children can elect to pick pictures of people who look like them. Additionally, they can label the emotions according to their own language or slang.

Cartoons, movies, songs, and TV shows are also helpful in promoting emotional expression. Similarly to the magazine photos, these other media offer a variety of models. A clip from movies or TV shows can be shown, paused at emotionally salient moments, and then processed with the child (How is this character feeling? How can you tell? Do you ever feel this way? When?).

Plush toys can also be quite useful. For example, Whitney was an 8-year-old girl who smeared feces to express her anger toward her mother. According to Whitney, smearing the feces was safer than telling mom she was angry because angry expression was prohibited in the family. Whitney then identified a red bull plush toy that she thought was mad. We then planned for her to leave the red bull rather than her feces around to signal her anger.

Once the children and adolescents can identify their emotions, they need to learn to scale them. For most children, scaling may be relatively plain and simple (e.g., on a scale from 1 to 10 or 1 to 100). For other children, you may have to dress it up a little. Various methods such as thermometers, rulers, speedometers, and traffic signals are used. Each of these instruments has a gradient that scales the emotional intensity on an easily identifiable measure. Friedberg and McClure (2002) also recommended using visual aids such as five clear plastic cups that are filled 100%, 80%, 50%, 25%, and 0% with either food, colored water, or colorful beads. Children then simply point to the cup that represents the intensity of feeling.

Innovative Methods

Mood Searcher

Mood Searcher is an emotional self-monitoring tool that makes use of a searcher analogy. Searcher is an apt metaphor because it is active. You have to seek out and look for mood shifts. In our electronic age, most young people know what it is to search for information on the Internet. The same deliberate process used in Internet searching can be applied when monitoring moods.

The Mood Searcher exercise includes one column where the mood is recorded and a second heading that signifies where the mood was found. The procedure helps children attend to their feelings and the circumstances in which they occur. Further, they learn to connect the mood to the activating circumstance. The mood searcher exercise is found in Form 6.2.

The following dialogue with Jay, a 10-year-old angry boy who believes his anger comes out of the blue, illustrates the use of the Mood Searcher (see Figure 6.3).

Therapist: Jay, we have to search for your moods.
Jay: Search? You mean like a treasure search?
Therapist: Exactly. The treasure is your feelings.
Jay: That's not real treasure. Real treasure is toys!
Therapist: I can understand that. But feelings are kind of like treasure because they are important and personal. How do you find things that are important to you?
Jay: You look for them in places you think they are or might be.
Therapist: Good. That's just what we do with the Mood Searcher exercise. See the first column. This is where you write your moods. So let's write a couple of your moods or feelings.
Jay: OK. Mad and sad.
Therapist: When you were mad, where were you?
Jay: At home.
Therapist: Who was there with you?
Jay: My mom.
Therapist: OK, let's write that down. Where were you sad?
Jay: At school on the playground during recess.
Therapist: Great job. Who was there?

Form 6.2 Mood Searcher

MOOD	WHERE DID YOU FIND IT?

Form 6.2   Mood Searcher

MOOD	WHERE DID YOU FIND IT?
Mad	At home with my mom.
Sad	At school on the playground during recess when I was alone.

Figure 6.3   Jay's—Mood Searcher.

Jay: I was alone. No one was playing with me. That's why I
      was sad.
Therapist: Wow, you are really becoming a good mood searcher.

This dialogue illustrates several points. The therapist col-
laborated and aligned with Jay by joining with the treasure
hunt idea. The therapist asked Jay short, simple questions to
help him complete the worksheet (i.e., "When you were mad,

where were you? Who was there?"). Finally, the therapist praised Jay's effort.

What's Your Wavelength?

A wave is a commonly used metaphor for emotions in CBT (Wagner, 2003). In fact, the wave metaphor is an explicit part of readying a patient for exposure (Chapter 10). The wave begins at a low level (0–1) and builds to an apex (9–10). Wavelength contains several lessons. It is a way to scale emotions and teaches children that emotions exist on a continuum. Moreover, emotions are linked to situations or time. Finally, like waves, feelings have an ebb and flow.

What's your wavelength is done in several phases. First, the notion of a wavelength is introduced. The introduction is presented in the following example.

> Emotions and feelings are kind of like waves. They build up to a high point and then they turn into smaller ripples. Every wave has a pattern. Some are big and last long. Others are small and last a short time. It's the same with feelings. Every person has their own wavelength. We have to find yours. How does this sound?

After the introduction, you pull out the wavelength form. Then, the x and y axes are completed. Then, the wavelength is drawn by connecting the data points. The following dialogue with Adam shows how (see Figure 6.4).

Therapist: OK, Adam. Here is where we graph your mad wave. See I put the numbers 1 to 10 here.

Adam: OK.

Therapist: Now down here we are going to write when you get mad at your mom. Let's put down a few points.

Adam: I get mad when she tells me it's time to come in.

Therapist: I'll write this here. Any other times?

Adam: When she tells me to do chores and nags me about homework.

Therapist: OK, I've got those recorded. What about other times?

Adam: I really get pissed when she corrects my work. Then when she erases my work that ticks me off.

Therapist: We're about half way there. How mad do you get at each of these points?

Adam: When she erases my work that ticks me at about a 10. When she corrects me, I'm ticked at an 8. I'm a 6 when

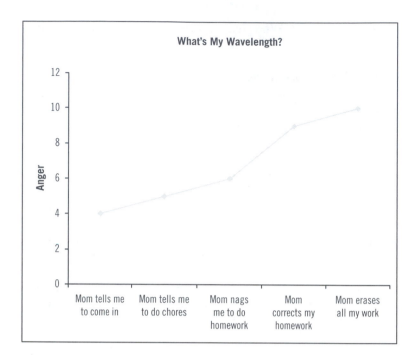

Figure 6.4   Adam's—What's My Wavelength?

she nags me to do my homework. Doing the chores
isn't too bad maybe a 5 and coming in is a 4.

Therapist: All we have to do now is connect the dots to find
your wavelength. (Adam connects the dots.) What do
you see?

Adam: My anger kind of builds up when she corrects me and
erases my work.

This dialogue serves several purposes. Both Adam and the
therapist worked collaboratively on the task. The therapist
was careful to break the task into phases. Finally, the therapist
asked a concluding synthesizing question (i.e., "What do you
see?").

Cognitive Self-Monitoring

Cognitive self-monitoring teaches children to increase awareness of thoughts and beliefs that are associated with particular situations and emotions. There are many ways to help
young people catch their thoughts. Friedberg and McClure
(2002) pointed out that the traditional question asked to access
a patient's thoughts is "What is going through your mind right

What is going through your mind right now?
What are you saying to yourself right now?
How are you seeing _____ in your mind's eye?
What's in your mind?
What is running through your head?
What is inside your head right now?
What is your private voice saying to you right now?
What jumped into your mind?
What do you make of that?
How do you understand that?
What is your mind saying to you?
What messages are you telling yourself?

Figure 6.5   A therapist's dozen questions to capture thoughts.

now?" Figure 6.5 provides you with a therapist's dozen questions to capture a variety of cognitive products.

When employing cognitive self-monitoring with children, the clinician may select from a number of tools that may be tailored to meet the needs of the individual young patient. Regardless of the type of thought diary, there are three essential tasks.

Three Steps in Completing a Thought Diary

Completing the situation. Situations or activating events need to be defined objectively and specifically. The event is the circumstance where the thoughts arise. Events could be environmental/contextual, circumstantial (e.g., "I saw Kaylee with another guy in the hall"), or internal experiences (e.g., shortness of breath, having bad thoughts). Care should be directed toward making sure the description of the situation is spelled out clearly. Figure 6.6 shows *No* (situations poorly defined or including an automatic thought) or *Go* (properly spelled out) examples of situational descriptions.

Completing the feeling column. Filling out the feeling or emotion column is based on your previous work identifying emotions described earlier in the chapter. Once the simple label is recorded, it should be scaled in intensity (e.g., 1–10, 1–100). Be wary about the common mistake of confusing thoughts with feelings. Friedberg, Mason, and Fidaleo (1992) recommended a system for making discriminations. Thoughts are the conclusions, interpretations, judgments, explanations, and images that run through your mind. Therefore, they are represented in sentences or phrases. Feelings are emotional states and most commonly expressed in one word. These one-word

John rejected me

Had a bad day at school

My mom is too bossy

John did not return my three calls

Got a 72 on a science test and
detention for not turning in
homework

Mom kept interrupting me when I
was on the Wii

Figure 6.6   No and Go situational descriptions.

Abandoned (it's a thought)

Helpless (it's a thought)

Empty (it's a thought)

In a bottomless pit (it's a thought)

Out of control (it's a thought)

Lonely, sad, angry

Sad, angry, hurt, anxious

Sad, lousy, crappy

Shitty, crappy, bad, sad, hopeless,
depressed, low

Anxious, angry, edgy

Figure 6.7   No and Go emotional descriptions.

emotional expressions are objective and consequently not
open to challenge or testing. Accurately identified feelings
are always valid. They simply are what they are. On the other
hand, since thoughts are judgments, they are always open to
testing because their accuracy is questionable. We only test
thoughts in CBT, not feelings. Figure 6.7 shows you the No and
the Go zones for the feeling columns on the thought diaries.

Completing the thought column. The thought column is where children's cognitions, assumptions, and beliefs are recorded. After you have elicited the automatic thoughts using the various questions in Figure 6.5, you need to check to make sure the thoughts and feelings match up on the content-specificity hypothesis (Chapter 2). If they do, you are golden and the thought diary is done. If not, you have more work to do.

Two hypotheses may explain why thoughts and feelings do not match up. First, the feelings may not be properly identified and recorded. If the feeling is identified according to the previous rubrics, then you may have caught a cold, irrelevant, or superficial cognition. In this circumstance, let the content specificity be your guide. Use the content specificity hypothesis to inform your questions in a technique called *laddering*. Figure 6.8 gives examples of content-specific questions that can lead you to hotter cognitions. The following dialogue illustrates laddering.

Therapist: Soledad, what goes through your mind when you call your friends and they do not call you back?
Soledad: It makes me feel bad.
Therapist: What feeling do you have?
Soledad: Sad, I guess.
Therapist: What do you say to yourself then?
Soledad: Just move on and call someone else.
Therapist: It must be hard to keep calling and not get a call back. I can see how it could make you feel really sad. What do you suppose it means about you that they don't call you back?
Soledad (teary): I guess I'm a loser and an outcast. Kind of a mutant or something.

Soledad responded with cold thoughts in her initial response to questions (i.e., "It makes me feel bad. Just move on and call someone"). The therapist amplified the emotional tone with an empathic statement (i.e., "It must be hard to keep calling and not get a call back"). Subsequently, the therapist asked a content-specificity-driven question (i.e., "What does that mean about you?") to elicit a hot thought associated with Soledad's sad mood.

Traditional Thought Diaries

Traditional thought diaries are very easy to construct. At the most basic level, you simply divide the paper into three

Emotion	Content-Specific Question
Depression	How do you see yourself?
	What does it mean about you?
	What are you saying to yourself about the kind of person you are?
	What critical things about yourself are going through your mind?
	In what ways are you blaming yourself?
	How do you see other people?
	What does this mean about your relationships?
	What goes through your mind about other people?
	What negative things are you saying to yourself about other people?
	How are you down on other people?
	How long do you think this will bother you?
	How permanent is_____?
	How changeable do you think_____is?
	What does this mean about your future?
Anxiety	What is the danger?
	What is the threat?
	What is the risk?
	What are you afraid of?
	What are you worried about?
	What is the scary thing?

Figure 6.8   Let the content specificity be your guide questions.

Anxiety (continued)	How likely do you think_____ is? (overestimation of the probability of the anger)
	How possible do you think_____ is? (overestimation of the probability of the danger)
	How sure are you that_____is going to happen? (overestimation of the probability of the danger)
	What is the catastrophe? (overestimation of the magnitude of the danger)
	How awful will it be? (overestimation of the magnitude of the danger)
	How bad do you expect it to be? (overestimation of the magnitude of the danger)
	How able do you see yourself to cope with_____? (underestimation of coping)
	How able do you see yourself to handle_____? (underestimation of coping)
	Who do you see as possibly helping you? (neglect of rescue factors)
	What people might help? (neglect of rescue factors)
	What might rescue you from the danger? (neglect of rescue factors)
	What do you suppose other people will think of you? (fear of negative evaluation)
	What do you predict other people will say or do? (fear of negative evaluation)

Figure 6.8   Let the content specificity be your guide questions. (**Continued**)

columns. You then label the columns, event/situation, feeling/intensity, and thought. A sample completed thought diary is presented in Figure 6.9.

Creative Thought Diaries

Creative thought diaries contribute to making cognitive self-monitoring tasks more engaging. The graphics and cartoons

Anger	What do you see as unfair?
	How unfair do you think_____ is?
	What doesn't seem right about_____?
	What provoked you?
	What rules were broken?
	What personal commandments were broken?
	What laws of living were broken?
	How much do you think _____ was done on purpose?
	How much do you think _____ deliberately did _____?
	What names did you call_____?
	What do you think of_____?
	How would you describe_____?

Figure 6.8 **(Continued)** Let the content specificity be your guide questions.

can reduce the idea that catching thoughts is a dull burdensome task. In addition to those presented next, creative
thought records can be found in Friedberg and McClure (2002),
Friedberg et al. (2001), Friedberg, McClure, and Garcia (2009),
and Kendall (1992).

Thought-Feeling Dragon

Thought-Feeling Dragon is a cartoon-based thought diary
that makes the idea of hot cognitions come to life for young
patients. Similar to other animals and cartoons, dragons are
ambiguous and therefore do not represent any specific gender or ethnicity. Thought-Feeling Dragon sets the table for a
cognitive restructuring exercise (Dragon Splasher in Chapter
8). Consequently, the graphic facilitates broader identification.
The thought is captured in the bubble enclosed in the flames
coming out of the dragon's mouth.

The first step is for children to record their feelings in the
blank alongside the dragon's face. They simply write the feeling they are experiencing in the space (sad, mad, worried,
etc.). In Step 2, they write the hot thought, the fire breathing

Situation	Feeling	Thought
Losing in a game	Sad (8)	Unless I am always the best at a thing, I am worthless.

Figure 6.9 Traditional thought diary.

drawing spits out. The following dialogue shows the way to complete the diary with Giovanni, an 11-year-old boy (see Figure 6.10).

Therapist: Giovanni, I remember you really like dragons.
Giovanni: They are really cool. I like how they look.
Therapist: Well, G. I have a worksheet where a dragon helps you catch your thoughts and feelings.
Givoanni: How can a dragon do that?
Therapist: Let's look (pulls out Form 6.3).
Giovanni: He looks cool!
Therapist: Look he's breathing fire.
Giovanni: It's really hot. Look at the flames.
Therapist: Just like the things that go through your mind. We call them hot thoughts. Write down what goes through your head when you are really hot with anger.
Giovanni: I hate it when kids don't play by the rules I know and they do things I don't like or want to do. I just can't stand it.

Giovanni and his therapist playfully completed the thought diary. The therapist used Giovanni's comments to fuel the processing. He also facilitated Giovanni's engagement in the task (i.e., "Look he's breathing fire"). Finally, the therapist asked the classic cognitive therapy question (i.e., '"What goes through your mind when you are really hot with anger?").

Thought-Feeling Asteroid

Thought-Feeling Asteroid is a daily thought record that makes use of the asteroid metaphor (see Form 6.4). Like all thought feeling diaries, the Thought-Feeling Asteroid fits nicely with the notion of hot thoughts. It also sets up the blaster of the universe self-talk intervention (Chapter 8).

The Thought-Feeling Asteroid is a diary that is completed in three parts. The first column is the activating event or situation, the second part is identifying the feeling, and the final

Form 6.3   Thought-Feeling Dragon

Feeling: _____

Form 6.3 Thought-Feeling Dragon

Feeling: Angry

I hate it when kids don't play by the rules that I know and they do things I don't like or want to do. I just can't stand it!

Figure 6.10 Giovanni's—Thought-Feeling Dragon.

phase is recording the thought. Children first write the activating event in the column provided. Next, they write their feeling label in the next column. Finally, they write in their hot thought by the asteroid. They may also color the asteroid a representative color (e.g., red for anger).

The following example with Colby, a 9-year-old boy with pervasive developmental disorder (PDD) who was fascinated with astronomy, illustrates the process (see Figure 6.11).

Therapist: Colby, I remember you really like asteroids.

Colby: I do. I am an expert in them. I know what they are made of and how fast they travel. I also know how you weigh them. I want to be an astronomer when I get out of high school.

Therapist: Then, this next worksheet should be interesting for you. It is called a Thought-Feeling Asteroid.

Colby: Huh, asteroids don't have thoughts and feelings! They are space matters.

Therapist: Well, sometimes your thoughts and feelings seem to come out at you really fast, maybe like the speed of an asteroid.

Form 6.4   Thought-Feeling Asteroid

Date _____

Event	Feeling	Thought

Form 6.4 Thought-Feeling Asteroid		
Date_____		
Event	**Feeling**	 **Thought**
Talking About Worksheet	Frustrated (7)	This isn't really right and I want it to look real and the way a real asteroid looks.
	Annoyed (7)	It's stupid.

Figure 6.11 Colby's—Thought-Feeling Asteroid.

Colby: They come at you fast but not that fast.

Therapist: And they seem to almost come from unknown directions, too.

Colby: I don't know much about that.

Therapist: So, this thought and feeling worksheet may help you be an expert with your own thoughts and feelings. Let me show you (pulls out worksheet). Here's the asteroid.

Colby: They don't look really like that! I can show you some better pictures.

Therapist: You sure are an expert but let's use this thought-feeling asteroid.

Colby: OK, but it isn't correct.

Therapist: We can even use the worksheet in our discussion. Look, I'll write what's happening in the event column. Now how are you feeling about what we are talking about?

Colby: Frustrated … This isn't right … The asteroid … It's annoying.

Therapist: You really like things just so and when things aren't the way you think is right, you feel very frustrated. How frustrated and annoyed are you on a scale from 1 to 10?

Colby: About a 7.

Therapist: The asteroid column shows what is going through your mind when you are frustrated?

Colby: This isn't really right. I want it to look real and the way a real asteroid looks. It's stupid.

Therapist: Colby, wow, you are becoming an expert at filling out this worksheet as well as astronomy. You are doing, great. Pick a color to color in the frustrated asteroid.

Colby: I'll use the rust color.

The dialogue with Colby illustrates several important points. The therapist introduced the task as a way to increase Colby's expertise (i.e., "This thought feeling worksheet may help you be an expert with your own thoughts and feelings"). Second, he used Colby's irritation with the task as a here-and-now way to complete the thought diary. Third, the therapist reinforced Colby's effort (i.e., "Wow, you are becoming an expert at filling out this worksheet").

Mind Your Mind

Mind Your Mind is a graphic-enhanced thought diary useful for older children and adolescents (see Form 6.5). Similar to the traditional thought diaries, it contains three columns: the event, emotion, and thought. The cartoon graphic of the mind is added to increase engagement in the task. The title, "Mind Your Mind," is interesting and provides a useful cue reminding youngsters to attend to their thoughts. Additionally, the Mind Menders exercise (Chapter 8) is based on this self-monitoring chapter.

Mind Your Mind is very simple to complete. The date, situation, and feeling are listed at the top of the page. The mind your mind column is marked by the brain drawing with a thought bubble over it. The youth then records the date and situation as well as the feeling and scaled intensity. Finally, in the mind your mind space, the patient writes in his or her thoughts.

The following example illustrates Mind Your Mind with Luciane, a 14-year-old bright young woman who is anxious and depressed due to peer rejection (see Figure 6.12). She is also the target of relational aggression (Crick & Dodge, 1996) where classmates spread rumors and try to disrupt her existing friendships.

Form 6.5 Mind Your Mind Diary

Date: _____

Situation:

Feeling:

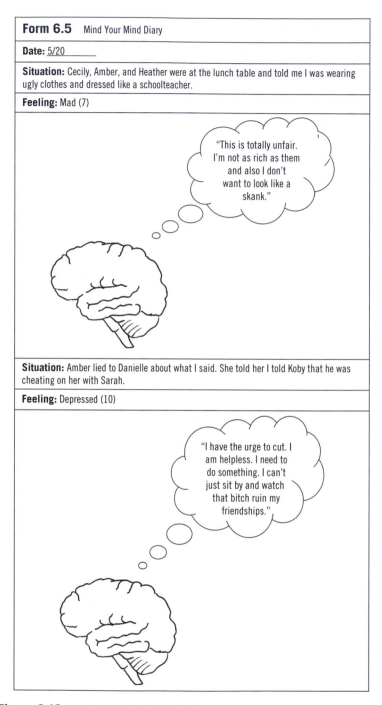

Form 6.5   Mind Your Mind Diary

Date: 5/20

Situation: Cecily, Amber, and Heather were at the lunch table and told me I was wearing ugly clothes and dressed like a schoolteacher.

Feeling: Mad (7)

"This is totally unfair. I'm not as rich as them and also I don't want to look like a skank."

Situation: Amber lied to Danielle about what I said. She told her I told Koby that he was cheating on her with Sarah.

Feeling: Depressed (10)

"I have the urge to cut. I am helpless. I need to do something. I can't just sit by and watch that bitch ruin my friendships."

Figure 6.12   Luciane's—Mind Your Mind Diary.

Therapist: You have a lot on your mind Luciane.

Luciane: I do. Sometimes it is hard to concentrate.

Therapist: I have this worksheet called minding your mind. It may help you sort things out.

Luciane: OK.

Therapist: There are several rows. Here you write the date. Next to the situation, you write what happened. Alongside the feeling, you write your emotion and rank it from 1 to 10. Finally, down here in the mind bubble column, you write down what is going through your head. How does that sound?

Luciane: Easy enough.

Therapist: OK. You said yesterday was a particularly rough day at school. So, let's write the date: 5/20. What happened?

Luciane: Cecily, Amber, and Heather were at the lunch table and told me I was wearing ugly clothes and dressed like I was a schoolteacher.

Therapist: Write that down in the situation. How did that make you feel?

Luciane: Mad.

Therapist: How mad on a scale of 1 to 10?

Luciane: Maybe a 7.

Therapist: Go ahead and write that down. Now, what went through your mind?

Luciane: This is totally unfair. I'm not as rich as them and also I don't want to look like a skank.

Therapist: Write that down in the minding your mind column.

Luciane: This was just one thing that happened.

Therapist: OK. We've got plenty of room on the paper. Let's write down what else happened.

Luciane: Amber lied to Danielle about what I said. She told her I told Koby that he was cheating on her with Sarah.

Therapist: That's a lot of drama.

Luciane: Welcome to my life.

Therapist: OK, so Amber lied to Danielle. How did that make you feel?

Luciane: Really depressed. I really thought Danielle and I were getting to be close. I started to get the urge to cut.

Therapist: Let's write depressed in this column. How depressed?

Luciane: A 10.

Therapist: You said you had the urge to cut.

Luciane: Yes.

Therapist: Did you?

Luciane: No, but I really felt like it.

Therapist: Let's write that in the thought column. What went through your mind when you had the urge to cut?

Luciane: I am helpless. I need to do something. I can't just sit by and watch that bitch ruin my friendships.

Therapist: So, you thought you should cut as a way to take action.

In this dialogue, the therapist and Luciane covered several emotionally provocative situations. Luciane was able to readily identify several hot cognitions during the process.

CONCLUSION

Self-monitoring is a keystone in CBP with children. Without this foundation, the subsequent CBP techniques rest on shaky ground. Remember to apply the behavioral, emotional, and cognitive self-monitoring in an emotionally salient context to get the best data. In sum, Bateson (1972) rightly noted that observing a phenomenon begins to change it.

Seven

Behavioral Techniques

INTRODUCTION

Behavioral approaches are founded exactly on the notion that learning theory is helpful in understanding and treating problematic behavior. Wilson (1981, p. 157) famously wrote that behavioral techniques involve "a systematic application of conditioning principles to clinical disorders." Conditioning is simply another way to say "learning." Behavioral techniques involve specific procedures for particular problems. Behavioral techniques emphasize doing rather than talking. Consequently, they focus on taking direct action. Westen (1996, p. 631) knowingly commented, "Whoever penned the proverb about the need to get back on the horse as soon as one has fallen off was a latent behavior therapist."

This chapter begins with descriptions of classical, operant, and social learning theory paradigms. Essential concepts in each paradigm are explained. Treatment rudiments based on learning models are presented. You will learn various techniques such as contingency management, relaxation, systematic desensitization, and social skills training.

RUDIMENTS

Classical Conditioning

Classical conditioning is the learning process for many fears, phobias, and aggressive behaviors (Domjan & Burkhard, 1986). Moreover, classical conditioning is the basic paradigm for treatment interventions such as systematic desensitization. In classical conditioning, people learn to make associations between stimuli and make new responses to these stimuli. Simply, classical conditioning demonstrates that strong emotional arousal to classes of stimuli can be learned. Essentially, learned emotional responding can be connected to ostensibly harmless stimuli in the same fashion as it is to apparently dangerous stimuli (Bandura, 1977b).

Classical conditioning involves several important variables. An *unconditioned stimulus* (US) is a stimulus that elicits reflexive behavior. The stimulus is considered unconditioned because it does not require prior learning to bring about the response. An *unconditioned response* (UR) is the reflexive or involuntary behavior elicited by the stimulus. For example, a puff of air directed at the eye (US) results in an eye blink (UR). No learning is occurring; there are just hardwired stimulus–response connections.

Classical conditioning occurs when a neutral stimulus called a *conditioned stimulus* (CS) begins to pull out the reflexive behavior due to repeated pairing with the US. The CS is paired with the US repeatedly until the CS presentation alone is able to elicit the response. Contemporary learning theorists believe that the capacity of the CS to bring out reflexive behavior is due to the fact that learners anticipate the US. Simply, the CS becomes a kind of signal or predictor of the US.

Let's say you want to use classical conditioning to teach an eye blink response to a tone. A puff of air (US) automatically produces an eye blink (UR). Then, you add a tone (CR) preceding the puff of air (US) to elicit the blink. After multiple pairings, the tone alone produces the blink. When this occurs, conditioning (learning) has occurred.

On the other hand, *extinction* involves active learning of an antagonistic, competing, or inhibitory response. Extinction in classical conditioning involves specific experiences with the conditioned stimulus (Domjan & Burkhard, 1986). Simply, extinction is an active process. Individuals learn that the CS does not predict the presence of the US. Consequently, the connection between the CS and CR is broken. In our view, extinction underlies many of the exposure techniques presented in Chapter 9.

Operant Conditioning

Operant conditioning is sometimes called instrumental conditioning or Skinnerian conditioning. Skinner, in his classic book *Beyond Freedom and Dignity* (1971), asserted that people do not exert influence on the world but rather the world acts upon them. There is heavy emphasis on environmental factors determining behavior. In the operant paradigm, an existing response is strengthened or weakened by external consequences. Behavior is shaped by its consequences or by what follows and comes after it. This prompted Bandura (1977b) to refer to operant conditioning as learning by consequent determinants. Responses are emitted rather than elicited as in classical conditioning (Sherman, 1979). Finally, operant conditioning works through cues and consequences.

There are four basic operant processes: positive reinforcement, negative reinforcement, punishment, and response cost. Reinforcers are determined by their effect on behavior (Craighead, Craighead, Kazdin, & Mahoney, 1994). Reinforcement is a process whereby responses are strengthened by the appearance of a pleasant stimulus (positive reinforcement) or the contingent disappearance of an aversive stimulus (negative reinforcement) (Skinner, 1938). Positive reinforcers are any pleasant stimuli that upon their presentation increase the frequency of the desired behavioral response. Negative reinforcement occurs when a desired behavior is strengthened by the removal of an aversive stimulus. Negative reinforcement occurs when something noxious, annoying, or otherwise bad is taken away and the desired behavior increases.

Lefrancois (1986) offered a simple way to remember negative reinforcement. He explained that negative reinforcement offers *relief*. Kazdin (2001) refers to negative reinforcement as turning off aversive stimuli. For example, a teenager who storms out of the house and sleeps all day to turn off (avoid) his mom's nagging is engaging in negative reinforcement. Leaving the house and hibernating is strengthened if it terminates the noxious nagging.

Response cost is an operant procedure that decreases the frequency of the behavior by the contingency removal of a reward (Masters, Burish, Hollon, & Rimm, 1987). Simply, undesirable responses *cost* a reward. Response cost procedures suppress the undesirable behaviors and these responses do not recover their strength after the response cost is discontinued. Additionally, these responses do not carry the aversive side effects of punishment (see later). Removal of rewards and privileges, and time-out are typical child behavior management strategies that are based on response cost.

Punishment refers to the presentation of an aversive stimulus that suppresses the frequency of an undesired behavior. Much to parents' dismay, punishment does not remove a behavior from a child's repertoire. Simply, punished behavior is not "lost" behavior. In fact, when punishment is removed, the behavior may recur. Moreover, if a behavior is well established, punishment is less effective (Masters et al., 1987). Further, Lefrancois (1986) commented that punishment does little to teach desirable behaviors.

Craighead et al. (1994) described unwanted side effects of punishment. Punishment increases the frequency of emotional responding. Thus, its application ramps up the emotional intensity of a situation. Second, punishment teaches children to avoid people who deliver aversive stimulation. Finally, children who are exposed to frequent and excessive punishment imitate these behaviors and become punishers themselves.

In general, consequences should occur immediately after a behavior in order to gain maximum effectiveness. This maxim is referred to as *temporal contiguity*. Essentially, temporal contiguity refers to the time elapsed between a response and the reinforcer (Domjan & Burkhard, 1986). In other words, the closer the consequence occurs to the response, the stronger the learning effect. Domjan and Burkhard (1986) argued that since behavior occurs in real time and is a continuous process, a delayed consequence may inadvertently become paired with an irrelevant behavior. In this way, possible confusion may occur and due to this ambiguity, individuals may attach the consequence to the behavior that was closest to it in time.

Reinforcements occur according to *contingencies*. Contingencies are if–then rules that are arranged according to various *schedules*. Schedules of reinforcement dictate the arrangement between responses and their consequences. They establish rules about how and when behaviors are reinforced. These laws of the land explain variations in the frequencies and patterns of behavior. There are five schedules of reinforcement. The arrangement of contingencies may indicate continuous or intermittent rates of reinforcement. They may also indicate whether the arrangement is fixed and unchanging, or variable (changing). Finally, contingencies may be based on the rate of behavior (ratio) or the time elapsed (interval) between delivery of reinforcement. Ratio schedules tend to produce strong rates of behavior. Variable schedules tend to produce very sturdy response rates that are resistant to extinction. The specific schedules of reinforcement are explained and illustrated next.

Ratio schedules. Ratio schedules are intermittent schedules that are based on the rate of behavior. They may either be fixed or variable. In a fixed ratio (FR) schedule, every nth response is reinforced. FR schedules may develop high rates of responding but may also contribute to premature extinction if the fixed rate is too high (Masters et al., 1987; Thorpe & Olson, 1997). In a variable ratio (VR) schedule, on average every nth response is reinforced. It produces a consistently high rate of responding and importantly provides training in delayed gratification. Since delayed reinforcement is a natural consequence in real-life functioning, this is another recommendation for VR schedules.

Interval schedules. Interval schedules (IS) are the second type of intermittent schedules. IS are based on time intervals. IS generally yield lower rates of behavior probably due to the fact that reinforcements are tied to time rather than behavior. In a fixed interval (FI) schedule, reinforcement is based on the time interval that elapses between delivery of reinforcements. FI schedules are characterized by a *scalloped* curve, which show that the rate of behavior gradually builds to a crescendo near the time of reinforcement and then declines somewhat. This is referred to as a *postreinforcement pause* (Sherman, 1979).

A course syllabus is a familiar fixed-interval schedule. Assignments are laid out over time and exams are scheduled. Students who mass their studying behavior or cram right before the exam intensify their behavior at the reinforcement point (e.g., the exam). They pull all-nighters and feverishly exhibit desired academic behaviors. Then, after the exam, their studying behavior declines to a much lower rate during the postreinforcement pause.

In addition to consequences, operant conditioning makes use of *cues*. While reinforcement and response cost processes are consequences, discriminative stimuli (SD) represent cues and represent another set of important variables in operant conditioning. Mahoney and Thoresen (1974) operationalized self-control by stating that it is determined by individuals' knowledge of and control over environmental factors. Simply, they offered the maxim "know thy controlling variables" (p. 22). SD emphasize the situation, context, and/or ambient conditions of the behavior. SD set the occasion and signal the situation is right for the behavior to be reinforced. SD marks the time and place for a response.

In operant conditioning, discrimination requires being able to discern the situations that are right for reinforcement from those that are not right for reinforcement (S^{Δ}). This is fundamental to healthy adjustment. When a behavior is directed by discriminative stimuli, the behavior is said to be under *stimulus control*. More specifically, the behavior occurs consistently to the SD and infrequently to the S$^\Delta$.

Consider the following family example. Eight-year-old Gary had trouble getting off to school in the morning on most weekdays. Specific questioning revealed that the worst days were the ones where his father readied him for the day. At breakfast, he refused nearly all the items offered by his father prolonging the morning meal. The father is highly indulgent and prepared whatever Gary chose. Moreover, he permitted Gary to watch TV while he dressed. Gary's mother is more directive, consistent, and organized when readying Gary. His food choices are limited and TV is contingent upon being ready for school. Dawdling was met with response cost (e.g., removal of rewards and privileges). Gary was a good learner. He recognized that Dad's behavior was a discriminative stimulus for dawdling. On the other hand, mother was S$^\Delta$ for dawdling. Consequently, Gary's dawdling behavior was considered under stimulus control.

Good adjustment requires keen alertness to these ambient or surrounding conditions (Thorpe & Olson, 1997). Indeed, failure to act properly in specific situations brings most children into treatment. Neglect of cues causes inappropriate behavior to bleed into improper situations. Often, this behavior is associated with children's and adolescents' desperate needs for reinforcement. The excessive motivation to meet their demands for reinforcement causes them to neglect situational cues (Rotter, Chance, & Phares, 1972).

Consider the example of 8-year-old Sophie. Sophie has a high demand for physical closeness, nurturance, and attention. Consequently, she hugs her teacher repeatedly during the day, hugs her peers during class, and at recess. All this hugging contributes to her being teased by her peers and ignored by the teacher.

Shaping is a laborious but generally effective way to develop new behaviors or increase the rate of low frequency behaviors. Shaping refers to the process where reinforcement is initially delivered to a response that resembles or approximates to a certain degree the desired behavior. Subsequent responses that become increasingly similar to the desired behavior are reinforced and the reward is withdrawn from the previous less similar behavior until the desired goal is realized.

The Premack principle may help in shaping desired behavior. The Premack principle is a learning principle, which states that more preferred activities can reinforce lesser preferred activities (Danaher, 1974). For example, studying first is reinforced by watching TV or playing video games later.

Extinction represents a decline in responsiveness as a function of nonreward. Behavior declines in frequency, intensity, and duration due to the absence of reinforcement. Strong emotional and behavioral arousal accompanies extinction. The emotionality associated with the extinction process is referred to as an *extinction burst*. An extinction burst is the temporary yet intense increase in behavioral intensity of the response due to deprivation of the reward. Tantrums and meltdowns represent children's protests at their behaviors being extinguished. Extinction bursts occur approximately 25% of the time (Lerman & Iwata, 1996). Spontaneous recovery occurs when there is a return of heretofore extinguished behaviors. However, spontaneous recovery is limited by the use of repeated extinction procedures (Domjan & Burkhard, 1986).

Social Learning Theory

Social learning theory (SLT) hypothesizes that behavior is a function of direct operant, classical conditioning as well as learning through observation (e.g., vicarious learning) (Bandura, 1977b). SLT rests on the assumption that behavior is learned through interactions with a meaningful environment, which adds a relational component to the theory (Sherman, 1979). Additionally, behavior is goal oriented and directional (Bandura, 1977b; Rotter et al., 1972). Expectancies about reinforcement are key concepts. Accordingly, a cognitive element is added to the learning paradigm. In a simple sense, SLT "explains how people acquire a set of complex behaviors in social settings" (Phares, 1988, p. 350).

People and environments are seen as reciprocally determining each other. Therefore, behavior does not occur in a vacuum. Rather, individuals act and react in situations and to others in a systematic manner. SLT posits that a child's behavior influences the parents' thoughts, feelings, and behaviors in a causally interactive fashion. For instance, Carla comes home upset that she is teased at school. Carla's mother reacts with anxiety, overcontrol, and overprotection motivated by the belief she should protect her daughter from all discomfort because she cannot handle it well. The mother's well-intentioned behavior fosters greater self-doubt and low perceived competence, which, in turn, fosters greater self-doubt and low perceptions of competence. Consequently, greater anxiety and self-criticism result. This increased distress then increases mother's overcontrollingness and overprotection.

Social learning theory also accounts for the rapid acquisition of new behaviors (Sherman, 1979). Behaviors are quickly acquired through social learning processes because it does not require trial and error. This is particularly adaptive and vital since some learning errors are harmful and fatal if done through trial and error (Sherman, 1979). Vicarious learning involves observation and then demonstrating this learning through imitation. Social learning theory emphasizes an individual's capacity for self-regulation through symbolic processes including cognition, language, goal setting, self-reinforcement, and expectancies (Bandura, 1977b; Rotter et al., 1972).

Self-efficacy (Bandura, 1977a) is a core construct in social learning theory. Self-efficacy refers to individuals' subjective perceptions that they can successfully perform a behavior or series of behaviors. In a simple sense, self-efficacy is a kind of self-confidence. Although there are a variety of sources for self-efficacy expectations, the most reliable and powerful basis is actual performance attainment (e.g., doing it). Bandura noted that self-efficacy earned through authentic mastery experiences is sturdy and enduring. Indeed, this theoretical construct is the basis for behavior and cognitive therapists' weighing of action over talk as a way to change behavior.

RUBRICS

Operant Conditioning Techniques

In this section, various clinical procedures based on operant conditioning are described. Teaching contingency management to parents is a common clinical task and is presented first. Pleasant activity scheduling is then explained. The section concludes with a discussion of graded task assignments.

Teaching Parents About Contingency Management: ABC Model of Parent Management

Contingency management increases desirable behavior (Kazdin, 2001). Anastopoulos (1998) noted that contingency management provides added motivation for reluctant and oppositional children to comply with requests. Contingency contracts are forms of social exchanges that require reciprocity (Wells & Forehand,

1981). As Wells and Forehand (1981) remarked, they are explicit *quid pro quo* (this for that) arrangements. Contingency management includes the dual processes of the presentation and withdrawal of rewards. A contingency is a rule that dictates what behavior under what circumstances merits a reward. Generally, stickers, charts, or other tokens are used to serve as a bridge between the response and a larger reward.

Additionally, contingency contracts work to reduce familial conflict by specifying expectations (Spiegler & Guevremont, 1998). Shapiro, Friedberg, & Bardenstein (2005) explained that "the essence of contingency contracting is its replacement of vague unstated reinforcement contingencies with clear, detailed information about the consequences of different behaviors" (p. 65). The ABC model is an understandable and efficient way to teach contingency management to children.

Functional analysis is central to individually tailored interventions and is founded on operant learning principles. Haynes, Leisen, and Blaine (1997) defined *functional analyses* as sets of probability-based statements that serve as "best estimates" of the purposes for individuals' behaviors (p. 337). Kazdin (2001) explained "cause" in behavioral terms is operationally defined as specifying the cues and consequences of behavior. Functional analyses tend to focus on present factors that influence the behavior rather than historical factors. Functional analysis helps clinicians teach parents to identify the causes or purposes of behavior.

Contingency management begins with functional analyses. The ABC model describes the antecedents and consequences that are associated with a particular behavior (Spiegler & Guevremont, 1998). Simply, they learn what comes before (antecedents) often cues their behaviors and what comes after (consequences) shapes the likelihood of their behavior occurring again. Children and families are taught to identify a target behavior; pay attention to it; and record information regarding the frequency, duration, and intensity of the target behavior. Friedberg and McClure (2002) recommended that the phrases "the things that come before" and "the things that come after" replace the technical terms "antecedents" and "consequences," respectively when teaching contingency management to parents.

In conclusion, the ABC model of parent training is a parsimonious form of functional analysis. Functional analysis specifies the context for behavior by identifying the antecedents (A) or cues for the behavior. Additionally, the parameters of the behavior (B) (e.g., frequency, intensity, duration) are also detailed. Third, the consequences (C) (reinforcement, response cost) that initiate, maintain, and exacerbate the behavior are spelled out.

Antecedents: Recommendations for Giving Good Cues and Commands

Kazdin (2001) rightly reminds us that behavior management is not just about delivering consequences. Rather, cues and commands are key training foci. Commands are the antecedents in the behavior management sequence. They represent the cues or the SD for the behaviors. Importantly, they set the stage for compliance. Accordingly, there are several important rudiments for effective antecedent commands.

Discuss the plan with the child or adolescent beforehand. Kazdin (2001) recommended collaboration and child involvement in any contingency contract. This practice ensures both parents and children know the rules of the game. Moreover, the contract holds each party accountable for playing by the rules. Finally, the collaboration prevents the contingency contract from being overly authoritarian and enables buy in by the child.

Prompt the child's attention. Many children with attention deficit hyperactivity disorder (ADHD)/attention deficit disorder (ADD), oppositional defiant disorder (ODD), and pervasive developmental disorder (PDD) spectrum disorders require prompts for desired behavior. Prompts are reminder cues for the behavior and initiate a desired response (Kazdin, 2001). Prompts are especially helpful when initially developing a new behavior or one with a low frequency behavior. They show children what to do, how to do it, and when to do it (e.g., "When you come in the house, take off your shoes and put them in the hall closet") (Kazdin, 2001). Once the behavior is well established, the prompt may be gradually withdrawn (faded).

Moreover, prompts guide attention (Kapalka, 2007). They also help children maintain eye contact. Kapalka (2007) emphasized that "there is something binding about human eye contact" (p. 40). Asking children to repeat commands or instruction is another form of prompting.

Create a climate change: Direct the child to do something they like. Early in the parent training process with very oppositional children and noncompliant children, Barkley, Edwards, and Robin (1999) suggested making a climate change. Parents are encouraged to give children commands to do activities they like in order to turn the icy, hostile family atmosphere warmer. Moreover, instructing children to do something they like or prefer and then praising their compliance establishes a successful command–compliance sequence.

There are several points to remember. First, the parental command must be genuine, sincere, and free from facetiousness. Second, compliance to the command should be accompanied by verbal praise from the parent or caregiver.

Commands should be short and understandable. Long, drawn out, and complex commands are easily tuned out. Children's attention is effortfully earned and hard to maintain. Lectures should be assiduously avoided. Accordingly, commands should be polite, respectful, but crisp and to the point. Kazdin (2008) encouraged the use of "please" commands. Ideally, specific commands communicate expectations. For example, an instruction to "try harder" is quite vague. What does this mean? How do children know they have fulfilled the expectation?

Chain commands where instructions follow like rapid fire bursts from an automatic weapon rarely hit the mark. Rather, multiple instructions should be broken down into component stages. Figure 7.1 gives you some examples and is a useful handout for parents.

Pay Your Dos: Give More Do Rather Than Stop Commands

I (RDF) learned this rudiment early in my career doing school consultations at the Children's Psychiatric Center at the Jewish Hospital of Cincinnati. I was working at an old Midwestern school building with a winding staircase with multiple landings separating the floors. While I was in the hall, a 5-year-old child went running down the stairs. As he reached the first

Soggy	Crisp
Get ready for school.	Please put your shoes on and get your book bag.
Be nice.	Please share your candy with your sister.
Don't bother me when I am on the phone.	Please wait until I am off the phone before you ask me a question.
Be careful with your juice cup.	Please hold the grape juice with two hands and stay in the kitchen while you drink it.

Figure 7.1 Crisp versus Soggy commands.

Don't Commands	Do Commands
Don't give me "attitude."	Please speak with me in a calmer voice and without swearing.
Don't make a mess.	Please lay down some newspaper before you start painting.
Don't get the dog all keyed up.	Play quietly with the dog now.
Don't forget your permission slip.	Please remember to put your permission slip in your book bag.
Don't leave your retainer on the kitchen table.	Please keep your retainer in its case in your bedroom.

Figure 7.2   Don't and Do commands.

landing, his teacher shouted after him, "Don't run." The boy dutifully stopped, paused for a few seconds, and then hopped down the next flight of stairs. The problem with the teacher's command was that it omitted the desired responses. Therefore, avoid don't- or stop-type commands and instead teach children what the expected response is (e.g., "Walk down the stairs, please"). Figure 7.2 illustrates do and don't commands and is another useful parental handout.

Allow time for compliance/response. Webster-Stratton (1986) recommended waiting 5 seconds or so for the children to comply. It is the rare child who hops to parental commands. Allowing some time for the child to comply increases the probability for success. Children need a little time to adjust and shift their attention and compliance.

Avoid question commands. Webster-Stratton (1986) reminds us that question commands are rarely effective. They are too vague and indirect. Moreover, they invite an explanation rather than behavior change (e.g., "Why don't you clean up now?"). Since they are indirect commands, the child's nonresponse cannot be explained as noncompliance. For example, a child who responds to the question, "Why don't you clean up?" by saying "Because I am not done playing" is actually engaging in appropriate conversation.

Decrease "let's" or "we" commands. Many parents unwittingly give let's or we commands. These commands are relatively passive and indirect requests. Let's commands imply wiggle room and create ambiguity surrounding the parental directive. On the other hand, we connote a joint effort. This is fine only if the parent intends to do the activity with the child.

Decrease unnecessary and rapid-fire commands. Dr. Donald J. Viglione, Jr., once aptly explained that parenting is always for the long-term. Although parents may have the urge to hang on to children like an old suit, compliance is not enhanced by unnecessary commands. Children become confused about what is important and parental voices become aversive stimuli. Parents need to prioritize and clarify what is considered the small stuff and behaviors that are truly important.

Form 7.1 helps parents not to sweat the small stuff. In the worksheet, parents mindfully list the behaviors or nuisances that are small stuff. Parents are then invited to let this small stuff be. The middle column requires more deliberation. These behaviors are the ones that are significant enough to be responded to but do not reach the threshold of major problems. This column calls for an intermediate level of response. Finally, the last column contains the major issues or problem areas. These behaviors demand immediate attention and parental intervention. The consequence for misbehavior in any of the columns should be proportionate but even in the big issue column physical punishment should be avoided.

Consequences: Suggestions for Reinforcements and Response Cost Procedures

Consequences are the C's in the ABC model. Reinforcement and response cost procedures are the consequences described in these next sections. Spiegler and Guevremont (1998) cogently summarized guidelines for delivering reinforcements. First, reinforcements should be clearly and explicitly connected to the completion of desired behavior ("Because you listened and followed my directions, I will read you an extra story"). Second, immediate reinforcement is preferable to delayed reinforcement especially in the early stages of change. Third, in the early stages of change, reinforcements should be given generously and then gradually leaned out. Fourth, you should rely on a variety of reinforcers so children do not habituate to them. Fifth, caretaking figures in children's lives need to be consistent and on the same page with the same target behavior and types of reinforcers. Finally, naturally occurring social reinforcers will foster greater generalization (e.g., praise, affection, playtime).

Figure 7.3 lists a variety of sample reinforcers. Selection of reinforcers should be a mindful and deliberate process.

Form 7.1 Don't Sweat the Small Stuff

Small Stuff	Middle Stuff	Big Stuff

Entertainment	Sports	Games	Choice	Trips	Social
TV time	Play football	Checkers	Choose a restaurant	Go to a museum	Praise
Watch a movie	Swim	Chess			Smiles
Listen to music	Play basketball	Scrabble	Choose a movie	Visit a pet store/shelter	Laughs
		Boggle			Hugs
Watch a puppet show	Lacrosse	Connect Four	Choose where to sit	Get a make over	High-fives
Go to a play	Tennis		Turn on the washing machine		Patting back
Go to a concert	Bocce Ball		Use the garage door opener		Kisses
	Hiking				
Surf the Net	Bowling				
CD downloads	Ping-pong		Use the remote control		
Puzzles	Air hockey				
Books	Fishing		Tune the car radio/CD player		
Sleepovers	Baseball				
Special classes (karate, dance, etc.)	Miniature golf				
	Arcade games				
Window shopping	Ice skating				
	Roller blading				
	Flashlight tag				

Figure 7.3   Types of reinforcements.

Contingency managers should have an array of reinforcers at their disposal. Moreover, different reinforcers have strengths and limitations (Kazdin, 2001). For example, Kazdin (2001) astutely noted that food's value as a reinforcer depends on the deprivation state. If children are not hungry or candy is in full supply, they will not work for candy. Second, Kazdin emphasized that administration and consumption of food may disrupt ongoing target behavior. Social reinforcers are far more portable, easy to administer, and more often than not in short supply in children's lives. Social reinforcers rarely interrupt the ongoing process of behavior and are quite powerful. For all these reasons, social rewards are highly preferable (Kazdin, 2001).

Rewards and privileges should match the difficulty of the task. Small prizes for short-term, relatively easy goals is the rule. Gifting the child with an expensive reward for a small achievement rarely works out well. Behaviorists know that an organism will not work for a reward in a satisfied state.

Consider this example. A mother and her 7-year-old son set up a point-based contingency chart. The child earned 2 points daily for feeding the dog, brushing his teeth before bed, and cleaning up toys by the second request. The child had the opportunity to earn 6 points daily and consequently 42 points per week. The initial criterion was for 32 points per week. A small reward (less than $2 toy, going to get ice cream) was to be delivered upon the child meeting the criterion.

After the first week, the child earned 36 points. The mother rewarded him with a $30 video game for his 36-point effort. His points for the second week sunk to 18 points. So what happened? The video game completely satisfied the child and he was satiated by reward. He could play the game all week so he did not care if he went for ice cream or earned a $2 toy.

Many parents will recoil from contingency management because they believe their child should not have an incentive to behave properly. Indeed, they may find the idea of reinforcement repugnant ("My father just told me to do things and I just did it"). However, the parents are engaging in selective attention and recall neglecting the reinforcers in their own situation (Masters et al., 1987). In these circumstances, you will need to guide the parents' attention to the importance of reinforcement by normalizing the notion of payoffs for positive behavior.

Clinical experience tells us that many parents may object to reinforcing children for behavior because they see it as a form of *bribery*. Masters et al. (1987) cogently stated, "Bribery refers to a payoff for irresponsible, undesirable, or morally offensive behavior" (p. 520). Bribery also occurs when rewards are offered at the wrong time for the wrong behavior. For instance, a parent who offers a trip to Wendy's to a sullen child who is stalling doing the homework is a bribe. The parent is bribing the child to stop being sullen and stalling. A bribe is offered when the child is misbehaving to stop the undesired response

("Here. I'll give you a stick of gum if you stop whining") whereas a reward is delivered when the child is doing the desired behavior in order to strengthen its frequency.

Differential reinforcement of other behavior (DRO). In differential reinforcement, wanted behaviors are positively reinforced and unwanted behaviors are ignored. There are two types of differential reinforcement of other behavior (DRO): One type is called differential reinforcement of incompatible behavior (DRI) and the other is labeled differential reinforcement of zero behavior (DRZ; Weis, 2008). DRI involves rewarding behaviors that are incompatible with the inappropriate behavior. In DRZ, children are reinforced for inhibiting an inappropriate behavior for a stipulated period of time.

Kazdin (2008) referred to DRO in a common-sensical way. He called this the "positive opposite." Kazdin explained, "When you get rid of a behavior by rewarding its opposite, the effects are stronger, last longer, and do not have undesirable side effects of punishment. So concentrate on the positive opposite and the principle of replacing what you don't want with what you do want" (p. 31).

Calling Penalties: Response Cost Procedures

Response cost procedures are behavioral consequences where children lose something (e.g., TV time, points, keys to the car). They are similar to fines, sanctions, and penalties (Kazdin, 2001). If you are a football fan, penalties are a useful way to understand the principles of response cost. If a team is off-sides, it loses 5 yards for the infraction. Holding or unnecessary roughness are more serious infractions so more yardage is sacrificed.

Tips from Kazdin's (2008) excellent parenting skills books guide application of response cost procedures. First, Kazdin recommends that if stickers or points are used, only a minimum amount should be taken away. If privileges are removed, they should be withdrawn only for a short period of time. Further, if a privilege is removed, it should be a highly valued one otherwise the response cost resembles a diluted time-out (discussed next). A privilege is a single reinforcer and if the child can replace it with something else of similar or even greater value, the response cost procedure is rendered ineffective. Finally, Kazdin proposed that the rate of any positive reinforcement to response cost ratio should be approximately 5:1.

Time-out. Time-out is a common yet misunderstood and misapplied child management strategy. Time-out refers to "time out for reinforcement" (Patterson, 1975, p. 73). Time-out is generally reserved as consequence for children ages 2 to 12 (Patterson, 1975). Time-out generally involves separation or isolation from other people or sources of reinforcement.

There are some key pivotal guidelines for using time-out (Patterson, 1975; Spiegler & Guevremont, 1998). First, the time-out spot should be dull and nonreinforcing. It can be a room, but it also can be a corner of room. Time-outs should range from 1 to 5 minutes. There is no additional benefit for longer time-out periods (Patterson & White, 1969). Time-out does not stop until the child is quiet (Webster-Stratton, 1986). Similarly, the child is never removed from time-out when they are having a tantrum, crying, or screaming. The child should not be scolded after time-out is over (Webster-Stratton, 1986). Rather the child should be praised as soon as he or she behaves appropriately after serving the time-out.

Ignoring. Ignoring is a commonly used behavior management technique. Ignoring is well suited to attention-seeking behaviors that are not self-injurious or dangerous. Additionally, it is a relatively easy technique to teach caregivers. Despite these advantages, there are several drawbacks to the technique (Spiegler & Guevremont, 1998). First, ignoring works slowly. Second, behavior is likely to get worse before it gets better when ignoring is first applied. Because it is an extinction procedure, there is a 25% chance of the burst. Third, Spiegler and Guevremont (1998) noted that extinction processes tend to generalize. Finally, spontaneous recovery is possible especially if DRO is not used.

Forehand and McMahon (1981) give pointers for ignoring. First, no eye contact or nonverbal cues are given during ignoring. They suggest turning your back to the child in a 90-degree angle. Second, there is no verbal communication. Finally, no physical contact occurs during ignoring. This may require the parent leaving the room.

Grounding. Grounding is seen as a very severe form of response cost (Barkley, Edwards, & Robin, 1999). Friedberg and McClure (2002) saw grounding as including elements of time-out and removal of rewards and privileges. Grounding should be monitored and relatively short in duration (Barkley, Edwards, & Robin, 1999). Barkley and his colleagues (1999) recommended the maximum length of two days. Similar to time-outs, grounding is best when it is relatively time limited. Moreover, they emphasize that a parent needs to be home to enforce the grounding. We agree with Barkley and colleagues' caution that grounding is not generally effective with children older than 15 years.

In sum, *contracts should be flexible and include negotiation.* Kazdin (2001) urged that if the reinforcers are not effective or the response demands are set too high or low, they should be collaboratively renegotiated. Contingency contracts are outcome driven. They are successful only if they increase the rate of desirable behavior. Rigidly adhering to contingencies that do not increase productive behavior is nonsensical. If a particular contract is not working, make changes so desirable behavior has a chance to increase.

Pleasant Activity Scheduling

Pleasant activity scheduling (PAS) is a time-honored and powerful behavioral intervention based on operant conditioning (Beck, Rush, Shaw, & Emery, 1979). Friedberg and McClure (2002) asserted that "pleasant activity scheduling is a valuable first line of defense against anhedonia, social withdrawal, and fatigue" (p. 200). The activity schedule is also useful when combined with the distress tolerance skills recommended in Chapter 8.

The basic pleasant activity schedule resembles a daily planner or appointment book. Days of the week are listed horizontally across the paper and time blocks are listed vertically on the left column. You want children and parents to consider the pleasant event scheduling as important as a prescription or an office visit. Youngsters then set aside a time when they engage in the pleasant activity. Children should be encouraged to rate their mood prior to and after completing the activity.

Some activities may require little time and no cost. There could be activities children can do on their own and other activities will need parental support and time to complete. Several excellent pleasant activity surveys are available (Daley, 1969; Phillips, Fischer, & Singh, 1977; Stark, 1990) and they could give you ideas for activities. Friedberg et al. (2001) suggested reviewing local newspapers and advertisements for activities that seem fun, interesting, accessible, and inexpensive (e.g., free concert at a local bookstore). These ads could be placed in an activity box and selected by the child.

Graduated Task Assignments: Setting Up the Patient for Success

Graduated tasks break big tasks into small ones. Taking baby steps is a popularized but nonetheless useful explanation.

Graduated tasks are designed to propel motivation so you want children to feel encouraged by their efforts. There are three important guidelines for helping patients with graduated tasks (Bandura, 1977b, 1986).

Task difficulty refers to outlining the precise type and level of effort needed to obtain a rewarding outcome (e.g., studying in a quiet room for 30 minutes from 7 to 7:30 P.M.) (Bandura, 1977b). Due to their detailed nature, these behaviors are easily observable and measurable. Consequently, they yield clear markers for progress.

Goal level defines the nature of the difficulty. For familiar and easy tasks, the standard for success should be set relatively high (Bandura, 1977b). For new and difficult tasks, the goal level should be set relatively lower. Bandura rightly noted that if a child tries hard but fails to reach to a high standard, they will get disappointed and surrender. Gradual tasks provide direction and increase self-confidence (Bandura, 1977b).

Goal proximity refers to how far into the future goals are projected. Daily goals are more motivating than goals projected further into the future (Bandura, 1977b). Thus, a goal for a C average at the end of a semester is not likely to increase motivation (remember the principle of temporal contiguity). Daily study goals are more motivating because they break the large task into smaller ones and lead to more immediate rewards.

Consider this example. Benny is a bright 17-year-old patient with PDD who lacks motivation for schoolwork. His baseline study behavior is approximately 10 minutes per day and his grades are dismal (all D's). Graduated tasks were assigned to help him increase time doing schoolwork. Recognizing the importance of task difficulty, goal level, and proximity, the therapist started with an easy task (i.e., studying for an extra 5 minutes per day). If Benny met his goal, he earned 5 extra minutes for computer time. After Benny achieved this level for 2 weeks, the goal level and task difficulty were increased (i.e., 10 minutes for the extra computer time).

Teaching a socially anxious child to increase the amount and frequency of social contacts is also accomplished via graduated tasks. Amber, an 11-year-old reclusive and inhibited girl rarely made eye contact and commonly offered barely audible hellos. Initial goals were making eye contact, saying an audible hello to two children at the bus stop, and noting their response on a chart. When Amber brought her chart to her mother, she received special mother–daughter time (e.g., makeovers, cooking, reading, crafts, etc.). As the goal level and task difficulty increased (more contact and conversation), the activities became intrinsically reinforcing as Amber was more included in social events.

Classical Conditioning Procedures

In this section, relaxation training and systematic desensitization are introduced and explained. The rudiments for conducting these procedures are detailed and ways to augment their effectiveness are outlined.

Relaxation Training

Relaxation training is a well-known and basic behavioral technique to reduce physiological arousal. Deep breathing is the simplest form of relaxation training. Clinical wisdom teaches us that many youngsters literally hold their breath when stressed. Indeed, this practice increases their physiological arousal.

Consequently, children need to recognize that releasing tensions will ultimately contribute to greater self-control. A *tornado metaphor* may be quite useful. For example, you could explain that a tornado possesses such force that any and all efforts to tighten, tie, nail, lock, or cover the windows paradoxically results in a house being blasted apart. On the other hand, what really helps is to open the windows and go down to the basement. Opening the windows is like loosening muscles and going to the basement is similar to engaging in coping imagery.

Controlled breathing is an easy and unobtrusive relaxation intervention. Breathing is something children can do throughout their day without drawing attention to themselves. Controlled diaphragmatic breathing involves learning to breathe deeply and slowly. A 5-point cycle is simple to teach. Children are taught to inhale for a count of 5, hold their breath for a count of 5, and then exhale through their mouth for a count of 5. The inhaling breaths should come from the diaphragm. You may demonstrate how to do the diaphragmatic breathing, reminding them that their stomachs need to fill up with air. You can also explain that their stomach should go out when they breathe in. Instructing the child to gently place their palm on their stomach is also a good strategy. In this way, they can give themselves feedback. The calming breaths should be done slowly or else they may hyperventilate.

Ten candles (Wexler, 1991) is an exercise where children imagine a row of 10 candles and then blow them out one by one.

Warfield (1999) recommended blowing bubbles with a commercial bubble solution and wand. Friedberg, McClure, and Garcia (2009) made use of a straw and cotton ball to teach deep breathing. In this procedure, the children are instructed to blow the cotton ball across the table with a straw to learn deep breathing.

Progressive muscle relaxation (Jacobson, 1938) is a more sophisticated relaxation procedure. Children are taught to tense and relax specific muscle groups. The systematic tension and relaxation phases are associated with inhaling and exhaling. We recommend several scripts for relaxation training for younger children, which include engaging metaphors and imagery (Geddie, 1992; Kendall et al., 1992; Koeppen, 1974; Ollendick & Cerny, 1981).

Systematic Desensitization

Systematic desensitization is a go-slow procedure where only low levels of distress are elicited in patients (McNally, 2007). The procedure presents patients with anxiety-producing stimuli while simultaneously experiencing a physiological state that inhibits anxiety (e.g., relaxation, laughter, and so on) (Foa, Steketee, & Ascher, 1980). Systematic desensitization includes three basic skills (King, Muris, & Ollendick, 2005). A hierarchy of anxiety-producing or aversive situations is constructed (Chapter 6). Children can draw or paste pictures from magazines on cards to represent each fear. Patients are schooled in muscle relaxation or some other counterconditioning agent (CCA). Humor, deep breathing, and emotive imagery are examples of other CCAs. Hierarchy items are then gradually paired with CCAs. Consequently, the items are encountered in a state of calm. Theoretically, the CCA inhibits the anxiety. Shapiro et al. (2005) cleverly explained that "systematic desensitization runs classical conditioning in reverse" (p. 59). Systematic desensitization then creates a fresh link between the fear-producing stimulus and the calming response (Friedberg, McClure, & Garcia, 2009).

Emotive imagery has been recommended as a CCA in systematic desensitization for children (King, Molloy, Heyne, Murphy, & Ollendick, 1998). King et al. (1998) claimed that relaxation training can be quite tedious and demanding for young children; therefore, emotive imagery is a useful alternative. Emotive imagery is viewed conceptually as a desensitization procedure because the imagery is juxtaposed with an anxiety-producing scene or situation (Shepherd & Kuczynski,

2009). Emotive imagery is well suited to imaginary worries and where *in vivo* exposure is contradindicated or not feasible (Shepherd & Kuczynski, 2009).

Emotive imagery as originally described by Lazarus and Abramovitz (1962) refers to imagery that carries an emotional payload of pride, power, self-efficacy, and humor. For instance, King et al. (1998) reported on their use of a Batman image where Batman joined forces with a child to battle fearful situations. Shepherd and Kuczynski (2009) used the Tasmanian Devil character to help a young child scare away ghosts. They augmented the procedure by encouraging the patient to draw a picture of Taz and post it in his room.

The process of pairing the scenes with a CCA is relatively straightforward. The first scene is presented when children are in a relaxed state. Morris and Kratochwill (1998) instructed children to "imagine the scene as if you were really there" (p. 100). If children experience anxiety, they signal by raising a finger. If they become anxious, they are told to stop imagining the scene and return to the relaxation. Once the children are able to hold a scene in their imagination without anxiety, they move onto the next item in the hierarchy. It is important to remember that in systematic desensitization, the experience with the fear stimuli ends when the youngster experiences the anxiety. Therefore, systematic desensitization is quite different from exposure (Chapter 10).

Morris and Kratochwill (1998) gave clinicians several recommendations for the procedure. First, each scene needs to be repeatedly presented (approximately three to four times). When the scenes are initially introduced, the children should hold onto the image for 5 to 10 seconds. Subsequent presentations should be approximately 10 to 15 seconds in duration. Finally, children should practice relaxation for 15 to 20 seconds between scenes.

There are several additional considerations to address when conducting systematic desensitization (Masters et al., 1987). These issues include the child's level of arousal and restlessness, their skills in applying the CCA, repeated signaling of anxiety to a scene, age, and number of fears.

Level of arousal and restlessness. Children who exhibit a great deal of psychomotor agitation are not good candidates for systematic desensitization. If these youngsters are overly restless or agitated, they will have difficulty maintaining images and practicing relaxation. Moreover, if they can't sit still their level of distraction works against the procedure. In these instances, you will want to consider some behavior management contracts as discussed in the previous section to reduce distractibility ad arousal.

Skill in applying the CCA and imagery skills. In order to progress through the hierarchy, children need to be skilled in both the CCA as well as imagery. It is important to make sure the CCA is calming to the child. Be careful not to rush through the relaxation training. Systematic desensitization will not be effective if the CCA is impotent.

Children or adolescents repeatedly signaling anxiety to a scene. Continued signaling of anxiety to a scene or situation may indicate several factors and call for creative trouble-shooting. First, the patient may have misjudged the intensity of the distress and made too low a subjective distress rating. In this case, the hierarchy needs to be rearranged. Second, if the systematic desensitization is imaginal, the patient may be changing the image to one approximating an item scaled higher in the hierarchy. Care should be directed toward checking in with the patient to see what he or she is imaging. If the image is changing you will need to rescale the item. Third, the patient may be engaging in anxiety-producing ruminations. Asking the patient, "What is going through your mind?" will elicit these ruminations. If ruminations are present, you will want to deal with them via the numerous techniques in Chapter 8.

Age and number of fears. There is little evidence support-ing the use of systematic desensitization in children under 9 (Morris & Kratochwill, 1998). Thus, the procedure is best reserved for older children and adolescents. Systematic desen-sitization is not indicated for children who have multiple fears (Masters et al., 1987). Systematic desensitization is best suited to very circumscribed fears (Foa et al., 1980).

Social Learning Procedures

This final section focuses on social skills training, which is firmly rooted in social learning theory. Various conventional and innovative social skills procedures are explained. Dialogues augment the descriptions and handy forms are also included.

Social Skills Training

Social skills training (SST) equips children and adolescents with core interpersonal competencies (Spiegler & Guevremont, 1998). Berger and Thompson (1995) characterized socially competent children as able to "cajole the adversary, use bar-gaining, suggest compromise or cooperation (like turn taking) and redirect conflict through humor" (p. 481). SST is involved in friend making, anger management, and handling teasing. There are some very handy texts totally devoted to social skills training (Asher & Gordon, 1998; Cartledge & Milburn, 1996; Robin, 1998).

Many social skills training packages are based on Euro-American standards and majority culture conventions. Therefore, we must recognize that these customs are not universal. Social skills should be taught in a context-dependent manner and tailored to individual characteristics. Cartledge and Milburn (1996) assembled a wonderful array of skills and is an excellent resource for designing cultural response social skills programs.

Social scripting or social stories is an emerging way to teach social skills to children with pervasive developmental disorders. Social scripts are used to enhance general social skills, on-task behavior, appropriate social/play behavior, social communication, and reduce disruptive behaviors (Ivey, Heflin, & Alberto, 2004; Reichow & Sabornie, 2009). Ivey et al. (2004) also noted that social scripts can teach children new social routines and prepare children for new situations.

Social Stories™ (Gray, 2000) are specific examples of social scripts. Social stories focus on explaining social concepts and nuances inherent in social situations. Additionally, they detail component skills and expected outcomes of social situations. The stories are individually constructed by children and written in the first-person perspective. Occasionally, drawings and photographs accompany them. Videotapes and audiotapes can also augment the stories.

Role-playing (also known as behavioral rehearsal) is a commonly used and fairly simple behavioral intervention to teach social skills. Role-playing is a procedure where you and the children act out a scene to practice new skills. Role-playing is like theatrical rehearsal in that it prepares children for actual performance (Fink, 1990). Role-playing is an active instructional procedure involving coaching, feedback, behavioral rehearsal, debriefing, and reinforcement (Beck et al., 1979). Friedman, Thase, and Wright (2008) recommended that the role-play should address the physical setting, antecedents of the interaction, and full descriptions of people involved in the interaction.

The similarity between role-playing and theatrical acting has long been documented (Goldfried & Davison, 1976). Integrating elements of theatrical method and instruction may provide an added dimension to the therapeutic role-playing. Method acting was developed in 1923 by Constantin Stanislavski in Russia. Method acting espouses "the virtue of truth in acting" (Andres-Hyman, Strauss, & Davidson, 2007, p. 85). The key is making the character believable and real. Vineberg (as cited in Andres-Hyman et al., 1991) delineated the tenets of method acting. Method acting presents the character in a psychologically sound and consistent manner. In method acting, genuine emotion is expressed and actors draw from their own personality. Frequently, method actors use spontaneity and improvisation to communicate with other actors. Bandelj (2003) wrote that "actors creatively respond to the contingencies of the moment" (p. 404).

Goldstein (2009) wrote that "acting teaches empathy, perhaps because actors must put themselves in the shoes of their character and feel that character's feelings" (p. 7). Indeed, recent work in teaching theory of mind (TOM) to children with PDD spectrum disorders focuses on helping them make accurate inferences about the thoughts, feelings, and intentions of others (Baron-Cohen & Howlin, 1998). Goldstein noted that effective role-playing helps actors read others' emotions and intentions. Further, Verducci (2000) noted that actors are taught to notice and adjust to other people's behaviors.

Most clinicians engage in some manner of role-playing and social skills training. There are several guidelines to keep in mind when role-playing. They include practicing patience, teaching hovering does not help, using direct instruction, employing a graduated approach, recognizing cues and consequences in the social interaction, and engaging in real-world practice.

Practice patience. Patience is a virtue in friendship making. SST teachers are well advised to teach youngsters to adopt a long-term view of relationships. Asher (1983) commented that skillful children recognize they should "not just start playing or even always come right out and ask to play. Instead, they wait, they kibbitz, and they can work their way slowly into the group" (p. 1429).

Hovering does not help. Putallaz and Wasserman (1989) defined *hovering* as observing and approaching a group from a moderate distance without making verbal overtures. Gottman (1977) concluded that hovering rarely leads to social inclusion.

Teach skill through direct instruction. Skill acquisition does not occur through osmosis. Skill sets need to be broken down into understandable components. Didactic material may be processed with children and adolescents. Skills may also be taught via videotaped displays like movies and TV shows. For instance, you may want to view a show with children and then highlight good examples of social skills. Fiction and non-fiction books are another source of social skills information. Finally, therapists demonstrating the social skills provide modeling displays for patients.

Krasny, Williams, Provencal, and Ozonoff (2003) urged social skills trainers to make the abstract concrete. For instance, they suggested that if–then social rules should be operationalized and include a menu of options (e.g., If someone compliments you, you could [a] look at them, smile, and say nothing; [b] look at them, smile, and say thank you; or [c] look at them, smile, say thank you, and say something nice about them).

Graduated practice with feedback. Simple skills need to be taught first and then progress to more complex skills. Bierman (2004) offered a number of easy-to-implement, creative, graduated practice group exercises. For example, individual children in a group are given separate ingredients for a trail mix. They then must talk with other members in order to share their ingredients for the trail mix. She also described cracker stackers, which is a creative variation of the trail mix exercise. Each child in a group is given a separate ingredient for a tasty snack (e.g., peanut butter, jelly, graham cracker, sprinkles, raisins, and so forth). The task is for everyone to make a complete cracker stacker with all the ingredients. Therefore, the children have to ask other members for ingredients and share their own in this cooperative task.

Krasny et al. (2003) described a clever use of a bingo game to increase practice seeing similarities between people and achieving a sense of belongingness. A printed card is handed out to group members. Common strengths and weaknesses of children who have Asperger's syndrome (AS) are recorded on the card. The group therapist calls out the characteristics and the children place a token on the space if they have the characteristic. If they get five in a row, they yell "bingo!" Krasny et al. (2003) noted that frequently multiple players get bingo and consequently they learn they share many characteristics with others.

Recognizing cues and consequences. Any social skills training program should help children and adolescents appreciate the cues that signal social situations are approachable or should be avoided or delayed. Moreover, thinking ahead or means-ends plans should be incorporated.

Cues for social entry and exit need to be explicitly identified. Children need to know which situations are welcoming and which situations are ripe for rejection. Further, they must realize when they are offensive, overbearing, or monopolizing conversations. Asher (1983) concluded that socially successful children are good at reading situational context and flexible enough to adapt to changing circumstances. They are able to go with the situational flow rather than redirecting it. Simply, skillful children are able to respond and follow others' leadership rather than always being in charge. Unskilled children try to enter a group and end up disrupting it, whereas skillful children make themselves relevant to the group activities, imitate group members' behaviors, and make group-oriented comments (Putallaz & Wasserman, 1989).

Figure 7.4 offers some simple educational information for social entry. Discriminative stimuli listed under the welcome column signal the situation is right for social entry.

Eye contact	Ignoring
Smiling	Frowning
Talking in an inviting way	Teasing
Moving closer	Turning away
Calling you by name	Interrupting
Giving you a compliment	Criticizing
Giving you a high-five or first bump	Whispering to others when you are around
Saying hi to you	Changing topics when you are talking
Saying good-bye when you are leaving	Taking things from you
Waving to you	Spreading rumors about you
Sitting by you when there is a choice of where to sit	Hurting you with words or actions
Giving you a chance to join the conversation by pausing	Rolling eyes when you walk by
Telling you a joke	
Helping you	
Asking for your help	
Making plans with you	

Figure 7.4 Welcome and Keep Out signs.

Discriminative stimuli listed under the keep away column indicate that social entry is not a good idea. This is a good handout for improving children's attention to cues and consequences.

Real-world practice. Social skills are typically rehearsed in role-play. Although these minidramas are quite useful, there are several cautions to this technique. First, role-play should approximate the emotional context in which the skills are to be applied. In this way, transfer of learning will occur.

Accordingly, when you role-play with children and adolescents, you will need to fully appreciate their stressful contexts. You should apply your empathy skills when you portray children's antagonists. This will require gathering information about how the children see the other characters in their scenes. When you play these characters, pay attention to their demeanor, emotions, thoughts, motives, and behaviors.

Role-playing may need to be augmented to approximate real-life scenarios. When training children and adolescents to role-play, cognitive behavioral therapists are well advised to teach the fundamentals of adopting a new role. Goldstein (2009) stated that a deep analysis of a character requires true understanding of other people. Therapeutic role-players should be trained to know what characters feel, how they act, and their motivations (Verducci, 2000). We argue that impactful therapeutic role-playing resembles method acting. Bandelj (2003) explained, "With patience and deep involvement, one acquires ease with and confidence about the new social role until one is not a mere performer but becomes that role" (p. 410).

Specific Procedures

Friendship 411

Children with social skills deficits and peer difficulties often do not know what it is to be a real friend and have a genuine friend. Therefore, you will need to provide some basic information about friendship. For instance, Feindler and Gerber (2007) offer a useful distinction between friendly and unfriendly teasing. *Friendly teasing* is defined as playful and governed by the motivation to relate, get closer, and join together. There is no malicious intent. On the other hand, unfriendly teasing focuses on exclusion, hurting others' feelings, and domination.

The simple exercise Friendship 411 (Form 7.2) is a checklist for friendship, and children rate the degree to which their

Form 7.2 Friendship 411

Action	You	Your Friend
A friend listens		
A friend cares about your ideas		
A friend cares about your feelings		
A friend cares about your opinions		
A friend respects your wishes		
A friend lets you be you		
A friend compromises		
A friend takes turns		

Action	You	Your Friend
A friend is honest		
A friend disagrees		
A friend is able to change plans		
A friend apologizes		
A friend is a good loser		
A friend is a good winner		
A friend sometimes does playful teasing		

friends or themselves possess the attribute. Dimensional ratings are used to deflate any absolutistic or all-or-none thinking
errors. Additionally, there are several blank spaces for children and adolescents to add in their own criteria.

Friendship 411 also serves as a handy friendship inventory
(Feindler & Gerber, 2007). This sheet also serves as basic information for friendship criteria. Feindler and Gerber (2007) recommended evaluating both the individuals' and their friends'
responsibilities in the relationship. Further, they suggested
children and adolescents consider the reasons for ending
friendships as well as the advantages and disadvantages for
no longer being friends.

Becoming a Friendship Scout

Becoming a Friendship Scout is a procedure that alerts children
to essential aspects of friend making (Form 7.3). You work with the
youth to identify (i.e., scout) a potential friend. Then, youngsters
identify the friend's attractive features. Next, friendship cues are
identified. The fourth step is completing the 2 × 2 matrix comparing the patient's likes and dislikes with the friend's preferences.
Finally, a conclusion and action plan is drawn.

The following dialogue illustrates the procedure with
Dexter, an 11-year-old boy who was lonely and reluctant to
approach peers (Figure 7.5). Dexter was very interested in military history and armed services. He excluded peers that had
differences from him.

Therapist: Dex, do you know what a scout is?
Dexter: It's like recon.
Therapist: Exactly. A scout does recon. What does he do?
Dexter: He collects information about a mission.
Therapist: Well, I am going to teach you how to be a friendship
              scout so you can go on a friend-making mission. How
              does this sound?
Dexter: Kind of cool.
Therapist: We have to make rules for our recon, so I'll use this
              sheet (pulls out Friendship Scout). So, who do you
              want to try to be friends with?
Dexter: Bobby. He's cool. He is nice to me.
Therapist: Good start on the recon. What do you like about
              Bobby?
Dexter: Like I said he is nice to me. He is smart and in my math
              group. He doesn't get too crazy in class and make a
              lot of noise. He's not rough on the playground.

Form 7.3 Being a Friendship Scout

Write down the name of a boy/girl you want to be friends with:

What is it you like about him/her?

What are the signs he/she wants to be friends with you?

Form 7.3 Being a Friendship Scout (Continued)

Things he/she likes to do:	Things I like to do:
Things he/she does not like:	Things I do not like:
What things that match can you do and talk about?	
How can you be friends with _____ even though there are some things that do not match?	
Action Plan	

Form 7.3   Being a Friendship Scout

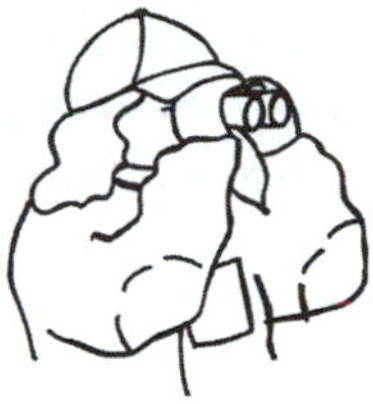

Write down the name of a boy/girl you want to be friends with.
Bobby

What is it you like about him/her?
He's cool. He's nice and smart in math. He's not too crazy. He does not make noise and is not rough.

What are the signs he/she wants to be friends with you?
Asked me to play Connect Four
Says hi
Smiles and asks me what I do on the weekend

Things he likes to do:	Things I like to do:
Play games	Read
Mario Kart	Music
Sports (baseball, football)	Mario Kart
Listen to music	Games
Math	Math
	Legos
	Hershey Park
	Star Wars
	Take electronic things apart

Things he does not like:	Things I do not like:
Getting into trouble	Sports
Getting bossed around	Disney movies
Hershey Park	Getting into trouble
Eat tomatoes	Dolls
Disney movies	Clowns
Legos	Eating with other kids

What things that match can you do and talk about?
Mario Kart, music, and math

How can you be friends with _____ even though there are some things that do not match?
We don't have to be exactly alike

Action Plan
I can get his phone number and call him to play

Figure 7.5   Dexter's—Friendship Scout Diary.

Therapist: What are some signs he wants to be friends with you?

Dexter: Signs?

Therapist: OK. Let me help you with the signs. When does he ask you to play with him or join him?

Dexter: He asked me to play a Connect Four game at indoor recess.

Therapist: What does he do when he sees you around school?

Dexter: He says, hi.

Therapist: Does he smile when he says it?

Dexter: Yes.

Therapist: What else does he say when he sees you?

Dexter: Sometimes he asks me what I did on the weekend.

Therapist: Now comes the hard part of the recon. Let's do this box. What things does Bobby like to do?

Dexter: I am not too sure.

Therapist: What does he do for fun?

Dexter: I think he plays games. I think he likes Mario Kart. That's my favorite game.

Therapist: OK, but let's keep focused on Bobby. What else does he like to do?

Dexter (disappointingly): I think he likes sports like baseball and football. I don't like sports though.

Therapist: Anything else he likes to do?

Dexter: He likes math. He likes to listen to county music like me.

Therapist: Let's add these things to our scout form. What doesn't he like to do?

Dexter: Hmm. He doesn't like to be in trouble. He doesn't like to be bossed around like me. He doesn't like to eat tomatoes. He doesn't like Disney movies. I'm like that too.

Therapist: Let's stay focused on Bobby for just a little more. What other things doesn't he like?

Dexter: Oh, he doesn't like Legos but I do.

Therapist: Anything else?

Dexter: He doesn't like Hershey Park but I do!

Therapist: It's really hard for you to stay focused on Bobby but it's important. Anything else he doesn't like?

Dexter: I don't know … I think that is all I know about him.

Therapist: Take a look at the boxes about you. What other things do you want to add in the favorite things category?

Dexter: Did I ever tell you how much I love to take electronics apart to see how they work? I really like to do that. I also have a collection of Star Wars books and figures I play with.

Therapist: How about some of your not so favorite things that we have forgotten?

Dexter: I hate eating with others. When other kids eat, it's disgusting when they put stuff on their face. Oh, I forgot, I love to read too.

Therapist: That's OK. I'll put that in the other box.

Dexter: I hate dolls and clowns.

Therapist: Anything else?

Dexter: I think that is it for now.

Therapist: Look at the boxes. Let's see where Bobby and you match.

Dexter: Hmm. We both like Mario Kart … music … math.

Therapist: So you can talk about games like Mario Kart and subjects like math. Maybe even you could play Mario Kart with Bobby.

Therapist: Let's look at the things that do not match. How can you be friends with someone even though there are some things that do not match?

Dexter: That's a hard one.

Therapist: Do you have to be exactly like someone to be friends with them?

Dexter: I guess we don't have to be exactly alike.

Therapist: I'll write that down for you. What action plan can you come up with?

Dexter: I don't know.

Therapist: Given what you know what can you do to become better friends with Bobby?

Dexter: Hmm … Maybe I could ask him to come over and play.

Therapist: Great. When would you do that?

Dexter: I could call him.

Therapist: Do you have his phone number?

Dexter: No.

Therapist: So what is your next step?

Dexter: Ask him for his phone number?

Therapist: Good. Remember to write it down. Anything else?

Dexter: Ask my mom if it is OK for him to come over?

Therapist: Great, now we have a plan.

This long dialogue with Dexter points out several critical elements. The therapist made use of Dexter's interests in the military. At times, Dexter was oblivious to various cues. The therapist then had to ask very specific and concrete questions (i.e., "What else does he say when he sees you?"). Dexter's egocentrism and self-absorption often threatened to derail the process. At these points, the therapist gently redirected him (i.e., "Let's stay focused on Bobby. It's really hard for you to stay focused on Bobby"). Finally, the therapist worked with Dexter to develop a very detailed action plan.

Two Can Rules

Two can rules (Form 7.4) is a social skills procedure that is well suited to children with PDD spectrum disorders. Children with PDD suffer a profound deficit in reciprocity. They are self-absorbed and governed by their own narrow interests. Further, these youngsters hold rigid idiosyncratic rules. Self-absorption, private rules, and lack of reciprocity combine to make relationships difficult. Krasny et al. (2003) recommended that social skills training with PDD children should emphasize other focused activities. They construct activities that foster reciprocity and a sense of belonging. For example, children make a craft or a picture for another or they serve another person a snack before they eat their own snack.

Two can rules uses a friendly toucan cartoon that guides patients into developing more consensual and reciprocal rules. Two can works through promoting the idea that two can have as much fun as one. The procedure is delivered in several phases. In the first phase, the toucan figure is presented. Second, toucan explains the importance of reciprocity. Third, the two can rules are presented and processed. Then, children add several of their own two can rules. Finally, their parents and themselves rate how well they follow the two can rules in relationships.

Friendship 911

Friendship 911 (Form 7.5) is a worksheet to help children and adolescents repair ruptured friendships. The worksheet contains several recommendations to fix broken friendships. The qualities are culled from a variety of sources (Asher & Gordon, 1998; Cooper & Widdows, 2008; Neenan, 2009; Randall & Bowen, 2008; Shapiro & Holmes, 2008a,b). Like Friendship 411, this procedure is a to-do list for children when their relationships become strained. Children simply review the ideas listed on the left side of the page and then check them if they tried the suggestion.

Form 7.4   Two Can Rules

Two Can Activity	My Rating of How Well I Followed the Two Can	Others Rating of How Well I Followed the Two Can
Share a toy or activity		
Ask another child what he/ she likes		
Practice seeing things from another person's side		
Help finish something someone else starts		
Listen to another person's ideas and think about what is good about their idea		
Follow another person's ideas		
Take turns		
Play a game someone else suggests		
Keep my ideas to myself until asked to share		
Give someone a high-five or pat on the back		
Cheer for another person		
Let others talk without interruption		
Look people in the eye as often as you can		
Stay on a topic that two can agree on		
Share a snack and let other people decide how much they want		

Now you come up with other *two can* rules:

Form 7.5   Friendship 911

Emergency Strategy	Check If You Tried
See your friend for who she/he is rather than who you want him/her to be	
Take a fresh look at things through your friend's eyes	
Let your friend be imperfect and make mistakes	
Think one bad day does not ruin a friendship	
Try to repair and not despair	
Let go of commands and demands	
Give friends gifts of second and third chances	
Think about what your friend wants to do	
Imagine how your friend feels	
Carefully choose what opinion to share with others	
Be brave enough to apologize	
Check to make sure that what bothered you about your friend was done on purpose and not by accident	

CONCLUSION

All the various procedures and techniques in this chapter should be fully embedded in a case conceptualization
informed by a grasp of various learning principles. Behavioral
procedures are a good place to start because they tend to be
straightforward, easy to implement, and nonintrusive. After
your success with some behavioral procedures, you are ready
to initiate some cognitive interventions.

Eight

Cognitive Restructuring and Problem-Solving Interventions

INTRODUCTION

This chapter presents the basics of first-line cognitive interventions such as cognitive restructuring and problem solving. Cognitive restructuring and problem solving are explained in the "Rudiments" section. The "Rubrics" section illustrates several conventional and innovative approaches to cognitive restructuring and problem solving.

RUDIMENTS

Gross and John (2002) wrote, "From violence in the schoolyards to deadly road rage on the highways, we regularly see the awful consequences of failures of emotional regulation" (p. 312). Cognitive restructuring and problem solving bolster a sturdy sense of self-control. Dahl (2004) referred to adolescence as a developmental period where the youth experiences "strong turbo-charged feelings with a relatively unskilled set of driving skills or cognitive abilities" (p. 17). The focus in any cognitive intervention is not the extinction of negative cognitions or distressing emotion but more of a shift toward productive problem solving and adaptive interpretations (Friedberg, McClure, & Garcia, 2009). Self-control works to modulate distressing emotions, irritating cognitions, and problematic behaviors (Overholser, 1996). Finally, self-control results in a sense of confidence earned when young people cope with emotional threats.

Kanfer and Phillips (1970) placed control in a literary context. They discussed Odysseus, the lead character in Homer's *The Odyssey*, who engaged in problem solving and

self-management to cope with stressors. When faced with
the Sirens' song, he ordered his men to plug their ears with
beeswax and instructed them to bind him to the mast. Kanfer
and Phillips noted that Odysseus took charge through effective action rather than passively relying on fate or powerful
others. Accordingly, self-control requires a relatively complex
set of self-management skills. Delaying impulses and modulating high intensity emotions in order to avoid adverse consequences is not an easy task. As Dahl (2004) explained, "The
ability to integrate these multiple components of behavior-
cognitive and affective in service of long-term goals involves
neurobehavioral systems that are among the last regions of the
brain to fully mature" (p. 18).

Private speech or *self-talk* directs attention and facilitates
discriminations among and between various stimuli (Masters,
Burrish, Hollon, & Rimm, 1987). Cognitive restructuring focuses
on changing "habits of thought" (Weisz, Southam-Gerow,
Gordis, & Connor-Smith, 2003; Weisz, Thurber, Sweeny, Proffitt,
& LeGagnoux, 1997). Developing healthy self-talk helps children
form hypotheses and guide their behavior (Meichenbaum, 1985).
These private speech patterns provide children and adolescents
with a map about their behavior and others' actions. Effective
cognitive restructuring helps children make sense of their
experiences, is believable, and decreases distress (Friedberg &
McClure, 2005). Cognitive restructuring translates unproductive internal messages into a language for coping (Deblinger,
Behl, & Glickman, 2006).

Successful cognitive restructuring relies on several guidelines (Friedberg, Friedberg, & Friedberg, 2001; Padesky, 1988;
Spiegler & Guevremont, 1998). Spiegler and Guevremont (1998)
recommended that cognitive restructuring help prepare individuals for stressors, refocus attention, direct adaptive behavior,
encourage persistence despite challenges, facilitate accurate
evaluation, and improve mood. It is crucial to remember that
effective cognitive restructuring involves functional but not
always 100% accurate positive alternative thoughts (Padesky,
1988). Finally, cognitive restructuring interventions build
a coping template that includes problem-solving strategies
and action plans (Kendall & Suveg, 2006). For example, a useful self-instruction for angry youngsters who are physically
aggressive is to have patients write, "When I feel like I am
going to hit someone, I can put my hands in my pocket and
fold them" (Sommers-Flannagan & Sommers-Flannagan, 1995).
Cognitive restructuring often profits from accompanying

cartoons, graphics, and metaphors. Coping cards augment cognitive restructuring. Coping statements can be written on index cards and serve as reminders. Kendall, Gosch, Furr, and Sood (2008) suggested the very creative idea of laminating the cards and putting them on a key ring. *Coping Cat Workbook* (Kendall, 1990), *Group Coping Koala Workbook* (Barrett, 1995), *Coping Power* (Lochman, Barry, & Pardini, 2003; Lochman, Wells, & Lenhart, 2008), *Therapeutic Exercises for Children* (Friedberg et al., 2001), and *Think Good, Feel Good* (Stallard, 2002) workbooks are all excellent examples of cartoon-aided cognitive restructuring procedures.

Problem Solving

Problem solving is aimed at providing children and adolescents with a greater sense of freedom. Bandura (1977b) noted that individuals who can rely on more options in a stressful situation experience a greater sense of self-control and freedom than others who count on fewer strategies. Problem solving equips youngsters with multiple alternatives. Friedberg and Friedberg (in press) pointed out that problem solving helps youngsters generate multiple alternatives, increase perspective taking, and reduce cognitive rigidity.

Kazdin (2001) noted that many referred children experience deficits in problem-solving skills. He found that distressed children frequently have trouble identifying alternate solutions to problems, anticipating consequences of their actions, and appreciating component steps to reaching a goal. Shapiro, Friedberg, and Bardenstein (2005) asserted that problem solving teaches children to slow down and think. Kazdin proposed three fundamental questions to cue problem solving (e.g., What am I required to do? What is my plan? How do I successfully complete my plan?). Padesky (2007) offered a creative alternative to this traditional problem solving. In her innovative approach, she also asks three simple questions (Does my strategy create a positive difference in my life? Is my behavior a compassionate way to treat myself? Is my behavior a compassionate way to treat others?).

The problem-solving component from the Treatment for Adolescents with Depression Study (TADS) protocol offers yet another treatment alternative (Rohde, Feeny, & Robins, 2005). In the TADS approach, RIBEYE was used as an acronym. (R) stands for learning to relax when facing a stressor. The second step is identifying the problem or stressor (I). Brainstorming (B) is the third step. Evaluating (E) each solution follows the brainstorming.

Making a choice or saying yes (Y) is the fifth step. Finally, encouraging (E) yourself provides a self-reward component.

RUBRICS

In the following sections, various problem solving and cognitive restructuring are illustrated. Forms, figures, and transcripts augment the explanations. The chapter concludes with a special section devoted to treating suicidal behavior.

Problem Solving

There are several basic components to problem solving. First, problems need to be broken down into specific, concrete, and measurable components (Nezu & Nezu, 1989). Be sure to tackle only one problem at a time and this problem should be within the individual's control (Butler & Hope, 2007). This makes problem solving more manageable and increases self-efficacy. Shapiro et al. (2005) reminded clinicians to view problem solving as a process that includes both brainstorming and a critical reasoning phase. Therefore, take care not to preempt the brainstorming process. In the brainstorming process, many solutions, even absurd ones, should be generated. Butler and Hope (2007) added that doing nothing is sometimes a solution. The critical reasoning part is realized by reviewing the potential short-term positive and negative consequences as well as long-term positive and negative consequences. Frequently, this is accomplished by creating a 2 × 2 matrix. Once the potential consequences are reviewed and evaluated, the youngster chooses the best option. Butler and Hope emphasized that both the child and therapist should exercise patience and give strategies time to work. Finally, a reward should follow successful experimentation with a constructive option. Figure 8.1 summarizes these central steps. In the following section, two specific problem-solving techniques are introduced and explained.

IRON Doesn't Melt

IRON Doesn't Melt is a rubric to help children reduce their emotional meltdowns (Form 8.1). In an emotional meltdown, the children's emotional reactions override cognitive mediation. In short, stopping and thinking becomes excruciatingly difficult. Therefore, a short memorable coping template may be quite effective. IRON Doesn't Melt is designed for just that purpose.

- Break down the problem into SPECIFIC, CONCRETE, MEASURABLE, OBSERVABLE COMPONENTS.
- Tackle problems ONE AT A TIME and that are CONTROLLABLE.
- BRAINSTORM many possible solutions including even absurd ones.
- Allow yourself to DO NOTHING.
- EVALUATE the long- and short-term positive and negative consequences (do a 2 × 2).
- Based on the evaluation, CHOOSE which option seems best.
- REWARD for successful experimentation with a new constructive option.
- Give yourself time to let the strategies WORK.

Figure 8.1   General problem-solving rubric.

A four-step coping process is contained in the mnemonic IRON. Iron was used because it is sturdy and does not weaken during periods of extreme heat. The worksheet also offers several cartoon graphics associated with each of the four steps. The first step calls for the identification of feelings and thoughts. Rethinking ideas and decreasing cognitive rigidity is a Step 2 target. Alternative solutions are generated in Step 3. Finally, cognitive and behavioral rehearsal is practiced in Step 4.

The following dialogue with Savina, an 11-year-old female patient, illustrates the process (see also Figure 8.2).

Therapist: Savina, how do you feel when you have a meltdown?
Savina: Really bad. I think I am weak.
Therapist: I understand. For someone who likes to be in charge so much that is a hard thing to deal with. How willing would you be to come up with a plan so you wouldn't melt down so much?
Savina: That would be OK with me.
Therapist: Do you know what iron is?
Savina: Some kind of strong metal, I think.
Therapist: That's right. Iron is so strong that it doesn't melt.
Savina: Cool.
Therapist: I use the word IRON to teach young people like yourself how to do problem solving instead of melting down because if you are IRON you don't melt! It begins with the letter I for identifying problems. Then of course, the next letter is R for rethinking.
Savina: Next comes O! What is that for?
Therapist: O is for opening a new can of options. Do you know what options are?
Savina: I'm not sure.

Form 8.1	IRON Doesn't Melt Worksheet

I

R

O

N

I	**Identify Your Thoughts and Feelings**

R	**Rethink Your Ideas**

O	**Open Up a Can of New Ways to Act**

N	**Now Practice Your New Behaviors**

Form 8.1   IRON Doesn't Melt Worksheet

I
R
O
N

I	**Identify Your Thoughts and Feelings**
	My sister took my book, marked it up, and colored on it. She messed it up.
R	**Rethink Your Ideas**
	She's just a little rug rat. She doesn't know any better.
O	**Open Up a Can of New Ways to Act**
	I could hide my good stuff.
	Close my door.
	Tell Mom and Dad.
	Only let her use my books when I am around.
N	**Now Practice Your New Behaviors**

Figure 8.2   Savina's—IRON Doesn't Melt Worksheet.

Therapist: Options are choices. N is for new ways of thinking and acting. Are you ready to try it out?

Savina: I think so.

Therapist: So, what was the problem that upset you?

Savina: My 8-year-old sister took my book, marked it up, and colored on the pages. She really messed it up.

Therapist: We'll write that in the *I* column. What's a new way to rethink the problem?

Savina: Hmm. She's just a little rug rat. She doesn't know any better.

Therapist: Let's put that down. Let's open up a new can of options.
Savina (laughs): That reminds me of opening up a can of
        whoop ass!
Therapist (smiles): Let's stay focused. What are your choices?
Savina: I could hide my good stuff.
Therapist: See if you can up with even more choices.
Savina: Close my door. Tell Mom and Dad.
Therapist: How about some more?
Savina: Only let her have my books when I am around.

The therapist began the procedure by communicating empathically (i.e., "For someone who likes to be in charge so much that is a hard thing to deal with"). Savina went a little off task but the therapist reeled her back into the technique. Finally, the therapist enabled Savina to generate multiple alternatives.

A GPS/Map for Problems

Many children and adolescents become lost in their problems. They are trapped and cannot find a productive way out of their respective dilemmas so they may give up or act out. Therefore, providing a road map for problem solving is helpful. Children and younger adolescents may enjoy the metaphors and graphics associated with a GPS and map. The map and GPS metaphor is useful because they provide directions and feedback. Moreover, a map is a good strategy since it promotes goal-directed activity. The GPS is a somewhat more complex procedure than IRON Doesn't Melt and should be reserved for older, higher functioning children and adolescents.

The GPS map includes multiple steps (Form 8.2). The first step identifies patients' goals. Then, the youth defines the steps necessary to get to the goal. It is likely that you will have to help the patient flesh out the appropriate steps. The third and fourth steps are very important. Here, you work with youngsters on a timeline. Children and adolescents are very impatient beings so helping them erect a realistic timeline is time well spent.

Step 5 represents the heart of the problem-solving process. Patients list the steps from Step 2 and predict the long-term and short-term positive and negative consequences for each step. To teach youngsters to think long-term and decrease impulsivity, long-term consequences are weighted more heavily (3 times more heavily).

After this analysis, the best routes are selected. The routes are then ranked according to the patients' perceptions of their frustration and difficulty. If the route is not seen as frustrating

Form 8.2   GPS for Problem Solving

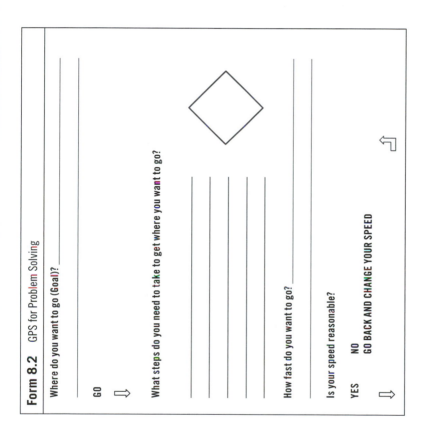

Where do you want to go (Goal)? _____

_____

GO

⇒

What steps do you need to take to get where you want to go?

_____

_____

_____

_____

How fast do you want to go? _____

Is your speed reasonable?

YES   NO

GO BACK AND CHANGE YOUR SPEED

⇒

Form 8.2 GPS for Problem Solving (Continued)

CHART A ROUTE OR PATH

Steps	Short-Term Positive Consequences	Short-Term Negative Consequences	Long-Term Positive Consequences	Long-Term Negative Consequences

Form 8.2 GPS for Problem Solving (Continued)

Pick Route With the Fewest Negative and Most Positive Consequences. Remember the Long-Term Consequences Count Three Times as Much as the Short-Term.

⟹

POSSIBLE ROUTES

1.

2.

3.

Form 8.2 GPS for Problem Solving (Continued)

DETOURS

Routes	How Frustrating	How Difficult

⇨

If the Routes Are Lower Than 4, Try Them!

If the Routes Are Higher Than 4, Stop and Come Up With a Plan to Cope With the Route Being Difficult and Frustrating and Then Try It.

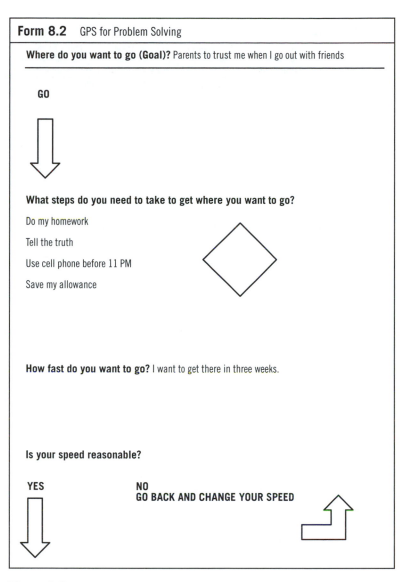

Form 8.2   GPS for Problem Solving

Where do you want to go (Goal)? Parents to trust me when I go out with friends

GO

What steps do you need to take to get where you want to go?

Do my homework

Tell the truth

Use cell phone before 11 PM

Save my allowance

How fast do you want to go? I want to get there in three weeks.

Is your speed reasonable?

YES

NO
GO BACK AND CHANGE YOUR SPEED

Figure 8.3   Completed GPS Problem-Solving Map.

or difficult, patients are then encouraged to experiment with the plan. On the other hand, if the plan is ranked high on the frustration and difficulty scale, a coping plan to tolerate the frustration needs to be developed. Figure 8.3 shows a completed GPS problem-solving map.

CHART A ROUTE OR PATH

Steps	Short-Term Positive Consequences	Short-Term Negative Consequences	Long-Term Positive Consequences	Long-Term Negative Consequences
Do my homework	Parents stop nagging Get better grades	Homework is boring Less TV time Less game time	Parents may increase trust No summer school	None
Tell truth	Parents like it	May be punished May feel worried	Increased trust	None
Use cell phone before 11 PM	Increased sleep Parents nag less	Less time talking to friends Less fun	Increased trust Increased rest	May not have as many friends
Save up my money	None	Don't get to buy stuff I want Less fun	Have more money Parents are happy Can do more stuff	None

PICK Route With the Fewest Negative and Most Positive Consequences. Remember the Long-Term Consequences Count Three Times as Much as the Short-Term.

POSSIBLE ROUTES

1. Do homework
2. Tell truth
3. Use cell phone before 11 PM
4. Save money

DETOURS

Routes	How Frustrating	How Difficult
Do homework	3	1
Tell truth	2	1
Use cell phone before 11 PM	3	3
Save money	3	3

If the Routes Are Lower Than 4, Try Them! If the Routes Are Higher Than 4, Stop and Come Up With a Plan to Cope With the Route Being Difficult and Frustrating and Then Try It.

Figure 8.3   **(Continued)** Completed GPS Problem-Solving Map.

Family Problem-Solving Interventions

Family problem solving with adolescents is recommended by Barkley, Edwards, and Robin (1999). The goal is for both parents and children to negotiate emerging psychological independence. The procedure involves operational definitions and distinguishing negotiable from nonnegotiable items. Additionally, teenagers are included in the deliberations for negotiable items and good communication skills are taught. Parents and adolescents are taught to develop realistic expectations about themselves and others.

Distinguishing negotiable from nonnegotiable items seems easier at first blush than when it is actually encountered. Frequently, parents send an inaccurate message that non-negotiable items are negotiable. For instance, telling a teenager "I don't care if you have sex just don't get pregnant" or "Do what you want outside of the house but you can't bring weed into this house" implicitly tells the child it is OK to do these things. When working with parents, it is important to check that the parent really believes sex and drugs are negotiable (e.g., Do you think it is OK to have sex at all?).

Once the nonnegotiable items are identified, the adolescent's input is actively sought. Collaboration with adolescents during problem solving is a developmentally sensitive intervention. First, achieving autonomy is highly sought by teenagers. Second, Barkley and his colleagues (1999) knowingly asserted that adolescents' compliance is more likely if they are invested in treatment. However, parents may expect their adolescent to submissively obey and absolutely submit to their authority. Nonetheless, including the adolescent in the negotiation can be a difficult sell to some parents. Some parents may believe in an authoritarian stance and a "benign dictatorship." Therefore adding some democratic elements could be a therapeutic struggle. Kazdin (2008) expertly remarked, "Negotiation is good for its own sake. Parents should look for ways to give up control, and kids should look for ways to address their parents' concerns" (p. 121).

We have found education about adolescent development quite helpful. I (RDF) often share Peter Blos's (1979) cogent and pithy remark that "adolescents do all the wrong things for the right reasons" to teach parents that in their search for their identities, teenagers revolt against parental authority (p. 147). Accordingly, I also sometimes refer to this process as revolution in the service of evolution. To quell some of this revolution, compromise and negotiation is necessary. You may also use some of the individual problem-solving methods described earlier in the section.

Parental control is most often motivated by anxiety. Authoritarian parents may overcontrol and intrude in their adolescents' lives due to fears about their children's evolving independence and identity. Barkley et al. (1999) identified "ruination" as a central distortion in parents' thinking. Ruination is a form of catastrophic all-or-none reasoning characterized by the prediction that if children have greater freedom, they will destroy their lives. Clearly, you will want to decrease parents' ruminations about ruination. Teenagers may also hold several dysfunctional beliefs about parental authority. First, they may absolutely believe that all rules are unfair and they must always get what they want (Barkley et al., 1999). In these instances, you will want to apply the cognitive restructuring techniques described later in the chapter or the rational analysis procedures in Chapter 9.

Cognitive Restructuring

In this section, various techniques aimed at cognitive restructuring are presented. Many of the procedures are aided by graphics. Illustrative transcripts augment the explanations.

Real or Right

Real or right is a cognitive restructuring technique for children and adolescents who tend to try to give clinicians "right" or "healthy" responses that are simply platitudes (Form 8.3; also see Figure 8.4). These patients seek the clinicians' approval, want to distract or derail the psychotherapy process, or avoid distress. They hide their genuine thoughts and feelings (what is real) in favor of superficial expression or disclosure. Sommers-Flanagan and Sommers-Flanagan (1995) believed that adolescents camouflage their experiences for a variety of reasons. They may intend to avoid responsibility, maintain a sense of invulnerability, and enhance their excitement and power. The foci of the real or right technique is threefold:

1. Identifying the pattern of posing right rather than being real
2. Clarifying the difference between the two
3. Bringing right and real into harmony

Form 8.3   Real or Right Worksheet

Real:

Right:

Activity	Real	Right

How do I bring Real and Right together?

Form 8.3 Real or Right Worksheet

Being Real:
My true feelings and thoughts that I keep private
My opinions and predictions that I believe in
Being myself
Doing things I feel interested and excited about

Posing Right:
Acting like people want
Agreeing even when I don't agree
Saying stuff just because I know people want to hear it
Pretending to be something I am not just to get someone off my back

Activity	Being Real	Posing Right
Listening quietly when being lectured		X
Not talking about how angry I am		X
Saying I agree with the meal plan		X
Secretly purging		X
Secretly exercising		X
Feeling hurt when criticized	X	

How do I bring Real and Right together? Text her instead of talking face to face.

Figure 8.4 Mischa's—Real or Right Worksheet.

Step 1 involves defining terms. In this stage, you elicit the specific view of what is "real" and what is "right." Various criteria are embedded in this definition. The children list their relevant activities and check whether these activities are real or right in Step 2. In Step 3, you discuss where there is congruence and difference between real and right. Finally, you collaboratively develop a productive action plan to bring real and right together.

The following example with Mischa, a 16-year-old female with anorexia marked by excessive purging, illustrates the procedure.

Mischa: Sometimes I feel like I am just going through the motions.

Therapist: Going through the motions?

Mischa: I have read just about everything about eating disorders and I know about my food plan. I know what everybody wants me to say and do. So, I just give them what they want.

Therapist: So, you have a sense you are posing or faking it?

Mischa: Yeah.

Therapist: What is that like for you?

Mischa: I don't know ... Good and bad I guess.

Therapist: How is it good?

Mischa: People don't bug me. They don't hover and watch everything I do.

Therapist: How is it bad?

Mischa: I feel false. People never see me for who I am so I never really am sure whether they like me for who I am or just this act.

Therapist: I can see how caught and trapped you see yourself to be. How would this be to work on?

Mischa: Good, I think.

Therapist: It sounds like you are caught and confused about what I call being "real" and being "right."

Mischa: What do you mean?

Therapist: Well, being real is being true to yourself. It's what you think and feel and acting in a way that honestly represents your thoughts, values, interests, and feelings.

Mischa: What about being right?

Therapist: That kind of goes to your perfectionism and wanting others to approve of you. Trying to act right is pretending to do and feel things just because others expect it or want it or you think it will get them to approve of you rather than how you really feel and think.

Mischa: Kind of like posing.

Therapist: Exactly. I have this form that may help you with this. Are you willing to check it out?

Mischa: OK.

Therapist: Let's list the things you feel are real and genuine about you.

Mischa: Hmm … my feelings and thoughts that I keep private … my opinions, predictions that I believe in, being myself, doing things I feel interested and excited about it.

Therapist: What about the things you do just because you think they are right?

Mischa: Umm … Acting like people want … agreeing even when I disagree, saying stuff because I know people want to hear it. Pretending to be something I am not just to get someone off my back.

Therapist: We are on a roll now. The next step is to list some behaviors you have done recently for being real or right. In this column, let's record some of the things you have talked about.

Mischa: I'm not sure I know what you want me to do.

Therapist: I'll get you started. You mentioned it bugged you when you just listened quietly and did not react to your mom's lecturing.

Mischa: Yeah …

Therapist: What about some other things like that?

Mischa: Like not talking about how angry I am.

Therapist: Sure.

Mischa: Saying I agree with the meal plan … secretly purging … secretly exercising … feeling hurt when my mother criticized me.

Therapist: Great job. Now check whether those things were examples of you being real or posing right.

Mischa: The only thing where I was real was feeling hurt when my mother criticized me.

Therapist: No wonder you feel false. We need an action plan so being real is safe and more common for you.

Mischa: That's going to be hard.

Therapist: Well, let's take it one step at a time. How can you feel comfortable being real when you are mad at your mother?

Mischa: Maybe I could text her at first and not tell her to her face.

Therapist: What are the downsides to that?

Mischa: I don't think there are many.

Therapist: Good. Experiment with that plan. How about the next one?

In this example of real or right, the therapist began with collaboration (i.e., "What is that like for you?" "How is it good?" "How is it bad?"). The collaboration promoted genuine empathy (i.e., "I can see how caught and trapped you see yourself to be"). The therapist then queried Mischa's willingness and began the procedure. At the end of the technique, the therapist and Mischa developed an action plan for being real.

Negative Feeling Superhero

Superheroes are a common metaphor in cognitive behavioral psychotherapy (Friedberg, McClure, & Garcia, 2009; Rubin, 2007). Superheroes provide fun coping models. Moreover, children realize that like them, superheroes have experienced some personal tragedy. Batman, for example, not only has suffered the loss of his parents but also overcame his fear of bats. Superheroes typically summon a power or skill or deal with stressors (Kendall et al., 1992).

Negative feeling superhero is a technique to help children who are emotionally avoidant. These youngsters believe strong emotions are to be avoided because they weaken them. The negative feeling superhero (Form 8.4) teaches skills that are direct ways to counter this avoidance. The superhero gains his or her power by tolerating negative feelings rather than releasing or avoiding them.

Negative feeling superhero combines drawing, imagery, and self-instructional processes. The procedure begins with the introduction of the superhero who is strengthened by negative emotions. There is a separate superhero for boys and girls. Like Spider-Man, Batman, and Batgirl, the superhero is masked so different ethnicities may identify with him. The power source of the superhero is the "heart" because this appeals to youngsters as the storage place for emotions. The hero's heart gets bigger the more she or he tolerates the emotional discomfort.

The child adds coping thoughts in the thought bubble floating above the hero's head. The following dialogue illustrates the process with Elian, a 9-year-old boy.

Form 8.4   Negative Feeling Superheroes

Therapist: Elian, I know you like superheroes.

Elian: I do.

Therapist: Look, what I have. This is a picture of our negative feeling superhero. What should we call him?

Elian: He doesn't have a name? ... I dunno.

Therapist: We are working together on anger, frustration, and anxiety. The superhero can help you deal with these feelings. Any ideas?

Elian: How about Captain Feeling?

Therapist: Sounds good. Now, let's look at Captain Feeling. Here's the key thing. Captain Feeling gains his power by having strong feelings and doing things about them that build him up. He gets stronger. The feelings work for him and not on him. Let's draw his heart. See his heart?

Elian: I'll make it really big.

Therapist: So, here is what you do. Depending on how big the feeling is, you color in the heart. If the feeling is little, you color in a small part very lightly. If the feeling is kind of strong, you color in about half a little darker. What if the feeling is really strong?

Elian: I color in his whole heart really dark so his heart is full of feelings.

Therapist: Exactly. Now look at the bubble above his head. What do you suppose that is for?

Elian: It is for what he says to himself.

Therapist: You are really understanding. The bubble is what he can say to himself that will help him be OK with strong feelings. Want to try it?

Elian: OK.

Therapist: Remember when you were getting frustrated when your older brother was beating you in the Wii game.

Elian: I got so fired up I threw the remote.

Therapist: Good. Captain Feeling might help you with this. Color in the heart to show how strong the feeling is.

Elian (colors): OK.

Therapist: You colored in the whole heart really dark. So remember Captain Feeling gets strength from having strong feelings. They work for him. What can he say so the feelings build him up rather than knocking him down?

Elian (pause): Hmm. Frustration is part of the game. I can turn it into something that helps me.

Therapist: Good start. How can it help?

Elian: Maybe it can help me concentrate more.

The example illustrates several key elements. First, Elian created an original name for the superhero (i.e., Captain Feeling). The therapist reinforced the connection between thoughts and feelings. Finally, Elian was able to construct a coping thought that included an action plan (i.e., "Frustration is part of the game. I can turn it into something that could help me").

It Stinks

Beck, Emery, and Greenberg (1985) discussed the notion of emotional acceptance. They saw acceptance as an active choice rather than a passive *que sera sera* stance. According to Beck and colleagues, this active choice propels a sense of mastery. For example, they offered the example of welcoming the negative feelings by saying hello to them. (e.g., "Hello again, my old friend anger"). In fact, their seminal AWARE acronym (accept, watch, act, repeat, expect the best) emphasizes active acceptance. For instance, the acceptance phase (Beck et al., 1985) encourages self-statements such as "Be with the experience. Don't fight it. Replace your rejection, anger, and hatred with acceptance" (p. 323). Moreover, the watch phase urges "Look at it (e.g., the distress) without judgment—not good, not bad. Don't look at it as an unwelcome guest" (p. 323). Kollman, Brown, and Barlow (2009) defined *acceptance* as a subtype of emotional regulation. They believed acceptance involves interpretations of acceptability of emotional arousal and giving oneself permission to experience emotion.

Many children and adolescents "melt down" when frustrated and distressed. Tolerating negative emotion is an important self-control skill. Parrott (2002) eloquently wrote, "There is more to emotions than pleasant or unpleasant feeling and there is more to human decision making than hedonism" (p. 341). Children believe they cannot stand the emotional unrest or they should never have to feel negative emotions. Often, helping children accept inevitable disappointment, frustration, and things not being just what they want decreases their exaggerated emotional responses. Dougher (1994) cogently noted that acceptance transcends mere inaction and instead requires endurance and tolerance. Gardner and Moore (2004) commented that acceptance implies actively experiencing dysphoric thoughts and feelings as a way to reach goals. Linehan (1993) emphasized that people do not have to like their experiences or judge them as good to accept them.

Borcherdt (2002) shared the example of a patient who believed the world stunk because he could not get what he wanted. Borcherdt replied by agreeing that the world did indeed stink but asked, "What do you think of getting used to the smell?" This is a humorous yet poignant way to communicate tolerance and acceptance of frustration. Moreover, getting used to the smell decreases demandingness. Therefore, employ the "it stinks" metaphor to help children tolerate unreasonable limits they mistakenly see as unfair. The procedure begins with an introduction of the metaphor, sample problem solving, and then generalization from the example to their real-life circumstances.

Jasper is a 12-year-old boy who suffered from peer rejection and often broke into tears at school, on the hockey rink, and at home when things did not go his way. In addition to this imperative, he also believed, "My needs should always be indulged" and "People should always make me feel good about myself." Not surprisingly, his life was punctuated by perceived assaults to his self-esteem (e.g., "The guys in my class don't ask me to join their group. I didn't finish the race in the top 10 and get a ribbon. I sit on the bench on my hockey team").

Jasper: I don't like the kids in my class. They think they are so cool. I stay away from them. My teacher pays attention to them and not me. That's why I hate this school. The teacher does not make me feel good about myself (tearfully).

Therapist: This is really painful for you. What hurts most about all this?

Jasper: This is like my dad says is a royal pain in the ass. The teacher picks the popular kids for all the special jobs. I was trying out for chorus and I think I have a great voice but the teacher didn't pick me. Then I am second string on the hockey team when I think I should be starting.

Therapist: It stinks when things don't go your way.

Jasper (tearily): I hate it. I can't stand it!

Therapist: Jasper, are you willing to try something different?

Jasper (sniffling): Like what?

Therapist: Maybe dealing with these situations where you feel bruised by these things without tears.

Jasper: How can I do that?

Therapist: Let me ask you something. Have you ever smelled something bad?

Jasper: I don't like it when there is cow manure from the farms around here.

Therapist: Any other times?

Jasper: The gym locker room stinks bad.

Therapist: So, how do you get used to it?

Jasper: I don't know what you mean.

Therapist: Well, did it smell as bad later as it did in the beginning?

Jasper: No, I guess not.

Therapist: How do you explain that?

Jasper: I got used to it, I guess.

Therapist: How did you get used to it?

Jasper: I guess I just stayed and the smell went away.

Therapist: So, the more you practiced smelling the bad odor, the more it helped you get used to it, and learn that you also got better at handling it or standing it.

Jasper: I guess.

Therapist: Well, it's just like those things that are not going your way. These things may stink but you have to train yourself to get used to the smell.

Jasper: So, how do I do that?

Therapist: Well, first we have to deal with a couple of things you are saying to yourself like "I can't stand it when things don't go my way because I must get what I want to feel good about myself."

Jasper: So, what are you saying? That I shouldn't feel good about myself?

Therapist: You are seeing it in kind of an all-or-none way. Most of the time you feel good but sometimes things don't go your way and this is part of being a 12-year-old. The problem comes in when you demand things go your way and believe you can't stand it when they don't.

Jasper: So, what do I do?

Therapist: Let's see if together we can come up with some things you can say to yourself to help you stand the stink.

Jasper: Like what?

Therapist: Well, how about I can stand the stink.

Jasper: That'll work.

Therapist: Good. Write it down. Now see if you can come up with one.

Jasper: I watched a TV show with army guys and they kept telling each other to embrace the suck. I thought that was cool.

Therapist: Sounds good but what do you think that means?

Jasper: Things were messed up and they were complaining about stuff ... so they just were telling each other to go with the flow.

Therapist: Sounds like someone else we know! You also came up with a third thought to stand the stink. Go with the flow.

Therapeutic work offered Jasper several meaningful lessons. First, empathy was communicated (i.e., "It stinks when things do not go your way"). Next, the therapist addressed Jasper's willingness to do the cognitive restructuring. Collaboration was diligently sought (i.e., "Let's see if together we can come up with some things you can say to yourself to stand the stink"). When Jasper struggled, the therapist modeled a coping statement (i.e., "I can stand the stink"). With gentle coaching and prompting, Jasper came up with his own coping thought.

Blaster of the Universe

Blaster of the Universe is a cognitive restructuring technique that is based on Thought-Feeling Asteroid (Chapter 6) and makes use of a space metaphor. Blaster capitalizes on the child's imagination and is ideal for children interested in space adventures. Children blast their distressing thoughts and come up with more adaptive coping thoughts in the procedure. The procedure is relatively straightforward and applicable to children 8 to 11 years old. The worksheet (Form 8.5) contains two columns and graphics. Children transfer the distressing thoughts identified in the Thought-Feeling Asteroid to the first column on the worksheet. Then, they work with the therapist to blast them and replace the thought with a more adaptive appraisal. The game begins with the therapist's introduction to cognitive restructuring as follows:

Therapist: We've talked about how thoughts and feelings are connected. By changing our thoughts, we can change how we feel. So, remember the Thought-Feeling Asteroid worksheet we worked on? We'll use it to play something called Blaster of the Universe. We're going to take the thoughts that you wrote down on your asteroids (pointing to the Thought-Feeling Asteroid worksheet), and blast them so they turn into thoughts that make you feel better. This means we get to make a worksheet that has a thought blaster on it. After we blast the thought asteroids, we're going to come up with more helpful thoughts, and write them down. That way, you will have helpful thoughts to practice thinking—ones that will make you feel better. How does that sound to you?

Colby: Fun!

Therapist: So Colby, here's your Thought-Feeling Asteroid worksheet. We found a bunch of your thoughts and feelings, didn't we? We're going to take these thoughts and put them in this column where it says thoughts to be blasted. Then we blast it and replace it with a different more helpful thought. Which thought from your Thought-Feeling Asteroid worksheet do you want to write here?

Colby: Things have to be just so. They have to look right.

Therapist: OK, let's write that here. What other thoughts do you have to blast?

Colby: When things are not done my way, I blow up. People should follow my rules.

Therapist: So, do you remember what we do next?

Colby: Yeah, I think we blast 'em!

Therapist: Let's blast them then. When we blast the rules that things have to be just right, what are we left with?

Colby: Scraps, I think.

Therapist: What are those scraps?

Colby: I don't know … Maybe things can look OK even if they are not just so.

Therapist: Let's write that down in this column. What is next to blast?

Colby: Let's blow it to smithereens!

Therapist: Which one?

Colby: People should follow my rules. I blast it! (Makes explosion sound.)

Therapist: You blew it up real good. (Laugh.) So what's left to put in this column?

Colby: I can blow up the rule instead of me blowing up. My thoughts don't always have to rule. I can try to give other people's rules a try.

Colby continued to use the Blaster of the Universe with several other thoughts (see Figure 8.5). The dialogue demonstrates several interesting points. First, Colby was very engaged in the procedure. Second, the blasting was followed by a cognitive repair procedure. The thought was not extinguished but rather

Form 8.5 Blaster of the Universe Worksheet	
	BANG!
Asteroid Thought to Be Blasted	**New Thought**

Form 8.5 Blaster of the Universe Worksheet

Asteroid Thought to Be Blasted	New Thought
Things have to be just so.	Maybe things can look OK even if they are not just so.
They have to look right.	I can blow up the rule instead of me blowing up. My thoughts don't always have to rule. I can try to give other people's rules a try.
When things are not done my way, I blow up. People should follow my rules.	

Figure 8.5 Colby's—Blaster of the Universe Worksheet.

reconstructed (i.e., "What are we left with?"). Colby came up with relativistic rather than absolute coping thoughts (i.e., "My rules don't have to always rule. I can give other people's rules a try").

Dragon Splasher

Dragon Splasher is an anger management strategy based on the Thought-Feeling Dragon diary (Chapter 6). Dragon Splasher cools down the hot thought the fire breathing dragon spits out (Form 8.6). The bucket of dragon splashers is used to douse the fire and provide self-instructions for anger management. Similar to Blaster of the Universe, Dragon Splasher is best suited to children ages 8 to 11.

Dragon Splasher begins with an introduction and relies on the completed Thought-Feeling Dragon diary (Chapter 6) for self-monitoring. The following dialogue shows how to use the Dragon Splasher with Giovanni who filled out the Thought-Feeling Dragon diary in Chapter 6.

Therapist: Giovanni, let's take a look at your Thought-Feeling Dragon diary. (Giovanni hands the therapist the diary.)
Giovanni: Here it is. (See Figure 8.6.)
Therapist: You did a good job capturing your hot thoughts. Now, we have to put out the fire.
Giovanni: Uh huh.

Form 8.6   Dragon Splashers

Chill! So, I don't strike out.

Be cool and don't play a fool.

Act calm and I'll be the bomb.

Being mad doesn't mean it's all bad.

Anger passes with time; I don't have to do anything right now.

I can stay in control even though I think being mad is awful.

Being cool-headed is the way to roll.

Just because I am mad doesn't mean I must hurt someone.

Think pink rather than red hot.

When the heat is on, cool down.

Keep my anger on the down low.

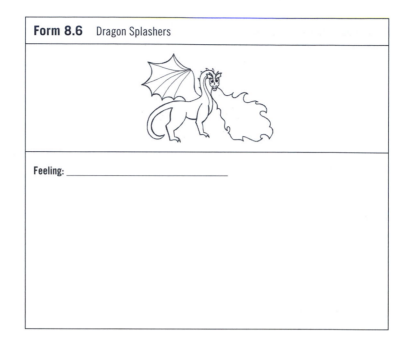

Figure 8.6   Giovanni's—Thought-Feeling Dragon Diary.

Therapist: We kind of have to splash some water on the hot
        thoughts the fire-breathing dragon has.

Giovanni: How do we do that?

Therapist: We use these dragon splashers (Form 8.6). Which
        ones do you think might cool off the dragon?

Giovanni: I like the short ones.

Therapist: OK. So we need to pick one that takes the fire out
        of the dragon. Write down a splasher on a piece of
        paper so we can cool it off.

Giovanni: I like "Being mad doesn't mean it's all bad."

Therapist: Now, let's see if you can add five more splashers of
        your own.

Giovanni: How about I can break my record of being able to
        stand my anger?

Therapist: That's a good one. How can you stand it?

Giovanni: I could use the things we talked about.

Therapist: Nice job adding an action plan. For homework, how
        about adding four more splashers.

In this dialogue, Giovanni was able to apply some cool coping thoughts to his anger. He preferred shorter coping thoughts

so the therapist began with them. Additionally, Giovanni created some original coping thoughts and then added an action plan.

Hip-Hop Self-Talk

Nelson, Finch, and Ghee (2006) recommended the rap music format for teaching self-instruction. According to Nelson et al., rap lyrics may provide potent messages that include themes of nonviolent empowerment and prosocial behavior. Employing a hip-hop/rap approach to cognitive restructuring emphasizes a strength-based approach and empowerment that increases self-efficacy (Kobin & Tyson, 2006). Hip-hop self-talk is suitable for a wide range of children and adolescents (ages 8 to 18 years).

Tyson (2002, 2003) developed his hip-hop therapy (HHT), which integrates cognitive behavioral techniques and psycho-education. HHT consists of seven steps including introducing hip-hop, distinguishing between positive and negative hip-hop, playing hip-hop verse, using guided discovery to interpret the lyrics, validating children and adolescents' values, identifying patients' goals, and eliciting feedback.

Hip-hop lyrics are essentially automatic thoughts and beliefs. You can select a song or have the patients bring in their favorite hip-hop song. You then listen to the selection and process the lyrics (e.g., what are the advantages and disadvantages of the beliefs in the song, what lyrics might be helpful or hurtful, what are the constructive and destructive lyrics). After you process the song with patients, you can invite the youngsters to create their own song, which supports adaptive coping.

The following dialogue illustrates the process with Justin, a 12-year-old boy with anger management problems.

Therapist: OK, Justin, we just went over your favorite song.
Justin: That was cool.
Therapist: What ideas did you get from it?
Justin: About what?
Therapist: A hip-hop song you can use to help you with your anger.
Justin: How do we do that?
Therapist: Let's start with a title.
Justin: I was thinking about "Forgivin' Ain't Forgettin'."
Therapist: Great title. Let's start with that line.
Justin: Forgivin' ain't forgettin'. But it's a place to start. Got to bounce. Got to flow. When I feel the pain.

Therapist: Justin, you are doing great. Let's add in a healthy
        action plan.
Justin: Forgivin' ain't weak. It makes me king. I rule when I
        walk. I rule when I shut you out.

   Justin and the therapist continued to develop several more
verses. For homework, Justin wrote two more verses and put
them on coping cards.

Mind Menders

Mind Menders is a cognitive restructuring intervention that
may follow from Mind Your Mind (Chapter 6) or any other
thought diary. After children and adolescents have identified
their thoughts and feelings, they replace their "broken" inaccurate thoughts with a mind mender. Some mind menders
are provided for the youths (Form 8.7) and the youngsters are
encouraged to create additional coping thoughts for themselves. Mind Menders is a rather basic intervention and can be
used with children 8 years and older.
   The following dialogue illustrates the process with Luciane
who filled out a minding your mind diary in Chapter 6.

Therapist: Luciane, you did a good job identifying your thoughts
        in your Mind Your Mind diary (Figure 8.7). Do you
        think the thoughts are helpful or hurtful to you?
Luciane: I feel bad when I have them so I would say they are
        hurtful.
Therapist: It is sometimes helpful to call these things you
        say to yourself broken thoughts. Does that seem to
        make sense?
Luciane: I think so.
Therapist: What's the thing to do if something is broken?
Luciane: Fix it, I guess.
Therapist: Right! Another word for fixing something is called
        mending. So, we have to come up with some mind
        menders to fix the broken thoughts.
Luciane: How do we do that?
Therapist: Let's take a look at the Mind Menders sheet. Which
        ones do you think fix your broken thoughts?
Luciane: Hmm. I like a couple of them.
Therapist: Which ones seem to heal up the belief about unfair-
        ness and not being rich enough?

Form 8.7   Sample Mind Menders

Discomfort does not equal disaster.

Likely and possible are two very different things.

Do something productive with the power or control you own.

Expect good results. Prepare for the worst. Accept what is likely.

Blindly do the task rather than actively worry about the results.

Effort and preparations are controllable: results and outcomes are less so.

Act on facts not feelings or others' opinions.

Protect my safety and do things that build me up rather than tear me down.

Respect who I am and question others' definitions of me.

Rescue my confidence by allowing myself to feel uncomfortable and dealing with it in healthy ways.

Flex a taste and try something new. I can creatively problem solve and come up with coping strategies.

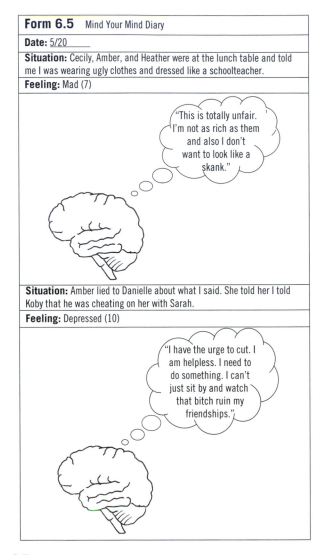

Form 6.5   Mind Your Mind Diary

Date: 5/20

Situation: Cecily, Amber, and Heather were at the lunch table and told me I was wearing ugly clothes and dressed like a schoolteacher.

Feeling: Mad (7)

"This is totally unfair. I'm not as rich as them and also I don't want to look like a skank."

Situation: Amber lied to Danielle about what I said. She told her I told Koby that he was cheating on her with Sarah.

Feeling: Depressed (10)

"I have the urge to cut. I am helpless. I need to do something. I can't just sit by and watch that bitch ruin my friendships."

Figure 8.7   Luciane's—Mind Your Mind Diary.

Luciane: I like the one about respecting who I am and questioning others' definitions of me. Also, I like the one about acting on facts rather than on others' opinions.

Therapist: Let's write that on one side of the card and your broken thought on the other side. How about the ones about being helpless and having the urge to cut.

Luciane: The word rescue is kinda cool. I like the one that says rescue my confidence by allowing myself to feel uncomfortable and dealing with it in healthy ways. The one about protecting my safety and doing things that build me up rather than tearing me down is good too.

Therapist: Good, let's write that one down too. Now here is the rough part. See if you can come up with some mind menders on your own.

Luciane (pause): I don't know. How about, "They're just scheming me. Think twice before you start thinking what they say is true."

Therapist: How helpful is that?

Luciane: Pretty helpful.

Therapist: Great. Write that one down too. For homework, let's see if you can come up with four more mind menders.

The therapist's work with Luciane demonstrates several points. First, the therapist reinforced the metaphor (i.e., "It is sometimes helpful to call these things you say to yourself broken thoughts"). Second, Luciane took the lead by identifying several mind menders. Finally, Luciane was able to come up with an original mind mender.

Immunity Boosters

Immunity boosters is a cognitive restructuring task that equates negative automatic thoughts with viruses and counter thoughts with immunity boosters. Immunity boosters are best used with children ages 11 or older. First, you begin with an introduction of the metaphor. Next, you help the child develop immunity boosters using the cognitive restructuring rubrics.

The following dialogue gives you an idea how to use the procedure with Natasha, a 12-year-old girl who is teased and excluded in her school.

Natasha: I don't understand what's so wrong with me. These girls make fun of me and I feel so bad. They call me really bad names and I can't help but cry. When that happens, my mom says I am losing control of my emotions. I'll never measure up.

Therapist: It's such a painful situation. It's enough to make you sick.

Natasha: That's how I feel ... sick ... before going to school.

Therapist: Do you know what a virus is? It is something that makes you feel bad. The things you are telling yourself are kind of like a virus. They zap your strength and make you feel bad. We need to come up with something to help you fight the viruses. The way you fight a virus is with a big word called immunity. Immunity protects you from viruses so we need to develop some messages you send yourself to fight off the negative things that go through your head. How does this sound?

Natasha: I'm not sure what your point is.

Therapist: Remember when you said I'll never measure up?

Natasha: Yeah.

Therapist: That's the virus; the thing that goes through your mind when you feel sick to your stomach.

Natasha: OK, I get it.

Therapist: So, how do you feel about coming up with a way to protect yourself from the virus?

Natasha: That would be great, but how?

Therapist: We have to boost your immunity.

Natasha: Like when I take a vitamin?

Therapist: Kind of. Let's come up with some immunity boosters for that bad virus saying you'll never measure up. First, list the ways you do measure up.

Natasha: Like what?

Therapist: What are some things about yourself you like and are proud of?

Natasha: I'm a good student. I always make the distinguished honor roll and sometimes the dumb honor roll.

Therapist: The dumb honor roll?

Natasha: You know … the regular one.

Therapist: Sounds like the virus creeping in. Let's put down the distinguished honor roll and regular honor roll. What else?

Natasha: I'm good at soccer and art. I'm in the honor choir.

Therapist: That's quite a list so far. Does it seem to describe someone who does not measure up?

Natasha: Not really.

Therapist: What does it say?

Natasha: I am pretty good at lots of different things.

Therapist: You just came up with an immunity booster. Write that down. Next, we have to come up with the sense that you will never measure up. We need to fight off that virus.

Natasha: So, some more thoughts that protect me from thinking I will never measure up.

Therapist: Ones that boost your wellness and block the virus.

Natasha: I try hard to be the best I can be.

Therapist: OK. Does that pressure help or hurt you?

Natasha: I think it sometimes hurts me.

Therapist: OK, then how do you make it an immunity booster that protects you?

Natasha: Not too sure.

Therapist: Let me see if I can help. When do you never measure up?

Natasha: I don't know.

Therapist: Do you have to measure up immediately or can you measure up over time?

Natasha: I never thought about it that way.

Therapist: Good, that's why we are doing this. So how can you be patient with yourself?

Natasha: I guess I can say I have time to prove myself.

Initially, Natasha struggled with the task (i.e., "I'm not sure what your point is"). The therapist systematically used some simple questions to help guide Natasha through the process (i.e., "Does it seem to describe someone who does not measure up? What does it say?"). Natasha also came up with an alternative thought (i.e., "I try hard to be the best I can be") that might hinder rather than help her. The therapist addressed the issue (i.e., "Does it help or hurt you?") and redirected the dialogue (i.e., "How do you make an immunity booster that protects you?").

Suicidal Ideation and Behavior

Due to the prevalence and severity of suicidal behavior, we have elected to devote a special section to suicidality. The section begins with a conceptual overview aimed at understanding suicidal behavior. The second subsection includes recommendations for increasing motivation, developing safety plans, implementing self-monitoring, processing reasons for living, and teaching distress tolerance and problem-solving skills.

Understanding Suicidal Behavior

In the seminal text on cognitive therapy for suicidal patients, Beck, Rush, Shaw, and Emery (1979) urged that "the therapist must be able to sense why the patient feels driven to kill himself and to experience, to some degree, the patient's despair and frenzy." Overall, we conceptualize suicide ideation as an ill-founded problem-solving strategy (Berk, Brown, Wenzel, & Henriques, 2008; Esposito, Johnson, Wolfsdorf, & Spirito, 2003; Wenzel, Brown, & Beck, 2008).

Suicidal ideation is often associated with helplessness and hopelessness. These youngsters have a sense of a foreshortened future. They see themselves caught in a miserable present with limited possibilities. Suicidal behavior is a misguided strategy to escape the helplessness. It is important to specifically identify and address the reason for helplessness. For some patients, they may feel helpless to control unwanted events. Drew was a 16-year-old boy who was torn by the breakup with his first girlfriend. He thought killing himself would make Ashlyn feel guilty and restore their relationship. Therefore, Socratic questions casting doubt on the efficacy of his problem-solving strategy were indicated (e.g., How guilty will Ashlyn feel? How long will she feel guilty? How long will you be dead? If guilt in fact does the trick in getting Ashlyn to come back, how can you be in a relationship if you are dead?).

Working with a functional analysis for suicidal ideation and behavior is often clinically productive. Brent (1997) identified interpersonal breakups and conflict as the most frequent precipitant for suicidal behavior in adolescents. For instance, parental conflict is the major stressor for younger adolescents, whereas romantic breakups are the modal interpersonal stressor for older adolescents. Persons (1989) urged practitioners to identify and intervene with motivations for suicide. Different motivations call for different interventions. Indeed, Persons noted that being angry yet unskilled in dealing with the emotion is frequently associated with suicide. Consequently, applying cognitive techniques for anger management is a good strategy.

Self-injury and parasuicidal behavior deserve special mention. Recent thinking shows that self-injury in adolescents serves four major functions (Nock & Prinstein, 2004; Nock, Teper, & Hollander, 2007). One function is relieving or escaping noxious internal states (e.g., "This pain is unbearable; I can't stand it"). A second function is to increase pleasant internal states (e.g., "Feeling pain means I am truly alive"). Klonsky and Muehlenkamp (2007) refer to this as "feeling generation" (p. 1050). Escaping or avoiding an undesirable event is a third function (e.g., "If I cut, I won't have to go to the party where my ex-boyfriend will be"). Finally, increasing the probability of a desired external event occurring is a fourth function. In this instance, the self-injury is a skewed communication strategy ("To show how much pain I am in"). Klonsky and Muehlenkamp wrote about the interpersonal boundary marking function of self-injury. They believed that the self-injurious behavior enables patients to communicate they are independent and distinct from others. Finally, Kennerley (2004) identified several beliefs associated with parasuicidal behavior. For instance, patients may see themselves as impotent, bad, trapped, unable to tolerate emotional distress, and uncared for.

Treating Suicidal Behavior With Specific Cognitive Restructuring Interventions

Increasing Motivation and Engagement

The overarching theme in treating suicidal youngsters is the seamless integration of safeguarding procedures with specific psychotherapeutic interventions (Rudd & Joiner, 1998). Daniel and Goldston (2009) reported on suicidal adolescents' ambivalence about treatment. They listed a number of factors contributing to the ambivalence including shame, embarrassment, wanting to move past discussing suicide, and a sense that being in treatment means they are different than their age mates. Frequently, increasing motivation and engagement means dealing directly with beliefs that "no one understands how badly I feel."

The first step is communicating your understanding. This is facilitated by your case conceptualization (Chapter 2) and augmented by the view of suicidal behavior presented earlier. Focusing on suicidal behavior as a maladaptive problem-solving strategy is helpful. Frequently, this will decrease the youth's shame, embarrassment, and sense of being deviant. The key here is the element of therapeutic patience and allowing youngsters' stories to unfold. Adolescents, in particular, dread adult lectures and being judged. Adopting the axiom "listen … listen … listen … and then respond" (Vaughn & Jackson, 2000) is a good strategy. Moreover, adhering the multiple stance variables presented in Chapter 3 will also help.

No-Suicide Contract

No-suicide contracts are frequently used by practicing clinicians. However, no-suicide contracts are questionable and controversial interventions. Brent (1997) believed that a no-suicide contract mobilizes patients' commitment to safety. Moreover, patients' response to the contract is a risk assessment procedure. According to Brent, the no-suicide contract should contain concrete alternatives to self-harm including access to 24-hour clinical backup. In his review, Brent strongly advocated for this backup due to findings that 24-hour availability resulted in lower frequency of attempts and threats.

Spirito and Esposito-Smythers (2006) offered useful questions for establishing a no-suicide contract. First, patients are asked to commit with 100% certainty that they can keep themselves safe for the length of the contract. Additionally, Spirito and Esposito-Smythers recommended considering the patients' living contexts. They assess whether the home environment is able to monitor and ensure the youth's safety. Parents' mental health or substance abuse problems limit their ability to monitor the child's safety. Additionally, Spirito and Esposito-Smythers suggested checking to see if the parent–child relationship is positive enough for the teen to disclose to the parents. Finally, the home environment should be scanned to see if neglect or abuse is present.

Although no-suicide contracts are part of clinical practice and lore, recent evidence casts considerable doubt on their effectiveness. Wenzel, Brown, and Beck (2008) cited research showing little empirical support for the no-suicide contract. Accordingly, no-suicide contracts should be used very cautiously.

Safety Plan

A safety plan is a viable alternative to a no-suicide contract. Wenzel et al. (2008) expertly detail the components of an effective safety plan. Warning signs, coping strategies, and ways for contacting responsible adults are essential. Phone numbers for the therapist, emergency department, and crisis hot lines should be written on the plan.

Berk et al. (2008) also advised the development of a family safety plan for family members also including warning signs. Additionally, the plan contains reminders for strategies for effective ways of communicating with adolescents when they are in crisis. The plan also has guidelines for monitoring the youth. Removal of lethal means for suicide should be included in any safety plan. Guns, knives, prescriptions as well as over-the-counter medicines, and ropes and belts may need to be removed. Locks can also be placed on windows. Finally, critical contact information for professionals and emergency departments should be included. Wenzel et al. (2008) have several excellent examples of safety plans in their seminal text.

Hope Box

Berk et al. (2008) designed a very creative intervention for suicidal adolescents called the hope box. The hope box contains items that are associated with positive feelings, coping skills, and reasons to live. Berk et al. suggested placing photographs of friends and loved ones, favorite CDs, movies, books, foods, scents, games, puzzles, letters, gifts, and trip souvenirs in the box. The box should be accessible. Therapists should assign the box as homework and review its contents on a regular basis.

Self-Monitoring

Self-monitoring skills (Chapter 6) are extremely valuable coping skills (Berk et al., 2008; Wenzel et al., 2008). Thermometers or other scaling devices help children and adolescents take their emotional temperatures (Wenzel et al., 2008). Wenzel et al. (2008) pointed out that degrees on the scale could be labeled boiling points, point of no return, points to take action, and calm points. The action point is the place on the scale where young patients can still carry out a coping strategy despite feeling distressed. When patients improve their self-monitoring skills, they can identify emotional trends and predict danger points. They can see when their mood is decreasing and become alert to crisis points.

More specifically, Walsh (2007) designed a very useful self-monitoring tool for self-injury and parasuicidal behavior. The form is quite comprehensive and addresses diverse contextual factors such as environmental conditions, psychological antecedents, and biological factors as well as situational parameters (place, start/end, alone or with others). Perceived consequences of the self-injurious behaviors are also noted (e.g., relief, pain, shame, and so on).

Reasons for Living

Reasons for living deal directly with suicidal adolescents' ambivalence (Overholser, 1995). Overholser (1995) eloquently stated that the reasons for living may "fan a spark of hope into a big flame of desire" (p. 199). Autonomy and greater personal freedom are highly valued in adolescence. Daniel and Goldston (2009) suggested including developmental milestones (e.g., dating, driving, college, work, and so forth) in a reasons for living list. Suicidal adolescents may have difficulty coming up with reasons to live on their own. Therefore, you will need to increase their attention to these factors through skillful questioning.

The Reasons for Living Inventory (Osman et al., 1996, 1998) can serve as a guide for your questions. You can focus your questions on accomplishments and aspirations (e.g., What do you hope to accomplish? What do you want to be? Before you were depressed, what did you hope to do as an adult?). A second set of questions could focus on the reaction of family members (e.g., What would your family lose? Who in your family depends on you? How would they cope with missing you? Who in your family would you hurt without meaning to? What lessons would you be teaching to your brothers and sisters?). The Reasons for Living Inventory also mobilizes potential moral objections to suicide (e.g., What does your religion say about _____?) Adolescents, in particular, are exquisitely sensitive to social approval and disapproval. Therefore, addressing friends' reactions is a useful avenue (e.g., What would your friends' reactions be? How would they view your decision?).

Finding meaning may be another developmental reason to live. Dahl (2004) referred to adolescence as a time of "igniting passions" and wrote "feelings of passion are rooted in the same deep brain systems as biologic drives and primitive elements of emotion" (p. 21). Moreover, adolescents demonstrate commitment to activities and causes. Daniel and Goldston (2009) recommended volunteerism as a way for suicidal adolescents to derive meaning from their experiences. They stated that volunteerism also increases social networking, develops an appreciation of one's value and strengths, and adds perspective. The clinical key is helping to channel these passions in healthy and productive ways.

Distress Tolerance Skills

Suicidal ideation and attempts may also be linked to a general intolerance for negative emotional experience (Berk et al., 2008; Linehan, 1993; Sidley, 1993). Corstorphine, Mountford, Tomlinson, Waller, and Meyer (2007) maintained that emotional intolerance spurs impulsivity and dysregulation. Therefore, distress tolerance skills (Layden, Newman, Freeman, & Morse, 1993; Linehan, 1993) are often helpful. Distress tolerance is different from distraction. Moreover, it is an active process. Linehan (1993) called distress tolerance the capacity to embrace negative emotional experiences and persist so adaptive problem solving can be realized. Layden et al. (1993) suggested that hitting oneself with pillows, crunching raw eggs on self, immersing hands into cold water, and reviewing old homework assignments may be alternatives to suicidal/parasuicidal behavior and increase emotional tolerance. Table 8.1 lists several distress tolerance skills.

Table 8.1   Distress Tolerance Skills

Skill
Hobbies
Sports/exercises
Cleaning
Attend community events
Visit a friend
Walk
Garden
Play computer games
Teach others a skill
Count leaves on a tree, colors in a painting
Work a puzzle, Sudoku
Read
Watch TV
Suck on a lemon
Listen to a nature sound
Eat a strong peppermint
Take a bubble bath
Pet a dog or cat
Put lotion on your body
Wear fur-lined gloves
Watch comedy shows
Crunch raw eggs on yourself
Cut tomatoes
Cut open ketchup packets
Drink hot tea

Problem-Solving Interventions

Daniel and Goldston (2009) encouraged clinicians to teach adolescents problem-solving skills that can be applied during emotionally powerful crisis points. They emphasized that since adolescents tend to be more present oriented rather than future oriented, problem-solving strategies should have a short-term focus. Dahl (2004) asserted that most adolescents are good problem solvers when their emotional arousal is low. However, suicidal youth who are experiencing intense emotional arousal are notoriously poor problem solvers. Brent (1997) commented, "What seems to be happening for many of these adolescents was that, as they felt increasingly under stress, they become more affectively labile and much less dispassionate and rational" (p. 283).

Wenzel et al. (2008) described the very creative idea of problem-solving letters based on the work of the CBT TASA Team (2008). The patients respond to letters as if they were an advice columnist or other expert problem solver. In this approach, the clinician creates a stock of fictionalized sample letters (e.g., feeling lonely and suicidal about the breakup of a relationship) and shares them with the patient. The patient then attempts to offer the writer a problem-solving strategy. Indeed, this is a time-honored cognitive behavioral therapy practice of objectifying the distress. Patients could follow up and extend this exercise by writing their own letter and trying to respond productively from the perspective of an expert problem solver.

As previously mentioned, suicidal behavior is a skewed problem-solving strategy. More specifically, suicide may be motivated by seeking revenge to resolve a problem. Therefore, clinicians need to address beliefs related to those behaviors. The following dialogue with Mara, a 16-year-old who is angry and resentful about parental criticism and control, is illustrative.

Therapist: Let's look back and see what got you thinking about killing yourself.

Mara: It's my parents. It's their f------ fault that I am a psycho. They have problems, too. If I killed myself, I could get even with them. Then they'll be sorry when they are rid of me.

Therapist: You are carrying around a lot of pain.

Mara: It's time someone else feels the pain I do. They are shit-heads and move on but I am stuck in the shit.

Therapist: It seems like you want things to be fairer and punishing your parents is a way to even things out.

Mara: Exactly.

Therapist: How will it even things out?

Mara: They'll suffer, they'll feel sorry.

Therapist: I see. Can I ask you more about this?

Mara: OK, knock yourself out.

Therapist: How long will they suffer?

Mara: I don't know. I haven't thought about that.

Therapist: Good, that's what we can use our time for.

Mara: I don't know what you mean.

Therapist: Will they suffer for a few days? Weeks? Months? Years? What do you think?

Mara (pausing): I don't know. Maybe 6 to 8 months.

Therapist: I see. And how awful will they feel on a scale from 1 to 10?

Mara: Oh, I think a 9 or a 10.

Therapist: Will they feel as bad in the first week as they feel in the eighth month?

Mara: Probably not.

Therapist: So, let me get this. Your plan will have the effect of your parents feeling really bad for at least a week and maybe 8 months but they will feel better over time.

Mara: I guess.

Therapist: And how long will you be dead?

Mara: What?

Therapist: How long does death last?

Mara: Forever, I guess.

Therapist: That's kind of how it works. I have a second question. How able will you be to enjoy your satisfaction of your parents' suffering if you are dead?

Mara (pausing): Uh ... I'm not sure ... I never thought about it.

Therapist: So, if I am understanding you'll be dead forever but your parents' suffering will last maybe 8 months and you are not sure if you will be able to enjoy their suffering. And you want things to be fair. How fair is that to you?

The Socratic dialogue with Mara illustrates several important points. The dialogue began with an empathic response (i.e., "You are carrying around a lot of pain. It seems like you want things to be fairer and punishing your parents is a way to even things out"). The therapist was careful and patient to guide the self-discovery in a nonjudgmental manner. Finally, the therapist aligned with Mara against the sense of unfairness.

Consider another example. Emma was a 15-year-old who was furiously angry yet terribly unskilled about dealing with it. Moreover, she believed, "Only bad and immoral people get angry at their parents." This rigid imperative led to a crippling sense of helplessness and painful self-recriminations. Persons (1989) saw these as very common beliefs and processes with suicidal individuals. Essentially, Emma saw suicide as a way to manage the problem of anger making her a despicable human being. Accordingly, interventions dealing with her hopelessness when experiencing anger as well as her self-punishing beliefs were employed.

Emma: I feel so bad that I have all these hateful feelings toward my mom and dad.

Therapist: What goes through your mind when you have these feelings toward your parents?

Emma: That I am a terrible person. Maybe even sinful for having these feelings toward my parents.

Therapist: I can see how painful that is.

Emma: I feel I should be punished because being mad is wrong and disrespectful.

Therapist: You see yourself as bad for having what you think are kind of evil feelings.

Emma: Um hmm.

Therapist: How would it be if we talked about some of these beliefs?

Emma: All right, I guess.

Therapist: We've talked about the things that make anger bad but what might be reasonable about your anger?

Emma: I don't know what you mean.

Therapist: Do you think most people your age get mad at their parents?

Emma: Most of my friends do.

Therapist: What do they get mad at their parents for?

Emma: Not being allowed to do things, friends, clothes, grades, that kind of stuff.

Therapist: On a scale of 1 to 10, how similar is that to the reasons that you get mad at them?

Emma: Pretty close. Maybe an 8 or 9.

Therapist: How much do you think they are immoral and should be punished?

Emma: Not at all.

Therapist: That's curious. Most of your friends get angry at their parents for the same things you do and you don't think they should be punished. So on a scale of 1 to 10, how reasonable is it for a 16-year-old to be angry at their parents?

Emma (pause): When you put it that way maybe a 9 or so.

Therapist: If it is completely reasonable, how deserving of punishment are you?

Emma: Not deserving.

The work with Emma points out several salient therapeutic issues. The therapist communicated an empathic summary statement gained through systematic questioning (i.e., "You see yourself as bad for having what you think are kind of evil feelings"). The therapist and Emma worked to discover the reasonableness of her anger. Once the foundation of reasonableness was established, the therapist juxtaposed it with punitiveness (i.e., "If it [your anger] were completely unreasonable how deserving of punishment are you?").

CONCLUSION

This chapter explained the basics of problem-solving and cognitive restructuring. Various rubrics that pervade all the different procedures provide a useful clinical compass. The technique, augmented by cartoons and metaphors, work to make the therapy accessible to children. As you progress to the next chapter, more sophisticated rational analysis techniques are outlined.

Nine

Rational Analysis

INTRODUCTION

Rational analysis procedures are more advanced cognitive behavioral therapy (CBT) techniques. Whereas cognitive restructuring changes the content of children's thoughts, rational analysis modifies children's thought processes. Cognitive restructuring teaches patients to say more productive and adaptive things to themselves, whereas rational analysis coaches young people to ask better questions of themselves. Overholser (1993a) explained rational analysis by writing, "In some ways, the process is similar to helping a child assemble a puzzle. If you hand the child a piece but the child cannot find the proper place, you do not keep handing the child the same piece. Instead you can give the child a few other pieces. As the picture starts to develop, the child can easily place the original difficult piece" (p. 72).

Rational analysis does not equal rationalization. Rational analysis focuses on developing specific and factually based conclusions (Friedman, Thase, & Wright, 2008). The goal is for children and adolescents to reflect thoughtfully on their expectations and assumptions in order to evaluate their accuracy. Through this process, self-knowledge and interpersonal understanding is achieved (Seligman, Reivich, Jaycox, & Gillham, 1995). Rationalization, on the other hand, is a defense mechanism that is focused on "explaining away actions in a seemingly logical way to avoid uncomfortable feelings especially guilt and shame" (Westen, 1996, pp. 438–439). In sum, rationalization is a intrapsychic mechanism that works to protect the patient from discomfort and blocks self-knowledge.

Lageman (1989) taught that Socrates is remembered for having a fervent commitment to self-examination and questioning assumptions. A. T. Beck, Rush, Shaw, and Emery (1979) wrote, "analysis of meaning and attitudes exposes the unreasonableness and self-defeating nature of the attitudes" (p. 154).

Rational analysis is based on the premise that children's beliefs are acquired logically and therefore are susceptible to Socratic evaluation (Bandura, 1986). Therefore, rational analysis makes use of Socratic dialogues. Overholser (1987, 1993a, 1993b, 1994, 1995, 1996) has written extensively on the Socratic method in psychotherapy and offers readers compelling clinical guidelines for conducting Socratic dialogues. Finally, applying the stance variables mentioned in Chapter 3 will propel your Socratic dialogue and rational analysis.

This chapter offers very specific rudiments and rubrics that break down the complexities associated with Socratic questioning into understandable elements. Specific examples, questions, dialogues, and exercises are explained.

RUDIMENTS

Eight Simple Rules for Rational Analysis

There is no one silver bullet question when doing rational analysis. Beginning cognitive behavioral therapists commonly think there is one question that can unlock children's rigid thinking. James, Morse, and Howarth (2010) explained, "Within cognitive therapy, questions are used to explore issues from different angles, create dissonance, and facilitate re-evaluation of beliefs whilst at the same time building more adaptive thinking styles" (p. 83). Therapeutic change most often is realized by building a Socratic dialogue characterized by systematic questions, flexibility, and empathy.

Many beginning cognitive behavioral psychotherapists sometimes like to act as if they are know-it-alls (Friedberg & McClure, 2002). Rational analysis is not a chance to poke holes in children's assumptions and show them how their thinking is silly. Rather, rational analysis provides the opportunity for creating doubt about and crafting fresh perspectives. Therefore, holster the urge to show off and remain curious.

The following eight simple rules for rational analysis provide guidelines for examining and modifying children's cognitive processes. The rules help you make rational analysis more accessible to children and maintain an advocacy stance rather than disputation and refutation.

1. *Initially rely on open-ended questions to lay out the foundation for the patient's beliefs.* In laying out the foundation, it is important not to preempt the "factual" basis for the children's beliefs. Unexpressed hidden or

implicit evidence needs to see the light of day. If you rush through this first step, you risk the conclusion being unbelievable to children or impotent in changing mood. Sample questions may include:

What makes you believe the other kids think you are a jerk?
What does your mom do that makes you certain she prefers your sister?
What convinces you that you are ugly?
How did you come to see your father as an asshole?

2. *Use short, simple questions.* Complex and abstract questions slow rational analysis. This is particularly true when working with younger children. Vaughn and Jackson (2000) nicely remind us to be crisp and say what is core in interpersonal interactions. Formulate short, concise questions that are pointed and straightforward. Figure 9.1 gives examples of rambling questions and their crisp alternatives.

3. *Ask one question at a time.* Compound questions are several questions embedded in one phrase (e.g., Do you think you are bad and others see you poorly?). Firing multiple fire questions that pound away at the patient makes you seem like an inquisitor. Often, this creates an adversarial relationship. Be patient. Go slow, ask single questions, and wait for a response. Further, be comfortable with silences. Allow the youngsters time to sit with the question, simmer, and stew until they are ready to respond.

4. *Use pacing.* Rational analysis also makes use of empathic responses as well as Socratic questions. Empathic responding amplifies emotion so rational analysis can take hold. Moreover, it communicates understanding so difficult questions can propel the rational analysis forward. Moreover, mixing in empathic responding provides a rest period for the patient. Padesky (1993) rightly noted that listening is half the battle when forming good rational analysis questions. The following short dialogue illustrates the proper use of pacing.

Devin: It's my fault that Dad left.
Therapist: When that goes through your mind, how do you feel?
Devin: Bad, I guess.

Rambling Questions	Crisp Alternative
In what types of situations and around who do you believe you are less than adequate?	What convinces you that you are less than adequate?
Your mother makes you do a lot of chores and checks your homework over and over.	What seems fair about your mother's behavior?
You get mad at her and get in trouble but that causes problems. So, what do you think about your mother's behavior that is unreasonable?	What seems unfair about your mother's behavior?
There are really a lot of things going on with you right now. You have been having sex with a lot of guys and you say you felt bad about yourself because of it and you call yourself a skank but you are still putting yourself in these situations. So, I am wondering what is really going on?	I can see you are confused by all that is going on. What seems to be confusing about your behavior?
There are many ways to think about yourself and your situation. You are blaming yourself for all the bad things that are happening in your family. You feel sad, depressed, angry, and worried. So, why are you blaming yourself?	What are all the other possible explanations for your family's problems?

Figure 9.1   Rambling and Crisp questions.

Therapist: It sure would make sense that you would feel sad and guilty if you thought Dad's leaving was all your fault.

Devin: It feels like crap.

Therapist: What convinces you that it's your fault?

Devin: Well, I hear them arguing about me. Maybe if I were doing better, they would still be together. My dad never spends time with me.

Therapist: I see. You've really got yourself convinced.

5. *Avoid assumption and presumption; it's OK to be dumb.* Freeman, Felgoise, and Davis (2008) claims therapists' narcissism promotes the myth that therapists know best. Narcissistic clinicians believe they know what is inside patients' head and show off to demonstrate how smart they are. Further, Rutter and Friedberg (1999) warned clinicians about inaccurately assuming you know the data upon which children's maladaptive beliefs are built without asking first. Therefore, remember the Columbo stance mentioned in Chapter 3. You might ask questions such as:

Help me see it as you do. What makes you a total freak?
I'm not sure I am following. What is it you guess your
teacher is thinking about you?

6. *Vary the type of question.* Similarly to the pacing
point, you should vary the type of question you ask.
Repeating the same question rarely is productive.
Einstein famously stated that insanity is doing the same
thing over and over and expecting a different result.
Therefore, repetitive stereotypical questioning is not
only ineffective but it may even be insane. Figure 9.2
provides you with different ways to ask evidence, attri-
bution, pro–con, and decatastrophizing questions.

7. *Get permission to test the thought.* Remember that
patients enter treatment with firmly held beliefs. They
rigidly adhere to the appraisals, interpretations, judgments, and conclusions because they are familiar and
make the world predictable. Therefore, patients may
not want to test or evaluate their beliefs. Changing
one's views can be threatening and even seem invasive.

Category	Einstein Questions
Evidence	What makes you think…?
	What are you using to come up with that conclusion?
	What is convincing you to make that judgment?
	Tell me how you saw it that way?
Attribution	What's another way to look at it?
	What's an alternative explanation?
	What's another reason?
Decatastrophizing	On a scale of 1 to 10, how catastrophic is it?
	On a scale of 1 to 10, how disastrous is it?
	What is the difference between a disaster and simply a bad event?
	How can you tell the difference between a catastrophe and something you just didn't wish to happen?
Advantages and Disadvantages	What are the pros and cons?
	What are the pluses and minuses?
	What are the costs and rewards?

Figure 9.2   Einstein-type questions.

Consequently, ask permission to test or question their beliefs before diving into the Socratic dialogue or rational analysis (Newman, 1994).

May I push you a little harder on this?
May I ask a difficult question?
Can we take a look at this question a little more?
May I check this out with you?

8. *Look at the thought through multiple angles and perspectives.* Doing rational analysis requires flexibility on the part of both the patient and the psychotherapist. Perhaps, the greater demand for flexibility falls upon the therapist. In order to shake or loosen tightly wound thinking patterns, you have to try to see things from many angles. When crafting a Socratic dialogue, take a many-sided view. Get a look at the conclusion from many vantage points. Dr. Christine Padesky used the analogy of climbing a spiral staircase when constructing a Socratic dialogue. Since the stairs are spiral and serpentine, you see different vistas at various turns. Each step offers a fresh look at the surroundings. Figure 9.3 offers questions from the spiral staircase that cast doubt on children and adolescents' automatic thoughts.

Automatic Thought	Line of Dialogue From the Spiral Staircase
I'm a total loser.	What do you do that a total loser would never do?
	What does a total loser do that you would never do?
	How do other people in a total loser's life treat them that people in your life never do?
It is horrible if people think badly about me.	What makes it horrible?
	How horrible is it on a scale of 1 to 10?
	How bad do you worry people think you are?
	On a scale of 1 to 10, what is the acceptable degree of how bad people think you are?
	How long do you worry people will have a negative judgment about you?

Figure 9.3   Questions from the Spiral Staircase.

RUBRICS

There are several rubrics for rational analysis (A. T. Beck, Emery, & Greenberg, 1985; J. S. Beck, 1995; Fennell, 1989; Overholser, 1987, 1991, 1993a, 1993b, 1994, 1995, 1996; Padesky, 1988; Seligman et al., 1995). These include test of evidence (TOE), reattribution, decatastrophizing, advantages and disadvantages, legal metaphors, and universal definitions. This section provides detailed descriptions of each rudiment replete with dialogues and examples. Finally, creative modifications of traditional methods are offered.

Test of Evidence

A Test of Evidence (TOE) evaluates whether conclusions are factually based and logically sound. Tests of evidence require considerable effort by cognitive behavioral therapists and their patients. The TOE is well-suited to children who engage in a variety of cognitive errors (all-or-none thinking, overgeneralization, etc.) and ill-founded inferences. A TOE requires a systematic deliberate approach. Although a TOE is quite sophisticated, it can be made child friendly with worksheets (Friedberg, Friedberg, Friedberg, 2001; Friedberg, Mason, & Fidaleo, 1992; Friedberg, McClure, & Garcia, 2009). Worksheets are helpful for beginning therapists because they help scaffold a systematic Socratic dialogue. Worksheets are also familiar to children and frequently add fun to the process.

There are six steps in constructing a proper TOE (Padesky, 1988). We have termed this the *Six Pack for Success.* First, you identify the thought to be tested via methods explained in Chapter 6. Second, the rate of belief is scaled (Chapter 6). Then, the two columns are labeled "Facts that completely (100%) support the thought" and "Facts that do not completely support the thought." As an alert reader, you should recognize that when the columns are labeled in this way, you only need one fact in the disconfirming column to cast doubt on the thought. It is important to make sure there are no automatic thoughts in either column. In Step 4, you check for alternate explanations of the facts other than the belief being tested. Similarly, all you need is a possible alternate explanation to cast doubt on the confirming piece of evidence.

Step 5 is the analytic and synthesizing level. Here, the facts supporting the belief, facts disconfirming beliefs, and alternative explanations are reviewed in order to come to a conclusion.

This is a very difficult phase and considerable effort needs to be allocated at this time. Helpful synthesizing questions may include:

> Looking at all three columns, what conclusion can you make?
> Taking in all this information, what do you make of this?
> What new belief seems to account for this information?

The Six Pack for Success is summarized in Figure 9.4 and a completed TOE is found in Figure 9.5.

Fact Hunter

Fact Hunter is a TOE for younger children (ages 8 to 12) along the lines of Private I (Friedberg & McClure, 2002) and clue snooping (Friedberg et al., 2001). Children with rigid beliefs center their search strategy on facts that confirm their inaccurate interpretation. They selectively attend to data consistent with their views and neglect contrary information. Due to these biases, cognitive behavioral therapists need to widen the hunt for data.

Fact Hunter is very similar to the traditional TOE for adolescents with just a few differences. First, it is a simpler form with no belief ratings or prompt for alternative explanation of facts. Second, the fact hunter graphic and metaphor are added to make the task more engaging for younger children. The Fact Hunter procedure is found in Form 9.1.

Miles is an 11-year-old boy with pervasive developmental disorder (PDD) and depression who believed he could never measure up to anyone his age and never did anything well. He loved hunting so the Fact Hunter was a good option for him. The facts supporting his belief were very easy for him to list (see Figure 9.6). However, the other fact-finding mission

---

1. Identify the thought to be tested.
2. Rate the degree of belief.
3. Label two columns: "Facts That Completely (100%) Support the Thought" and "Facts That Do Not Completely Support the Thought."
4. Check for an alternate explanation of the facts that support the conclusion.
5. Review the facts supporting the belief, facts not supporting the beliefs, alternative explanations, and come to a conclusion.
6. Re-rate the mood based on a new conclusion.

Figure 9.4   Six Pack for Success.

Thought: Without Tomas as a boyfriend, I am a loser.
Degree of Belief: 10
Feeling: Depressed (10)

Facts That Completely (100%) Support the Thought	Alternative Explanations	Facts That Do Not (100%) Support the Thought
People invited me to more parties after I was with Tomas.		My grades were higher when I didn't have a boyfriend.
Most other girls in my class have boyfriends.	← Maybe it was because I felt more confident.	I cut myself every time we had sex.
More girls were friendly to me.		I felt bad when I saw him talking to another girl.
I was busy pretty much every weekend.		I played harder at field hockey practice before I met him.
I was texting and talking to my friends much more.		I hung out with my teammates from field hockey and student council more.
I didn't feel so alone when I was walking down the hall.		
My mother didn't annoy me as much.	← Maybe it was because I did not feel as depressed.	I was elected as an officer in several clubs before I met him.
I felt happier.		

Conclusion: Although many things changed for the better for me when I was with Tomas, there were some negatives as well. I had a lot of things going for me before I met him. So, I'm probably not as much of a loser as I think.

Figure 9.5   Completed Test of Evidence.

looking for disconfirming data was excruciatingly difficult. Therefore, we augmented the procedure with an activity.

Miles believed that because he didn't see much positive about himself, these qualities did not exist. We added a penlight flashlight to a fact-hunting trip in the clinic. His parents wrote strengths and skills on slips of paper and placed them in hidden places in a dark room in the clinic. Miles then had to find them with just his penlight shedding a narrow beam of light. Of course, this was time consuming and difficult for Miles.

We turned on the lights in the room for Miles and he readily found the "facts." Miles was able to derive two important conclusions. First, just because he didn't see the facts did not mean the strengths were not there. Second, he needed a bigger flashlight to find his strengths. Subsequently, he was able to complete the Fact Hunter procedure and derive a conclusion (see Figure 9.6).

Form 9.1   Fact Hunter

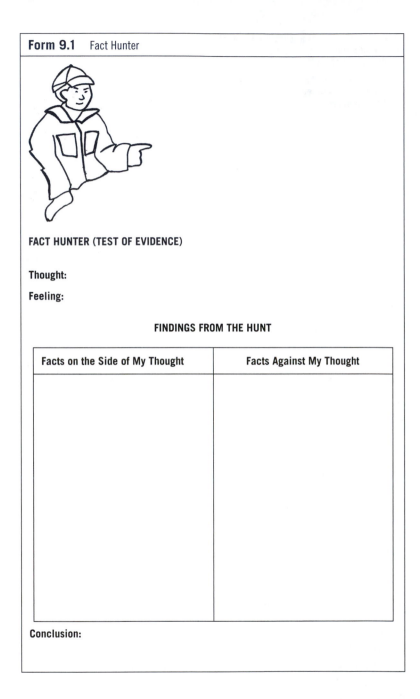

FACT HUNTER (TEST OF EVIDENCE)

Thought:

Feeling:

FINDINGS FROM THE HUNT

Facts on the Side of My Thought	Facts Against My Thought

Conclusion:

Form 9.1   Fact Hunter

FACT HUNTER (TEST OF EVIDENCE)

Thought: I will never measure up.

Feeling: Sad

FINDINGS FROM THE HUNT

Facts on the Side of My Thought	Facts Against My Thought
I stay after school a lot.	My grades are A's and B's.
My teacher yells at me.	I am sometimes asked to do special activities and help with other kids.
Other kids make fun of me and call me stupid.	I have two friends.
Other kids shut me out of their conversation.	Craig invited me for a sleepover.
Kids make faces when I sit down at the lunch table with them.	Ed asked me to be on his team for Math Olympics.

Conclusion: Just because other kids shut me out or tease me doesn't mean that I will never measure up. My grades are good, I have a few good friends, and my teacher seems to think well of me.

Figure 9.6   Miles's—Fact-Hunter Diary.

Reattribution

Attributions work to answer fundamental why questions (e.g., Why did this happen?). Harvey and Weary (1981) defined *attributions* as explanatory rules about commonplace and extraordinary events. Explanatory accuracy is a central goal in CBP and consequently this perceptual accuracy is facilitated through reattribution procedures.

Reattribution does not focus on the facts themselves but rather tests whether the explanations based on the facts are accurate. Reattribution simply asks, "What is another explanation?" (A. T. Beck et al., 1985). This form of rational analysis seeks to loosen rigid thinking patterns and create more divergent thinking. You are teaching your patients to see things from multiple angles. Reattribution is an especially nice intervention for youngsters who are excessively self-critical, self-blaming, and inaccurately personalize their responsibility for events beyond their control. A. T. Beck et al. (1979) reminds us that in reattribution, "the point is not to absolve the patient of all responsibility but to define the multitude of extraneous factors contributing to an adverse experience" (p. 158).

The basic reattribution process is completed in five sequential steps (Take Five, Figure 9.7). The first step is to base the reattribution on the cognition captured in a thought diary (Chapter 6). Attributional search is initiated in Step 2 by a variety of open-ended questions. Then, the plausibility of each step is rated (e.g., How possible is the alternative explanation on a scale of 1 to 10, 1 to 100?). Step 4 is the synthesizing stage where patients form a conclusion based on the interpretation

---

1. Base the reattribution on a thought diary or its variation (Chapter 6).
2. Search for alternate explanation:

   What's another explanation?
   What's another way to look at _____?
   What else could _____ mean?
   What's another angle to look at that from?
   What's another conclusion?
   What's another way to see this?
   What's another way to think about it?
   What's a fresh way to see _____?

3. Rate the plausibility of each step.
4. Make a conclusion.
5. Re-rate the mood.

Figure 9.7 Take Five steps in reattribution.

of data generated in Steps 2 and 3. Finally, they re-rate their mood associated with the new conclusion.

Various authors use a responsibility pie for reattribution (Greenberger & Padesky, 1995; Seligman et al., 1995). The responsibility pie is especially useful for children who engage in personalization, all-or-none thinking, overgeneralization, and excessive self-blame. The responsibility pie involves the therapeutic use of a pie chart. Patients complete the reattribution process by apportioning pieces of the pie to specific causes. Responsibility pies profit from the fact they are concrete and quite graphic.

There are several basic steps to completing a responsibility pie. First, therapists and patients brainstorm to list all possible reasons, causes, or interpretations. The original thought to be tested is accounted for in the pie analysis but it is included last. The thought is included to increase believability of the counterthought but it is considered last to derail the automatic bias in information processing.

Next, a pie is drawn. Each explanation is given a percentage and the pie is divided accordingly. Once the entire pie is sliced, the therapist makes sure the patient is satisfied with the allotments (e.g., What portions do you want to change?). Then, the synthesizing stage begins where the patient derives a conclusion based on the portions associated with each cause. Finally, the patients rate their mood associated with the reattribution. A completed Responsibility Pie is found in Figure 9.8.

"Mom and dad's arguing is all my fault."

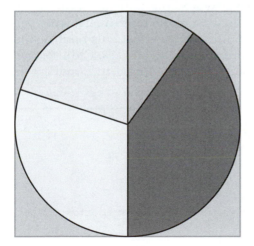

Figure 9.8   Responsibility Pie.

Decatastrophizing

Decatastrophizing is a rational procedure that tests children's and adolescents' predictions of doom. Decatastrophizing is not a logical test but instead adds perspective to narrow catastrophizing by putting circumstances in relative context. As you recall from Chapter 2, anxious children overestimate the magnitude and probability of threats, neglect, rescue factors; and underestimate their own coping skills. This is recently referred to as being a "disaster forecaster" (Friedberg, McClure, & Garcia, 2009). Decatastrophizing works to modify the overestimations of the magnitude and probability of dangers, and maximizes attention to rescue factors and coping resources.

Similar to TOE and reattribution, decatastrophizing requires systematic questioning. The decatastrophizing process is built upon nine pillars (Figure 9.9). Like the other rational analysis procedures, the first pillar is capturing the catastrophic thought in a thought diary (Chapter 6). Brainstorming all the things that are worse than the predicted disaster represents Pillar 2. In Pillar 3, patients assign a likelihood rating (from 0 [impossible] to 100 [certain]) to each prediction. Pillar 4 lists all the best outcomes and in Pillar 5, these events are assigned a probability rating. Pillar 6 records the most likely outcomes. Patients develop a problem-solving strategy for the worst possibilities in Pillar 7. This problem-solving component is important because it sets up an important Socratic question to decrease decatastrophizing (i.e., If you have a problem-solving strategy, how catastrophic can the event be?). Pillar 8 is the synthesizing phase where the patients form conclusions based on their evaluation of the most likely, worst, and best outcomes. The final pillar involves patients rerating their mood based on the decatastrophizing process. Child-friendly decatastrophizing procedures can be found in Friedberg and

1. Record the decatastrophizing in a thought diary or its variations.
2. List things that are worse than the catastrophic thought.
3. Rate the likelihood of these new catastrophes.
4. List the best things that can happen in the situation.
5. Rate the likelihood of the best things happening.
6. Make a problem-solving plan for the worst things.
7. List the most likely things to happen.
8. Make a conclusion based on the evaluation of the most likely, worst, and best outcomes.
9. Re-rate the mood.

Figure 9.9 Pillars of Decatastrophizing.

McClure (2002) ("dreadful iffy") and Friedberg, McClure, and Garcia (2009) ("master of disaster").

Advantages and Disadvantages

Some cognitive behavioral therapists refer to examining advantages and disadvantages as a cost–benefit analysis. Examining advantages and disadvantages is well-suited to increasing patients' motivation to change (Chapter 3) and addressing medication issues (Chapter 11). Simply, patients divide a sheet of paper into two columns. One column is headed "Advantages" and the other "Disadvantages." Patients then review each column and come up with a reasoned conclusion. In this section, two creative advantages and disadvantages procedures are explained. Magic Shop combines experiential learning with advantages–disadvantages analyses. The Ball Is in Your Court couples advantages and disadvantages with cartoon graphics.

Magic Shop

Magic Shop (Wiener, 1994) is a role-playing game that adds an experiential component to the advantages–disadvantages procedure. Magic Shop is rooted in psychodrama but is easily integrated with rational analysis. The therapist sets up the "shop" and stocks it with items the family or children want to obtain (e.g., greater self-control, friendship, independence, courage, success in school, compliance). The "items" could be placed on shelves and labeled for a more realistic look. For instance, the patients could make the labels (e.g., independence, friendship, and so on) and paste them on a box or package. The therapist plays the shop owner and sets the price for the items (e.g., not being able to do what I want all the time, one hour less of computer time). Then, the store owner and customer barter about the price for the item (e.g., What are you willing to pay for friendship? It costs not having your own way all the time. Do you still want it?).

The Ball Is in Your Court

The Ball Is in Your Court is a graphic augmented example of the advantages and disadvantages technique. The procedure makes use of a basketball metaphor and includes a form representing a basketball court with hoops at each end. The advantages bucket is at one end and the disadvantages lie at the other end of the court. In the center of the court, there is a large basketball where a conclusion is recorded. Children fill in the hoops at each end with the advantages and disadvantages.

After mindful deliberation, the children make a conclusion at center court.

The following example with Hazel, an 11-year-old girl who was torn between passively letting overly critical peers boss her around and self-assertion, illustrates the procedure.

Hazel: I just don't know what to do. I hate it when these girls tell me what to do or not to do. They criticize my clothes, the way I talk, my drawing, and even the way I sit. I want to do the right thing but I just don't know.

Therapist: There really isn't a rule book, Hazel. What to do is pretty much up to you. I do have something that may help straighten things out for you. Look at this (brings out Form 9.2). It's called the ball's in your court. At one end, this hoop is for the advantages and the other hoop is for the disadvantages. After you think about both hoops, you write down your decision at center court. How does this sound?

Hazel: I'm willing to try it.

Therapist: OK. What do you see as the disadvantages of letting the girls know how you feel about their comments?

Hazel: They could get mad and spread rumors about me. Maybe they will get the other girls on their side. They might not let me sit at their lunch table.

Therapist: Any other things on the down side of telling them?

Hazel: I might feel guilty.

Therapist: What do you see as advantages?

Hazel: They might stop. I might feel better about myself. I wouldn't feel so sick at lunch.

Therapist: Anything else?

Hazel: No, I don't think so.

Therapist: Now, here is the hard part. The ball is in your court now. Looking at the two hoops, what is your plan?

Hazel: It's hard. The negatives are bad and the positives are good.

Therapist: How likely are some of the disadvantages?

Hazel: I think I would feel guilty for a while. I don't think they can turn girls against me. It wouldn't be so bad if they didn't let me sit at the table. I could sit with Kelsey and Morgan.

Therapist: The worst and most likely thing is you would feel guilty.

Hazel: I think so.

Form 9.2   The Ball Is in Your Court

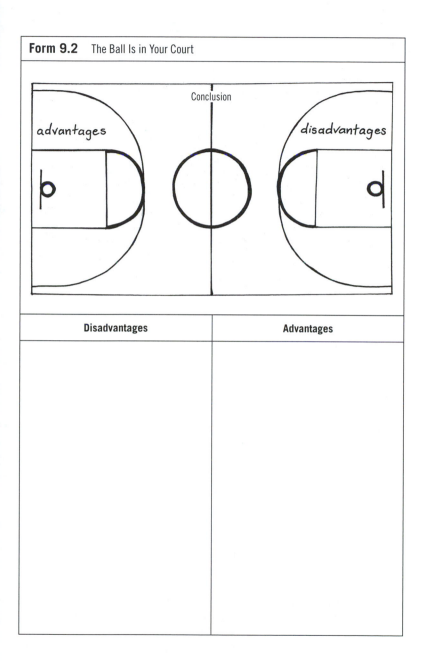

Disadvantages	Advantages

Form 9.2   The Ball Is in Your Court

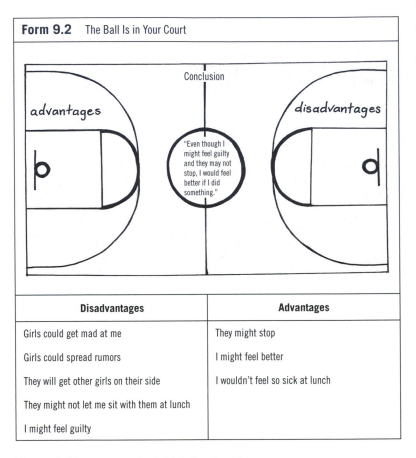

Disadvantages	Advantages
Girls could get mad at me	They might stop
Girls could spread rumors	I might feel better
They will get other girls on their side	I wouldn't feel so sick at lunch
They might not let me sit with them at lunch	
I might feel guilty	

Figure 9.10   Hazel's—The Ball Is in Your Court form.

Therapist: How likely are the advantages?

Hazel: I would be surprised if they stopped … But I think I would feel better if I did something.

Therapist: Now, what do you think?

Hazel: Even though I might feel guilty and they may not stop, I would feel better if I did something.

Hazel's work with The Ball Is in Your Court illustrates several critical points (see Figure 9.10). The therapist began with identifying the disadvantages then moved to listing advantages. Finally, considerable effort was directed toward helping Hazel synthesize the advantages and disadvantages (Now, here is the hard part. The ball is in your court now. Looking at the two hoops, what is your plan?). The therapist coached Hazel to examine the likelihood of the advantages and disadvantages.

Universal Definitions

Universal definitions are other lines of rational analysis. Overholser (1994) explained that universal definitions offer a description or conceptualization that is unchanged by circumstances. Accordingly, there are no exceptions in a universal definition. Overholser (1994) remarked there are several functions of universal definitions. Universal definitions identify whether a piece of data belongs to a specific category (e.g., worthlessness). Second, universal definitions test cause–effect relationships (e.g., any imperfection causes unacceptability). Defining and operationalizing terms involves specifying the precise meaning of language and imagery reported by patients. Operational definitions break down general, abstract concepts (e.g., dork, loser) into their molecular point-at-ables (e.g., no date for the prom, picked last for teams, excluded from lunch table). Universal definitions are also involved in labels and standards (e.g., loser, attractive, competent, dirty, and so on). Finally, the definitions help patients evaluate the generalizations they use.

In this section, two procedures for developing universal definitions are described. Proper Chemistry relies on a paper and pencil approach. Label Fable is more of an action-oriented exercise. Proper Chemistry is most appropriate for adolescents ages 15 and older, whereas Label Fable is appropriate for a wider age range (8 years and older).

Proper Chemistry

Children and adolescents often construct overly narrow definitions of themselves and others. Chemistry is concerned with the composition, structure, and properties of substances (*Webster's Ninth New Collegiate Dictionary*, 1991). Young people's conclusions about themselves, their world, other people, and their experiences are compounds built upon arbitrary inferences, spurious correlations, and specious explanations. Chemistry is also a good metaphor because solutions are frequently involved. Solutions, by definition, are homogeneous mixtures. Proper Chemistry is well suited to older children who make all-or-none generalizations about themselves, others, and their experiences. The proper chemistry technique is a rational analysis procedure that unpacks children's attributions that define themselves and others.

Proper chemistry begins with identifying the thought to be tested. The procedure is set up as creating a formula for a solution (Form 9.3). A formula expresses a general truth, fact, or universal principle. Then, therapists ask youngsters what will be necessary to redefine explanations. The third step is developing the proper ingredients or compounds that go into the definition. Finally, the therapist and patient derive a conclusion (e.g., the formula). Ingredients are placed in one of three beakers. The first beaker on the left side of the worksheet contains the data supporting the all-or-none solution. The second beaker is a container filled with alternative data. The second beaker is filled by eliciting information about what someone defined by the all-or-none label would do that the person in question (self or other) would never do as well as information about what the person in question does that someone defined by the universal definition would never do. The third beaker represents the final solution and is formed by subtracting the second from the first beaker.

The following dialogue illustrates the process with 16-year-old Ashley.

Therapist: Ashley, you and your mother have some really bad chemistry going on between you.
Ashley: I know. I don't think we get along very well.
Therapist: I am wondering if we can take a closer look at the chemistry.
Ashley: Whatever, I guess.
Therapist: What do you know about chemistry?
Ashley: I have to take it and it is boring.
Therapist: It can be a drag but it may be a way we can help your relationship with your mother.
Ashley: What? I don't understand.
Therapist: Well, in chemistry, you make solutions.
Ashley: Sure.
Therapist: Well, a solution is an all-or-none mixture and sometimes you may make all-or-none mixtures about your mom. How do you feel when you make all-or-none solutions like your mother is a controlling bitch?
Ashley: Pretty angry I guess.
Therapist: What do you say to the idea of trying to mix up another solution?
Ashley: OK, I guess.
Therapist: Here's the process of doing proper chemistry.
Ashley: Looks complicated.

Therapist: I understand. We'll break it down together. The first step is write down all the things that convince you your mother is a total bitch.

Ashley: That could take a long time.

Therapist: Good. So let's get started. What goes into this beaker?

Ashley: My mom does a lot of criticizing and correcting of the things I do. She tries to get me to be like her. She doesn't like my clothes, friends, or music or anything. It seems like she doesn't let me be me.

Therapist: You've got a lot of stuff stored up inside you about this.

Ashley: No kidding. She wants to pick classes for me and even topics for papers. And you know what? She listens into my calls. That's why I only give my friends my cell phone number.

Therapist: That's a lot of ingredients in the beaker. Anything else you want to add?

Ashley: No, I think we can go on.

Therapist: OK, in the next beaker, think about things a controlling bitch does that your mother would never do.

Ashley: Hmm. That is really tough … I don't know.

Therapist: It is sometimes hard to come up with new ingredients. How involved does she get with what you eat?

Ashley: Not much. She's fat and doesn't really pay attention to what I eat.

Therapist: So, if she was a totally controlling bitch, would she let that alone?

Ashley: Thank God for small miracles.

Therapist: Can we put that in a beaker?

Ashley: I guess.

Therapist: What else does a totally controlling bitch do that your mother would never do?

Ashley: I don't have a lot of chores.

Therapist: We'll put that in here. Anything else?

Ashley: Like what?

Therapist: A simple way to jump start this is to ask yourself what about your mother does not bug you.

Ashley: She can be forgiving … She's really good when I am sick … She usually gives me money for stuff.

Therapist: Would a totally controlling bitch do any of that?

Ashley: I guess not.

Therapist: We've filled two beakers. Now we are down to the final solution. If we take the original solution that your mother is a total controlling bitch and subtract

Form 9.3 Proper Chemistry

Formula:

Data for All-or-None View	Alternatives	Final Solution
−	=	

Figure 9.11   Ashley's—Proper Chemistry form.

what we put in the second beaker, what do we come up with?

Ashley: I'm confused.

Therapist: OK, let's break it down. If we compare and subtract what is in the second and third beaker from your first solution, does it stay so pure and absolute?

Ashley: I guess not.

Therapist: Then what do you make of that?

Ashley: My mother is sometimes bitchy and controlling but not all the time.

This long dialogue illustrates several important points. First, the therapist established the metaphor (i.e., "You and your mother have some bad chemistry going on," "A solution is an all or none mixture"). Ashley and her therapist worked diligently through both beakers (see Figure 9.11).

Throughout the procedure, the therapist mixed in questions with empathic responses (i.e., "You've got a lot of stuff stored up inside you"). Finally, coming up with a conclusion synthesizing the disparate data was difficult for Ashley. The therapist then simplified the process with a concise question (i.e., "If we compare and subtract what is in the second and third beaker from your first solution, does it stay so pure and absolute?").

Label Fable

Children and adolescents frequently place arbitrary labels on themselves (Chapter 2). These labels yield constricting all-or-none self-definitions and are associated with contingent self-worth appraisals.

The Label Fable exercise is a metaphor inspired by a scene in the movie, *The Express* (Fleder, Coplan, Dauchy, Davis, & Schmidt, 2008). Label Fable focused on teaching children and adolescents how false labels do not genuinely define content, content exists independently of labels, and testing labels is important.

You will need cans of soda, several Styrofoam cups, and a permanent marker. The following dialogue with Jordi, a 14-year-old anxious, perfectionistic, and self-critical girl, illustrates the process. Jordi was plagued by much self-doubt about her goodness and attractiveness. When others criticized her, she unquestionably accepted the label and nosedived into a spiral of anxiety and depression.

Therapist: Jordi, you like soda, right?
Jordi: I do. I like root beer, coke, and birch beer.
Therapist: Would you be willing to do an experiment with this that might help you with the labels others put on you and the ones you place on yourself?
Jordi: OK.
Therapist: Here's what we are going to do. I am going to pour soda into each of these cups. I want you to close your eyes so you do not see which cup has which soda. Are you willing to do that?
Jordi: Sure, then can I drink some? (Laughs.)
(The therapist then poured Pepsi in both cups but labeled one cup "Pepsi" and the other cup "Root Beer.")
Therapist: OK, open your eyes. Do you see the cups?
Jordi: Yeah.
Therapist: Are they labeled correctly?

Jordi: I guess so.

Therapist: Well, how do you know?

Jordi: You wrote them on the outside.

Therapist: So, the way you know they are labeled correctly is to take somebody's word for it?

Jordi: Sure, why not?

Therapist: Well, let's test it out. Take a drink from each cup.

Jordi: Hey, they are both Pepsi. There is no root beer!

Therapist: How do you know that?

Jordi: I could taste it and smell it.

Therapist: So the labels were wrong?

Jordi: Yeah. Can I have some more Pepsi?

Therapist: In a second. Let me understand this. The label I wrote on the outside was wrong. Did the label change what was truly on the inside?

Jordi: No. It stayed Pepsi.

Therapist: Hmm. So how much power does a label have to change what is inside?

Jordi: None, I guess.

Therapist: Let's write that down. Now, Jordi, I want you to properly label the cups.

(Jordi corrects the labels.)

Therapist: Now you put the right labels on?

Jordi: Yep, I did.

Therapist: When were you more in control, when I labeled what was inside or when you tested out the insides and came up with your own definition?

Jordi: When I did.

Therapist: What do you make of that?

Jordi (pause): I guess when I check things out and find out stuff, I can come up with correct labels.

Therapist: Do you think this applies to the labels others put on you and you accept?

Jordi: You know I think it does.

Therapist: Then let's write down that conclusion too.

The dialogue with Jordi highlights several points. The therapist crafted a systematic line of dialogue. The questions were simple and sequential (i.e., Are they labeled correctly? How do you know? Did the label change what was truly inside? So, how much power does label have to change what is truly inside?). Finally, the therapist worked with Jordi to write down new statements developed through the rational analysis.

Legal Metaphors

Leahy (2001) advocates the use of legal theory in cognitive and behavioral interventions. Rational and objective analysis of events is part of both legal and cognitive behavioral processes. In this section, three metaphors based on legal concepts are described.

Reasonable Person Rule

Leahy (2001) invoked the reasonable man doctrine for use in cognitive therapy. It is a legal term that basically assesses what a reasonable person would know or do. Second, Leahy offered a compelling question such as, "What are the traditional expectations about a person's behavior in the same situation?" Additionally, he recommends examining the behavioral intent and considering whether the action was deliberately malicious. The reasonable person rule and its accompanying questions are especially useful with adolescents carrying a strong sense of guilt, regret, and shame.

The Trial

De Oliveira (2008) proposed an innovative way to deal with self-accusations, which he termed *the trial*. De Oliveira based the approach on the Kafka (1925) novel of the same name. The trial is a clever adaptation of a test of evidence. The procedure also integrates role-playing, which adds an experiential component. During the therapeutic process, patients play the prosecutor, the defense attorney, and the jury. Situations, feelings, and thoughts are recorded on three columns. The prosecutor's evidence (data confirming the belief) is presented in column 4 and the defense attorney's evidence is listed in column 5. De Oliveira (2008) recommends telling the patient, "As a defense attorney you don't have to believe in the client's innocence, you only have to remain committed to creating reasonable doubt. The jury's role is evaluating the arguments" (p. 18). De Oliveira offered several very useful processing questions for jury deliberations:

> Whose arguments are more convincing?
> Who presented more evidence?
> Who made fewer distortions? (p. 18)

Fruit of the Poisonous Tree

Legal scholars and casual viewers of the *Law and Order* television series are familiar with the fruit of the poisonous tree doctrine. The fruit of the poisonous tree is a legal metaphor (Acker & Brody, 2004; Dressler, 2002). Simply, the fruit of the poisonous tree is an exclusionary rule that states that if the source of information or "evidence" is tainted, any additional evidence is similarly soiled (Acker & Brody, 2004). As such, the metaphor is apt for testing evidence of maladaptive beliefs.

The metaphor is quite vivid and flexible enough to be used with older elementary children. For younger children, the metaphor lends itself nicely to illustration (Form 9.4 and Figure 9.12). Similar to the other interventions, the metaphor is introduced and explained. Then, the source of the belief is identified (i.e., the tree). Derivative beliefs (the falling fruit) are collected and recorded. Third, therapists and patients Socratically process the thoughts. Finally, the patients make a conclusion.

The following example with Dana, a 12-year-old girl with obsessive-compulsive disorder (OCD), is informative.

Therapist: Dana, I am thinking of a new way to help you with your obsessive thoughts. How does that sound?

Dana: What is it?

Therapist: It's something called the fruit of the poisonous tree.

Dana: That sounds a little scary and freaky.

Therapist: Let me tell you about it and then we'll see what you think, OK?

Dana: OK.

Therapist: The fruit of the poisonous tree is something that lawyers and judges use to cast doubt on evidence. In simple terms, it says if your conclusions or beliefs are grounded on a wrong basis, they are inaccurate.

Dana: I'm not sure I understand.

Therapist: Another way to put it is that if the root or source of information has holes or flaws in it, then anything based on it is flawed.

Dana: Kind of like if someone spreads a rumor and people start to believe it spreads to other things. That's when my mom says consider the source.

Therapist: Exactly. So, let's put your source right here in the tree. What does your OCD say?

Dana: I am careless and a danger to others. I am a menace.

Therapist: Good, write that in your tree. Now, what thoughts and action come from the tree?

Dana: I think I have to be careful or I might hurt someone accidentally. I worry that I left the stove on or if I left the milk out too long and it will poison someone. I worry

Form 9.4 Fruit of the Poisonous Tree

Belief:

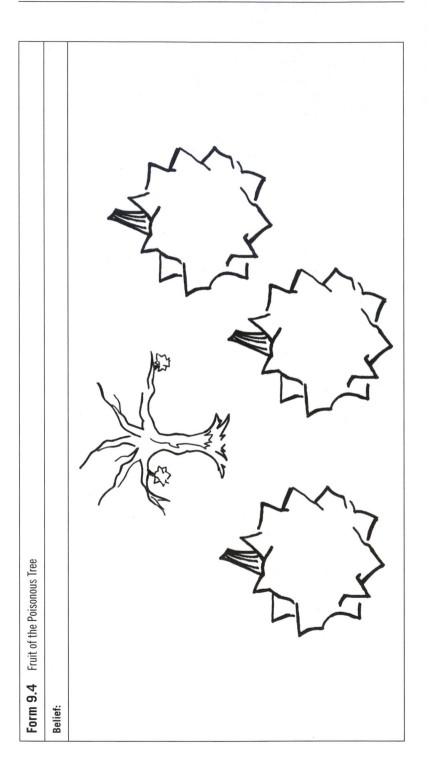

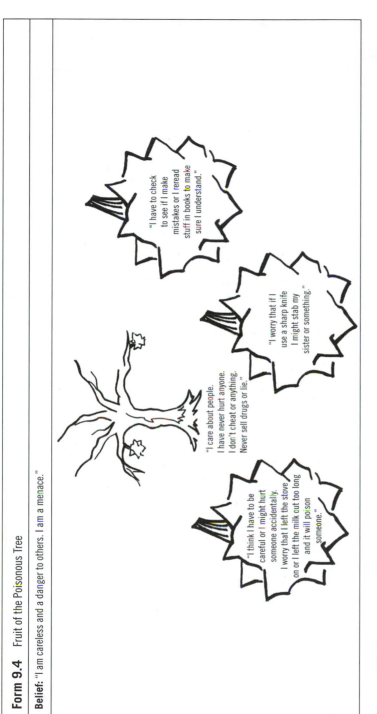

Form 9.4 Fruit of the Poisonous Tree

Belief: "I am careless and a danger to others. I am a menace."

"I have to check to see if I make mistakes or I reread stuff in books to make sure I understand."

"I worry that if I use a sharp knife I might stab my sister or something."

"I care about people. I have never hurt anyone. I don't cheat or anything. Never sell drugs or lie."

"I think I have to be careful or I might hurt someone accidentally. I worry that I left the stove on or I left the milk out too long and it will poison someone."

Figure 9.12 Dana's—Fruit of the Poisonous Tree.

that if I use a sharp knife I might stab my sister or something.

Therapist: How about the careless part?

Dana: I have to check to see if I make mistakes or I reread stuff in books to make sure I understand.

Therapist: These are all fruit from the tree. I am writing them in the fruit shapes. Which makes sense to you: to test all the fruit or to see if the source of the tree is poisoned?

Dana: See if the tree is poisoned.

Therapist: I agree. So let's look at what is in the poisonous tree. It says you are a danger to others and careless. How accurate do you see that to be?

Dana: I'm not sure.

Therapist: Well, let's look at the menace and danger to other parts. What do you do that a dangerous menace would not do?

Dana: I care about people. I have never hurt anyone. I don't cheat or anything.

Therapist: OK, go on. What does a dangerous menace do that you would never do?

Dana: Maybe sell drugs. Hurt people. Lie. Stuff like that.

Therapist: Now, I am going to write those things under the roots of the tree. Does this tree grow from those roots?

Dana: Hmm. I never saw it like that. I guess not.

Therapist: So, what do you make of that?

Dana: Huh … Maybe my thoughts and feelings may be poisoned. There's really no root to them.

Dana's work with her therapist is illustrative. First, she personalized the metaphor (i.e., "Kind of like if someone spreads a rumor and people start to believe it spreads to other things. That's when my mom says consider the source"). She then identified the belief that propelled various problematic behaviors, subsequent obsessions, and anxiety. Next, Dana and her therapist evaluated the source (e.g., the roots supporting her belief). Finally, Dana constructed a new conclusion.

CONCLUSION

Rational analysis is a difficult therapeutic exercise. You will likely have to stretch your skill set to flex your therapeutic muscle in this area. Practice, practice, practice, and patience are the rules in learning rational analysis. Remain mindful and faithful to the rubrics and rudiments as you progress through this skill set.

Ten

Behavioral Experiments and Exposure

INTRODUCTION

Behavioral experiments and exposure provide the *action* in cognitive behavioral psychotherapy (CBP). Experiments and exposure are based on experiential learning. Data is gained firsthand by the patient and then internalized via new interpretations, judgments, and conclusions. These direct personal encounters with heretofore dreaded and avoided circumstances create new life lessons for young patients and their families.

Although behavioral experiments and exposures may initially sound quite scientific, arcane, and perhaps a little daunting, they are firmly based in a common-sense rationale. The necessity of facing difficult moments and engaging in productive action rather than avoiding them is advocated by professionals and lay people alike. Eleanor Roosevelt's quote, "Do one thing every day that scares you" lives ubiquitously on posters, magnets, buttons, and greeting cards. In the closing song from the new musical, *The Addams Family* (Lippa, 2010), the characters urge, "When you face your nightmares, then you'll know what is real." Gilbert and Leahy (2007) remarked that graduated exposure is embedded in many cultural practices and worldviews. For example, they wrote that "in Buddhist practice, if you have a fear of death you might be encouraged to meditate on a corpse and to focus on the thought that all things decay" (p. 6).

This chapter deals with the rudiments and rubrics associated with these action-based strategies. Experiments and exposures are defined. Additionally, misconceptions regarding exposure are debunked. Requirements for clinicians doing exposure are outlined. The "Rubrics" section provides information on educating patients about exposure and offers several guidelines for implementing good experiments. Specific examples of exposures and their application to different problems are explained.

RUDIMENTS

Definitions and Functions of Experiments

Behavioral experiments and exposures are based on the concept of *enactive attainment* (Bandura, 1986). Bandura (1977b) wrote, "performance accomplishments provide the most dependable source of efficacy expectations because they are based on one's own personal experiences" (p. 81). Behavioral experimentation changes levels of emotional arousal, loosens rigid thinking patterns, and decreases firmly held patterns of avoidance (Rouf, Fennell, Westbrook, Cooper, & Bennett-Levy, 2004). A. T. Beck (1976) wrote that "the experiential approach exposes the patient to experiences that are in themselves powerful enough to change misconceptions" (p. 214). In the unified theory of emotional disorders, Barlow, Allen, and Choate (2004) emphasized that exposure and experiments develop new action tendencies. Typically, these new action tendencies are adaptive coping strategies. Simply, experiments and exposure help patients test their newly acquired skills in emotional evocative contexts (Purdon & Clark, 2005).

Exposure is a present-oriented experience. Exposure and experiential learning are here-and-now procedures (Richard, Lauterbach, & Gloster, 2007). Exposures require the self-regulation of attention. Consequently, the process is a mindful experience that demands "being very alert to what is occurring in the here and now" (Bishop et al., 2004, p. 232). The in-session exposure/experiment is a common way for youngsters to show the therapist they can perform the behavior in the context of emotional arousal.

Exposure increases perceived sense of emotional control. More specifically, exposure serves emotional regulation by "fostering the belief that one can continue to meet life's demands in the presence of aversive internal experiences" (Kollman, Brown, & Barlow, 2009, p. 233). Exposure and experiments help create added order in young people's chaotic inner worlds (Mineka & Thomas, 1999). Mineka and Thomas (1999) argued this increased control is a safety signal. Essentially, they learn they are in charge of the anxiety rather than the fear being in charge of them. Exposure and experiments rely on showing rather than telling.

At times, patients and therapists become too comfortable talking in therapy and neglect the components associated with acting differently (Waller, 2009). Vernon (2007) wrote "action often speaks louder than words and children and adolescents frequently remember what they have experienced more accurately than what they talked about" (p. 120). Accordingly, cognitive behavioral psychotherapists focus on helping patients practice and experiment with new behaviors (Rosenbaum & Ronen, 1998). A. T. Beck, Emery, and Greenberg (1985) believed that patients should engage in as much anxiety producing behavior as possible in session.

Experiential avoidance impacts many young patients. In fact, experiential avoidance is associated with substance use, trauma spectrum disorders, generalized anxiety disorder (GAD), and trichotillomania (Chawla & Ostafin, 2007). Valuable emotional resources are wasted when children expend time and effort trying to escape aversive private experiences (Kashdan, Barrios, Forsyth, & Steger, 2006). Anhedonia is a consequence of experiential avoidance (Gross & John, 2003). Moscovitch, Antony, and Swinson (2009) asserted that experiential acceptance is a central part of exposure treatment.

Exposure and experiments are emotionally evocative. Barlow (1988) referred to behavioral experiments and exposures. Exposure changes patients' view of emotions and their perceived capacity to deal with them (Leahy, 2007). They learn that emotions are not strange phenomena that have an unrelenting stranglehold over them (Samoilov & Goldfried, 2000). Because these experiments are emotionally provocative, they build self-corrective action tendencies. Hannesdottir and Ollendick (2007) urged, "It is one thing to teach children strategies in a relaxed office and quite another to actually use them in a stressful situation" (p. 286).

Experiments and exposures change attitudes. Experiments decrease the believability of negative assumptions and help build new expectations (Moses & Barlow, 2006; Rouf et al., 2004). Exposure provides a powerful disconfirming experience for children, adolescents, and their families (Bandura, 1977a). Most important, they achieve this realization by action and their own performance accomplishment. Rosqvist (2008) emphasized, "Exposure forces the system to recognize its error, through giving it the opportunity to encounter better evidence for what is truly dangerous and what is not" (p. 41).

Exposure is collaborative. Experiments and exposures are done with rather than to young patients. Therefore, they are always collaborative. Few avoidant people will want to face their distress. The collaboration is focused on the *willingness* to look dreaded circumstances in the eye (Hayes, Strosdahl, & Wilson, 1999; Huppert & Baker-Morissette, 2003). Empowering children to design their own experiments and following their lead allows children a greater sense of being in charge of their distress (Ginsburg & Kingery, 2007). Franklin and Foa (2008) instructed that "therapists should assure the patient that he or she would not use force to implement the exposure and that no exposure will be planned without the patient's consent" (p. 191). Velting, Setzer, and Albano (2004) recommended to therapists that the pace of exposure is greatly influenced by a child's motivation, age, and level of distress. Education regarding the exposure process is a key first step in fostering collaboration. Modeling also is a good way to enhance collaboration. Bieling, McCabe, and Antony (2006) noted that if people observe a trusted individual engage in the feared task first, they are more likely to approach the exposure.

Consider this example. Adam was an 18-year-old male patient with obsessive-compulsive disorder (OCD). He feared contamination by chemicals. Therefore, he avoided anyone or anything that came into contact with chemical agents such as household cleansers. In one exposure trial, I (RDF) filled a cup with liquid dish detergent and modeled dipping a finger into the solution.

Exposure results in new learning. Traditional notions of exposure treatment emphasize that exposure should continue until there is a 50% decline in anxious responding (Beidel & Turner, 2006; Podell, Mychailyszyn, Edmunds, Puleo, & Kendall, 2010). However, recent data and reviews suggest that the decline in emotional responding is not as important as creating new learning. The main point of exposures and experiments is to gain confidence and comfort in distressing situations.

Craske and Mystowski (2006) demonstrated that the degree of fear reduction and physiological habituation within an exposure trial are not consistently associated with better outcomes. This finding led Craske and Barlow (2008) to assert that tolerating anxiety, gaining a sense of increased self-efficacy, and building increased perceptions of control are pivotal. Learning a new relationship with the stimulus and emotional responding is central. Craske and Barlow (2008) emphasized, "We have moved away from the model of 'Stay in the situation until the anxiety has declined' to 'Stay in the situation until you have learned what you need to learn, and sometimes that means learning you can tolerate the fear'" (p. 30).

Graduated exposures approximate real-life circumstances. Exposure and experiments are based on transfer of learning. Transfer of learning is best facilitated when the emotional contexts of situations are most similar (Safran & Muran, 2001). The state dependent learning hypothesis informs us here. Coping skills acquired in similar circumstances to the one in which they are required are more likely to be successfully applied. Massad and Hulsey (2006) concluded that exposure intervention should resemble the circumstances surrounding the original learning context as much as possible. Fidaleo, Friedberg, Dennis, and Southworth (1996) showed that if you create an exposure designed to decrease a snake phobia by exposing the patient to a worm, it is unlikely to work well because the worm and the snake do not share the same dangerous properties.

Types of Exposure and Experiments

Graduated exposure. Graduated exposure/graded practice helps the patient lean into discomfort with small steps toward avoided circumstances. Graduated exposures are consistent with a skills-building approach (Allen & Rapee, 2005; Kendall & Suveg, 2006). Nonetheless, any exposure is difficult for children but graduated exposures do not overwhelm them (Silverman & Kurtines, 1996). Graduated exposure has the advantage of not scaring off patients with too intense encounters quickly (Craske & Barlow, 2001). Hierarchies constructed with Subjective Units of Distress (SUDS) ratings (Chapter 6) guide the way. By mastering their distress via successive steps, children gain confidence in their coping skills and their sense of control increases. In graduated exposure, starting at a moderate level of anxiety is a recommended strategy (Bieling et al., 2006).

Imaginal exposure. Imaginal exposure/experiments involve performing coping responses in one's mind's eye rather than in actuality (e.g., *in vivo*). Imaginal exposures may be done gradually or by flooding. They also can be used as a stepping stone paving the way toward *in vivo* exposure. There are several ways to augment the power of imaginal exposure. Dolls, puppets, toys, photos, videos, music, audiotapes of voices and sounds, and articles of clothing are helpful props (Deblinger, Behl, & Glickman, 2006; Faust, 2000; Saigh, 1987). Finally, incorporating vivid detailed scenes punctuated by strong sensory experience is a good idea (e.g., You smell _____. You see _____. The temperature is _____) (Padesky, 1988; Richard et al., 2007).

In vivo *exposure*. Kendall et al. (2005) refers to *in vivo* exposure as encountering stressors "live and in person" (p. 141). Essentially, *in vivo* experiments help children apply their acquired skills in their natural environment (Craske & Barlow, 2001). The majority of the tasks described later in the chapter are *in vivo* exposures. *In vivo* exposures may be presented gradually or in full.

Flooding. Flooding is sometimes erroneously seen as synonymous with exposure, but flooding is a subtype of exposure. "Flooding is a method in which the client is exposed to the maximum intensity fear-producing situation directly without any graduated approach" (Agras, Kazdin, & Wilson, 1979, p. 31). Therefore, no hierarchies are used and patients remain in contact with the most intense stimuli until their anxiety decreases. Not surprisingly, flooding is far more distressing to patients and harder to endure than graduated exposure (D'Eramo & Francis, 2004). Therefore, greater attrition may occur. Additionally, long-term gains are suspect (Rosqvist, 2005).

Implosive therapy. Implosive therapy (Hogan, 1968; Stampfl & Levis, 1968) deserves a brief mention mainly because our experience indicates it is often confused with flooding and exposure. Implosive therapy is actually based on psychodynamic tenets. Implosive therapy is an imagery-based approach based upon images supplied by the therapist emphasizing unconscious conflict areas such as fears, humiliations, deprivations, orality, anality, sexual concerns, aggression, rejection, loss of impulse control, and guilt. Generally, cognitive behavioral therapists eschew implosive therapy.

Response prevention/ritual prevention. Response prevention (RP) is the technical term for preventing patients' typical escape or avoidance response (Masters, Burish, Hollon, & Rimm, 1987). RP is useful for reducing compulsive behaviors. The focus of RP is to disrupt the connection between engaging in ritualistic behavior and sense of safety (Franklin, Riggs, & Pai, 2005). According to Richard et al. (2007), RP prevents maladaptive behavior and reinforces adaptive behavior. RP refers to children's own efforts at resisting efforts rather than the therapist forcing the patient to refrain.

What Is Required of the Therapist?

There are several requirements of clinicians doing exposure and behavioral experiments. Embedding the exposure and experiment in an accurate case conceptualization (Chapter 2) is a sine qua non. Clearly adhering to the stance variables in Chapter 3 is a launching point. Strong "psychological presence" is a requirement. Greenberg (2007) referred to presence as a state of undivided attention where therapists are fully focused on their patients' emotional experiences. "This means that therapists need to let go of their own specific concerns, the quarrel with their spouse in the morning, the falling value of the dollar or an upcoming vacation and truly show up for their session" (Greenberg, 2007, p. 54).

Grounding the technique in case conceptualization and surrounding it with a sound grasp of learning principles adds to a clinician's confidence. The beneficial effect of therapeutic confidence is well documented (Frank, 1961). Clinicians may worry that exposures and experiments may spin out of control. Pasteur noted that chance favors a prepared mind. Preparation may bolster a sense of control.

Accordingly, appreciate that experiments and exposures are deliberately planned interventions. We suggest clinicians develop a mental checklist for themselves when conducting experiments. Rouf et al. (2004) offered a comprehensive review of the critical issues in the various stages of experiments. Additionally, we integrated Rouf and colleagues' consideration with our clinical experiences to derive twelve points of experiments (POE). They are summarized in Table 10.1.

Table 10.1   Twelve Points of Experiments (POE)

1. Does the patient understand the rationale for exposure/experiments?
2. Is the exposure target properly specified?
3. Is the experiment/exposure graduated?
4. Does the graduated experiment approximate the real circumstance, so transfer of learning is facilitated?
5. How will data be collected?
6. Has the patient made specific, testable predictions?
7. Have possible problems been anticipated and prepared for?
8. Is the experience a no-lose situation?
9. Does the experiment address behavioral, somatic, cognitive, emotional, and interpersonal issues?
10. Are there medical concerns or possible contraindications?
11. Has the patient's doubts and worries about the procedure been processed?
12. How will the patient's maladaptive avoidance and safety-seeking behavior be addressed?

Misconceptions About Exposure and Experiments

Silverman and Kurtines (1997) argued that exposure is a common factor to all successful psychotherapies. Nonetheless, too many therapists do not provide exposure-based treatment when it is indicated (Hembree & Cahill, 2007; Waller, 2009). Becker, Zayfert, and Anderson (2004) reported that therapists tend to be unnecessarily uncomfortable with exposures and consequently avoid applying the procedure. Some of this reluctance can be traced to a lack of training and experience, but twisted clinical lore about exposure accounts for a large amount of the remaining unwillingness. This finding led Becker et al. to predict the use of exposure-based practices will greatly depend on clinicians' attitudes and beliefs. Several recent important articles have specifically tackled the myths surrounding exposure (Kendall et al., 2009; Olatuniji, Deacon, & Abramowitz, 2009).

You will need to be clear about what exposure is and is not. Upon learning that I (RDF) was doing exposure with a young patient, a former colleague wondered aloud and incredulously asked me, "Why would you want to do *that*?" thinking I was going to torment the young phobic child. She was fundamentally misinformed about the nature, purpose, and process of exposure. Exposure is one psychosocial intervention with extremely strong empirical support. Not applying the technique to appropriate clinical conditions would seem inhumane. Many professionals who are naïve about the procedure assume exposure is a form of torture. Although patients are initially distressed and quite uncomfortable during the early stages, no one is tortured. Remember you always obtain informed consent, and patients guide the process and have the option to end the procedure. The goal is to teach rather than torment.

Exposures are typically graduated, co-engineered therapeutic adventures that follow from the acquisition of facilitative coping skills (Chapters 6 through 9). Patients experience similar distress in exposure that they encounter on a regular basis in daily life and commonly bring them into treatment. The difference is during exposure, they face the distress in a controlled environment gently guided by therapist who helps them apply their acquired skills. For instance, a patient with OCD faces contaminated surfaces all the time. Developing a systematic series of treatment experiments focused on touching surfaces does not introduce the patient to an unfamiliar threat. Unfortunately, circumstances included in the exposure are all too familiar. The key difference is that as a therapist, you are helping the patient face rather than avoid his or her distress as well as constructing a genuine mastery experience.

Friedberg and McClure (2002) explained that many therapists may mistakenly believe exposure makes psychotherapy an "unsafe place." This is an example of the cognitive distortion process (e.g., all-or-none thinking, mental filtering). Therapists who hold this view are advocating that successful therapy is characterized by predominantly positive feelings and comfort (e.g., "happy talk"). However, CBP and most other established forms of psychotherapy (psychodynamic, gestalt, emotion-focused, etc.) recognize the importance of experiential enactment. Patients need to feel free to encounter negative emotions. For example, whenever one of my young patients experiences strong emotions in session, I (RDF) advise them that the clinic is the best place to have strong emotions (e.g., "This is what we are here for"). Richard and Gloster (2007) made the cogent point that aversive biomedical procedures such as chemotherapy and bone marrow treatments are commonly prescribed. These interventions are seen as efficacious ways to treat the patient. However, their use is generally unquestioned despite their unpleasant nature.

Many clinicians worry that exposure treatment damages the therapeutic relationship. Kendall et al. (2009) found that exposure trials did not adversely influence therapeutic alliance. Negative alliance ratings did not increase after the introduction of the in-session exposure. If experiments and exposures are properly designed and implemented, they demonstrate the clinicians' exquisite understanding of a patient's experience. Therefore, the therapeutic relationship may profit from effective exposures rather than becoming damaged by them.

RUBRICS

Exposure and Experiments Begin With Psychoeducation

There are several specific elements that should be included in psychoeducation regarding exposure (Hembree, Rauch, & Foa, 2003). Patients should learn that avoidance is worse than the anxiety. Further, they need to be aware that the anxiety will decrease with repeated practice. Youngsters and their families are being taught that persistence in the face of distress is a learned skill. Finally, therapists should teach young patients that successful exposure increases a sense of self-efficacy and perceived control.

Waves and alarms are common metaphors for psychoeducation about anxiety. The wave metaphor is a frequently used method to teach patients about the nature of anxiety and exposure (Pincus, Ehrenreich, & Spiegel, 2008; Shenk, 1993; Wagner, 2003). The wave metaphor can also be modified to a worry hill (Wagner, 2000, 2003). The steep part of the hill represents the incline where anxiety gets worse during the exposure before it gets better. However, with tolerance and endurance, habituation occurs. Wagner (2003) explains the worry hill in the following way:

> Learning to stop the OCD is like riding your bicycle up and down a hill. At first facing your fears and stopping your rituals feels like riding up a big "Worry Hill" because it is tough and you have to work very hard. If you keep going and don't give up, you get to the top of the Worry Hill. Once you get to the top, it's easy to coast down the hill. But you can only coast down the hill if you first get to the top. (p. 294)

Castro-Blanco (2010) offered a very illustrative but different wave metaphor. He compared distress to a child playing in the ocean. Waves, at times, will crest over the child's head. "The wave will pass and the child will remain unharmed if she or he realizes being overwhelmed is temporary and will quickly change. If he or she is able to remain calm and focus on the next wave, then the child can resurface and recover without further incident" (p. 132).

Alarms are useful metaphors for teaching about anxiety (A. T. Beck, 1976; A. T. Beck et al., 1985; Piacentini, Langley, & Roblek, 2007a, 2007b; Shenk, 1993). The simple axiom that the alarm is worse than the fire is a good way to show patients that anticipatory anxiety and avoidance is worse than the feared situation (A. T. Beck et al., 1985). Further, false alarms mark anxiety. False alarms are signals that inaccurately predict danger. Piacentini, March, and Franklin (2006) explained a false alarm as "even though there is no fire, the loud noise makes everyone nervous and they want to leave the situation" (p. 309).

Exposures Should Be Explicitly Processed

Exposures are constructed, conducted, and then debriefed with patients so they can draw their own conclusions and inferences (Rouf et al., 2004; Zinbarg, 2000). Boal (2002) insisted that emotions should not simply be experienced; they also must be understood and interpreted. This is a pivotal procedure because as previously mentioned the key is new learning. Wells (1997) developed a useful guideline as a rubric for processing exposure and experiments. The four steps are summarized via the acronym PETS. (P) reflects the preparation phase where patients and their families are oriented to the rationale of exposure, make predictions, and develop self-monitoring scales (SUDS, Chapter 6). The second phase (E) is the actual experiment or exposure. T follows the exposure and patients test their predictions. In the final stage (S), patients and their therapists synthesize and summarize the results with a conclusion.

Exposures and Experiments Should Be Developmentally Sensitive

Experiments and exposures should be tailored to fit children's and adolescents' capabilities (Gosch, Flannery-Schroeder, Mauro, & Compton, 2006). Friedberg, McClure, and Garcia (2009) argued that stimulating children's curiosity and adventuresome spirit is key. Using child-friendly language when describing exposure and experiments is another way to become developmentally sensitive. Terms such as therapeutic adventures, emotional showdowns, or behavioral throwdowns may be helpful. Rewards may be delivered contingently on children's attempts at experiments and exposures. Visual reminders such as videotapes and DVDs (Kendall, Choudhury, Hudson, & Webb, 2002) and photographs (Kearney & Albano, 2007) of the children's approach behaviors are rewarding.

Creative and fun exposures are recommended (Kendall & Suveg, 2006). Many exposures may incorporate games, puppets, and toys (Hirshfeld-Becker & Biederman, 2002). Ideas for fun exposures can come from unlikely sources. The television show *Minute to Win It* (Plestis, Puntillo, Olsson, & Millgardh, 2010) requires contestants to perform frustrating and unfamiliar tasks under time pressure. Accordingly, these games are engaging ways for children to apply their acquired skills. Several of these games are explained in the "Rudiments" section for angry and aggressive youngsters.

Consider this example. Jeremy is a 5 1/2-year-old boy diagnosed with pervasive developmental disorder (PDD). He had a very severe fear of "ghosts." His therapist decided to design an exposure that made use of his strong interest in trains and was within his developmental capacities. To capitalize on the imaginal component of his fear, Jeremy first drew a picture of a scary ghost. You can consider the describing and drawing of the frightening image as a form of graduated exposure. After the picture was drawn, Jeremy cut out the ghost with scissors. Next, Jeremy drew a picture of a train complete with an engine, passenger cars, and a caboose.

After all the drawings were made, the therapist put tape on the back of the ghost and stuck it on a wall inside the clinic that represented where Jeremy's train would pick up the scary passenger. Jeremy's train stopped at the station and picked up the ghost. The therapist then asked Jeremy, "You are the engineer and so you are in control of how far you take the ghost. Do you want to drop him off far away?" The train then travelled to the farthest corner of the clinic and the ghost was dropped off at a remote location. The therapist and Jeremy processed the experiment (e.g., "Who's in control, you or the ghost?" "Who decides when to pick up or leave the ghost?"). The experiment plus the processing yielded a greater sense of control for Jeremy and was developmentally sensitive.

Exposure Should Be Repeated and Prolonged

Once is never enough. Exposure needs to be repeated or prolonged (Barlow & Cerny, 1988; Craske & Barlow, 2008; Persons, 1989; Richard et al., 2007). Thus, in-session exposures should be augmented regularly with experiments between sessions in real-world contexts. Moreover, Moscovitch et al. (2009) advised that the best treatment outcome involves moderate levels of in-session arousal. Accordingly, they recommended multiple exposures should occur across contexts.

Daily practice is highly recommended. For instance, Tim, an adolescent male with obsessive-compulsive symptoms associated with overresponsibility and perfectionism, experimented with purposefully putting paper in the recycling bin at home and recyclables in the trash on a daily basis and then tolerating the possibility of disapproval for these actions.

Examples of Experiments and Exposures
Family Crafts

Craft-making kits are good behavioral experiments for family CBP (Friedberg, McClure, & Garcia, 2009). The family craft demands that family members cooperate to reach a goal. Family members must work to complete, for example, a necklace, lanyard, or bracelet. These craft kits can be purchased at toy stores as well as craft/hobby shops. Various roles are assigned during the craft (e.g., a person who gives the directions, person with beads, person with key chain, etc.). Regardless of the actual craft set you use, there are several clinical considerations.

Decide which family member is responsible for giving directions. To unsettle the family dynamics, you will likely want to select the more passive parent to give the directions. This will create necessary anxiety and ignite revealing thoughts, feelings, and behavior patterns. The other parent should be instructed to simply observe and complete a daily thought record (Chapter 6).

Explicitly process here-and-now thoughts and feelings. Friedberg (2009) explained, "The experiment ignites salient emotional reactions. Frequently, cognitive and emotional sparks fly when the craft is carried out. For example, beads spill, messes are made, and directions are imperfectly followed" (p. 6). Watch for emotionally salient moments during the task. When you identify these moments, capture the hot thoughts and then apply the cognitive restructuring or rational analysis techniques in the present context.

Experiment with different roles and ways of negotiating the craft and exercise. The key in this exercise is changing the way family members routinely function. Therefore, after the thoughts and feelings are identified in the previous steps, invite the family to do the task differently. This may include revising roles; experimenting with different approaches for task completion; or performing the task while modifying their expectations, beliefs, and assumptions.

Help the family draw conclusions. As previously stated, experience alone is not an efficient teacher. Meaning must be extracted from the experience. Accordingly, each family member should be encouraged to draw a conclusion or lesson from the experience. These conclusions could be written on index cards.

Board Games/Play Activities

Simple board games, which most mental health professionals have in their toy closet, are good exposure activities. Essentially, any game that produces a winner or loser is emotionally evocative. Games governed by rules also elicit children's problematic thoughts, feelings, and behaviors. Games have an ebb and flow, which tests children's frustration tolerance, performance fears, flexibility, and adherence to rules. Fortunately, in our clinic, a Wii game was donated. The Wii is both engaging and able to elicit competition and frustration. Nerf Hoops is also a favorite activity for experiments and exposures.

Survey Experiments

Rouf et al. (2004) explained that survey experiments collect a "broad sample of factual information or opinion about a question relevant to the patient's concerns" (p. 28). Survey experiments are essentially behavioral tests of evidence. First, children make predictions. Second, children and therapists craft nonleading survey questions to test the predictions. Third, children "go public" with the survey and gather data. Finally, after the survey data, children compare their predictions to the observed results.

Corbin was a 17-year-old with OCD marked by scrupulosity obsessions and compulsions. He lived a very restricted life. He became highly anxious around his peers when they did things he saw as immoral such as listening to rap music or watching sexy MTV videos. To loosen these moralistic imperatives, Corbin and his therapist designed several survey experiments.

Corbin believed if he told people he saw comedies like the *Hangover*, *Pineapple Express*, and *American Pie* they would see him as a "lawless out of control teenager who has sex and drugs on his mind." He then did a survey within the clinic asking "respondents" whether they had seen the movie and what opinion they had about him after he told them he saw the movie. He carried out the assignment in his home environment as well. After completing the survey, he compared his predicted to observed results. Subsequently, he was able to derive a conclusion that few people will judge him harshly after knowing he saw these typical teen movies.

Narrative Exposure

Narrative exposure involves writing about the trauma. Narrative exposure is most commonly used in trauma-focused cognitive behavior therapy (TF-CBT; Cohen, Deblinger, Mannarino, & Steer, 2004; Cohen & Mannarino, 2008). Narrative exposure and cognitive reprocessing help youngsters cope with traumatic memories, identify and modify cognitive errors, and place the trauma in a larger context (Cohen & Mannarino, 2008). This contextualization occurs because the narrative contains information about the child before and after the trauma. More specifically, the narrative may take various forms such as a book, poem, song, artwork, and even dance (Cohen & Mannarino, 2008). Generally, the written narratives are first-person accounts of the trauma. Narrative exposure also promotes social sharing of trauma (Van der Oord, Lucassen, Van Emmerik, & Emmelkamp, 2010). Writing about the trauma is also accompanied by Socratic questioning and cognitive restructuring.

Theater Games

The therapeutic use of theater games in CBP was first introduced in Chapter 7. Theater games are also excellent activities for exposures and experiments. Improvisational theater is an exciting medium for experiential learning because action occurs in real-time urgent circumstances that are unscripted (Landy, 2008). Fink (1990) emphasized that improvisation targets action rather than thoughts and feelings and keeps participants present focused. Wiener (1994) wrote that the fundamental risk is to "experience and act in the moment fully and without reservation" (p. 241). Improvisation encourages authentic and genuine expression (Boal, 2002). Therefore, it is well-suited as an experiment or exposure task.

Wiener (1994) listed a number of reasons improvisational exercises are recommended for psychotherapy. Improv lessens the demands for verbal processing and includes productive rules for interpersonal conduct as well as a heightened awareness of social norms. Wiener stated that improv teaches patients to pay attention to others' cues and support other people. Improvisational games propel cooperation, listening, speaking, problem solving, and flexibility. Kisiel et al. (2006) argued that theater-based approaches are multimodal and allow for application and acquisition of new cognitive and behavioral skills. Bedore (2004) wrote that "since our daily lives are unscripted, we are really doing improv all the time." Accordingly, improv theater helps children change rigid behavioral routines. Bedore (2004) and Friedberg, McClure, and Garcia (2009) recommended these activities for developing social skills, emotional tolerance, impulsivity, and emotional constriction. Bedore (2004), Rooyackers (1998), and Wiener (1994) are extremely robust resources stocked with numerous exercises.

Urban Improv (Freelance Players, 2004; Kisiel et al., 2006; Magis, 2004) is a violence prevention program for inner-city youth in Boston. Urban Improv consists of nine weekly sessions lasting 75 minutes each. A director and four actors run the program. The curriculum for fourth-graders includes friendship, self-esteem, imagination, peer pressure, fairness, violence/conflict resolution, sharing, and family. Urban Improv utilizes behavioral rehearsal, impulse control methods, assertiveness, and cooperation skills. Outcome evaluation showed that Urban Improv reduced aggression, enhanced prosocial behaviors, and increased self-control skills (Kisiel et al., 2006).

Applications to Different Clinical Problems

The chapter concludes with specific applications of the previous material to different clinical problems. Experiments and exposures for fear of emotions, fear of internal sensations, perfectionism, fear of negative evaluation, obsessions, separation, low frustration tolerance, and truncated perspective-taking are offered.

Fear of Emotions

Exposure and experiential methods may be applied to fear of emotions. Leahy (2007) claimed this emotional avoidance is mediated by fears of losing control and beliefs about the acceptability of emotions. Some perfectionistic children and adolescents see aversive negative emotions as personal flaws. Trosper, Buzzella, Bennett, and Ehrenreich (2009) discussed the role of emotion as a way to enhance emotional regulation. They recommended adopting a graduated approach. For instance, they suggested listening to songs, watching TV or movie vignettes, or reading a passage that elicits strong emotion. Patients are invited to note their reactions to the emotional arousal, which in turn increases their present awareness. Subsequently, patients progress to situational emotional exposure whereby they gradually approach specific situations where the avoided emotions are encountered.

In-session emotion exposure is useful for emotionally avoidant children, adolescents, and their families (Holland, 2003). A. T. Beck et al. (1979) advocated in-session emotional arousal to deal with "hot" problems and make use of state dependent learning. Noted emotional expression can be promoted by calling attention to feelings experienced in-session and empathic responses amplify the response. Typically, in these circumstances, the treatment relationship is a medium for the exposure.

Kari is a 6-year-old girl who was highly experientially avoidant. She referred to herself as a "fashion girl." The therapist and Kari then decided to do a feeling fashion show. The first step involved cutting doll clothes out of paper and designing an emotion to go with the clothes. She labeled the clothes (mad, sad, ashamed, afraid, and happy). After the clothes were labeled and colored with a crayon, a paper clip hanger was pasted on the top of the "outfit." Kari and her mother's homework included making a closet for each feeling. At the next meeting, Kari arranged each feeling in the closet with the easiest feeling to wear hanging in the front and the more difficult feeling to show pushed to the back of the closet. Kari and the therapist then processed the reasons for Kari's arrangement. Essentially, Kari and her therapist were creating a hierarchy for emotional displays.

The next stage of the experiment was the fashion show. In this graduated task, Kari picked a feeling from the front of the closet and shared times she "wore" the emotional outfit with others. Initially, she shared the feelings with the therapist and her mother. Next, she shared it with other clinic staff who were invited to the show. Finally, for homework, she shared her feeling fashions with other family members.

Fear of Internal Sensations

Many children and adolescents fear internal sensations. This is particularly true for youngsters with panic disorder (see content-specificity hypothesis described in Chapter 2). However, children who have an overly valued sense of control as well as a sort of physiological perfectionism may also fear their interoceptive sensations. In our clinical experience, these physiological perfectionists believe they never deviate from a "normal" or typical bodily state. They scan the body for signs of danger such as changes in temperature, itching, or a tickle in their throat causing them to cough. Children with sensory sensitivities may also be considered for interoceptive exposures.

Several clever and easy experiments are described in the literature. Antony, Ledley, Liss, and Swinson (2006) recommended breathing through a straw for 2 minutes to simulate hyperventilation. McKay and Moretz (2008) designed a very creative experiment to induce a sense of derealization. They invited patients to wear 3-D glasses for approximately 30 minutes while sitting in a chair. McKay and Moretz explained that the glasses promote visual hazing and "lead to the perception of prismatic light in the periphery" (p. 436). In their seminal chapter, Craske and Barlow (2008) suggested several interoceptive exposures including shaking the head from side to side for 30 seconds (dizziness), spinning in a swivel chair for

60 seconds (dizziness), and staring at the self in the mirror for 90 seconds (derealization).

Otto and Hinton (2006) implemented a culturally specific exposure trial for Cambodian refugees based on the game Hung. In Hung, players have to get a stick that is thrown a considerable distance away and bring it back to the base. However, the players have to hold their breath while running and come back to the starting point while making a "hung" sound. Otto and Hinton stated that the game resulted in light-headedness and dyspnea.

Consider this example. Greg was a 14-year-old male with panic disorder. He believed literally that people should never see you sweat. Similar to most other panic disordered patients, he believed anxiety itself was a harbinger of bad things to come. He was quite sensitive to changes in room temperature and highly attuned to his physiological sensations. Whenever he became warm, he checked his body for perspiration. If he felt himself perspire, he would automatically conclude, "I'm out of control. Something bad is going to happen."

Greg and his therapist collaboratively designed a simple and easy experiment for Greg's heat sensitivity. Greg gradually increased the thermostat in the therapist's office and focused his bodily sensations associated with the increased room temperature. He was also instructed to note the therapist's reaction to his increased perspiration. Finally, as the temperature rose, Greg agreed to hold a mirror in front of his face and scan for signs of perspiration and flushing.

Lucas was a 7-year-old boy with PDD who hated the sensation of crumbs on his hands. For instance, if he went to a fast-food restaurant and ordered french fries, ate them with his fingers, and got crumbs on his hands, his acute sensory sensitivity would kick in. Consequently, he would engage in furious hand shaking, licking his fingers, and screaming. A graduated series of experiments were designed. In session, Lucas agreed to dip his fingers in a cup filled with salt and tolerate the sensation of the granules on his hands. As his coping increased, Lucas increased the amount of salt on his hands and the length of time tolerating the sensation. Over the course of repeated trials, Lucas learned his temporary minor discomfort was not disastrous.

Perfectionism

Abramowitz (2001) recommended a number of excellent experiments for patients with obsessions and rigid rules about morality and perfectionism. For example, filling out a negative comment card in a restaurant or store, leaving a shopping cart in the parking lot instead of returning it to its cage, and laughing at a tasteless joke.

Improv theater games are well suited to perfectionism. Wiener (1994) described an easy game in which individuals interact with others and call common objects by the wrong name. Gibberish encounter (Wiener, 1994) is another theater game useful for anxious, rule-governed young people. In this exercise, the patient and you engage in a gibberish conversation. If you want to increase the challenge, you could go public with the gibberish encounter. Predictions could be made before going public. Then reactions could be observed and compared with the predictions.

Fear of Negative Evaluation

Many children with social anxiety and generalized anxiety disorder are approval seeking and consequently fear negative evaluation. They are often "too nice." These children may dread ever arriving late to any activity. Velting et al. (2004) suggested an experiment inviting a child to arrive 5 minutes late to a birthday party. Additionally, you could have the child plan to arrive 5 to 10 minutes late to your appointment. The child could make predictions about what would happen if they are late, then arrive late, and in session compare the observed to the predicted results.

Kendall et al. (2005) suggested asking for directions as an exposure for negative evaluation. Although this may seem to be a relatively benign task to people without social anxiety, genuinely social anxious youth will find it quite challenging. Consider this example. Tricia was a 17-year-old with rather severe social anxiety. She became quite distressed at going to Philadelphia on a trip with her school choir and the possibility of asking a policeman for directions. On her graduated hierarchy, this activity earned a SUDS rating of 7 on a 10-point scale. When asked about her beliefs about the experiment, Tricia replied, "I think the policeman will think we are up to no good."

Giving negative feedback is another graduated exposure task for youngsters who fear negative evaluation. The feedback component (Chapter 4) in each session gives patients regular practice. However, other simple assignments are also ways to develop new thought–feeling–action patterns. Placing a negative comment in a suggestion box is an example of a graduated task. Ordering in a restaurant, returning the food, trying on clothes and not buying them in a store, exchanging/returning items in a store are other examples.

Elaina was a 12-year-old socially anxious girl who was very uncomfortable asking store clerks about trying on clothes in the fitting room. She worried they thought the clothes were inappropriate or would not look good on her. Additionally, she worried that she might mistakenly exceed the number of items allowed in the fitting room. Accordingly, an experiment was designed where Elaina deliberately chose items that obviously were too small or big for her and carried in too many items into the fitting room.

Consider yet another example. Ruben was a 15-year-old young man who placed strict demands on himself always to be proper. Any social mistake or faux pas however small was unacceptable and created much distress. Ruben and his therapist constructed some simple experiments aimed at creating new learning. During one session, Ruben planned to call different extensions within the clinic and admit he dialed a wrong number. He made predictions about what others' reactions would be, called the number, and then recorded their actual reactions.

Separation Anxiety

Santucci, Ehrenreich, Trosper, Bennett, and Pincus (2009) described a treasure hunt procedure to help young children decrease their separation anxiety. Treasures (small prizes) were placed at various locations throughout the treatment facility. Children were required to separate from their parents to search for prizes. Podell et al. (2010) also described a scavenger hunt game in the clinic to help with separation.

Obsessive-Compulsive Disorder (OCD) Symptoms

Caron and Robin (2010) shared a number of engaging exposures for patients with OCD. For example, they created taste tests using an adolescent's favorite candies and sodas to help with excessive self-doubting. McKay, Storch, Nelson, Morales, and Moretz (2009) treated a young girl who avoided magazines, computers, newspapers, and TV shows for fear of seeing ads for sexual things that were specified as ads for Viagara and Levitra. Accordingly they designed an experiment where the patient would browse through magazine racks in a bookstore.

Marien, Storch, Geffken, and Murphy (2009) described a case of a 13-year-old female with OCD. Specifically, her obsessions dealt with her fear of being a homosexual and were activated by "sexual" stimuli such as movies, television shows, and going to beaches or malls where people dressed in revealing clothing. They designed exposure sessions where the patient watched a prohibited movie (e.g., *Dirty Dancing*), looked at taboo magazines (e.g., Victoria Secret catalogue), and sat across from a person in the food court who was wearing a short skirt.

Randi was a 7-year-old girl who experienced symmetry obsessions and compulsions. For Randi, clothes with elastic waistbands, socks, and shoelaces had to look and feel right. Using March and Mulle's (1998) recommended practice of distancing the child from the OCD, Randi renamed her OCD, "Mr. Just Right." Randi began to oppose Mr. Just Right's symmetry rules ("dissing him") with several experiments. Randi and her family put on fashion shows where she could wear her knee socks pulled up to different levels, shoelaces tied crookedly, and blouses tucked into shorts or skirts creating a "bunched up" look. Randi would then model these messed up outfits and then refrain from fixing them.

Low Frustration Tolerance and Poor Anger Management

Anger management procedures suffer from the classic skill application problem. Young patients are quite able to acquire anger management skills but struggle to apply them when they are pissed off. As Friedberg, McClure, and Garcia (2009) remarked, the trick is to help angry youngsters practice their skills in the raw and urgent circumstances when their anger is pumped up. The Coping Power program (Boxmeyer, Powell, Barry, & Pardini, 2007; Larson & Lochman, 2002; Lochman, Boxmeyer, Powell, Barry, & Pardini, 2010; Lochman & Wells, 2002a, 2002b) offers a number of excellent methods for practicing anger management.

Several *Minute to Win It* (Plestis et al., 2010) games provoke children's and adolescents' frustration and irritation. For example, a game titled "Movin on Up" is a fun experiment for children who are impulsive, disorganized, easily frustrated, or challenged by performance pressures. A player is given 49 blue plastic cups and 1 red cup. The cups are arranged with the red cup on the bottom of the stack. The child has to move the red cup up to the top by holding the stack in their hands and continuously raising the red cup up to the top of the stack by moving the blue cup from the top of the stack to the bottom of the stack. The child must alternate between their left and right hands. If they drop the stack of cups or neglect to alternate their hands, the game is over. "Loner" is another game that evokes frustration. An unsharpened pencil is placed on its end at the far side of a long table. The child is then seated at the opposite end of the table and given 20 tries in a minute to knock over the pencil by rolling a marble.

Imogene was a 12-year-old girl whose aggressive behavior was triggered by her 8-year-old sister's verbal and nonverbal behavior. If Imogene's sister tattled on her to her mother, Imogene would become enraged and physically attack her sister. Imogene was also quite sensitive to her sister's nonverbal behavior. For instance, if her sister looked smug or superior to Imogene, it would prompt assaultive behavior from Imogene. Following the acquisition of self-instructional anger management skills, Imogene agreed to an experiment.

Imogene and her sister played a game in the office with the therapist and their mother. It was explained to Imogene that the game rules would be slanted to favor her sister. Imogene was instructed to use her anger coping strategies when she felt her anger growing. The therapist and mother acted as coaches during the process. The experiment was graduated with the therapist supplying the sister with mildly to moderately provocative taunts to say during the game. When Imogene looked angry, she was prompted to apply coping thoughts.

Increasing Flexibility and Perspective Taking

Improv theater games are excellent ways to gain perspective. Wiener (1994) created an improvisational theater game called unfortunately/fortunately. The game can be played individually with a family or in a group. Simply, one person starts with a statement beginning with *fortunately* (e.g., Fortunately, I love football). The partner counters with a statement beginning with unfortunately (e.g., Unfortunately it is not football season). The exercise continues with the next person returning to fortunately and moving to the next person (unfortunately) until the game cannot continue.

Sofronoff and Beaumont (2009) described a very creative game called the secret agent transmission device. Children play with walkie-talkies and listen to a transmission trying to guess the speaker's emotion or perspective from their voice pitch, volume, and pace. Several board games are also helpful in increasing flexibility. *Too Much, Too Little, Just Right* (Weiss, Singer, & Feigenbaum, 2006) is specifically designed for children with PDD. Children adopt two roles: sender and receiver. They deliver and receive verbal and nonverbal messages that differ in the amount of emotional intensity (too much, too little, and just right). The game gives children experiential practice in detecting and sending subtle messages. Moreover, they receive feedback from others on their performance.

CONCLUSION

Exposures and experiments encourage young patients to take productive action. All the procedures included in this chapter are designed to yield new learning. In general, exposure and experiments help young patients learn that difficulty and discomfort do not equal disaster. This key module bolsters self-confidence by teaching children they can face down their emotional challenges. Experiments invite young people to "take their skills to the street" and test them in increasingly real circumstances.

Eleven

Incorporating Cognitive Behavioral Therapy Concepts Into Medication Management

INTRODUCTION

This chapter guides your integration of the previous cognitive behavioral psychotherapy (CBP) techniques explained in earlier chapters with medication management. Rudiments focus on the easy fit between pharmacotherapy and CBP as well as the importance of adopting a functional view of medication compliance. Rubrics include adhering to therapeutic stance variables, remaining mindful regarding cultural and familial context as well as remembering the modular format.

RUDIMENTS

The Easy Fit Between Pharmacotherapy and Cognitive Behavioral Psychotherapy

In her autobiography, Elizabeth Wurtzel wrote (1994),

> The secret I sometimes think that only I know is that Prozac really isn't that great. Of course, I can say this and still believe that Prozac was once the miracle that saved my life and jump started me out of a full time state of depression, which would seem to most people reason enough to think of the drug as manna from heaven. But after six years on Prozac, I know it is not the end but the beginning. (p. 304)

Her hard earned balanced view speaks to key points about integrating CBP into medication checks.

In his seminal work, A. T. Beck (1985) saw pharmacotherapy and CBP as points along an identical continuum. More specifically, he viewed biological and cognitive perspectives as examining neurochemical and information-processing paradigms reflecting the same phenomena from different angles. CBP is especially well suited to medication compliance because it is so active and solution focused (Marcinko, 2003; Wright, Basco, & Thase, 2006). Gabbard (2006) wrote, "Psychiatrists who do medication checks have long recognized that psychotherapeutic work with the patient may improve compliance with the medication regimen" (p. 317). In sum, the ideal child psychiatrist is seen as able to integrate CBP and pharmacotherapy (Ginsburg, Albano, Findling, Kratochvil, & Walkup, 2005).

Wright (2007) summarized the easy fit between CBP and pharmacotherapy. He cogently noted that both CBP and pharmacotherapy enjoy strong empirical support. Moreover, both approaches tend to be pragmatic, action focused, and outcome driven. Finally, both CBP and pharmacotherapy are applicable to multiple clinical populations.

Various outcome studies and practice parameter guidelines advocate combined treatment (Bernstein & Shaw, 1997; Pediatric OCD Treatment Study [POTS] Team, 2004; Treatment for Adolescents with Depression Study [TADS] Team, 2004). Combined CBP and pharmacotherapy is recommended for diverse disorders including obsessive-compulsive disorder (OCD; POTS Team, 2004) and most other anxiety disorders (Bernstein & Shaw, 1997). Moreover, combined treatment for adolescent depression is also indicated (March, Silva, Vitiello, & TADS Team, 2006; TADS Team, 2004). Seligman (1995) noted that combined psychotherapy and pharmacotherapy is favorably seen by consumers.

Using CBP techniques and procedures during medication checks is a form of integrated treatment. Riba and Balon (2009) referred to integrated treatment as combined pharmacotherapy and psychotherapy delivered by a single provider. Integrated treatment appears to avoid arbitrary distinctions between biology and behavior. Gabbard and Kay (2001) advocated that psychiatrists who can combine psychotherapeutic skills with pharmacotherapy are well suited to understand and process assumptions about medication. Nonetheless, providing both medication management and therapy can be challenging. We recommend the medication not be overvalued such that important functional and self-regulatory skills are ignored.

Adopt a Functional Analysis of the Behavior

Similar to much of the other conditions described in this book, medication noncompliance is seen as predominantly a learned behavior. Accordingly, Marcinko (2003) reminds us to examine the functional value or purpose of the medication noncompliance (Chapter 7). In addition to examining the actual antecedents and consequences of noncompliance, Marcinko recommends identifying the expected or hoped-for consequences of noncompliance or compliance. Various cognitive behavioral therapists see medication compliance as due to a number of psychological and practical factors (J. S. Beck, 2001; Marcinko, 2003). Practical issues may include poor access to medications, side effects, and misunderstanding of the prescription.

Consider this example. When I (RDF) was directing a brief therapy program housed in an internal medicine clinic, we would regularly receive referrals from the internists that were usually associated with medication compliance. An uneducated gentleman from a poor rural agricultural area was referred to the clinic for medication noncompliance. He arrived and presented in a perplexed manner. When asked what brought him into treatment, he held up several rectal suppositories and complained, "For the life of me no matter how much water I drink I can't ever swallow these gosh darn things." Was this medication noncompliance? No, he simply did not understand the prescription. Thus, a practical rather than a psychological reason mediated his noncompliance.

Psychological or emotional issues include worries about negative evaluation by others because of the medication, discomfort with the diagnosis, the expectation that emotional distress should be eliminated by the medication, or that problems should be handled without the medication. Exploring the triggers or cues for medication noncompliance is essential in developing an effective intervention plan. Moreover, examining the consequences (positive reinforcement, negative reinforcement, response cost, punishment) explained in Chapter 7 will give you clues how to interrupt the noncompliance.

RUBRICS

Adhere to Therapeutic Stance Variables

Adhering to the stance variables espoused in Chapter 3 will help you during med checks. These alliance-building skills will create an atmosphere of openness where families can discuss their beliefs about the illness, medications, themselves, and their clinician. Gabbard and Kay (2001) recommended that psychiatrists should always expect obstacles to medication compliance. Gabbard (2006) explained the "psychiatrist must be able to shift flexibly from the realm of automatic thoughts, core beliefs, meanings, object relations, and fantasies to the realm of neurotransmitters, side effects, and medical comorbidity" (p. 317).

Collaboration is a stance variable that is fundamentally relevant to medication checks. Recall from Chapter 3 that interventions are collaboratively constructed via consensus rather than through authoritarian fiat. Collaboration's cousin, guided discovery, emphasizes dialogue over debate. Guided discovery honors patients' subjective experiences. The third point mentioned in Chapter 3 (harvesting open and flexible attitudes) propels problem solving. Teaching there are many ways to solve problems is especially important when dealing with medication concerns.

Chapter 3 emphasized that trust is best earned the hard way through minute-to-minute transactions with patients rather than from a position of power. Omitting why questions from your repertoire is useful in both CBP and medication checks. Why questions push people to defensiveness and force them to rationalize their positions. Remember the why question drives relationships toward confrontation rather than collaboration.

Remain Mindful of Familial and Cultural Context Issues

Clay, Mordhorst, and Lehn (2002) reminded us that treatment that is not compatible with cultural context is doomed to poor adherence and outcome. Prescribing medicine, like CBP, takes place in a familial and cultural context. Adult caregivers often carry the responsibility of buying, monitoring, and sometimes administering the medicine.

The American healthcare system often reflects separate and unequal treatment for patients based on race and socioeconomic status. For instance, African Americans suffer higher rates of illnesses and death from all health conditions (Shelton, 2000). Brown and Sawyer (1998) reported that children from lower socioeconomic statuses are referred for medication more often than their more affluent counterparts. Moreover, Brown and Sawyer reviewed multiple studies demonstrating differential benefits, adverse side effects, and dose responses for specific medications for various racial and ethnic groups. In their review, they cited the National Institutes of Health's mandate for clinical populations to include at least 19% of underrepresented groups in their sample. Alarmingly,

Brown and Sawyer found only a single study that met this criterion.

Mayberry, Mili, and Ofili (2000) noted there is evidence that African Americans, Asian Americans, Hispanic Americans, and Native Americans are not benefiting from advances in healthcare. Mayberry et al. (2000) wrote, "The history of medical care in the United States is replete with examples of discriminatory practices that denied ethnic minorities access to services based on skin color. Thus, the medical care system of the past is correctly described as a racist institution and the legacy of racism should not be minimized" (p. 134). Thomas and Quinn (1991) pointed out that the Tuskegee syphilis study and its vestiges fomented mistrust of the American healthcare system and fueled worries that medicines will have a toxic effect. The take-away message is that mistrust has a legitimate foundation and needs to be sensitively addressed in a culturally responsive manner.

Gaw (2009) identified several sociocultural factors related to pharmacological treatment including physician biases, religious beliefs, and cost. Chaudhry, Neelam, Duddu, and Husain (2008) reported that there are variations in both diagnoses and prescription practices that are shaped by physician biases associated with patients' ethnocultural background. For instance, an African American has a greater chance of being diagnosed with a psychotic condition and prescribed a depot medication. Moreover, when using cost containment measures, drug formularies may neglect data on ethnocultural variations.

Marcinko (2003) noted that in many Latino families, mental illness and taking medicine is seen as weakness and recovery is in God's hands. Consequently, shame is associated with taking medication. Gaw (2009) noted that certain religious groups are not inclined to accept medications. Poverty is its own unique stressor and cultural group. Poverty also shapes medication compliance. Gaw said that limited financial resources force patients to make difficult choices between necessities (food, rent) and perceived luxuries (medicine).

Adopting a culturally responsive stance encouraged in Chapter 2 is recommended. In addition to addressing general ethnocultural issues impacting CBP, you will want to discuss any sociocultural issues germane to pharmacotherapy. Useful questions might include:

What cultural beliefs do you hold about medication?
How does your ethnic or religious group view medication?

What financial concerns about the medication do you
have?
Does the name, color, size, or form of the medication have
any special meaning for you?

Maintain Session Structure

Session structure (Chapter 4) is quite applicable to medication
checks. Friedman, Wright, Jarrett, and Thase (2006) stated that
session structure can unite both CBP and pharmacotherapy.
Remember that session structure fuels efficient and organized
work. This is particularly useful when pressed for time during
time-limited medication checks. Review of mood states and
agenda setting set the table for the content of your med check.
This will highlight crucial areas for clinical attention and
alert you toward trouble shooting. Moreover, collaboratively
setting agendas puts you and your patients on the same page.
Finally, eliciting feedback and summaries enhance the therapeutic alliance and limit potential for misunderstandings.

Remember the Modular Content

Psychoeducation

Psychoeducation about medications and disorders is a key concept in your medication management (Compton, Kratochvil, &
March, 2007; Singh, Pfeifer, Barzman, Kowatch, & DelBello,
2007). The processes described in Chapter 5 are helpful when
doing medication checks. For instance, Friedman et al. (2006)
suggested using videos, readings, and computer-assisted learning to teach parents and children about medication.

A critical factor to consider is the patient's and family's ability to tolerate risk. Any medication trial will incur some degree
of risk ranging from unpleasant side effects to worsening of the
presenting concerns. These risks will cause stress; different
families are able to deal with stress with varying degrees of
competence. Families may be in your office primarily because
of their difficulty coping with stress that is revealing itself in
the child's mood and behavior. Careful consideration needs
to be given to how a family may tolerate an adverse outcome.
Even expected side effects can have the potential to derail an
entire treatment plan if a particular family is unprepared for
or unable to deal with such stress.

Consider the following case example. Beth is a 10-year-old
girl who presents with symptoms consistent with posttraumatic
stress disorder following a fire that destroyed her family

home. Her parents appear to have been equally traumatized by the fire but are not seeking treatment secondary to financial constraints. Beth is experiencing severe hyperarousal, daily nightmares, and frequent flashbacks, which are significantly impairing her schoolwork as well as interfering with her friendships. Her family agrees to weekly individual therapy and a trial of sertraline for Beth's initial treatment plan. Beth experiences some increased restlessness with the initial doses of sertraline. Her parents become highly distressed and are not reassured that this restlessness will be, most likely, a short-lived effect while Beth is adjusting to the medication. They stop giving her the medication and cancel all of her scheduled therapy sessions.

It appears that the somewhat typical and to be expected side effects Beth experienced while adjusting to the medication were not tolerable to Beth's parents. Their own levels of untreated anxiety may have made it impossible to deal with any additional stress no matter how seemingly small or transient. More information about potential side effects and their likely duration as well as frequent contact by the physician's office may have aided the parents through the stress of Beth's adjustment to the medication and preserved the overall treatment plan. A simple psychoeducational intervention may have avoided this rupture in the treatment.

Another important point to consider involves split families. With the prevalence of divorce in our society and the high levels of contentiousness, dispute, and expressed emotion involved in many cases, it is imperative that psychoeducation be done for all parties involved. Otherwise, you risk alienating at least one of the parties, thus almost ensuring noncompliance in families with split custody or, perhaps even worse, compliance in one household and not in the other. Common topics to discuss include family members' differing opinions regarding the problematic symptoms, diagnoses, beliefs and views regarding medications, tolerance of potential and actual side effects, and goals for treatment. Addressing all parties' questions and concerns, helping them find common ground, and keeping them focused on the ultimate goal of relief of symptoms increases the probability of a positive outcome.

Consider the following case example. Aaron is a 9-year-old boy who presents to the clinic with his parents for symptoms of attention deficit hyperactivity disorder (ADHD) that clearly interfere with his ability to succeed in the school setting as his grades are consistently low despite testing that indicates a superior IQ. His parents are divorced and he spends every other week alternating between his mother's and father's house as both parents live in the same school district. After reviewing the risks and benefits of a stimulant trial, his mother readily consents to the medication trial. Aaron's father, clearly not as enthusiastic, expresses his consent as well anyway. The physician notices the father's apparent reservations about the medication but, pressed for time, does not probe further and prescribes methylphenidate.

During the monthly follow-up session, attended only by Aaron's mother, she states that the medication seems to work well and the school notices improvement, but comments that she gets reports that his behavior in school is more disruptive and he seems less focused on certain days. She thinks the father may not be giving Aaron the medication during his weeks with him, and Aaron has told her as much. Concerned, the physician calls Aaron's father, who states he has not been giving Aaron the medication because he hears it can make his son look like a zombie, lose weight, and make it difficult for him to sleep. He doesn't want to put his son through that.

The father agrees to come in for a session to discuss his concerns further. At that session, the physician listens to the father's concerns and then provides more detailed information on the medication and reassures the father that he will be monitoring for such side effects on a very regular basis and that if they occur, they can adjust the medication or even try something else. After the discussion, Aaron's father felt satisfied that his concerns had now been addressed and began giving the medication regularly. Aaron started consistently doing well in school. Had the physician not addressed the father's concerns and taken the time to provide psychoeducation on the medication and the process of regular reassessments of the effects of the medication, Aaron likely would have continued to have alternating weeks of baseline symptoms and improvement, which while better, is not the best outcome possible and would have deprived Aaron the opportunity to reach his full potential academically.

When working with children and adolescents, it is critical to determine the agendas for each person involved in the child's or adolescent's life. Concerns raised by a teacher or school personnel may be very different than the main concerns offered by the parents who often have differing opinions even between themselves. It is crucial to elicit the concerns from the child or adolescent as well. Having an understanding of the competing agendas will allow for clarification for the role of medication in the child's or teen's treatment and create opportunities to educate "the team" about appropriate expectations for this aspect of the treatment.

Consider the following case example: Jared is a 14-year-old young man with newly diagnosed bipolar II disorder. During the evaluation process, Jared's parents complained of his severe anger outbursts at home that are frightening to Jared's younger siblings and have resulted in damage to the family home. Jared's teachers are concerned about his disruptive behaviors in the classroom, which include frequent calling out, monopolizing class time with off-topic comments, poor attention span, and extreme fidgetiness. One teacher wrote in the comments section of the questionnaire provided, "He has the worst case of ADHD I have ever seen in my 20 years of teaching." Jared himself complains of racing thoughts, extreme irritability when with his friends, and trouble concentrating when he plays his guitar or video games, which are his two favorite pastimes. However, he also likes the "high" feelings he sometimes has and is afraid of losing that.

Having elicited these concerns from Jared and his team, the psychiatrist was able to tailor her explanation of bipolar II disorder and its treatment to address Jared's, his parents', and his teachers' concerns. By tailoring this explanation to include details from Jared's experiences, he and his parents were more comfortable with the treatment recommendations, which included a trial of valproic acid in addition to individual and family therapy. Similarly, education was provided to Jared's teachers about the overlap between ADHD and bipolar symptoms, which enabled them to be more supportive of Jared and to enact some behavioral strategies, including the opportunity to take breaks and nonverbal cues to help him monitor his calling out, and to ease his stress in the classroom.

Without clarification of the differing concerns and agendas, an opportunity would have been lost to understand how Jared's illness is impacting the different areas of his life. This understanding allows the psychiatrist to frame Jared's illness in a manner that allows him to more readily endorse the treatment plan and will help with treatment compliance. Similarly, the school team is able to enact behavioral strategies to help Jared be more successful in school as a result of understanding his challenges in the classroom and clarifying the school team's understanding of his needs.

Psychoeducation about the medication should minimally address the reasons for the medication; a description of the medication; information on dosage, timing, and ways to take the medication; timelines for assessing the efficacy; discussion of side effects; and ways of dealing with these side effects. Compton et al. (2007) reminds us that whenever medication is being considered, patients should be educated about its risks and benefits. Therefore, doing a benefit–risk analysis with patients is a good strategy. Indeed, this is conceptually similar to the advantages and disadvantages technique explained in Chapter 8. Compton and colleagues encouraged clinicians to provide medication guides for patients and their families. Information on medications can be found at: www.fda.gov/drugs or www.medlineplus.gov. Medscape (www.medscape.com) provides physicians extensive information about medications. Pamphlets tailored for patients and their families with customized information, including the physician's or practice name as well as telephone numbers families should use to address medication concerns, can be printed from the site once a free registration is completed.

For family or school team members wishing to learn more about medication use, *Straight Talk About Psychiatric Medications for Kids* (3rd ed.) by Wilens (2008) is a good reference. Most pharmaceutical companies maintain Web sites for their brand-name medications, which can include useful educational materials and monitoring tools. Make sure you are thoroughly familiar with the Web site before you endorse it to a family and stress that you are referencing the site only for the useful material it provides. If you fear there may be a perceived conflict of interest, either provide the material directly (realizing it will be prominently branded with the medication name) or elect to obtain similar materials elsewhere. The American Academy of Child and Adolescent Psychiatry also offers fact sheets for families on medications.

Self-Monitoring

When considering a medication trial, it is important to agree on outcome measures to evaluate the efficacy of the medication. Wright et al. (2006) recommended systematically adopting a strategy to address specific obstacles and set measurable goals for improved adherence. Regular check-ins on medication compliance and response are key. Knowing what type of data to collect can be challenging. Collecting the wrong data can make an effective medication appear ineffective and lead to faulty clinical decisions. Parent or teacher rating scales can be used to monitor outcomes. Self-report measures such as the Children's Depression Inventory (CDI) can be effective measures of progress. Daily thought records are useful ways to help parents and children identify expectations and assumptions associated with medication issues.

Behavioral

Evaluating behavioral targets (e.g., in-seat behavior) is a helpful strategy because they can be objective measures of progress. As mentioned in Chapter 6, behavioral targets should be easily operationalized in multiple environments. Remember the behavior should be clearly described so that observers in different settings, such as school and home, can measure the behavior similarly. A baseline of the target behavior should be obtained before starting any medication trial. It can be tempting to skip this step particularly when a patient is presenting with significant symptoms, but the absence of a baseline makes interpretation of medication efficacy difficult at best and near meaningless at worst.

Consider the following case example. Ethan is a 5-year-old boy with Asperger's syndrome. He attends a traditional kindergarten class with the assistance of an aide. He is doing well academically but is struggling in meeting the classroom rules and expectations. He also has difficulty getting along with the other children at school and his siblings at home. When Ethan encounters something he does not like or another child speaks to him, he throws behavioral tantrums where he throws himself to the ground, yelling and screaming. He also becomes assaultive and self-injurious when highly agitated. These behaviors are jeopardizing his current school placement and causing severe problems at home. Multiple behavioral plans have been implemented with no reported improvement.

Ethan's parents agreed to a trial of risperidone. Baseline data of number of minutes per day on the floor during tantrums as well as daily attempts at hitting others and himself were obtained over 2 weeks' time. The family and school team agreed to continue his current behavioral plan without modification for the next 2 months. At the 4-week medication follow-up appointment after beginning risperidone, Ethan's teachers and parents expressed frustration at his continuing tantrums and aggressive behaviors. Analysis of the data revealed a 40% reduction in number of minutes per day on the floor having a tantrum and a reduction of average attempts at hurting others from 4 per day to 1.5 per day. However, he was no longer attempting to hit himself. Based on these results, Ethan's parents and the treatment team agreed to continue the current dose of risperidone for another 4 weeks. If the data did not improve over that time frame, consideration was given to increasing the dose at the next follow-up appointment. Fortunately, Ethan's behavior continued to improve at the 4-week follow-up appointment.

Without the support of the behavioral data, Ethan's parents' and teacher's frustration at his continuing tantrums and attempts to hurt others might have led to a misstep in his treatment. If the baseline and current data were missing, the treating physician could have been influenced by their expressed frustration to change course. The effort in obtaining the baseline data paid off in demonstrating the partial treatment effect of the initial dose of risperidone. Continued data collection assessed the ongoing efficacy of the trial and was useful in determining whether an increased dose may be indicated. Data collection can be utilized in determining the appropriateness of attempted reductions in medication when a period of stability has been achieved. Further, data is reassuring to parents and providers that progress is being made and when combined with anecdotal reporting can reliably guide treatment decisions.

Emotional

Mood charting is a recommended practice for tracking depressed and manic moods (Singh et al., 2007). Moreover, regular monitoring of depressed moods and suicidal ideation via a CDI or Beck Depression Inventory (BDI)-II is a clinically responsive way to respond to the Food and Drug Administration (FDA) black box warnings about antidepressant use in pediatric populations. Referring to the measures listed in Chapter 2 should be quite helpful.

Consider the following case example. Joey was a 14-year-old boy who initially presented with severe depression. Initial therapy efforts were unsuccessful in lowering his CDI score below 20. A trial of fluoxetine was initiated at a dose of 10 mg/day after discussing the medication's potential side effects with Joey and his parents. Joey's CDI score lowered to 12 after 4 weeks of the medication and continuing therapy. Joey's parents requested that the medication be stopped because they felt it was ineffective. They were frustrated that he remained irritable when they asked him to make his bed or made other requests of him.

The family considered the medication trial to be a failure despite Joey reporting a significant decrease in vegetative symptoms because they were expecting a better relationship with him as an outcome of this intervention. The physician working with Joey and his family was able to point to the reduction in the CDI score as a positive indicator of the treatment progress. Without this, an effective intervention might have been abandoned. Clarifying appropriate expectations for fluoxetine (which do not include fixing adolescents' disdain of chores) through cognitive self-monitoring would help the family more accurately evaluate the effectiveness of this trial.

Cognitive

In the initial CBP manual on depression, A. T. Beck, Rush, Shaw, and Emery (1979) warned that patients' negative cognitions contribute to medication noncompliance. Beck et al. noted that dysphoric patients selectively attend to medication side effects. Moreover, dealing with the patients' and families' expectations about the medication is fundamental (Tasman, Riba, & Silk, 2000). Therefore, using thought diaries (Chapter 6) to capture beliefs is crucial.

Behavioral Interventions

Contingency contracting is an effective way to impel medication compliance (Lemanek, Kamps, & Chung, 2001). Designing and implementing a contingency contract according to the rudiments recommended in Chapter 7 is a reasonable starting point. Taking the medication properly is the target behavior. Tokens, stickers, or points are added or subtracted based on the compliance. Small prizes and privileges can be exchanged when short-term goals are met. Larger rewards follow attaining longer-term compliance rates.

Prompts (Chapter 7) and behavioral aids are also useful. For instance, weekly or monthly pill boxes, which can be purchased at local pharmacies, are effective pill counters and reminders. Calendars and activity schedules (Chapter 7) are other potential tools. Pairing taking the medication with pleasant activities (e.g., watching cartoons, drinking favorite soft drink, listening to music, etc.) is also reinforcing.

For children who are afraid of swallowing a pill, graduated tasks are productive ideas. Children might start with trying to swallow an ice cream sprinkle, progress to a Tic Tac breath mint, and so on until they reach the goal of swallowing the actual pill. Empty gelatin capsules can be prescribed in different sizes to further desensitize children who struggle with pill swallowing. A size 4 capsule is average sized (remember the smaller the number, the bigger the capsule). Relaxation training (Chapter 7) is another means to decrease the anxiety associated with pill swallowing.

Cognitive Interventions

Processing children's and parents' misgivings about medication is important. Newman (2003) urged, "We cannot merely patronize our patients by giving them rote platitudes about the need to take their medication without also striving to understand their fears, misgivings, and opinions about the matter" (p. 156). Indeed, dealing with the patient and family's expectations about the effectiveness of the medications is fundamental (Tasman et al., 2000).

Marcinko (2003) cogently summarized various cognitive restructuring interventions for medication compliance. For example, she suggested using prediction when processing children's and their families' beliefs about medication (e.g., What do you think will happen with or without medicine? What side effects do you imagine will happen? How bad or uncomfortable might they be?). Then, these predictions could be tested by inviting patients and their families to chart the effects over time. Additionally, tests of evidence (Chapter 9) can be applied to assumptions about medicine (e.g., What is the evidence for and against people being weak if they take medicine?). Following are common examples of children's and parents' beliefs and ways to test them.

"*Taking medicine means my child is worse than I thought.*" As a CB psychotherapist, you recognize this belief as an inaccurate cause-and-effect relationship. Parents believe the medicine magnifies the problem. A test of evidence is indicated. You might construct a dialogue using some of the following questions:

> When your child is not taking medicine, how well is he or she doing?
> What happens to your child's behavior and functioning when she or he is not taking medicine?
> If taking medicine means he or she is worse, what would you see in his or her behavior when on or off medication?

What positive effects of medicine could be experienced?
If medication improves your child's mood and behavior, how can she or he be worse on the medication?

"Medication is a crutch for my child. He should just cowboy up!" In this instance, you can rely on universal definitions and other rational analysis techniques (Chapter 9). It would seem important to define what the parent means by "crutch" and "cowboy up." Helping the parent define terms and adopt a third-person perspective with some of the following Socratic questions is a good strategy.

What does a crutch mean to you?
How are you defining a crutch?
What are some positive aspects of a crutch?
If someone broke an ankle, would using a crutch be a bad idea?
Are people who have broken ankles and try to walk without a cast, better, stronger, and more in control individuals?

"I don't need medicine." As a CB psychotherapist, you recognize this as a hypothesis that is based on an empirical question. Adopting a curious, collaborative approach that remains faithful to scientific mindedness is far better than arguing with the patient. Moreover, the treatment alliance is strengthened by this stance. Your job here is to invite the patient to design an experiment replete with data collection methods to evaluate the question. Patients will need to be educated about the symptoms and the effects of medication or lack of medication on them. Additionally, information on the use of outcome measures to track progress will need to be provided. Questions to discuss with the patient might include:

How will you know that you need medication or not?
What type of data or information should be collected?
What reliable and objective measures should we use?
When should we start tracking symptoms?
How long should we track the symptoms?
What should the goal be?

"My child will become a zombie and not have any emotions." You readily see this thought as a form of catastrophizing, labeling, and all-or-none thinking. First, you will want to help the parent develop universal definitions (Chapter 9).

Second, you will address the all-or-none view of emotions. Finally, applying a decatastrophizing intervention (Chapter 9) is a good strategy. Helpful Socratic questions might be:

> What do you mean by a zombie?
> In what ways do you see him possibly acting like a zombie?
>> In what ways would he be different from a zombie?
> What emotions would be eliminated?
> Let's list all of his potential emotions. Now let's rate how strongly he feels them now without medicine. Next, let's make predictions about how strongly he will feel these emotions on the medication. Would you be willing to experiment for ____ weeks and see if these predictions come true?

"Medications will solve all my child's problems." When considering medications for a patient, there are a number of factors to weigh, the most important being the meaning taking medication will have for the patient and his or her family. It is important that medication be viewed as another tool in the patient's toolbox and not simply a passive means of obtaining relief from the presenting concerns. The framing of appropriate expectations is critical for an accurate evaluation of a medication trial's efficacy. Therefore, useful questions might be:

> What problems do you think the medication will solve?
> What problems are likely to remain even after the medication is introduced?
> When problems remain after the initiation of the medicine, what will that mean to you?
> How can you deal with problems that are still present after the introduction of the medicine?

CONCLUSION

Integration of CBP techniques with medication management can significantly enhance the therapeutic relationship between the physician and the patient, thus increasing adherence to the treatment plan and increasing the probability of a successful outcome. Following the rudiments and rubrics laid out in this chapter and the earlier parts of the book, you should have the beginnings of a solid foundation that will allow for successful combination of these treatment modalities. With physicians being increasingly pressed for time to follow up with patients, having the ability and skills to incorporate CBP techniques into a medication follow-up appointment becomes immensely valuable.

One of the most stressful challenges a family can face is the illness of a child. When the child is struggling with a mental illness, families often have the added burden of dealing with their preconceived ideas about the disorder and its treatment, particularly when part of the treatment entails medication. Child mental health professionals have the unique perspective of dealing with these disorders on a daily basis; we sometimes forget the impact our work has on the lives of these families. What might be just another med check to us can be a monumental decision for the families we are treating. The considerations and steps outlined in this chapter not only promote better treatment outcomes, they ensure that families are cared for in the process.

Twelve

Improving as a Cognitive Behavioral Psychotherapist

INTRODUCTION

Improving as a cognitive therapist requires self-reflection. Reflection is essential for flexible adaptation into an independent professional context (Sheikh, Milne, & MacGregor, 2007). Further, Bennett-Levy (2006) argued that self-reflection is the main way psychotherapists earn clinical wisdom and self-improvement. According to Bennett-Levy (2006), reflection requires focused attention and may be prompted by discomfort, curiosity, a supervisor's questions, or formal learning.

Nonetheless, self-reflection is anxiety producing. Consequently, improving as a cognitive behavioral psychotherapist requires a bit of courage to travel outside your comfort zones. Courage, for Overholser (1999), is the commitment to act upon accurate beliefs even when fearful. More specifically, courage is demonstrated by the conviction to face one's fears even when avoidance is a genuine option. Overholser (1999) emphasized that courage is fundamental to "boldness of action" (p. 140), which involves relying upon tolerance of discomfort and determination to directly meet challenges. We encourage you to be both bold and brave in your clinical work.

Friedberg, McClure, and Garcia (2009) reminded clinicians, "Cognitive therapy is work, not magic" (p. 292). In this chapter, we offer guidelines for self-reflection and improving as a cognitive behavioral psychotherapist. The tips focus on accurately defining competence and dealing with pressures associated with the work. The overriding emphasis is placed on committing to do cognitive behavioral psychotherapy (CBP) on yourself. Rubrics help you embrace being imperfect, deal with rejection and disapproval, manage fears of loss of control, earn emotional tolerance, tolerate doubt and ambiguity, address fears of patients' anger, work with doubts about competence, avoid burnout, resist drift, and step into lifelong learning.

RUDIMENTS

Worries About Competence

Barber, Sharpless, Klosterman, and McCarthy (2007) saw competence as a process where knowledge, techniques, and reasoning is acquired and applied. Moreover, they defined competence in dimensional rather than in categorical terms. Competence is seen as a relative rather than an all-or-none process. You own a place on a competence continuum rather than in a competent or incompetent box. Consequently, we encourage you to focus on improving your level of competence in CBP rather than making absolute judgments.

Frequently, new CBP therapists base their competence on their subjective emotional state. Schmidt (1979) found that beginning therapists make errors in using their feelings of confusion, boredom, anxiety, or anger to support the faulty belief that "good therapists don't have these negative feelings about their work." This is a form of emotional reasoning. Schulte, Bochum, and Eifert (2002) reported that cognitive behavioral practitioners changed treatment strategies based on their subjectively felt emotion. Waller (2009) urged cognitive behavioral practitioners to be mindful of their emotional state in order to not be misled by them. Thus, while your emotions can be good cues in CBP, be cautious about basing your decisions predominantly on your emotions.

Less competent therapists tend to overestimate their competence (Brosnan, Reynolds, & Moore, 2008). More specifically, Brosnan et al. (2008) found this inaccuracy was most pronounced in the interpersonal and cognitive behavioral techniques domains. Finally, they concluded that this naïve overestimation was a function of attention to irrelevant cues such as patients' appreciation of therapy. On the other hand, competent therapists based their self-appraisals on judgments regarding the quality of guided discovery.

Working With Dysfunctional Beliefs: Do Cognitive Behavioral Psychotherapy on Yourself

Burns (2002) in a humorous but compelling article on trainees' beliefs wrote,

> In specific situations where one's therapy competencies are or are perceived as being evaluated, some pretty spooky things happen. Underlying this is the propensity to process all incoming information in a therapist-referent mode which is distorted by a number of information processing biases including dichotomous thinking, arbitrary inference, emotional reasoning, and generally scaring the shit out of oneself. (p. 367)

Freeman, Pretzer, Fleming, and Simon (1990) identified a number of specific distorted beliefs that challenge CBP clinicians. For instance, they noted beginning therapists may think "I must be successful with all my patients," "If I fail, I am a lousy therapist and person," "I must succeed with impossible clients where others have failed," "I must be greatly respected, admired, and approved of by all my patients," "I shouldn't have to do any work, reading, thinking, or preparation outside of the therapy session." Does any of this sound familiar?

Remember psychotherapeutic work is stressful and emotionally messy. In the original manual for cognitive therapy of depression, A. T. Beck, Rush, Shaw, and Emery (1979) encouraged psychotherapists to remain vigilant in addressing their own thoughts and feelings. Burns (1989) wrote, "We bring our own vulnerabilities and shortcomings to the therapeutic process" (p. 510). Rosenbaum and Ronen (1998) emphasized that cognitive behavioral therapists must explore their therapeutic selves by examining their inner experiences. Finally, Lombardo, Milne, and Proctor (2009) argued that therapists' negative thoughts and feelings during the course of CBP compromise concentration and truncate motivation.

Rosenbaum and Ronen (1998) asserted, "We believe that CBT is not only a profession but also a philosophy of life; a way of living. You cannot ask your clients (or your supervisees) to practice this approach while you do not live according to its principles" (p. 224). Therefore, one of the best ways to improve your CBP skills is to try them on yourself (J. S. Beck, 1995; Bennett-Levy, 2001; Nezu, Saad, & Nezu, 2000; Padesky, 1996; Reilly, 2000; Rosenbaum & Ronen, 1998). Sudak, Beck, and Wright (2003) remarked that psychiatric residents who did cognitive therapy on themselves tended to have a fuller appreciation of the techniques than residents who did not apply the techniques to themselves. Further, Bennett-Levy (2003) found that self-practice increased application of cognitive behavioral techniques in sessions including assigning homework, designing behavioral experiments, and facilitating guided discovery. Self-practice also helped therapists prepare for inevitable difficult moments in therapy. Not surprisingly, therapists who applied CBP to themselves were more flexible and adaptable in their clinical work.

Avoiding the Procrustean Bed

Kuyken, Padesky, and Dudley (2008b) reminded us that the Procrustean fable teaches that one size never fits all. According to Greek mythology, Procrustes was a sort of inn keeper who offered travelers a meal and a night's rest in his very special bed. Once guests reclined on the bed, Procrustes cut off their legs if they were too long for the bed or stretched them out on the rack if they were too short. We must mindfully address individual differences and unique contexts if we are to avoid the Procrustean bed. Throughout this book, we advocated an approach that embraces individual differences mediated by cultural and developmental differences. Alertness to cultural and developmental variations in both CBP and medication management diminishes a one-size-must-fit-all mentality.

RUBRICS

Developing a Learning Outcomes List

You have already learned about the importance of goal setting (Chapter 7). Developing your own learning goals and crafting ways to measure progress toward your goals is a good first step toward increasing confidence and competence. A learning outcomes list is commonly used in clinical supervision (Milne, 2008).

Similar to other goals, learning outcomes need to be operationalized. Step 1 involves identifying the general goal (e.g., improving with agenda setting). Next, you need to break down the goal into essential components (e.g., setting agendas in sessions 90% of the time; checking in and obtaining collaboration 90% of the time). Third, develop a rating scale for meeting your goal (e.g., 0–4). Finally, decide on a period for evaluation (e.g., rate myself daily for 3 weeks). Form 12.1 gives you a template for recording your progress.

Tolerating Doubt and Ambiguity

Javert, the driven and rigid moralist in the classical musical *Les Misérables* (Kretzmer, 1988), honors certainty when he

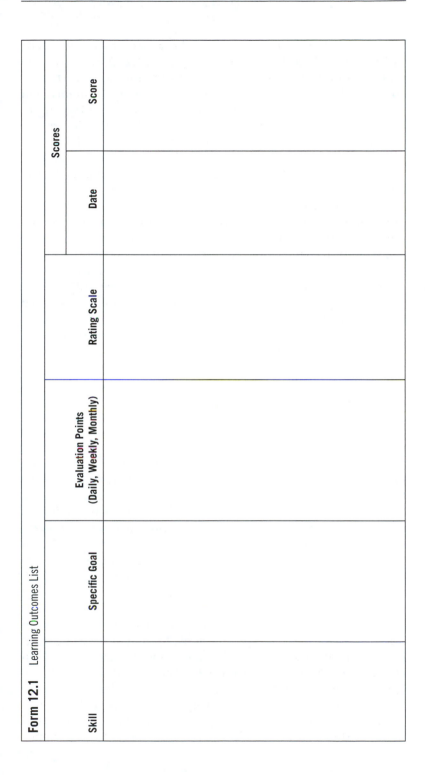

Form 12.1 Learning Outcomes List

Skill	Specific Goal	Evaluation Points (Daily, Weekly, Monthly)	Rating Scale	Scores	
				Date	Score

proclaims, "Stars in your multitudes/Scarce to be counted/
Filling the darkness/With order and light/You are the
sentinels/Silent and sure." Although stars maintain certainty,
cognitive behavioral psychotherapists cannot. As mentioned
in Chapter 1, tolerance of ambiguity and doubt is a key ingredient in the recipe for a good cognitive therapist. Trying to
excessively limit ambiguity prompts an overly reductionis-
tic approach to CBP. Additionally, this propels a stance that
tries to fit the patient into the model rather than matching the
model to patients' circumstances and characteristics.

When thinking about encountering intolerance for ambiguity, Angela Gorman (one of the contributors to this book)
recalled working with a depressed adolescent patient who presented with passive suicidal ideation and often complained, "I
wish I could just go away from here." Gorman monitored the
patient's progress with Beck Depression Inventory (BDI)-II and
the Beck Hopelessness Scale (BHS). Over time, the scores failed
to change and prompted Gorman to think she was not helping
her. Gorman believed, "Her scores must decrease immediately
and dramatically." When Gorman reviewed progress with her
patient, she suggested a psychiatric consult and the young
woman replied, "Why? I'm good just seeing you. You've helped
me a lot. I'm still here." After evaluating the progress, Gorman
became overly focused on the concrete numerical scores and
neglected the ambiguity associated with them. Small signs
of progress were ignored. Benign reasons for lack of change
were also overlooked. For instance, how did the constancy
of the scores fit with the patient's presentation? (e.g., Did she
believe that if she improved therapy might end? People might
then expect more of her?). The lesson from the example is that
although it is excellent practice to monitor progress with concrete scales, scores are sometimes ambiguous. At times, you
may be able to resolve the ambiguity and still in other circumstances the reasons for scores may not be readily apparent.
Remaining curious and accepting ambiguity is difficult but
necessary in these circumstances.

Intolerance for ambiguity and doubt may drive you to an
undue reliance on cookbook methods. In their early work, A. T.
Beck et al. (1979) cautioned therapists about becoming infatu-
ated with cookbooks and gimmicks. They urged that the "therapist should never lose sight of the fact that he [sic] is engaged
with another human being in a very complicated task" (p. 27).

Intolerance for ambiguity also propels rushing patients and
their families. Young et al. (2003) extolled the virtue of patience

in CBP. Rushing the child or family may preempt important data collection as well as potent therapeutic processes. Hurrying to provide solutions to patients may also risk patronizing them. Creed and Kendall (2005) found that impatience ruptures treatment progress.

We all strive for that aha moment when patients put things together. Occasionally, these moments are few and far between. Although major changes are expected, progress is seldom easy. In your everyday clinical practice, you will likely see complex patients with difficulties in several domains and possibly parents, who because of their own pathology, will work against therapy. Under such circumstances slower incremental change is more the rule. It will feel like you are treading water. Frequently, a small seed is planted and is not actualized for weeks or months. This slowness can feel like you are just wasting their time, and you may think you are inept.

You must remember that psychotherapy is an inherently creative process (Kuehlwein, 2000). Mooney and Padesky (2000) remarked that ambiguity and doubt facilitate the search for possibilities. More specifically, Mooney and Padesky (2000) wrote, "We reframe ambiguity and doubt as signposts that we are in new territory and not just rehashing the predictable old system" (p. 152).

There are several ways to help you better tolerate doubt and ambiguity. First, completing an advantages/disadvantages list (Chapter 8) on your belief that doubt must always be resolved is a good step. Additionally, conduct a test of evidence (Chapter 9) on beliefs relating to intolerance of ambiguity and impatience (e.g., change must happen quickly and in large amounts). Finally, decatastrophizing (Chapter 9) is also helpful with beliefs such as "bad things happen in ambiguous situations."

Working With Your Perfectionism: Embrace Being Ragged

Professionals entrusted with the care of children tend to be highly perfectionistic professionals who place a great deal of pressure on themselves to help others (Pretorius, 2006). Perfectionism is paralyzing, creates anxiety, and fuels self-doubt. Perfectionistic individuals rarely achieve confidence because the goal is unattainable. Moreover, perfection induces inertia. You are frozen in place by the fear of making a mistake. Burns (1980) emphasized that you should "never give up your capacity for being wrong because then you lose the ability to move forward" (p. 333).

Vaughn and Jackson (2000) called accepting your mistakes "embracing being ragged." Beal and DiGuiseppe (1998) argued that errors are expected and understandable when learning psychotherapy. Shapiro (2009) also endorsed the advantages of being ragged. He disclosed, "one of the potential advantages of clinical practice over research therapy is that practitioners can engage in mid-course correction; they can change their strategies any time they want to, even in the middle of a session" (p. 51). Thus, being ragged propels innovation and flexibility.

When you find yourself subjectively experiencing inordinate doubt and anxiety in situations that are objectively within your competence level, you may want to engage in a decatastrophizing procedure. In this case, refer to the nine pillars of decatastrophizing (Chapter 9). If you find yourself plagued by perfectionistic beliefs, Friedberg and Taylor (1994) suggested asking:

What are the advantages and disadvantages of making a mistake?
Do you know any good therapists who make mistakes?
What is the relationship between learning and making mistakes?
What am I avoiding by perfectionism?
Is competence achieved through flawless practice?
Is perfection the ultimate criterion for competence?
How is my CBP practice negatively influenced by my perfectionistic behavior? (p. 149)

Dealing With Fear of Rejection and Disapproval

Excessively seeking patients' approval and admiration is dangerous. Burns (1980) warned that excessive approval seeking sets individuals up for emotional blackmail. Many beginning therapists dread disapproval from their patients. Additionally, others may yearn for admiration (e.g., "You're the best doctor ever"). As you know, obtaining and processing negative and positive feedback from patient is part of a cognitive behavioral psychotherapist's job description. Nonetheless, hearing either a negative or positive feedback may be quite uncomfortable.

Therapists who fear their patients' rejection and disapproval show passivity and indecisiveness in their clinical work. Additionally, they exhibit an urge to prematurely refer or discharge the patient (Persons, 1989). As Persons (1989) pointed out, the impulse to rid oneself of the patient is governed by the need to maintain self-esteem and escape discomfort. Simply, this is therapists' safety-seeking behavior. As previously stated, the ability to tolerate and manage emotional discomfort is a fundamental skill in CBP (Chapters 1 and 3).

Waller (2009) identified therapists' excessive niceness as a safety behavior that acts to reduce the therapists' anxiety surrounding disapproval. Alliance or relationship ruptures are a naturally occurring and even necessary process in CBP (Chu, Suveg, Creed, & Kendall, 2010; Safran & Muran, 2000). Indeed, Safran and Muran (2000) posited that alliance ruptures may actually ignite therapeutic momentum.

Examining the advantages and disadvantages (Chapter 8) for your excessive approval-seeking behavior with patients is a useful strategy (Burns, 1980). Burns (1980) offers the idea of listing the reasons that disapproval is unpleasant but not disastrous. Additionally, he suggests asking yourself useful questions such as: How long will the disapproval last? How complete is the disapproval? How long will the discomfort last? Decatastrophizing (Chapter 9) can also help (e.g., What's the worst that could happen if I am disapproved of?).

Managing Fear of Loss of Control

Many high achieving individuals equate their competence to maintaining absolute control. They are typically take-charge individuals. Chances are you may be like that. Therefore, the prospect of losing control is quite threatening. However, control is an illusion in psychiatry and psychology. Although there is a degree of predictability and control offered by the science of CBT, the art of CBP is managing the variables beyond your control. This realization led one of my (RDF) supervisees to remark, "Cognitive therapy is the ultimate thrill ride in Disneyland." Like roller coasters, therapy has tremendous inclines building up to breathtaking plunges.

Persons (1989) rightly stated that therapists fear loss of control when working with patients. First, it is important to accept the fact that the actual degree of control you have over a patient is limited. An inflated sense of responsibility is related to fears of loss of control. Persons reminds us that as clinicians we are only responsible for acting in an ethical and clinically alert fashion. Creating a responsibility pie for reattribution (Chapter 9) is merited.

Overpersonalizing and assuming too much responsibility is a common cognitive error (Chapter 2). A way to decrease this personalization involves objectively accepting the limits of your own control (Form 12.2). Divide a piece of paper into three

Form 12.2   Accepting Limits of Personal Control

Clinical Issues I Believe I Am Responsible For	How Responsible (1–10)	How Much Control (1–10)

columns. List all the things you believe you hold responsibility for. Label the first column "Clinical Issues I Believe I Am Responsible For." Label the second column "How Responsible" and the third column "How Much Control." Next, rate on a 1 to 10 scale how much responsibility you own. Then, rate the degree to which you are in control of each item.

Many therapists equate competence with control. Consequently, this inaccurate definition can strangle CBP. Anytime therapists experience a lack of control they begin to feel threatened. Accordingly, they might act to preempt the patient's emotional exploration in a misguided attempt to restore order. Using universal definitions (Chapter 9) to correct this inaccuracy is a good idea.

Here are a few additional questions to help you unplug control from competence:

> What factors go into competence other than control?
> On scale of 1 to 10, how much am I doing these factors?
> What is the evidence that a competent therapist is not preoccupied with control?

Earning Emotional Tolerance

At times, CBP may seem too much for beginning psychiatrists and you may want to withdraw into the subjective comfort of doing only med checks (Chapter 11). Gabbard and Kay (2001) warned that

> biological reductionism may appeal to all of us when immersing ourselves in human suffering is too much to bear. An exclusive focus on dosage adjustment may provide the psychiatrist with a buffer against painful empathic awareness of the patient's despair as well as offering an illusion of mastery over the complexities of psychiatric illness. (p. 1959)

Dobson and Shaw (1993) asserted that tolerating negative affect in session is a key feature for the competent cognitive therapist. Padesky (1996) wrote that "therapists who are not willing to participate in highly interactive therapy relationships are poor candidates for cognitive therapy training" (p. 270). A common but ineffective and partial compensatory strategy for emotional intolerance used by beginning therapists is to withdraw from the treatment process. Psychotherapy is an emotionally intimate process (Chapter 3) and this creates discomfort in many beginning therapists. In her personal account of cognitive therapy supervision, Paolo (1998) found that "intimacy requires close emotional connection with other people" (p. 159).

Conduct-disordered adolescents commonly induce strong emotional reactions in psychotherapists. Frequently, you might feel guilt, anger, and exasperation when working with these youngsters. Developing an empathic attunement may become excruciatingly difficult. Nonetheless, you will need to transcend these reactions and move past them to effectively intervene.

Another example from Angela Gorman's experience is illustrative. During her training in CBP, she worked with a female adolescent who suffered from depression and carried a history of severe sexual trauma. Since the patient had recently disclosed her trauma and was hospitalized for suicidal behavior, Gorman viewed her as exquisitely vulnerable and mistakenly thought that the most effective treatment absolutely hinged on her ability to build a strong rapport. Rapport building was equated with approval and avoidance of negative affect. Due to this equation, much time in the initial sessions was spent chatting and engaging in small talk. Further, collusion with the patient's beliefs about personal frailty and the value of avoidance occurred ("It's OK not to talk about negative experiences, feelings, thoughts, and problems. I can't talk about real issues because I can't handle them").

With greater self-reflection, Gorman learned emotional tolerance. In the later course of treatment, the patient became more directly emotionally expressive. Through this experience, the patient disclosed that trust increased because she learned that the therapist helped her manage her emotions in the urgent context of strong negative emotional arousal.

In order to earn greater emotional tolerance, you might ask:

What emotions are hard for me to tolerate in myself and others?
What makes this tolerance so hard to achieve?
How am I avoiding these emotions in my CBP work?
What needs to happen for me to be comfortable with these emotions?

Addressing Fear of the Patient's Anger

Fear of the patient's anger is quite common in beginning therapists. Raymond A. Fidaleo is a cognitive therapist who in my opinion (RDF) is one of the best clinicians in dealing with angry patients, and often speaks about respecting a patient's anger but not fearing it. Respecting the patient's anger means recognizing the psychopathology that is present as well as the accompanying levels of impulse control, judgment, and risk for acting out. Once you own a healthy respect for the patient's anger, your fear becomes more manageable and you are better able to deal with a child's or parent's anger toward you.

As difficult as it may be, drawing out the patient's anger and trying to understand the specific nature of their dissatisfaction is vital. Preempting and cutting off patients' expression sabotages treatment. Burns (1989) reminds therapists, "When you and your patient feel the angriest and the most defeated, you may be the closest you have ever been to each other and the source of the difficulty" (p. 521).

Similarly to other issues, CBP procedures in the book can be applied to helping you address patients' anger. Considering the advantages and disadvantages of addressing patients' anger is useful. Tests of evidence may be applied to thoughts such as "It's bad that the patient is mad at me" or "When a patient is mad, it means I am a bad therapist." Reattribution techniques could be used for beliefs such as "If the patient is mad, I must have done something wrong." Finally, decatastrophizing is merited for still other beliefs such as, "It is disastrous for the patient to be angry with me."

Working With Doubts About Competence and Inexperience

Newman (1997) recommended flash cards and self-statements for therapists such as "Solve the problem, don't catastrophize! Stay centered. My worth as a therapist does not hinge on my client's believing everything I say, doing everything I suggest, and being respectful to me in session" (pp. 11–12).

"I'm too inexperienced and unfamiliar with CBT to help this patient" is a common belief expressed by many beginning cognitive behavioral therapists. Tests of evidence and reattribution (Chapter 9) procedures are quite helpful with these automatic thoughts.

A good series of questions to ask includes:

How absolute is the relationship between experience and successful treatment outcome?

Has any patient been helped by an inexperienced therapist?

Has any patient not been helped by an experienced
therapist?

If there is any evidence that inexperienced therapists
help patients, what factors other than experience contribute to outcome?

Which of these factors are present in your work?

Resist Drift

Waller (2009) discussed drift in terms of moving away from key
CBP processes and procedures (e.g., collaborative empiricism,
guided discovery, daily thought records, homework assignments, behavioral experiments, exposures) over the course of
treatment. Indeed, he stated that this moves CBP from a doing
therapy to a talking therapy.

Dr. Susan Jasin, a former supervisor of mine (RDF), often
stated, "Practice makes permanent." The more you rehearse
an activity, the more it is planted in your repertoire. Thus,
practice patterns are reinforced through use. Both positive
and negative clinical habits are strengthened by repeated
practice.

During the course of your busy clinical schedule, you may
find yourself starting to drift off course in cognitive therapy.
When no one is watching, critical theoretical and clinical
tenets may fade from your memory and behavior. Therefore,
careful self-monitoring (e.g., self-reflective learning) is key
for course correction. Additionally, periodic consultation
with colleagues and continued supervision is helpful. If this
is not possible, we recommend you regularly rate yourself
on the Cognitive Therapy Scale (Young & Beck, 1980). The
CTS is available at various Internet sites (www.academyofct.
org).

Avoiding Burnout

The superhero dad in the movie *The Incredibles* (Bird, 2004)
famously lamented, "No matter how many times you save
the world, it always manages to get back in jeopardy again.
Sometimes I just want it to stay saved! You know, for a little
bit? I feel like the maid; I just cleaned up this mess! Can we
keep it clean for ... for ten minutes!" Thus, even superheroes
bend due to pressures and are vulnerable to burnout.

Wright, Basco, and Thase (2006) warned that due to the
taxing nature of cognitive behavioral psychotherapy, therapists may experience burnout. Kail and Cavanaugh (2009)

described burnout being associated with decreased energy, motivation, idealism, and a sense of exploitation. Burnout is most common in the helping professions (Cordes & Dougherty, 1993). Waller (2009) emphasized the unfortunate circumstance where clinicians work at an untenable fatigue or stress level. He reminded us that fatigue decreases energy for case conceptualization and treatment planning as well as clinical flexibility. Waller recommends cognitive behavioral practitioners allocate time to reflect on cases, refine techniques, and build new skills.

Wright and his colleagues recommend assiduous scheduling time to care for your own needs. Developing a wide range of interests outside of work is an important strategy. Second, establish limits for hours of patient care. Be careful not to overschedule patients and overwhelm your resources. Rest including sufficient sleep helps with burnout. Further, seeking supervision is another antidote to burnout.

Stepping Into Lifelong Learning

Maintaining and improving critical thinking skills is key to the responsible use of the techniques described in this book. Research demonstrated that the best psychotherapists are ones who continually seek out new learning opportunities and experiences for professional growth (Orlinksy & Ronnestad, 2005). Overholser (1999) discussed wisdom as a virtue. For him, wisdom is a general concept and transcends specific knowledge bases. Instead, wisdom is a broad reasoning ability that is applied to ambiguous questions where answers are less than clear cut. Wisdom also involves recognizing the limits of one's knowledge.

Friedberg, McClure, and Garcia (2009) argued that achieving competency in CBP is a dynamic process rather than a static ending point. In an article titled "How *Not* to Learn Cognitive-Behavioral Therapy," Trinidad (2007) stated that beginning therapists should not be a casual student but rather immerse themselves in the literature. Sheikh et al. (2007) reported that in order to progress as a cognitive behavioral psychotherapist, novice clinicians must commit to learning through active internalization of information. In short, you have to *own* your progress. Therefore, continuing education via reading, training, attending conferences, and joining professional organizations is vital. Table 12.1 lists various organizations, conferences, and CBP training centers that offer continuing training in CBP.

Table 12.1　Selected Training Resources

Conferences and Organizations	Training Centers
Academy of Cognitive Therapy	Center for Cognitive Therapy (Huntington Beach, California)
International Association of Cognitive Therapy	Beck Institute for Cognitive Therapy and Research
Association of Behavioral and Cognitive Therapy	La Jolla Center for Cognitive Therapy
British Association of Cognitive and Behavioral Therapy	Cognitive Therapy Institute of San Diego
	Cognitive Therapy Center of Denver
European Association of Cognitive and Behavioral Therapy	Center for Cognitive Therapy (Oakland, California)
	Washington (DC) Center of Cognitive Therapy
Latin American Association of Cognitive Psychotherapy	Florida Center for Cognitive Therapy
	American Institute for Cognitive Therapy (New York)
American Psychiatric Association	Cognitive Therapy Center of New York
American Psychological Association	Center for Cognitive Therapy (Newton Centre, Massachusetts)
American Academy of Child and Adolescent Psychiatry	Cognitive Therapy of New Jersey
	Atlanta Center for Cognitive Therapy
American Association of Directors of Psychiatric Residency Training	Center for Cognitive Therapy–Northwestern University
Anxiety Disorders Association of America	CBT Program–University of Illinois, Department of Psychiatry
World Congress of Behavioral and Cognitive Therapy	Kentucky Center for Cognitive Therapy, University of Louisville School of Medicine
	Baltimore Center for Cognitive Therapy
Argentina Association of Cognitive Therapy	Cognitive Therapy Center (Chevy Chase, Maryland)
	Cleveland Center for Cognitive Therapy
Brazilian Society of Cognitive Therapy	Columbus Center for Cognitive Therapy
	Toronto Center for Cognitive Therapy (Canada)
	Anxiety Treatment and Research Centre (Hamilton, Ontario, Canada)
	Belfast Center for Cognitive Therapy (Ireland)
	Oxford Cognitive Therapy Centre (United Kingdom)
	Institute of Psychiatry, Kings College (London)

CONCLUSION

Self-reflection is crucial to self-improvement, professional growth, and earning the clinical wisdom necessary to serve as an effective cognitive behavioral therapist. However, the process of self-reflection produces emotional discomfort and anxiety. You will need considerable courage and commitment to propel your progress. In this chapter, several recommendations were made for the purpose of enhancing self-reflection, decreasing your performance fears, and modulating distressing thoughts and emotions.

As you navigate your journey as a cognitive therapist, self-reflection is undeniably one of the most powerful therapeutic tools in your toolbox. Although the course of self-reflection may be bumpy, rough, and full of hazards, the trip is worthwhile. We hope this book is a stop you will return to repeatedly during your continuing practice of CBP.

References

Aarons, G. A. (2004). Mental health provider attitudes toward adoption of evidence based practice: The Evidence Based Practice Attitude Scale (EBPAS). *Mental Health Services Research, 6,* 61–74.

Abramowitz, J. S. (2001). Treatment of scrupulous obsessions and compulsions using exposure and response prevention: A case report. *Cognitive and Behavioral Practice, 8,* 79–85.

Achenbach, T. M. (1991a). *Manual for Child Behavior Checklist/4-18 and 1991 profile.* Burlington: University of Vermont, Department of Psychiatry.

Achenbach, T. M. (1991b). *Manual for the Teacher's Report Form and 1991 profile.* Burlington: University of Vermont, Department of Psychiatry.

Achenbach, T. M. (2007). Applications of the Achenbach System of empirically based assessment to children, adolescents, and their parents. In S. R. Smith & L. Handler (Eds.), *The clinical assessment of children and adolescents: A practitioner's handbook* (pp. 327–344). Mahwah, NJ: Lawrence Erlbaum.

Achenbach, T. M., & Rescorla, L. A. (2001). *Manual for the AESBA school-age forms and profiles.* Burlington: University of Vermont Research Center for Children, Youth, and Families.

Acker, J. R., & Brody, D. C. (2004). *Criminal procedure: A contemporary perspective* (2nd ed.). Boston: Jones & Bartlett.

Addis, M. E. (2002). Methods for disseminating research products and increasing evidence-based practice: Promises, obstacles, and future directions. *Clinical Psychology: Science and Practice, 9,* 367–378.

Agras, W. S., Kazdin, A. E., & Wilson, G. T. (1979). *Behavior therapy: Toward an applied science.* San Francisco: WH Freeman.

Alford, B. A., & Beck, A. T. (1997). *The integrative power of cognitive therapy.* New York: Guilford Press.

Allen, J. L., & Rapee, R. M. (2005). Anxiety disorders. In P. J. Graham (Ed.), *Cognitive behavior therapy for children and families* (2nd ed., pp. 300–319). New York: Cambridge University Press.

American Psychological Association. (1993). Guidelines for providers of psychological services to ethnic, linguistic, and culturally diverse populations. *American Psychologist, 48,* 45–58.

Anastopoulos, A. D. (1998). A training program for children with attention deficit/hyperactivity disorder. In J. M. Briesmeister & C. E. Schaefer (Eds.), *Handbook of parent training: Parents as co-therapists for children's behavior problems* (2nd ed., pp. 27–60). New York: John Wiley.

Andres-Hyman, R. C., Strauss, J. S., & Davidson, L. (2007). Beyond parallel play: Science befriending the art of method acting to advance healing relationships. *Psychotherapy: Theory, Research, Practice, and Training, 44,* 78–89.

Antony, M. M., Ledley, D. R., Liss, A., & Swinson, R. P. (2006). Responses to symptom induction exercises in panic disorder. *Behavioral Research and Therapy, 44,* 85–98.

Arnold, C., & Walsh, B. T. (2007). *Next to nothing.* New York: Oxford University Press.

Aronson, E., Wilson, T. D., & Akert, R. M. (1997). *Social psychology* (2nd ed.). New York: Addison Wesley Longman.

Asher, M. J., & Gordon, S. B. (1998). *The AD/HD forms book.* Champaign, IL: Research Press.

Asher, S. R. (1983). Social competence and peer status: Recent advances and future directions. *Child Development, 54,* 1427–1434.

Attwood, T. (2004). Cognitive behavior therapy for children and adults with Asperger's syndrome. *Behaviour Change, 21,* 147–161.

Bandelj, N. (2003). How method actors create character roles. *Sociological Forum, 18,* 387–416.

Bandura, A. (1977a). Self-efficacy: Toward a unifying theory of behavior change. *Psychological Review, 84,* 191–215.

Bandura, A. (1977b). *Social learning theory.* Englewood Cliffs, NY: Prentice-Hall.

Bandura, A. (1986). *Social foundations of thought: A social cognitive theory.* Englewood Cliffs, NJ: Prentice-Hall.

Barber, J. P., Sharpless, B. A., Klosterman, S., & McCarthy, K. S. (2007). Assessing intervention competence and its relation to therapy outcome: A selected review derived from the outcome literature. *Professional Psychology: Research and Practice, 38,* 493–500.

Barkley, R. A. (1995). *Taking charge of ADHD.* New York: Guilford Press.

Barkley, R. A., & Benton, C. M. (1998). *Your defiant child: Eight steps to better behavior.* New York: Guilford Press.

Barkley, R. A., Edwards, G. H., & Robin, A. L. (1999). *Defiant teens: A clinician's manual for assessment and family intervention.* New York: Guilford Press.

Barkley, R. A., Robin, A. L., & Benton, C. M. (2008). *Your defiant teen: 10 steps to resolve conflict and rebuild your relationship.* New York: Guilford Press.

Barlow, D. H. (1988). *Anxiety and its disorders: The nature and treatment of anxiety and panic.* New York: Guilford Press.

Barlow, D. H., Allen, L. B., & Choate, M. L. (2004). Toward a unified treatment for emotional disorders. *Behavior Therapy, 35,* 205–230.

Barlow, D. H., & Cerny, J. A. (1988). *Psychological treatment of panic.* New York: Guilford Press.

Baron-Cohen, S., & Howlin, P. (1998). *Teaching children with autism to mind-read: A practical guide for teachers and parents.* New York: Wiley.

Barrett, P. B. (1995). *Group Coping Koala Workbook.* Unpublished manuscript, School of Applied Psychology, Griffith University, Brisbane, Australia.

Bateson, G. (1972). *Steps to an ecology of mind.* New York: Dutton.

Beal, D., & DiGuiseppe, R. A. (1998). Training supervisors in rational emotive behavior therapy. *Journal of Cognitive Psychotherapy, 14,* 215–229.

Beck, A. T. (1976). *Cognitive therapy and the emotional disorders.* New York: International Universities Press.

Beck, A. T. (1985). Cognitive therapy, behavior therapy, psychoanalysis, and pharmacotherapy: A cognitive continuum. In M. J. Mahoney & A. Freeman (Eds.), *Cognition and psychotherapy* (pp. 325–347). New York: Plenum Press.

Beck, A. T. (1996). *Beck Depression Inventory-II.* San Antonio, TX: Psychological Corporation.

Beck, A. T., & Clark, D. A. (1988). Anxiety and depression: An information processing perspective. *Anxiety Research, 1,* 23–36.

Beck, A. T., Emery, G., & Greenberg, R. L. (1985). *Anxiety disorders and phobias: A cognitive perspective.* New York: Plenum.

Beck, A. T., Rush, A. J., Shaw, B. F., & Emery, G. (1979). *Cognitive therapy for depression.* New York: Guilford.

Beck, A. T., Steer, R. A., & Brown, G. K. (1996). *Beck Depression Inventory manual* (2nd ed.). San Antonio, TX: Psychological Corporation.

Beck, A. T., Weissman, A., Lester, D., & Trexler, L. (1974). The measurement of pessimism: The Hopelessness Scale. *Journal of Consulting and Clinical Psychology, 42,* 861–865.

Beck, J. S. (1995). *Cognitive therapy: Basics and beyond.* New York: Guilford.

Beck, J. S. (2001). A cognitive therapy approach to medication compliance. In J. Kay (Ed.), *Review of psychiatry: Integrated treatment of psychiatric disorders* (Vol. 20). Washington, DC: American Psychiatric Press.

Beck, J. S., Beck, A. T., & Jolly, J. (2001). *Beck Youth Inventories.* San Antonio, TX: Psychological Corporation.

Beck, J. S., Beck, A. T., Jolly, J. B., & Steer, R. A. (2005). *Beck Youth Inventories for children and adolescents* (2nd ed.). San Antonio, TX: Psychological Corporation.

Becker, C. B., Zayfert, C., & Anderson, E. (2004). A survey of psychologists' attitudes towards and utilization of exposure for PTSD. *Behaviour Research and Therapy, 42,* 277–292.

Becker, W. C. (1971). *Parents and teachers.* Champaign, IL: Research Press.

Bedore, B. (2004). *101 Improv games for children and adults.* Alameda, CA: Hunter House.

Beidel, D. C., & Turner, S. M. (2006). *Shy children, phobic adults* (2nd ed.). Washington, DC: American Psychological Association.

Beidel, D. C., Turner, S. M., & Morris, T. L. (1995). A new inventory to assess childhood social anxiety and phobia: The Social Phobia and Anxiety Inventory for Children. *Psychological Assessment, 7,* 73–79.

Bender, S., & Messner, E. (2003). *Becoming a therapist: What do I say and why.* New York: Guildford.

Bennett-Levy, J. (2001). The value of self-practice of cognitive therapy techniques and self-reflection in the training of cognitive therapists. *Behavioural and Cognitive Psychotherapy, 29,* 203–220.

Bennett-Levy, J. (2003). Mechanisms of change in cognitive therapy: The case of automatic thought records and behavioral experiments. *Behavioral and Cognitive Psychotherapy, 31,* 261–277.

Bennett-Levy, J. (2006). Therapist skills: A cognitive model of their acquisition and refinement. *Behavioural and Cognitive Psychotherapy, 34,* 57–78.

Bennett-Levy, J., Lee, N., Travers, K., Pohlman, S., & Hamernik, E. (2003). Cognitive therapy from the inside: Enhancing therapist skills through practicing what we preach. *Behavioral and Cognitive Therapy, 31,* 145–163.

Berg, B. (1986). *The assertiveness game.* Dayton, OH: Cognitive Counseling Resources.

Berg, B. (1989). *The anger control game.* Dayton, OH: Cognitive Counseling Resources.

Berg, B. (1990a). *The anxiety management game.* Dayton, OH: Cognitive Counseling Resources.

Berg, B. (1990b). *The depression management game.* Dayton, OH: Cognitive Counseling Resources.

Berg, B. (1990c). *The self-control game.* Dayton, OH: Cognitive Counseling Resources.

Berg, B. (1992a). *The conduct management game.* Los Angeles: Western Psychological Services.

Berg, B. (1992b). *The feelings game.* Los Angeles: Western Psychological Services.

Berg, B. (1992c). *The self-concept game.* Los Angeles: Western Psychological Services.

Berger, K. S., & Thompson, R. A. (1995). *The developing person through childhood and adolescence* (4th ed.). New York: Worth.

Berk, M. S., Brown, G. K., Wenzel, A., & Henriques, G. R. (2008). A cognitive therapy intervention for adolescent suicide attempters: An empirically informed treatment. In C. W. LeCroy (Ed.), *Handbook of evidence-based treatment manuals for children and adolescents* (2nd ed., pp. 431–455). Oxford, England: Oxford.

Berman, S. (1997). *A comparison of dialogue and debate.* Mimeograph. Boston, MA: Educators for Social Responsibility.

Bermudes, R. A., Wright, J. H., & Casey, D. (2009). Techniques of cognitive-behavioral therapy. In G. O. Gabbard (Ed.), *Textbook of psychotherapeutic treatments* (pp. 201–237). Arlington, VA: American Psychiatric Publishing.

Bernstein, G., & Shaw, K. (1997). Practice parameters for the assessment and treatment of children and adolescents with anxiety disorders. *Journal of the American Academy of Child and Adolescent Psychiatry, 36,* 695–845.

Betan, E. J., & Binder, J. F. (2010). Clinical expertise in psychotherapy: How expert therapists use theory in generating case conceptualizations and interventions. *Journal of Contemporary Psychotherapy, 40,* 141–152.

Beutler, L. E., Brown, M. T., Crothers, L., Booker, K., & Seabrook, M. K. (1996). The dilemma of factitious demographic distinctions in psychological research. *Journal of Consulting and Clinical Psychology, 64,* 892–902.

Bieling, P. J., & Kuyken, W. (2003). Is cognitive case formulation science or science fiction? *Clinical Psychology: Science and Practice, 10,* 52–69.

Bieling, P. J., McCabe, R. E., & Antony, M. M. (2006). *Cognitive-behavioral therapy in groups.* New York: Guilford.

Bierman, K. L. (2004). *Peer rejection: Developmental processes and intervention strategies.* New York: Guilford.

Binder, J. L. (1999). Issues in teaching and learning time-limited psychodynamic psychotherapy. *Clinical Psychology Review, 19,* 705–719.

Bird, B. (Director). (2004). *The Incredibles* [Motion picture]. United States: Walt Disney Pictures and Pixar Animation.

Bird, H. R., Gould, M. S., & Staghezza, B. (1992). Aggregating data from multiple informants in child psychiatry epidemiological research. *Journal of American Academy of Child and Adolescent Psychiatry, 31,* 78–85.

Birmaher, B., Khetarpal, S., Brent, D. A., Cully, M., Balach, L., Kaufman, J., & Neer, S. M. (1997). The Screen for Child Anxiety Related Emotional Disorders (SCARED): Scale construction and psychometric characteristics. *Journal of American Academy of Child and Adolescent Psychiatry, 36,* 545–553.

Bishop, S. R., Lau, M., Shapiro, S., Carlson, L., Anderson, N. D., Carmody, J., ... Devins, G. (2004). Mindfulness: A proposed operational definition. *Clinical Psychology: Science and Practice, 11,* 230–241.

Blos, P. (1979). *The adolescent passage: Development issues.* New York: International University Press.

Boal, A. (2002). *Games for actors and non-actors* (2nd ed.). New York: Routledge.

Borcherdt, B. (2002). Humor and its contributions to mental health. *Journal of Rational-Emotive and Cognitive-Behavior Therapy, 20,* 247–257.

Bose-Deakins, J. E., & Floyd, R. G. (2004). A review of the Beck Youth Inventories of emotional and social impairment. *Journal of School Psychology, 42,* 333–340.

Boxmeyer, C. L., Lochman, J. E., Powell, N., Yaros, A., & Mojnaroski, M. (2007). A case study of the Coping Power Program for angry and aggressive youth. *Journal of Contemporary Psychotherapy, 37,* 165–175.

Brems, C. M. (1993). *A comprehensive guide to child psycho-therapy.* Boston: Allyn & Bacon.

Brent, D., Emslie, G., Clarke, G., Wagner, K., Asarnow, J., Keller, M., ... Zelazny, J. (2008). Switching to another SSRI or to Venlafaxine with or without cognitive behavioral therapy for adolescents with SSRI-resistant depression: The TORDIA randomized controlled trial. *Journal of the American Medical Association, 299,* 901–913.

Brent, D. A. (1997). Practitioner review: The aftercare of adolescents with deliberate self-harm. *Journal of Child Psychology and Psychiatry, 38,* 277–286.

Brent, D. A., & Birmaher, B. (2002). Adolescent depression. *New England Journal of Medicine, 347,* 667–671.

Brent, D. A., Holder, D., Kolko, D., Birmaher, B., Baugher, M., Roth, C., ... Johnson, B. A. (1997). A clinical psychotherapy trial for adolescent depression comparing cognitive, family, and supportive treatments. *Archives of General Psychiatry, 54,* 877–885.

Brew, L., & Kottler, J. A. (2008). *Applied helping skills: Transforming lives.* Thousand Oaks, CA: Sage.

Briere, J. N., & Scott, C. (2006). *Principles of trauma therapy: A guide to symptoms, evaluation, and treatment.* Thousand Oaks, CA: Sage.

Brock, S. E., Jimerson, S. R., & Hansen, R. L. (2009). *Identifying, assessing, and treating ADHD at school.* New York: Springer.

Brooks, S. J., & Kutcher, S. (2001). Diagnosis and measurement of adolescent depression: A review of commonly used instruments. *Journal of Child and Adolescent Psychopharmacology, 11,* 341–376.

Brosnan, L., Reynolds, S., & Moore, R. G. (2008). Self-evaluation of cognitive therapy performance: Do therapists know how competent they are? *Behavioral and Cognitive Pschotherapy, 36,* 581–587.

Brown, R. T., & Sawyer, M. G. (1998). *Medications for school-age children.* New York: Guilford.

Burns, D. D. (1980). *Feeling good: The new mood therapy.* New York: Springer.

Burns, D. D. (1989). *The feeling good handbook: Using the new mood therapy in everyday life.* New York: William Morrow & Company.

Burns, M. (2002). Cognitive therapy training stress disorder: A cognitive perspective. *Behavioral and Cognitive Psychotherapy, 30,* 365–374.

Burum, B. A., & Goldfried, M. R. (2007). The centrality of emotion to psychological change. *Clinical Psychology: Science and Practice, 14,* 407–413.

Butler, G., & Hope, T. (2007). *Managing your mind: The mental fitness guide.* Cambridge, UK: Oxford.

Cantet, L. (Director). (2008). *The Class* [Motion picture]. France: Haut et Cout.

Cardemil, E. V., & Battle, C. L. (2003). Guess who's coming to therapy: Getting comfortable with conversations about race and ethnicity in psychotherapy. *Professional Psychology: Research and Practice, 3,* 278–286.

Caron, A., & Robin, J. A. (2010). Engagement of adolescents in cognitive-behavioral therapy for obsessive-compulsive disorder. In D. Castro-Blanco and M. S. Karver (Eds.), *Elusive alliance: Treatment strategies with high-risk adolescents* (pp. 95–122). Washington, DC: American Psychological Association.

Carroll, K. M., & Nauro, K. F. (2002). One size cannot fit all: A stage model for psychotherapy manual development. *Clinical Psychology: Science and Practice, 9,* 367–378.

Carter, M. M., Sbrocco, T., & Carter, C. (1996). African-Americans and anxiety disorders research: Development of a testable theoretical framework. *Psychotherapy, 33,* 449–463.

Cartledge, G. C., & Feng, H. (1996a). Asian Americans. In G. C. Cartledge & J. F. Milburn (Eds.), *Cultural diversity and social skills instruction: Understanding ethnic and gender differences* (pp. 87–132). Champaign, IL: Research Press.

Cartledge, G. C., & Feng, H. (1996b). The relationship of culture and social behavior. In G. C. Cartledge & J. F. Milburn (Eds.), *Cultural diversity and social skills instruction: Understanding ethnic and gender differences* (pp. 13–44). Champaign, IL: Research Press.

Cartledge, G. C., & Milburn, J. F. (Eds.). (1996). *Cultural diversity and social skills instruction: Understanding ethnic and gender differences.* Champaign, IL: Research Press.

Castro-Blanco, D. (2010). TEEN: Techniques for enhancing engagement through negotiation. In D. Castro-Blanco and M. S. Karver (Eds.), *Elusive alliance: Treatment strategies with high-risk adolescents* (pp. 95–122). Washington, DC: American Psychological Association.

Chambless, D. L., & Ollendick, T. H. (2001). Empirically supported psychological interventions: Controversies and evidence. *Annual Review of Psychology, 52,* 685–716.

Chansky, T. E. (2000). *Freeing your child from obsessive-compulsive disorder.* New York: Three Rivers Press.

Chartrand, M. M., Frank, D. A., White, L. F., & Shope, T. R. (2008). Effect of parents' wartime deployment on the behavior of young children in military families. *Archives of Pediatric and Adolescent Medicine, 162,* 1007–1014.

Chaudhry, I. B., Neelam, K., Duddu, V., & Husain, N. (2008). Ethnicity and psychopharmacology. *Journal of Psychopharmacology, 22,* 673–680.

Chawla, N., & Ostafin, B. (2007). Experiential avoidance as a functional dimensional approach to psychopathology: An empirical review. *Journal of Clinical Psychology, 63,* 871–890.

Chi, T. C., & Hinshaw, S. P. (2002). Mother-child relationships of children with ADHD: The role of maternal depressive symptoms and depression-related distortions. *Journal of Abnormal Child Psychology, 30,* 387–400.

Chorpita, B. F. (2003). The frontier of evidence-based practice. In A. Kazdin & J. R. Weisz (Eds.), *Evidence-based psychotherapies for children and adolescents* (pp. 42–59). New York: Guilford.

Chorpita, B. F. (2006). *Modular cognitive-behavior therapy for child anxiety disorders.* New York: Guilford.

Chorpita, B. F., Barlow, D. H., Albano, A. M., & Daleiden, E. M. (1998). Methodological strategies in child clinical trials: Advancing the efficacy and effectiveness of psychosocial treatments, *Journal of Abnormal Psychology, 26,* 7–16.

Chorpita, B. F., Daleiden, E. L., & Weisz, J. R. (2005a). Identifying and selecting the common elements of evidence-based interventions: A distillation and matching model. *Mental Health Services Research, 7,* 5–20.

Chorpita, B. F., Daleiden, E. L., & Weisz, J. R. (2005b). Modularity in the design and application of therapeutic interventions. *Applied and Preventive Psychology, 11,* 141–156.

Chu, B. C., Suveg, C., Creed, T. A., & Kendall, P. C. (2010). Involvement shifts, alliance ruptures, and managing engagement over therapy. In D. Castro-Blanco and M. S. Karver (Eds.), *Elusive alliance: Treatment strategies with high-risk adolescents* (pp. 95–122). Washington, DC: American Psychological Association.

Clark, D. M., & Beck, A. T. (1988). Cognitive approaches. In C. G. Last & M. Hersen (Eds.), *Handbook of anxiety disorders* (pp. 362–385). Elmsford, NY: Pergamon Press.

Clark, L. (2005). *SOS: Help for parents* (3rd ed.). Bowling Green, KY: Parents Press and SOS Programs.

Clay, D. L., Mordhorst, M. J., & Lehn, L. (2002). Empirically supported treatments in pediatric psychology: Where is the diversity? *Journal of Pediatric Psychology, 27,* 325–337.

Cobain, B. (2007). *When nothing matters anymore.* Minneapolis, MN: Free Spirit Press.

Cognitive Behavioral Therapy Treatment of Adolescent Suicide Attempters (CBT TASA) Team. (2008). *Cognitive behavioral therapy for adolescent suicide attempts teen manual.* Unpublished manuscript, National Institute of Mental Health.

Cohen, J. A., Deblinger, E., Mannarino, A. P., & Steer, R. (2004). A multi-site, randomized controlled trial for children with sex abuse-related PTSD symptoms. *Journal of the American Academy of Child and Adolescent Psychiatry, 43,* 393–402.

Cohen, J. A., & Mannarino, A. P. (2008). Trauma-focused cognitive behavioral therapy for children and parents. *Child and Adolescent Mental Health, 13,* 158–162.

Compton, S. N., Kratochvil, C. J., & March, J. S. (2007). Pharmacotherapy for anxiety disorders in children and adolescents: An evidence-based medicine review. *Psychiatric Annals, 37,* 504–517.

Conners, C. K. (2000). *Conners' Rating Scales—Revised: Technical Manual.* North Tonawanda, NY: Multi Health Systems.

Cooper, B., & Widdows, N. (2008a). *Knowing yourself, knowing others.* Oakland, CA: New Harbinger.

Cooper, B., & Widdows, N. (2008b). *The social success workbook for teens.* Oakland, CA: New Harbinger.

Cordes, C. L., & Dougherty, T. W. (1993). A review and integration of research on job burnout. *Academy of Management Review, 18,* 621–656.

Corstorphine, E., Mountford, V., Tomlinson, S., Waller, G., & Meyer, C. (2007). Distress tolerance in the eating disorders. *Eating Behaviors, 6,* 91–97.

Cozza, S., Chun, R., & Polo, J. (2005). Military families and children during Operation Iraqi Freedom. *Psychiatric Quarterly, 76,* 371–378.

Craighead, L. W., Craighead, W. E., Kazdin, A. E., & Mahoney, M. J. (1994). Principles of behavior and cognitive change. In L. W. Craighead, W. E. Craighead, A. E. Kazdin, & M. J. Mahoney (Eds.), *Cognitive and behavioral interventions* (pp. 29–46). Boston: Allyn & Bacon.

Craske, M. G., & Barlow, D. H. (2001). Panic disorder and ago-raphobia. In D. H. Barlow (Ed.), *Clinical handbook of psychological disorders: A step-by-step treatment manual* (3rd ed., pp. 1–59). New York: Guilford.

Craske, M. G., & Barlow, D. H. (2008). Panic disorders and ago-raphobia. In D. Barlow (Ed.), *Clinical handbook of psychological disorders* (4th ed., pp. 1–64). New York: Guilford.

Craske, M. G., & Mystkowski, J. L. (2006). Exposure therapy and extinction: Clinical studies. In M. G. Craske, D. Hermans, & D. Vansteenwegen (Eds.), *Fear and learning from basic processes to clinical implications* (pp. 217–233). Washington, DC: American Psychological Association.

Creed, T. A., & Kendall, P. C. (2005). Therapist alliance building within a cognitive behavioral treatment for anxiety in youth. *Journal of Consulting and Clinical Psychology, 73*, 498–505.

Crick, N. R., & Dodge, K. A. (1996). Social information processing mechanisms in reactive and proactive aggression. *Child Development, 67*, 993–1002.

Cuijpers, P., Munoz, R. F., Clarke, G. N., & Lewinsohn, P. M. (2009). Psychoeducational treatment and prevention of depression: The coping with depression course thirty years later. *Clinical Psychology Review, 29*, 449–458.

Curry, J. F., & Becker, S. J. (2009). Better but not well: Strategies for difficult-to-treat youth depression. In D. McKay & E. A. Storch (Eds.), *Cognitive-behavior therapy for children: Treating complex and refractory cases* (pp. 231–258). New York: Springer.

Curry, J. F., & Reinecke, M. A. (2003). Modular therapy for adolescents with major depression. In M. Reinecke, F. M. Dattilio, & A. Freeman (Eds.), *Cognitive therapy with children and adolescents: A casebook for clinical practice* (2nd ed., pp. 95–127). New York: Guilford.

Curry, J. F., & Wells, K. C. (2005). Striving for effectiveness in the treatment of adolescent depression: Cognitive behavioral therapy for multisite community intervention. *Cognitive and Behavioral Practice, 12*, 177–185.

Dahl, R. E. (2004). Adolescent brain development: A period of vulnerabilities and opportunities. *Annals of the New York Academy of Sciences, 1021*, 1–22.

Daley, M. F. (1969). "The reinforcement menu." Finding effective reinforcers. In J. D. Krumboltz & C. E. Thorson (Eds.), *Behavioral counseling: Cases and techniques* (pp. 42–45). New York: Holt, Rinehart, & Winston.

Danaher, B. G. (1974). Theoretical foundations and clinical applications of the Premack principle: Review and critique. *Behavior Therapy, 5,* 307–324.

Daniel, S. S., & Goldston, D. B. (2009). Interventions for suicidal youth: A review of the literature and developmental considerations. *Suicide and Life-Threatening Behavior, 39,* 252–268.

Deblinger, E., Behl, L. E., & Glickman, A. R. (2006). Treating children who have experienced sexual abuse. In P. C. Kendall (Ed.), *Child and adolescent therapy: Cognitive-behavioral procedures* (3rd ed., pp. 383–418). New York: Guilford.

De Los Reyes, A., & Kazdin, A. E. (2005). Informant discrepancies in the assessment of childhood psychopathology: A critical review, theoretical framework, and recommendations for future study. *Psychological Bulletin, 131,* 483–509.

DeLucia-Waack, J. L. (2006). *Leading psychoeducational groups for children and adolescents.* Thousand Oaks, CA: Sage.

de Oliveira, I. R. (2008). Trial-based thought record (TBTR): Preliminary data on a strategy to deal with core beliefs by combining sentence reversion and the use of analogy with a journal process. *Revista Brasileira de Psiquiatria, 30,* 12–18.

D'Eramo, K. S., & Francis, G. (2004). Cognitive-behavioral psychotherapy. In T. L. Morris & J. S. March (Eds.), *Anxiety disorders in children and adolescents* (pp. 305–328). New York: Guilford Press.

Dobbins, J. E., & Skillings, J. H. (2000). Racism as a clinical syndrome. *American Journal of Orthopsychiatry, 70,* 14–27.

Dobson, K. S., & Shaw, B. F. (1993). The training of cognitive therapists: What have we learned from treatment manuals. *Psychotherapy, 30,* 573–577.

Domjan, M., & Burkhard, B. (1986). *The principles of learning and behavior* (2nd ed.). Pacific Grove, CA: Brooks/Cole.

Dougher, M. J. (1994). The act of acceptance. In S. C. Hayes, N. S. Jacobson, V. M. Follette, & M. J. Dougher (Eds.), *Acceptance and change: Content and context in psychotherapy* (pp. 46–53). Reno, NV: Context Press.

Dozois, D. J. A., & Covin, R. (2004). The Beck Depression Inventory-II, Beck Hopelessness Scale, and Beck Scale for Suicidal Ideation. In M. Hersen (Series Ed.), D. L. Segal, & M. Hilsenrotn (Vol. Eds.), *Comprehensive handbook of psychological assessment: Vol. 2. Personality assessment and psychopathology.* New York: Wiley.

Dozois, D. J. A., Dobson, K. S., & Ahnberg, J. L. (1998). A psychometric evaluation of the Beck Depression Inventory-II. *Psychological Assessment, 10,* 83–89.

Dressler, J. (2002). *Understanding criminal procedure* (3rd ed.). Newark, NJ: Matthew Bender and Company.

Drinkwater, J. (2004). Cognitive case formulation. In P. Graham (Ed.), *Cognitive behavior therapy for children and families* (2nd ed., pp. 84–99). Cambridge, UK: Oxford.

Drummet, A. R., Coleman, M., & Cable, S. (2003). Military families under stress: Implications for family life education. *Family Relations, 52,* 279–287.

Ehrenreich, J. T., Fairholme, C. P., Buzzella, B. A., Ellard, K. K., & Barlow, D. H. (2007). The role of emotion in psychological therapy. *Clinical Psychology: Science and Practice, 14,* 422–428.

Eisen, A. R., & Engler, L. B. (2006). *Helping your child overcome separation anxiety or school refusal.* Oakland, CA: New Harbinger.

Eisen, A. R., & Engler, L. B. (2007). *Helping your socially vulnerable child: What to do when your child is shy, socially anxious, withdrawn, and bullied.* Oakland, CA: New Harbinger.

Ellison, R. (1952). *Invisible man.* New York: Random House.

Esposito, C., Johnson, B., Wolfsdorf, B. A., & Spirito, A. (2003). Cognitive factors: Hopelessness, coping, and problem-solving. In A. Spirito & J. C. Overholser (Eds.), *Evaluating and treating adolescent suicide attempters: From research to practice* (pp. 89–112). New York: Academic Press.

Evans, D. L., & Andrews, L. W. (2005). *If your adolescent has depression or bipolar disorder.* New York: Guilford Press.

Faust, J. (2000). Integration of family and cognitive behavioral therapy for treating sexually abused children. *Cognitive and Behavioral Practice, 7,* 361–368.

Feindler, E. L., & Gerber, M. (2007). TAME: Teen anger management education. In R. W. Christner, J. L. Stewart, & A. Freeman (Eds.), *Handbook of cognitive-behavior group therapy with children and adolescents* (pp. 367–388). New York: Routledge.

Fennell, M. J. V. (1989). Depression. In K. Hawton, P. M. Salkovskis, J. Kirk, & D. M. Clark (Eds.), *Cognitive behavior therapy for psychiatric problems: A practical guide* (pp. 169–234). Oxford, England: Oxford University Press.

Fidaleo, R. A., Friedberg, R. F., Dennis, G., & Southworth, S. (1996). Imagery, internal dialogue, and action: An alternative treatment for PTSD. *Crisis Intervention, 3,* 143–155.

Fink, S. O. (1990). Approaches to emotion in psychotherapy and theatre: Implications for drama therapy. *The Arts in Psychotherapy, 17*, 5–18.

Finkel, L. B., Kelley, M. L., & Ashby, J. (2003). Geographic mobility, family, and maternal variables as related to the psychosocial adjustment of military children. *Military Medicine, 168*, 1019–1024.

Fiske, S. T., & Taylor, S. E. (1991). *Social cognition.* New York: McGraw Hill.

Flannery-Schroeder, E. (2005). Treatment integrity: Implications for training. *Clinical Psychology: Science and Practice, 12*, 388–390.

Flannery-Schroeder, E., & Kendall, P. C. (2000). Group and individual cognitive behavioral treatments for youth with anxiety disorders: A randomized clinical trial. *Cognitive Therapy and Research, 24*, 251–278.

Fleder, G. (Director), Coplan, A. (Co-producer), Dauchy, D. (Executive producer), Davis, J. (Producer), & Schmidt, A. L. (Executive producer). (2008). *The Express* [Motion picture]. United States: Davis Entertainment, IDEA Film Productions, & Relativity Media.

Foa, E. B., & Andrews, L. W. (2006). *If your adolescent has an anxiety disorder.* New York: Oxford University Press.

Foa, E. B., Steketee, G. S., & Ascher, L. M. (1980). Systematic desensitization. In A. Goldstein & E. B. Foa (Eds.), *Handbook of behavioral interventions* (pp. 38–91). New York: John Wiley.

Ford, E. B., Liebowitz, M., & Andrews, L. W. (2007). *What you must think of me.* New York: Oxford University Press.

Forehand, R. L., & McMahon, R. J. (1981). *Helping the non-compliant child: A clinician's guide to parent training.* New York: Guilford.

Frank, A. (1953). *The diary of a young girl.* New York: Pocket Books.

Frank, J. (1961). *Persuasion and healing: A comparative study of psychotherapy.* New York: Schocken Books.

Franklin, A. J., & Boyd-Franklin, N. (2000). Invisibility syndrome: A clinical model of the effects of racism on African-American males. *American Journal of Orthopsychiatry, 70*, 33–41.

Franklin, M. E., & Foa, E. B. (2008). Obsessive-compulsive disorder. In D. H. Barlow (Ed.), *Clinical handbook of psychological disorders* (4th ed., pp. 164–215).

Franklin, M. E., Riggs, D. S., & Pai, A. (2005). Obsessive-compulsive disorder. In M. M. Antony, D. R. Ledley, & R. G. Heimberg (Eds.), *Improving outcomes and parenting relapse* (pp. 128–173). New York: Guilford.

Freelance Players. (2004). *Urban improve educational services.* Chatsworth, CA: Aims Multimedia.

Freeman, A. (1990). Technicians, magicians, and clinicians. *Behavior Therapist, 13,* 169–170.

Freeman, A., & Dattilio, F. M. (1992). Cognitive therapy in the year 2000. In A. Freeman & F. M. Dattilio (Eds.), *Comprehensive casebook of cognitive therapy* (pp. 375–379). New York: Plenum.

Freeman, A., Felgoise, S. H., & Davis, D. D. (2008). *Clinical psychology: Integrating science and practice.* New York: John Wiley.

Freeman, A., Pretzer, J., Fleming, B., & Simon, K. M. (1990). *Clinical applications of cognitive therapy.* New York: Plenum.

Freiheit, S. R., & Overholser, J. C. (1997). Training issues in cognitive-behavioral psychotherapy. *Journal of Behavior Therapy and Experimental Psychiatry, 28,* 79–86.

Friedberg, R. D. (2006). A cognitive behavioral approach to family therapy. *Journal of Contemporary Psychotherapy, 36,* 159–165.

Friedberg, R. D. (2009). Staying faithful to our roots: Experiential learning in cognitive behavioral psychotherapy. *The Brown University Child and Adolescent Letter, 25,* 1, 6.

Friedberg, R. D., & Brelsford, G. (In press). Using cognitive behavioral interventions to help children cope with parental military deployments. *Journal of Contemporary Psychotherapy.*

Friedberg, R. D., & Clark, C. C. (2006). Supervision of cognitive therapy with youth. In T. K. Neill (Ed.), *Helping others help children: Clinical supervision of child psychotherapy* (pp. 109–122). Washington, DC: American Psychological Association.

Friedberg, R. D., & Friedberg, R. J. (in press). Field of dreams and sometimes nightmares: Enhancing young athletes' emotional well-being. In F. Columbus (Ed.), *Sport Psychiatry.* Hauppauge, NY: NOVA Science.

Friedberg, R. D., Friedberg, B. A., & Friedberg, R. J. (2001). *Therapeutic exercises for children: Guided self-discovery using cognitive behavioral techniques.* Sarasota, FL: Professional Resource Press.

Friedberg, R. D., & Gorman, A. A. (2007). Integrating psychotherapeutic processes with cognitive behavioral procedures. *Journal of Contemporary Psychotherapy, 37,*
185–193.

Friedberg, R. D., Gorman, A. A., & Beidel, D. B. (2009). Training
psychologists for cognitive behavioral therapy in the raw
world: A rubric for supervisors. *Behavior Modification,
33,* 104–123.

Friedberg, R. D., Mason, C., & Fidaleo, R. A. (1992). *Switching
channels: A cognitive behavioral work journal for
adolescents.* Sarasota, FL: Psychological Assessment
Resources.

Friedberg, R. D., & McClure, J. M. (2002). *Clinical practice of
cognitive therapy with children and adolescents: The nuts
and bolts.* New York: Guilford Press.

Friedberg, R. D., & McClure, J. M. (2005). Adolescents. In N.
Kazantzis, F. P. Deane, K. R. Ronan, & L. L'Abale (Eds.),
*Using homework assignments in cognitive behavior ther-
apy* (pp. 95–116). New York: Brunner Routledge.

Friedberg, R. D., McClure, J. M., & Garcia, J. H. (2009). *Cognitive
therapy techniques for children and adolescents.* New
York: Guilford Press.

Friedberg, R. D., & Taylor, L. A. (1994). Perspectives on supervision in cognitive therapy. *Journal of Rational-Emotive and
Cognitive-Behavior Therapy, 12,* 147–162.

Friedberg, R. D., Viglione, D. J., Fidaleo, R. A., Celeste, B. L.,
Lovette, J., Street, G., ... Beal, K. G. (1998). Measuring how
we preach what we practice: Psychoeducational change
in depressed inpatients. *Journal of Rational-Emotive and
Cognitive-Behavior Therapy, 16,* 45–57.

Friedman, E. S., Thase, M. E., & Wright, J. H. (2008). Cognitive
and behavioral therapies. In A. Tasman, J. Kay, J. A.
Lieberman, M. B. First, & M. Maj (Eds.), *Psychiatry* (3rd
ed., pp. 1920–1947). New York: John Wiley.

Friedman, E. S., Wright, J. H., Jarrett, R. B., & Thase, M. E.
(2006). Combining cognitive therapy and medication for
mood disorders. *Psychiatric Annals, 36,* 320–328.

Fristad, M. A. (2006). Psychoeducation treatment for school-
aged children with bipolar disorder. *Development and
Psychopathology, 18,* 1289–1306.

Fristad, M. A., & Goldberg-Arnold, J. S. (2004). *Raising a moody
child.* New York: Guilford Press.

Gabbard, G. O. (2006). The rationale for combining medication
and psychotherapy. *Psychiatric Annals, 36,* 315–319.

Gabbard, G. O., & Kay, J. (2001). The fate of integrated treatment: Whatever happened to the biopsychosocial psychiatrist. *American Journal of Psychiatry, 158,* 1956–1963.

Gardner, F. L., & Moore, Z. E. (2004). A mindfulness-acceptance-commitment-based approach to athletic performance enhancement: Theoretical considerations. *Behavior Therapy, 35,* 707–725.

Garland, A. F., Hurlburt, M. S., & Hawley, K. M. (2006). Examining psychotherapy processes in a services context. *Clinical Psychology: Science and Practice, 13,* 30–46.

Gaw, A. C. (2009). Cultural issues. In R. E. Hales, S. C. Yodofsky, & G. O. Gabbard (Eds.), *Textbook of clinical psychiatry* (5th ed.). Washington, DC: American Psychiatric Association. Retrieved July 28, 2009, from www.psychiatryonline.com.

Geddie, L. (1992). *Dinosaur relaxation script.* Unpublished manuscript, University of Oklahoma Health Sciences Center, Oklahoma City, OK.

Gilbert, P., & Leahy, R. L. (2007). Introduction and overview. In P. Gilbert & R. L. Leahy (Eds.), *The therapeutic relationship in the cognitive behavioral psychotherapies* (pp. 3–23). London: Routledge.

Ginsburg, G. S., Albano, A. M., Findling, R. L., Kratochvil, C., & Walkup, C. (2005). Integrating cognitive behavioral therapy and pharmacotherapy in the treatment of adolescent depression. *Cognitive and Behavioral Practice, 12,* 252–262.

Ginsburg, G. S., & Kingery, J. N. (2007). Evidence-based practice for childhood anxiety disorders. *Journal of Contemporary Psychotherapy, 37,* 123–132.

Gluhoski, V. L. (1995). Misconceptions of cognitive therapy. *Psychotherapy, 31,* 594–600.

Golan, O., Baron-Cohen, S., & Golan, Y. (2008). The reading the mind in film task (child version): Complex emotional and mental state recognition in children with and without Autism Spectrum Conditions. *Journal of Autism and Developmental Disorders, 38,* 1534–1541.

Goldfried, M. R. (2003). Cognitive-behavior therapy: Reflections on the evolution of a therapeutic orientation. *Cognitive Therapy and Research, 27,* 53–69.

Goldfried, M. R., & Davila, J. (2005). The role of the relationship and technique in therapeutic change. *Psychotherapy: Theory, Research, Practice, and Training, 42,* 421–430.

Goldfried, M. R., & Davison, G. C. (1976). *Clinical behavior therapy.* New York: Holt, Rinehart, & Winston.

Goldman, C. R. (1988). Toward a definition of psychoeducation. *Hospital and Community Psychiatry, 39,* 666–668.

Goldstein, T. R. (2009). Psychological perspectives on acting. *Psychology of Aesthetics, Creativity, and the Arts, 3,* 6–9.

Gosch, E. A., Flannery-Schroeder, E., Mauro, C. F., & Compton, C. N. (2006). Principles of cognitive-behavioral therapy for anxiety disorders in children. *Journal of Cognitive Psychotherapy, 20,* 247–262.

Gottman, J. (1977). Toward a definition of social isolation in children. *Child Development, 48,* 513–517.

Graham, P. (2005). Cognitive behavior therapies for children: Passing fashion or here to stay? *Child and Adolescent Mental Health, 10,* 57–62.

Gray, C. (2000). *Writing social stories with Carol Gray.* Arlington, TX: Future Horizons.

Greenberg, L. S. (2007). Emotion in the therapeutic relationship in emotion-focused therapy. In P. Gilbert & R. L. Leahy (Eds.), *The therapeutic relationship in the cognitive behavioral psychotherapies* (pp. 43–62). New York: Guilford.

Greenberg, L., & Elliot, J. (1997). Varieties of emotional expression. In A. Bohart & L. Greenberg (Eds.), *Empathy reconsidered: New directions in theory, research, and practice.* Washington, DC: American Psychological Association.

Greenberger, D., & Padesky, C. A. (1995). *Mind over mood: Changing how you feel by changing the way you think.* New York: Guilford Press.

Greene, R. W. (2001). *The explosive child: A new approach for understanding and parenting easily frustrated, chronically inflexible children* (2nd ed.). New York: HarperCollins.

Greenspan, S. (1993). *Playground politics.* Reading, MA: Addison Wesley.

Greenspan, S., & Greenspan, N. T. (1985). *First feelings.* New York: Penguin Books.

Greenspan, S., & Greenspan, N. T. (1989). *The essential partnership.* New York: Penguin Books.

Gross, J. J., & John, O. P. (2002). Wise emotion regulation. In L. F. Barrett & D. Salovey (Eds.), *The wisdom in feeling* (pp. 297–318). New York: Guilford.

Gross, J. J., & John, O. P. (2003). Individual differences in two emotional processes: Implications for affect, relationships, and well-being. *Journal of Personality and Social Psychology, 64,* 970–986.

Guidano, V. F., & Liotti, G. (1983). *Cognitive processes and emotional disorders: A structural approach to psychotherapy.* New York: Guilford.

Guidano, V. F., & Liotti, G. (1985). A constructionalist foundation for cognitive therapy. In M. J. Mahoney & A. Freeman (Eds.), *Cognition and psychotherapy* (pp. 101–142). New York: Plenum Press.

Haft, S. (Producer), Witt, P. J. (Producer), Thomas, T. (Producer), & Weir, P. (Director). (1989). *Dead poets society* [Motion picture]. USA: Touchstone Pictures.

Hamil, S. (2008). *My feeling better workbook.* Oakland, CA: New Harbinger.

Hammen, C., & Zupan, B. A. (1984). Self-schemas, depression, and the processing of personal information in children. *Journal for Experimental Child Psychology, 37,* 598–608.

Hannesdottir, D. K., & Ollendick, T. H. (2007). The role of emotion regulation in the treatment of child anxiety disorders. *Clinical Child and Family Psychology Review, 10,* 275–293.

Hart, K. J., & Morgan, J. R. (1993). Cognitive-behavioral procedures with children: Historical context and current status. In A. J. Finch, W. M. Nelson, & E. S. Ott (Eds.), *Cognitive-behavioral procedures with children and adolescents* (pp. 1–24). Boston: Allyn & Bacon.

Harvey, J. H., & Weary, G. (1981). *Perspectives on attributional processes.* Dubuque, IA: W.C. Brown.

Hayes, S. C., Strosahl, K. D., & Wilson, K. G. (1999). *Acceptance and commitment therapy.* New York: Guilford Press.

Haynes, S. N., Leisen, M. B., & Blaine, D. D. (1997). Design of individualized behavioral treatment programs using functional analytic clinical case models. *Psychological Assessment, 9,* 334–348.

Haynes, S. N., & O'Brien, W. H. (2000). *Principles and practice of behavioral assessment.* New York: Kluwer.

Hays, P. A. (1995). Multicultural applications of cognitive-behavior therapy. *Professional Psychology: Research and Practice, 26,* 309–315.

Hays, P. A. (2001). *Addressing cultural complexities in practice: A framework for clinicians and counselors.* Washington, DC: American Psychological Association.

Hays, P. A. (2009). Integrating evidence-based practice, cognitive-behavior therapy, and multicultural therapy: Ten steps for culturally competent practice. *Professional Psychology: Research and Practice, 4,* 354–360.

Hays, P. A., & Iwamasa, G. Y. (Eds.). (2006). *Culturally responsive cognitive-behavioral therapy: Assessment, practice, and supervision.* Washington, DC: American Psychological Association.

Hembree, E. A., & Cahill, S. P. (2007). Obstacles to successful implementation of exposure therapy. In D. C. S. Richard & D. L. Lauterbach (Eds.), *Handbook of exposure therapies* (pp. 389–408). San Diego: Academic Press.

Hembree, E. A., Rauch, S. A. M., & Foa, E. B. (2003). Beyond the manual: The insider's guide to prolonged exposure to PTSD. *Cognitive and Behavioral Practice, 10,* 22–30.

Himle, M. B., & Franklin, M. E. (2009). The more you do it, the easier it gets: Exposure and response prevention for OCD. *Cognitive and Behavioral Practice, 16,* 29–39.

Hirshfeld-Becker, D. R., & Biederman, D. R. (2002). Rationale and principles for early intervention with young children at risk for anxiety disorders. *Clinical Child and Family Psychology Review, 5,* 161–172.

Hogan, R. A. (1968). The implosive technique. *Behaviour Research and Therapy, 6,* 423–432.

Holland, S. J. (2003). Avoidance of emotion as an obstacle to progress. In R. L. Leahy (Ed.), *Roadblocks in cognitive-behavioral therapy* (pp. 116–134). New York: Guilford.

Hudson, J. L., & Kendall, P. C. (2005). Children. In N. Kazantzis, F. P. Deane, K. R. Ronan, & L. L'Abale (Eds.), *Using homework assignments in cognitive behavior therapy* (pp. 75–94). New York: Brunner Routledge.

Huebner, D. (2006). *What to do when you worry too much: A kid's guide to overcoming anxiety.* Washington, DC: Magination Press.

Huebner, D. (2007a). *What to do when you grumble too much: A kid's guide to overcoming negativity.* Washington, DC: Magination Press.

Huebner, D. (2007b). *What to do when your brain gets stuck: A kid's guide to overcoming OCD.* Washington, DC: Magination Press.

Hughes, J. N. (1988). *Cognitive behavior therapy with children in schools.* New York: Pergamon.

Huppert, J. D., & Alley, A. C. (2004). The clinical application of emotion research in generalized anxiety disorder: Some proposed procedures. *Cognitive and Behavioral Practice, 11,* 387–392.

Huppert, J. D., & Baker-Morissette, S. L. (2003). Beyond the manual: The insider's guide to panic control treatment. *Cognitive and Behavioral Practice, 10,* 2–13.

Ingram, R. E., & Kendall, P. C. (1986). Cognitive clinical psychology: Implications of an information-processing perspective. In R. E. Ingram (Ed.), *Information processing approaches to clinical psychology* (pp. 3–21). Orlando, FL: Academic Press.

Irwin, C., Evans, D. L., & Andrews, L. W. (2007). *Monochrome days.* Oxford, UK: Oxford University Press.

Ivey, M. L., Heflin, J., & Alberto, P. (2004). The use of social stories to promote independent behaviors in novel events for children with PDD-NOS. *Focus on Autism and Other Developmental Disabilities, 19,* 164–176.

Jacobson, E. (1938). *Progressive relaxation.* Chicago: University of Chicago Press.

James, I. A., Morse, R., & Howarth, A. (2010). The science and art of asking questions in cognitive therapy. *Behavioral and Cognitive Psychotherapy, 38,* 83–93.

Jamieson, P. E. (with Rynn, M. A.). (2006). *Mind race.* New York: Oxford University Press.

Johnston, C., & Mah, J. W. T. (2008). Child attention deficit/hyperactivity disorder. In J. Hunsley & E. J. Mash (Eds.), *A guide to assessments that work* (pp. 17–40). New York: Oxford.

Jolly, J. B. (1993). A multimethod test of the content-specificity hypothesis in young adolescents. *Journal of Anxiety Disorders, 7,* 223–233.

Jolly, J. B., & Dyckman, R. A. (1994). Using self-report data to differentiate anxious and depressive symptoms in adolescents: Cognitive content specificity and global distress. *Cognitive Therapy and Research, 18,* 25–37.

Jolly, J. B., & Kramer, T. A. (1994). The hierarchical arrangement of internalizing cognitions. *Cognitive Therapy and Research, 18,* 1–14.

Kafka, F. (1925). *The trial.* Berlin, Germany: Schocken.

Kail, R.V., & Cavanaugh, J. C. (2009). *Human development* (5th ed.). Florence, KY: Wadsworth.

Kamphaus, R. W., VanDeventer, M. C., Brueggemann, A., & Barry, M. (2006). Behavior Assessment System for Children. In S. R. Smith & L. Handler (Eds.), *The clinical assessment of children and adolescents* (2nd ed., pp. 311–326). New York: Erlbaum.

Kanfer, F. H., & Phillips, J. S. (1970). *Learning foundations of behavior therapy.* New York: John Wiley.

Kant, J. D., Franklin, M., & Andrews, L. W. (2008). *The thought that counts: A firsthand account of one teenager's experience with obsessive-compulsive disorder.* NY: Oxford University Press.

Kapalka, G. M. (2007). *Parenting your out of control child: An effective, easy-to-use program for teaching self-control.* Oakland, CA: New Harbinger.

Kashdan, T. B., Barrios, V., Forsyth, J. P., & Steger, M. F. (2006). Experiential avoidance as a generalized psychological vulnerability comparison with coping and regulation strategies. *Behaviour Research and Therapy, 54,* 1301–1320.

Kazdin, A. E. (2001). *Behavior modification in applied settings* (6th ed.). Stanford, CT: Wadsworth.

Kazdin, A. E. (2008). *The Kazdin method for parenting the defiant child.* Boston: Houghton Mifflin.

Kazdin, A. E., Rodgers, A., & Colbus, D. (1986). The Hopelessness Scale for Children: Psychometric characteristics and concurrent validity. *Journal of Consulting and Clinical Psychology, 54,* 241–245.

Kazdin, A. E. & J. R. Weisz (Eds.). (2003). *Evidence-based psychotherapies for children and adolescents.* New York: Guilford Press.

Kearney, C., & Albano, A. M. (2007). *When children refuse to go to school.* Oxford, England: Oxford University Press.

Kearney, C. A. (2007). *Getting your child to say "yes" to school.* New York: Guilford Press.

Kearney, C. A., & Silverman, W. K. (1993). Measuring the function of school refusal behavior: The School Refusal Assessment Scale. *Journal of Clinical Child Psychology, 22,* 85–96.

Keegan, K. (with Moss, H. B.). (2008). *Chasing the high.* New York: Oxford University Press.

Kendall, P. C. (1990). *Coping cat workbook.* Ardmore, PA: Workbook.

Kendall, P. C. (1992). *Coping cat workbook.* Ardmore, PA: Workbook.

Kendall, P. C. (1998). Directing misperceptions: Researching the issues facing manual-based treatments. *Clinical Psychology: Science and Practice, 5,* 396–399.

Kendall, P. C. (2006). Guiding theory for therapy with children and adolescents. In P. C. Kendall (Ed.), *Child and adolescent therapy: Cognitive behavioral procedures* (3rd ed., pp. 3–30). New York: Guilford Press.

Kendall, P. C., Aschenbrand, S. G., & Hudson, J. L. (2003). Child-focused treatment of anxiety. In A. E. Kazdin & J. R. Weisz (Eds.), *Evidence-based psychotherapies for children and adolescents* (pp. 81–100). New York: Guilford.

Kendall, P. C., & Beidas, R. (2007). Smoothing the trail for dissemination of evidence-based practices for youth: Flexibility within fidelity. *Professional Psychology: Research and Practice, 38*, 13–20.

Kendall, P. C., Chansky, T. E., Kane, M. T., Kim, R. S., Kortlander, E., Ronan, K., ... Siqueland, L. (1992). *Anxiety disorders in youth: Cognitive-behavioral interventions.* Boston: Allyn & Bacon.

Kendall, P. C., Choudhury, M., Hudson, J. L., & Webb, A. (2002). *The C. A. T. Project.* Ardmore, PA: Workbook Publishing.

Kendall, P. C., Chu, B., Gifford, A., Hayes, C., & Nauta, M. (1998). Breathing life into a manual. *Cognitive-Behavioral Practice, 5*, 89–104.

Kendall, P. C., Comer, J. S., Marker, C. D., Creed, T. A., Puliafico, A. C., Hughes, A. A., ... Hudson, J. (2009). In session exposure tasks and therapeutic alliance across the treatment of childhood anxiety disorders. *Journal of Consulting and Clinical Psychology, 77*, 517–525.

Kendall, P. C., Flannery-Schroeder, E., Panichelli-Mindel, S. M., Southam-Gerow, M., Henin, A., & Warman, M. (1997). Therapy for youths with anxiety disorders: A second randomized trial. *Journal of Consulting and Clinical Psychology, 65*, 366–380.

Kendall, P. C., Gosch, E., Furr, J., & Sood, E. (2008). Flexibility within fidelity. *Journal of American Academy of Child and Adolescent Psychiatry, 47*, 987–993.

Kendall, P., Robin, J., Hedtke, K., Suveg, C., Flannery-Schroeder, E., & Gosch, E. (2005). Considering CBT with anxious youth? Think exposures. *Cognitive and Behavioral Practice, 12*, 136–150.

Kendall, P. C., & Suveg, C. (2006). Treating anxiety disorders in youth. In P. C. Kendall (Ed.), *Child and adolescent therapy: Cognitive behavioral procedures* (3rd ed., pp. 243–294). New York: Guilford Press.

Kennerley, H. (2004). Self-injurious behavior. In J. Bennett-Levy, G. Butler, M. Fennell, A. Hackmann, M. Mueller, & D. Westbrook (Eds.), *Oxford guide to behavioural experiments in cognitive therapy* (pp. 373–392). Oxford, UK: Oxford.

King, N. J., Molloy, G. N., Heyne, D., Murphy, G. C., & Ollendick, T. H. (1998). Emotive imagery treatment for childhood phobias: A credible and empirically validated intervention. *Behavioral and Cognitive Psychotherapy, 26,* 103–113.

King, N. J., Muris, P., & Ollendick, T. H. (2005). Childhood fears and phobias: Assessment and treatment. *Child and Adolescent Mental Health, 10,* 50–56.

Kisiel, C., Blaustein, M., Spinazzola, J., Schmidt, C. S., Zucker, M., & Van der Kolk, B. (2006). Evaluation of a theater-based youth violence prevention program for elementary school children. *Journal of School Violence, 5,* 19–36.

Klonsky, E. D., & Muehlenkamp, J. J. (2007). Self-injury: A research review for the practitioner. *Journal of Clinical Psychology, 63,* 1045–1056.

Knell, S. M. (1993). *Cognitive-behavior play therapy.* Northvale, NJ: Jason Aronson.

Kobin, C., & Tyson, E. (2006). Thematic analysis of hip-hop music: Can hip-hop therapy facilitate empathic connection when working with clients in urban settings? The *Arts in Psychotherapy, 33,* 343–356.

Koeppen, A. S. (1974). Relaxation training for children. *Journal of Elementary School Guidance and Counseling, 9,* 14–21.

Kollman, D. M., Brown, T. A., & Barlow, D. H. (2009). The construct validity of acceptance: A multitrait-multimethod investigation. *Behavior Therapy, 40,* 205–218.

Kovacs, M. (1985). The Children's Depression Inventory. *Psychopharmacology Bulletin, 21,* 995–998.

Kovacs, M. (1992). *Children's Depression Inventory.* North Tonawanda, NY: Multi-Health Systems.

Krain, A. L., & Kendall, P. C. (2000). The role of parental emotional distress in parent report of child anxiety. *Journal of Clinical Child Psychology, 29,* 328–335.

Krasny, L., Williams, B. J., Provencal, S., & Ozonoff, S. (2003). Social skills interventions for the autism spectrum: Essential ingredients and a model curriculum. *Child and Adolescent Psychiatric Clinics of North America, 12,* 107–122.

Kretzmer, H. (1988). *Stars.* [CD: Les Miserables] United Kingdom: Alain Boubil Music Ltd.

Kuehlwein, K. T. (2000). Enhancing creativity in cognitive therapy. *Journal of Cognitive Psychotherapy, 14,* 175–188.

Kuyken, W., Padesky, C. A., & Dudley, R. (2008a). *Collaborative case formulation working effectively with clients in cognitive-behavioral therapy.* New York: Guilford.

Kuyken, W., Padesky, C. A., & Dudley, R. (2008b). The science and practice of case conceptualization. *Behavioral and Cognitive Psychotherapy, 36,* 757–768.

Lageman, A. G. (1989). Socrates and psychotherapy. *Journal of Religion and Health, 28,* 219–223.

LaGravenese, R. (Director). (2007). *Freedom writers.* [Motion picture]. USA: Paramount Pictures, Double Feature Films, MTV Films, Jersey Films, Kernos Film Productions Gesellschalf & Co.

LaGreca, A. M., & Stone, W. L. (1993). Social Anxiety Scale for Children—Revised: Factor structure and concurrent validity. *Journal of Clinical and Child Psychology, 22,* 7–27.

Lamb-Shapiro, J. (2000). *The bear who lost his sleep.* Plainview, NY: Childswork/Childsplay.

Landy, R. J. (2008). *The couch and the stage.* New York: Guilford Press.

Larson, J., & Lochman, J. E. (2002). *Helping school children cope with anger: A cognitive behavioral intervention.* New York: Guilford.

Last, C. G. (2006). *Help for worried kids.* New York: Guilford Press.

Laurent, J., & Stark, K. D. (1993). Testing the cognitive content-specificity hypothesis with anxious and depressed youngsters. *Journal of Abnormal Psychology, 102,* 226–237.

Layden, M. A., Newman, C. F., Freeman, A., & Morse, S. (1993). *Cognitive therapy of borderline personality disorder.* Boston: Allyn & Bacon.

Lazarus, A., & Fay, A. (1975). *I can if I want to.* New York: Warner Books.

Lazarus, A. A., & Abramovitz, A. (1962). The use of "emotive imagery" in the treatment of children's phobias. *Journal of Mental Science, 108,* 191–195.

Leahy, R. L. (2001). *Overcoming resistance in cognitive therapy.* New York: Guilford.

Leahy, R. L. (2007). Emotion and psychology. *Clinical Psychology: Science and Practice, 14,* 353–357.

Lefrancois, G. R. (1986). *Of children* (5th ed.). Belmont, CA: Wadsworth.

Lemanek, L., Kamps, J., & Chung, N. B. (2001). Empirically supported treatments in pediatric psychology: Regimen adherence. *Journal of Pediatric Psychology, 26,* 253–275.

Lerman, D. C., & Iwata, B. A. (1996). Developing a technology for use of operant extinction in clinical settings: An examination of basic and applied research. *Journal of Applied Behavioral Analysis, 29,* 345–382.

Lezine, D. A., & Brent, D. (2007). *Eight stories up.* New York: Oxford University Press.

Lincoln, A., Swift, E., & Shorteno-Fraser, M. (2008). Psychological adjustment and treatment of children with parents deployed in military combat. *Journal of Clinical Psychology, 64,* 984–992.

Linehan, M. M. (1993). *Cognitive behavioral treatment for borderline personality disorder.* New York: Guilford Press.

Liotti, G. (1987). The resistance to change of cognitive structures: A counter proposal to psychoanalytic metapsychology. *Journal of Cognitive Psychotherapy, 1,* 87–104.

Lipmann, W. (1992). *Public opinion.* New York: Harcourt Brace.

Lippa, A. (2010). *Move toward the darkness.* New York: Lippa Songs.

Lochman, J. E., Barry, T. D., & Pardini, D. A. (2003). Anger control training for aggressive youth. In A. E. Kazdin, & J. E. Weisz (Eds.), *Evidence-based psychotherapies for children and adolescents* (pp. 263–281). New York: Guilford Press.

Lochman, J. E., Boxmeyer, C. L., Powell, N. P., Barry, T. D., Pardini, D. A. (2010). Anger control training for aggressive youth. In J. R. Weisz & A. E. Kazdin (Eds.), *Evidence-based psychotherapies for children and adolescents* (2nd ed., pp. 227–242). New York: Guilford.

Lochman, J. E., & Wells, K. C. (2002a). Contextual social cognitive mediators and child outcome: A test of the theoretical model in the Coping Power program. *Developmental and Psychopathology, 14,* 945–967.

Lochman, J. E., & Wells, K. C. (2002b). The Coping Power Program at middle school transition: Universal and indicated prevention effects. *Psychology of Addictive Behaviors, 16,* 540–554.

Lochman, J. E., Wells, K. C., & Lenhart, L. A. (2008). *Coping Power program.* New York: Oxford University Press.

Lock, J., & LeGrange, K. (2005). *Help your teenager beat an eating disorder.* New York: Guilford Press.

Lockshin, S. B., Gillis, J. M., & Romanczyk, R. G. (2005). *Helping your child with autism spectrum disorder: A step by step workbook for families.* Oakland, CA: New Harbinger.

Loeber, R., Green, S. M., Lahey, B. B., & Stouthamer-Loeber, M. (1991). Differences and similarities between children, mothers, and teachers as informants on disruptive child behavior. *Journal of Abnormal Child Psychology, 19*, 75–95.

Lombardo, C., Milne, D., & Proctor, R. (2009). Getting to the heart of clinical supervision: A theoretical review of emotions in professional development. *Behavioral and Cognitive Psychotherapy, 37*, 207–219.

Magis, W. (2004). Urban improv: A portrait of an educational drama organization. *Youth Theater Journal, 18*, 30–44.

Mahoney, M. J., & Thoresen, C. E. (1974). *Self-control: Power to the person*. Monterrey, CA: Brooks/Cole.

March, J. (1997a). *MASC: Multidimensional Anxiety Scale for Children technical manual*. North Tonawanda, NY: MHS.

March, J. S. (1997b). *Multidimensional Anxiety Scale for Children*. New York: Multi-Health Systems.

March, J. S. (with Benton, C. M.). (2007). *Talking back to OCD*. New York: Guilford Press.

March, J. (2009). The future of psychotherapy for mentally ill children and adolescents. *Journal of Child Psychology and Psychiatry, 50*, 170–179.

March, J. S., & Franklin, M. E. (2006). Cognitive-behavioral therapy for pediatric OCD. In B. O. Rothbaum (Ed.), *Pathological anxiety: Emotional processing in etiology and treatment* (pp. 147–165). New York: Guilford Press.

March, J. S., & Mulle, K. (1998). *OCD in children and adolescents*. New York: Guilford Press.

March, J. S., Parker, J. D. A., Sullivan, K., Stallings, P., & Connors, K. (1997). The Multidimensional Anxiety Scale for Children (MASC): Factor structure, reliability, and validity. *Journal of the American Academy of Child and Adolescent Psychiatry, 40*, 780–786.

March, J., Silva, S., Vitiello, B., & the TADS Team. (2006). The treatment for adolescents with depression study (TADS): Methods and message at 12 weeks. *Journal of American Academy of Child and Adolescent Psychiatry, 45*, 1393–1403.

March, J. S., Sullivan, K., & James, P. (1999). Test-retest reliability of the Multidimensional Anxiety Scale for Children. *Journal of Anxiety Disorders, 13*, 349–358.

Marcinko, L. (2003). Medication compliance with difficult patients. In R. L. Leahy (Ed.), *Roadblocks in cognitive-behavioral therapy* (pp. 318–340). New York: Guilford.

Marien, W. E., Storch, E. A., Geffken, G. R., & Murphy, T. K. (2009). Intensive family-based cognitive-behavioral therapy for pediatric obsessive-compulsive disorder: Applications for treatment of medication partial- or nonresponders. *Cognitive and Behavioral Practice, 16*, 304–316.

Marsella, A. J., & Yamada, A. M. (2000). Culture and mental health: An introduction and overview of foundations, concepts, and issues. In I. Cuellar & F. A. Paniagua (Eds.), *Handbook of multicultural mental health: Assessment and treatment of diverse populations* (pp. 3–44). San Diego, CA: Academic Press.

Mash, E. J., & Dozois, D. J. A. (2003). Child psychopathology: A developmental-systems perspective. In E. J. Mash & R. A. Barkley (Eds.), *Child psychopathology* (2nd ed., pp. 3–71). New York: Guilford Press.

Massad, P. M., & Hulsey, T. L. (2006). Exposure therapy renewed. *Journal of Psychotherapy Integration, 16*, 417–428.

Masters, J. C., Burish, T. G., Hollon, S. D., & Rimm, D. C. (1987). *Behavior therapy: Techniques and empirical findings* (2nd ed.). San Diego, CA: Harcourt Brace Jovanovich.

Mayberry, R. M., Mili, F., & Ofili, E. (2000). Racial and ethnic differences in areas of medical care. *Medical Care Research and Review, 57*, 108–145.

McAuliffe, G. (2008). What is culturally alert counseling? In G. McAuliffe (Ed.), *Culturally alert counseling: A comprehensive introduction* (pp. 2–44). Thousand Oaks, CA: Sage.

McAuliffe, G., Gomez, E., & Grothaus, T. (2008). Race. In G. McAuliffe (Ed.), *Culturally alert counseling: A comprehensive introduction* (pp. 105–145). Thousand Oaks, CA: Sage.

McAuliffe, G., Kim, B. S. K., & Park, Y. S. (2008). Ethnicity. In G. McAuliffe (Ed.), *Culturally alert counseling: A comprehensive introduction* (pp. 84–104). Thousand Oaks, CA: Sage.

McHolm, A. E., Cunningham, C. E., & Vanier, M. K. (2005). *Helping your child with selective mutism: Practical steps to overcome a fear of speaking*. Oakland, CA: New Harbinger.

McIntosh, P. (1998). White privilege and male privilege: A personal account of coming to see correspondence through work in women's studies. In M. L. Anderson & P. H. Collins (Eds.), *Race, class, and gender: An anthology* (pp. 94–105). New York: Wadsworth.

McKay, D., & Moretz, M. W. (2008). Interoceptive cue exposure for depersonalization: A case series. *Cognitive and
Behavioral Practice, 15,* 435–439.

McKay, D., Storch, E., Nelson, B., Morales, M., & Moretz, M.
(2009). Obsessive-compulsive disorder in children and
adolescents: Treating difficult cases. In D. McKay & E. A.
Storch (Eds.), *Cognitive-behavior therapy for children:
Treating complex and refractory cases* (pp. 81–113). New
York: Springer Publishing Co.

McMahon, R. J., & Kotler, J. S. (2006). Conduct problems. In
D. A. Wolfe & E. J. Mash (Eds.), *Behavioral and emo-
tional disorders in adolescents* (pp. 153–225). New York:
Guilford Press.

McNally, R. J. (2007). Mechanisms of exposure therapy: How
neuroscience can improve psychological treatments
for anxiety disorders. *Clinical Psychology Review, 27,*
750–759.

Meichenbaum, D. H. (1985). *Stress inoculation training.* New
York: Pergamon Press.

Milne, D. (2008). CBT supervision: From reflexivity to spe-
cialization [Special issue]. *Behavioural and Cognitive
Psychotherapy., 36(6),* 779–786.

Mineka, S., & Thomas, C. (1999). Mechanisms of change in
exposure therapy for anxiety disorders. In T. Dagleish
& M. Power (Eds.), *Handbook of cognition and emotion*
(pp. 747–764). New York: Wiley.

Mooney, K. A., & Padesky, C. A. (2000). Applying client creativity to recurrent problems: Constructing possibilities and
tolerating doubt. *Journal of Cognitive Psychotherapy, 14,*
149–162.

Morris, R. J., & Kratochwill, T. R. (1998). Childhood fears and
phobias. In R. J. Morris & T. R. Kratochwill (Eds.), *The
practice of child therapy* (3rd ed., pp. 91–132). Boston:
Allyn & Bacon.

Moscovitch, D. A., Antony, M. M., & Swinson, R. P. (2009).
Exposure-based treatments for anxiety disorders: Theory
and process. In M. M. Antony & M. B. Stein (Eds.), *Oxford
handbook of anxiety and related disorders* (pp. 461–475).
New York: Oxford.

Moses, E. B., & Barlow, D. H. (2006). A new unified treatment
approach for emotional disorders based on emotion science. *Current Direction in Psychological Science, 15,*
146–150.

Muris, P., Merckelbach, H., Van Brakel, A., & Mayer, B. (1999). The revised version of the Screen for Child Anxiety Related Emotional Disorder (SCARED-R): Further evidence for its reliability and validity. *Anxiety, Stress, and Coping, 12*, 411–425.

Murphy, V. B., & Christner, R. W. (2006). A cognitive-behavioral case conceptualization approach for working with children and adolescents. In R. B. Mennuti, A. Freeman, & R. W. Christner (Eds.), *Cognitive-behavioral interventions in educational settings* (pp. 37–64). New York: Routledge.

Myers, K., & Winters, N. C. (2002). Ten-year review of rating scales: II. Scales for internalizing disorders. *Journal of the American Academy of Child and Adolescent Psychiatry, 41*, 634–659.

Myles, B. S. (2003). Behavioral forms of stress management for individuals with Asperger syndrome. *Child and Adolescent Psychiatric Clinics of North America, 12*, 123–141.

Najman, J. M., Williams, G. M., Nikles, J., Spence, S., Bor, W., & O'Callaghan, M. (2000). Mothers' mental illness and child behavior problems: Cause-effect association or observation bias? *Journal of the American Academy of Child and Adolescent Psychiatry, 39*, 592–602.

Nass, M. (2000). *The lion who lost his roar*. Plainview, NY: Childswork/Childsplay.

Neenan, M. (2009). *Developing resilience: A cognitive-behavioral approach*. London: Routledge.

Nelson, W. M., & Finch, A. J. (2000). *Children's Inventory of Anger (CHIA): Manual*. Los Angeles, CA: Western Psychological Services.

Nelson, W. M., Finch, A. J., & Ghee, A. C. (2006). Anger management with children and adolescents: Cognitive behavioral therapy. In P. C. Kendall (Ed.), *Child and adolescent therapy: Cognitive-behavioral procedures* (3rd ed., pp. 114–168). New York: Guilford.

Newman, C. F. (1994). Understanding client resistance: Methods for enhancing motivation to change. *Cognitive and Behavioral Practice, 1*, 47–70.

Newman C. F. (1997). Maintaining professionalism in the face of emotional abuse from clients. *Cognitive Behavioral Practice, 4*, 1–30.

Newman, C. F. (2003). Bipolar disorder. In R. L. Leahy (Ed.), *Roadblocks in cognitive behavioral therapy: Transforming challenges into opportunities for change* (pp. 153–174). New York: Guilford.

Nezu, A. M., & Nezu, C. M. (1989). Clinical decision making in the practice of behavioral therapy. In A. M. Nezu & C. M. Nezu (Eds.), *Clinical decision making in behavior therapy* (pp. 57–113). Champaign, IL: Research Press.

Nezu, A. M., Saad, R., & Nezu, C. M. (2000). Clinical decision making in behavioral supervision: "...And how does that make you feel?" *Cognitive and Behavioral Practice, 7*, 338–342.

Nock, M. K., & Prinstein, M. J. (2004). A functional approach to the assessment of self-mutilative behavior. *Journal of Consulting and Clinical Psychology, 72*, 885–890.

Nock, M. K., Teper, R., & Hollander, M. (2007). Psychological treatment of self-injury among adolescents. *Journal of Clinical Psychology, 63*, 1081–1089.

Novaco, R. W. (2003). *The Novaco Anger Scale and Provocation Inventory (NAS-PI).* Los Angeles, CA: Western Psychological Services.

Oatley, K., & Keltner, D., & Jenkins, J. M. (2006). *Understanding emotions.* New York: Blackwell.

Olatuniji, B. O., Deacon, B. J., & Abramowitz, J. S. (2009). The cruelest cure: Ethical issues in the implementation of exposure-based treatments. *Cognitive and Behavioral Practice, 16*, 172–180.

Ollendick, T. H. (1983). Reliability and validity of the Revised Fear Survey Schedule for Children-R. *Behavior Research and Therapy, 21*, 395–399.

Ollendick, T. H., & Cerny, J. A. (1981). *Clinical behavior therapy with children.* New York: Plenum Press.

Ollendick, T. H., King, N. J., & Frary, R. B. (1989). Fears in children and adolescents: Reliability and generalizability across gender, age, and nationality. *Behaviour Research and Therapy, 27*, 19–26.

Ong, S. H., & Caron, A. (2008). Family-based psychoeducation for children and adolescents with mood disorders. *Journal of Child and Family Studies, 17*, 809–822.

Orlinsky, D. E., & Ronnestad, M. H. (2005). *How psychotherapists develop: A study of therapeutic work and professional growth.* Washington, DC: American Psychological Association.

Osman, A., Downs, W. R., Kopper, B. A., Barrios, F. X., Baker, M. T., Osman, J. R., ... Linehan, M.M. (1998). The Reasons for Living Inventory for Adolescents (RFL-A): Development and psychometric properties. *Journal of Clinical Psychology, 54*, 1063–1078.

Osman, A., Kopper, B. A., Barrios, F. X., Osman, J. R., Besett, T., & Linehan, M. M. (1996). The Brief Reasons for Living Inventory for Adolescents (BRFL-A). *Journal of Abnormal Child Psychology, 24,* 433–443.

Otto, M., & Hinton, D. (2006). Modifying exposure-based CBT for Cambodian refugees with posttraumatic stress disorder. *Cognitive and Behavioral Practice, 13,* 261–270.

Overbeck, J. R. (2010). Concepts and historical perspectives on powers. In A. Guinote & T. K. Vescio (Eds.), *The social psychology of power* (pp. 19–45). New York: Guilford.

Overholser, J. C. (1987). Facilitating autonomy in passive-dependent persons: An integrative model. *Journal of Contemporary Psychotherapy, 17,* 251–269.

Overholser, J. C. (1991). The Socratic method as a technique in psychotherapy supervision. *Professional Psychology, 22,* 68–74.

Overholser, J. C. (1993a). Elements of the Socratic method: I. Systematic questioning. *Psychotherapy, 30,* 67–74.

Overholser, J. C. (1993b). Elements of the Socratic method: II. Inductive reasoning. *Psychotherapy, 30,* 75–85.

Overholser, J. C. (1994). Elements of the Socratic method: III. Universal definitions. *Psychotherapy, 31,* 286–293.

Overholser, J. C. (1995). Cognitive-behavioral treatment of depression, part I: Assessment of depression and suicide risk. *Journal of Contemporary Psychotherapy, 25,* 185–204.

Overholser, J. C. (1996). Elements of the Socratic method: V. Self-improvement. *Psychotherapy, 4,* 549–559.

Overholser, J. C. (1999). Elements of the Socratic method: VI. Promoting virtue in everyday life. *Psychotherapy, 36,* 137–145.

Padesky, C. A. (1988). *Intensive training series in cognitive therapy.* Workshop series presented at Newport Beach, CA.

Padesky, C. A. (1993, September). *Socratic questioning: Changing minds or guided discovery.* Keynote address at the meeting of the European Congress of Behavioral and Cognitive Psychotherapies, London, UK.

Padesky, C. A. (1994). Schema change processes in cognitive therapy. *Clinical Psychology and Psychotherapy, 1,* 267–278.

Padesky, C. A. (1996). Developing cognitive therapist competency. Teaching and supervision models. In P. M. Salkovskis (Ed.), *Frontiers of cognitive therapy* (pp. 266–292). New York: Guilford.

Padesky, C. A. (2004). Behavioral experiments: At the crossroads. In J. Bennett-Levy, G. Butler, M. Fennell, A. Hackman, M. Mueller, & D. Westbrook (Eds.), *Oxford guide to behavioral experiments in cognitive therapy* (pp. 433–438). Oxford, UK: Oxford University Press.

Padesky, C. A. (2007, July). *The next frontier: Building positive qualities with cognitive behavior therapy*. Invited address presented at the 5th World Congress of Behavioral and Cognitive Therapies, Barcelona, Spain.

Paolo, S. B. (1998). Receiving supervision in cognitive therapy: A personal account. *Journal of Cognitive Psychotherapy, 12*, 153–162.

Parrott, W. G. (2002). The functional utility of negative emotions. In L. F. Barrett & P. Salovey (Eds.), *The wisdom of feeling* (pp. 341–362). New York: Guilford.

Patterson, G. R. (1975). *Families: Applications of social learning to family life* (2nd ed.). Champaign, IL: Research Press.

Patterson, G. R. (1976). *Living with children.* Champaign, IL: Research Press.

Patterson, G. R., & White, G. D. (1969). It's a small world: The application of "Time-out from positive reinforcement." *Oregon Psychological Association Newsletter, 15(Suppl.),* 2.

Patterson, H. O., & O'Connell, D. E. (2003). Recovery maintenance and relapse prevention with chemically dependent adolescents. In M. A. Reinecke, F. M. Dattilio, & A. Freeman (Eds.), *Cognitive therapy with children and adolescents* (2nd ed., pp. 70–94). New York: Guilford.

Pediatric OCD Treatment Study (POTS) Team. (2004). Cognitive-behavior therapy, sertraline, and their combination for children and adolescents with obsessive-compulsive disorder: The Pediatric OCD Treatment Study (POTS) randomized controlled trial. *Journal of the American Medical Association, 292,* 1969–1976.

Pelham, W. E., Fabiano, G. A., & Massetti, G. M. (2005). Evidence-based assessment of attention deficit hyperactivity disorder in children and adolescents. *Journal of Clinical Child and Adolescent Psychology, 34,* 449–476.

Perris, C. (1989). *Cognitive therapy with schizophrenic patients.* New York: Guilford.

Persons, J. B. (1989). *Cognitive therapy in practice.* New York: Norton.

Persons, J. B. (1995, November). *Cognitive-behavioral case for-mulation*. Workshop presented at the annual meeting of the Association for Advancement of Behavior Therapy, Washington, DC.

Persons, J. B. (2008). *The case formulation approach to cogni-tive-behavioral therapy*. New York: Guilford Press.

Phares, E. J. (1988). *Introduction to personality* (2nd ed.). Glenview, IL: Scott, Foresman, and Company.

Phillips, D., Fischer, S. C., & Singh, R. (1977). A children's rein-forcement survey schedule. *Journal of Behavior Therapy and Experimental Psychiatry, 8,* 131–134.

Phinney, J. S. (1990). Ethnic identity in adolescents and adults: Review of research. *Psychological Bulletin, 108*, 499–514.

Phinney, J. S., & Chavira, V. (1995). Parental ethnic socialization and adolescent coping with problems related to ethnicity. *Journal of Research on Adolescence, 5*, 31–53.

Piacentini, J., & Bergman, R. L. (2001). Developmental issues in cognitive therapy for childhood anxiety disorders. *Journal of Cognitive Psychotherapy, 15*, 165–182.

Piacentini, J. C., Langley, A. K., & Roblek, T. (2007a). *Cognitive-behavioral treatment of childhood OCD: It's only a false alarm (Therapist guide)*. New York: Oxford University Press.

Piacentini, J. C., Langley, A. K., & Roblek, T. (2007b). *Cognitive-behavioral treatment of childhood OCD: It's only a false alarm (Workbook)*. New York: Oxford University Press.

Piacentini, J. C., March, J. S., & Franklin, M. E. (2006). Cognitive-behavioral therapy for youth with obsessive-compulsive disorder. In P. C. Kendall (Ed.), *Child and adolescent ther-apy: Cognitive-behavioral procedures* (3rd ed., pp. 297–321). New York: Guilford Press.

Pincus, D. B., Ehrenreich, J. T., & Spiegel, D. A. (2008). *Riding the wave*. Oxford, England: University Press.

Pinderhughes, E. (1989). *Understanding race, ethnicity, and power: The key to efficacy in clinical practice*. New York: Free Press.

Plestis, C., Puntillo, T., Olsson, M., & Millgardh. J. (Executive producers). (2010). *A minute to win it* [Television series]. Los Angeles, CA: NBC.

Plizka, S. R. (2003). *Neuroscience for the mental health clini-cian*. New York: Guilford.

Podell, J. L., Mychailyszyn, Edmunds, J., M., Puleo, C. M., & Kendall, P. C. (2010). The coping cat program for anx-ious youth: The FEAR plan comes to life. *Cognitive and Behavioral Practice, 17,* 132–141.

Pretorius, W. M. (2006). Cognitive behavioral supervision: Recommended practice. *Behavioral and Cognitive Psychotherapy, 34,* 413–420.

Purdon, C., & Clark, D. A. (2005). *Overcoming obsessive thoughts.* Oakland, CA: New Harbinger.

Putallaz, M., & Wasserman, A. (1989). Children's naturalistic entry behavior and sociometric status: A developmental perspective. *Developmental Psychology, 25,* 297–305.

Quinn, P. O., & Stern, J. M. (1993). *The putting on the brakes activity book for young people with ADHD.* Washington, DC: Magination Press.

Quinn, P. O., & Stern, S. M. (Eds.). (2000). *50 activities and games for kids with ADHD.* Washington, DC: Magination Press.

Rachman, S. (1977). The conditioning theory of fear acquisition: A critical examination. *Behavior Research and Therapy, 15,* 375–387.

Randall, K., & Bowen, A. (2008). *Mean girls: 101½ strategies and activities for working with relational aggression.* Chapin, SC: Youthlight.

Reddy, L. A., & De Thomas, C. (2007). Assessment of Attention Deficit/Hyperactivity Disorder with children. In S. R. Smith & L. Handler (Eds.), *The clinical assessment of children and adolescents* (pp. 367–390). New York: Guilford.

Reichow, B., & Sabornie, E. J. (2009). Brief report: Increasing verbal greeting intimations for a student with autism via a social story™ intervention. *Journal of Autism and Developmental Disorders, 39,* 1740–1743.

Reilly, C. E. (2000). The role of emotion in cognitive therapy, cognitive therapists, and supervision. *Cognitive and Behavioral Practice, 7,* 343–345.

Reiner, R. (Director). (1992). *A few good men* [Motion picture]. United States: Castle Rock Entertainment and Columbia Pictures.

Reynolds, C. R., & Kamphaus, R. W. (2004). *Behavior Assessment System for Children-2 (BASC-2).* Circle Pines, MN: American Guidance Services.

Reynolds, W. M. (1987). *Suicidal Ideation Questionnaire.* Odessa, FL: Psychological Assessment Resources.

Reynolds, W. M. (1988). *Suicidal Ideation Questionnaire: A professional manual.* Odessa, FL: Psychological Assessment Resources.

Riba, M. B., & Balon, R. (2009). Combining psychotherapy and pharmacotherapy. In R. E. Hales, S. C. Yodofsky, & G. O. Gabbard (Eds.), *Textbook of clinical psychiatry* (5th ed.). Washington, DC: American Psychiatric Association. Retrieved July 28, 2009, from www.psychiatryonline.com.

Richard, D. C. S., & Gloster, A. T. (2007). Exposure therapy has a public relations problem: A dearth of litigation amid a wealth of concern. In D. C. S. Richard & D. L. Lauterbach (Eds.), *Handbook of exposure therapies* (pp. 409–425). San Diego, CA: Academic Press.

Richard, D. C. S., Lauterbach, D., & Gloster, A. T. (2007). Description, mechanisms of action, and assessment. In D. C. S. Richard & D. Lauterbach (Eds.), *Handbook of exposure therapies* (pp. 1–28). New York: Academic Press.

Ridley, C. R., Chih, D. W., Olivera, R. J. (2000). Training in cultural schemas: An antidote to unintentional racism in clinical practice. *American Journal of Orthopsychiatry, 70,* 65–72.

Robin, A. L. (1998). *ADHD in adolescents: Diagnosis and treatment.* New York: Guilford.

Rogers, G. M., Reinecke, M. A., & Curry, J. F. (2005). Case formulation in TADS CBT. *Cognitive and Behavioral Practice, 12,* 198–208.

Rohde, P., Feeny, N. C., & Robins, M. (2005). Characteristics and components of the TADS CBT approach. *Cognitive and Behavioral Practice, 12,* 186–197.

Ronen, T. (1997). Linking developmental and emotional elements into child and family cognitive-behavioural therapy. In P. J. Graham (Ed.), *Cognitive-behaviour therapy for children and families* (pp. 1–17). New York: Cambridge University Press.

Rooyackers, P. (1998). *Drama games for children.* Alameda, CA: Hunter House.

Rosenbaum, M., & Ronen, T. (1998). Clinical supervision from the standpoint of cognitive-behavior therapy. *Psychotherapy, 35,* 220–230.

Rosqvist, J. (2005). *Exposure treatments for anxiety disorders: A practitioner's guide to concepts, methods, and evidence-based practice.* New York: Routledge.

Rosqvist, J. (2008). *Exposure treatments for anxiety disorders.* New York: Routledge Communications.

Rotter, J. B. (1982). *The development and applications of social learning theory.* New York: Praeger.

Rotter, J. B., Chance, J. E., & Phares, E. J. (1972). *Applications of a social learning theory of personality*. New York: Holt, Rinehart, & Winston.

Rouf, K., Fennell, M., Westbrook, D., Cooper, M., & Bennett-Levy, J. (2004). Devising effective experiments. In J. Bennett-Levy, G. Butler, M. Fennell, A. Hackmann, M. Mueller, & D. Westbrook (Eds.), *Oxford guide to behavioral experiments in cognitive therapy* (pp. 21–58). Oxford, England: Oxford.

Rubin, L. C. (Ed.). (2007). *Using superheroes in counseling and play therapy*. New York: Springer.

Rudd, M. D., & Joiner, T. E. (1998). An integrative conceptual framework for assessing and treating suicidal behavior in adolescents. *Journal of Adolescence, 21*, 489–498.

Rutter, J. G., & Friedberg, R. D. (1999). Guidelines for the effective use of Socratic dialogue in cognitive therapy. In L. Vandecreek & T. L. Jackson (Vol. Eds.), *Innovations in clinical practice: A sourcebook* (Vol. 17, pp. 481–490). Sarasota, FL: Professional Resource Press.

Safran, J. D., & Muran, J. C. (2000). Resolving therapeutic alliance ruptures: Diversity and integration. *Journal of Clinical Psychology, 56*, 233–243.

Safran, J. D., & Muran, J. C. (2001). A relational approach to training and supervision in cognitive psychotherapy. *Journal of Cognitive Psychotherapy, 15*, 3–16.

Saigh, P. A. (1987). The use of in vitro flooding package in the treatment of traumatized adolescents. *Journal of Developmental and Behavioral Pediatrics, 10*, 17–21.

Samoilov, A., & Goldfried, M. R. (2000). The role of emotion in cognitive behavior therapy. *Clinical Psychology: Science and Practice, 7*, 373–385.

Santucci, L. C., Ehrenreich, J. T., Trosper, S. E., Bennett, S. M., & Pincus, D. B. (2009). Development and preliminary evaluation of a one-week summer treatment program for separation anxiety disorder. *Cognitive and Behavioral Practice, 16*, 317–331.

Schmidt, J. P. (1979). Psychotherapy supervision: A cognitive-behavioral model. *Professional Psychology: Research and Practice, 9*, 278–283.

Schulte, D., Bochum, R. U., & Eifert, G. H. (2002). What to do when manuals fail? The dual model of psychotherapy. *Clinical Psychology: Science and Practice, 9*, 312–328.

Seligman, M. E. P. (1995). The effectiveness of psychotherapy: The Consumer Reports Study. *American Psychologist, 50*, 965–973.

Seligman, M. E. P., Reivich, K., Jaycox, L., & Gillham, J. (1995). *The optimistic child.* Boston: Houghton & Mifflin.

Shapiro, J. P. (2009). Integrating outcome research and clinical reasoning in psychotherapy planning. *Professional Psychology: Research & Practice, 40,* 46–53.

Shapiro, L. E., & Holmes, J. (2008). *Let's be friends.* Oakland, CA: New Harbinger.

Shapiro, R., Friedberg, R. D., & Bardenstein, K. K. (2005). *Child and adolescent therapy.* New York: Wiley.

Shaw, J., & Barzvi, A. (2005). *Who invented lemonade?: The power of positive perspective.* New York: Universe Inc.

Sheikh, A. I., Milne, D. L., & MacGregor, B. V. (2007). A model of personal professional development in the systematic training of clinical psychologists. *Clinical Psychology and Psychotherapy, 14,* 278–287.

Shelton, D. L. (2000). African-American health study in black in white. *American Medical News, 43.*

Shenk, J. (1993, January). *Cognitive-behavioral therapy of obsessive-compulsive disorder.* Grand rounds presentation at Mesa Vista Hospital, San Diego, CA.

Shepherd, L., & Kuczynski, A. (2009). The use of emotive imagery and behavioral techniques for a 10-year-old boy's nocturnal fear of ghosts and zombies. *Clinical Case Studies, 8,* 99–112.

Sherman, M. (1979). *Personality: Inquiry and application.* New York: Pergamon Press.

Shirk, S., & Karver, M. (2006). Process issues in cognitive-behavioral therapy for youth. In P.C. Kendall (Ed.), *Child and adolescent therapy* (pp. 465–491). New York: Guilford.

Shirk, S. R. (1999). Integrated child psychotherapy: Treatment ingredients in search of a recipe. In S. W. Russ & T. H. Ollendick (Eds.), *Handbook of psychotherapies with children and families* (pp. 369–385). New York: Plenum Press.

Sidley, G. L. (1993). Parasuicide. In N. Tarrier, A. Wells & G. Haddock (Eds.), *Treating complex cases.* New York: John Wiley.

Siegel, D. J. (1999). *The developing mind.* New York: Guilford.

Silverman, W. K., & Kurtines, W. M. (1996). *Anxiety and phobic disorders.* New York: Plenum.

Silverman, W. K., & Kurtines, W. M. (1997). Theory in child psychosocial treatment research: Have it or had it? *Journal of Abnormal Child Psychology, 25,* 359–366.

Silverman, W. K., & Ollendick, T. H. (2005). Evidence-based assessment of anxiety and its disorders in children and adolescents. *Journal of Clinical Child and Adolescent Psychology, 34*, 380–411.

Silverman, W. K., & Rabian, B. (1999). Rating scales for anxiety and mood disorders. In D. Shaffer, C. P. Lucas, & J. E. Richters (Eds.), *Diagnostic assessment in child and adolescent psychopathology* (pp. 127–166). New York: Guilford Press.

Singh, M. K., Pfeifer, J. C., Barzman, D., Kowatch, R. A., & DelBello, M. P. (2007). Pharmacotherapy for child and adolescent mood disorders. *Psychiatric Annals, 37*, 465–476.

Skinner, B. F. (1938). *The behavior of organisms.* New York: Appleton-Century-Crafts.

Skinner, B. F. (1971). *Beyond freedom and dignity.* New York: Knopf.

Sloan, D. M., & Kring, A. M. (2007). Measuring changes in emotion during psychotherapy: Conceptual and methodological issues. *Clinical Psychology: Science and Practice, 14*, 307–322.

Sofronoff, K., & Beaumont, R. (2009). The challenges of working with young people diagnosed with Asperger syndrome. In D. McKay & E. A. Storch (Eds.), *Cognitive-behavior therapy for children: Treating complex and refractory cases* (pp. 421–443). New York: Springer Publishing Co.

Sommers-Flanagan, J., & Sommers-Flanagan, R. (1995). Psychotherapeutic techniques with treatment-resistant adolescents. *Psychotherapy, 32*, 131–140.

Southam-Gerow, M. (2004). Some reasons that mental health treatments are not technologies: Toward treatment development and adaptation outside labs. *Clinical Psychology: Science and Practice, 11*, 186–189.

Southam-Gerow, M., & Kendall, P. C. (2000). A preliminary study of the emotion understanding of youth referred for treatment of anxiety disorders. *Journal of Clinical Child Psychology, 29*, 319–327.

Spiegler, M. D., & Guevremont, D. C. (1998). *Contemporary behavior therapy* (3rd ed.). Pacific Grove, CA: Brooks/Cole.

Spirito, A., & Esposito-Smythers, C. (2006). Addressing adolescent suicidal behavior: Cognitive-behavioral strategies. In P. C. Kendall (Ed.), *Child and adolescent therapy: Cognitive-behavioral procedures* (3rd ed., pp. 217–242). New York: Guilford.

Stallard, P. (2002). *Think good, feel good: A cognitive behavior workbook for children and young people.* Chichester, UK: Wiley.

Stallard, P. (2005). Cognitive behaviour therapy with prepubertal children. In P. Graham (Ed.), *Cognitive behaviour therapy for children and families* (2nd ed., pp. 121–135). Cambridge, UK: Cambridge University Press.

Stampfl, T. G., & Levis, D. G. (1968). Implosive therapy: A behavioral therapy? *Behavioural Research and Therapy, 6,* 31–36.

Stark, K. D. (1990). *Childhood depression: School-based depression.* New York: Guilford Press.

Steer, R. A., Kumar, G. T., Beck, A. T., & Beck, J. S. (2005). Dimensionality of the Beck Youth Inventories with child psychiatric outpatients. *Journal of Psychopathology and Behavioral Assessment, 27,* 123–131.

Sudak, D. M., Beck, J. S., & Wright, J. (2003). Cognitive behavioral therapy: A blueprint for attaining and assessing psychiatry resident competency. *Academic Psychiatry, 27,* 154–159.

Sue, S. (1998). In search of cultural competence in psychotherapy and counseling. *American Psychologist, 53,* 440–448.

Sue, D. W., & Sue, D. (1999). *Counseling the culturally different: Theory and practice.* New York: John Wiley.

Suveg, C., Kendall, P. C., Comer, J. S., & Robin, J. (2006). Emotion-focused cognitive-behavioral therapy for anxious youth: A multiple-baseline evaluation. *Journal of Contemporary Psychotherapy, 36,* 77–86.

Swanson, J. M., Sandman, C. A., Deutsch, C. K., & Baren, M. (1983). Methylphenidate hydrochloride given with or before breakfast: I. Behavioral, cognitive, and electrophysiologic effects. *Pediatrics, 72,* 49–55.

Tasman, A., Riba, M. B., & Silk, K. R. (2000). *The doctor–patient relationship in pharmacotherapy.* New York: Guilford.

Tharp, R. G. (1991). Cultural diversity and treatment of children. *Journal of Consulting and Clinical Psychology, 59,* 799–812.

Thase, M. E., & Beck, A. T. (1993). Overview of cognitive therapy. In J. H. Wright, M. E. Thase, A. T. Beck, & J. W. Ludgate (Eds.), *Cognitive therapy with inpatients* (pp. 3–34). New York: Guilford.

The Freedom Writers (with Gruwell, E.). (1999). *The Freedom Writers Diary.* New York: Broadway Books.

Thomas, S. B., & Quinn, S. C. (1991). The Tuskegee Syphilis Study, 1932–1972: Implications for HIV education and AIDS risk education programs in the black community. *American Journal of Public Health, 81,* 1498–1505.

Thompson, T. L. (2002). *Loud lips Lucy.* Citrus Heights, CA: Savor Publishing House.

Thompson, T. L. (2003). *Worry wart Wes.* Citrus Heights, CA: Savor Publishing House.

Thompson, T. L. (2007). *Busy body Bonita.* Citrus Heights, CA: Savor Publishing House.

Thorpe, G. L., & Olson, S. C. (1997). *Behavior therapy* (2nd ed.). Needham Heights, MA: Allyn & Bacon.

Tolin, D. (2009). Alphabet soup: ERP, CT, and ACT for OCD. *Cognitive and Behavioral Practice, 16,* 40–48.

Tompkins, M. A. (1999). Using a case formulation to manage treatment non-response. *Journal of Cognitive Psychotherapy, 13,* 317–330.

Tompkins, M. A. (2004). *Using homework in psychotherapy: Strategies, guidelines, and forms.* New York: Guilford.

Treatment for Adolescents with Depression Study (TADS) Team. (2003). Treatment for adolescents with depression study: Rationale, design, and methods. *Journal of the American Academy of Child and Adolescent Psychiatry, 42,* 531–542.

Treatment for Adolescents with Depression Study (TADS) Team. (2004). Fluoxetine, cognitive-behavioral therapy, and their combination for adolescents with depression. *Journal of the American Medical Association, 292,* 807–820.

Treatment for Adolescents with Depression Study (TADS) Team. (2005). The treatment for adolescents with depression study (TADS): Demographic and clinical characteristics. *Journal of the American Academy of Child & Adolescent Psychiatry, 44,* 28–40.

Treatment for Adolescents with Depression Study (TADS) Team. (2007). Treatment for adolescents with depression study: Long-term effectiveness and safety outcomes. *Archives of General Psychiatry, 64,* 1132–1143.

Trinidad, A. C. (2007). How not to learn cognitive-behavioral therapy. *American Journal of Psychotherapy, 61,* 395–403.

Trochim, W., & Donnelly, J. P. (2006). *The research methods knowledge base.* Mason, OH: Atomic Dog.

Trosper, S. E., Buzzella, B. A., Bennett, S. M., & Ehrenreich, J. T. (2009). Emotion regulation in youth with emotional disorders: Implications for a unified treatment approach. *Clinical Child and Family Psychology Review, 12,* 234–254.

Tyson, E. H. (2002). Hip-hop therapy: An exploratory study of a rap music intervention with at-risk and delinquent youth. *Journal of Poetry Therapy, 15,* 131–144.

Tyson, E. H. (2003). Rap music in social work practice with African-American and Latino youth. *Journal of Human Behavior in the Social Environment, 8,* 1–21.

Van der Oord, S., Lucassen, S., Van Emmerik, A. P., & Emmelkamp, P. M. G. (2010). Treatment of Post-traumatic Stress Disorder in children using cognitive behavioral writing therapy. *Clinical Psychology and Psychotherapy, 17,* 240–249.

Vaughn, B. E., & Jackson, G. (2000, June). *Managing emotional race and ethnic relations training.* Workshop presented at the Annual National Conference on Race and Ethnicity (NCORE) Conference, Santa Fe, NM.

Velting, O. N., Setzer, N. J., & Albano, A. M. (2004). Update on and advances in assessment and cognitive-behavioral treatment of anxiety disorders in children and adolescents. *Professional Psychology Research and Practice, 35,* 42–54.

Verducci, S. (2000). A moral method? Thoughts on cultivating empathy through method acting. *Journal of Moral Education, 29,* 87–99.

Vernon, A. (2007). Application of rational emotive behavior therapy to groups within classrooms and educations settings. In R. W. Christner, J. L. Stewart, & A. Freeman (Eds.), *Handbook of cognitive-behavior group therapy with children and adolescents* (pp. 107–127). New York: Routledge.

Vernon, A., & Al-Mabuk, R. (1995). *What growing up is all about.* Champaign, IL: Research Press.

Waddington, L. (2002). The therapy relationship in cognitive therapy: A review. *Behavioural and Cognitive Psychotherapy, 30,* 179–191.

Wagner, A. P. (2000). *Up and down the worry hill: A children's book about obsessive-compulsive disorder.* Rochester, NY: Lighthouse Press.

Wagner, A. P. (2003). Cognitive behavioral therapy for children and adolescents with obsessive-compulsive disorder. *Brief Therapy and Crisis Intervention, 3,* 291–306.

Waller, G. (2009). Evidence-based treatment and therapist drift. *Behavior Research and Therapy, 47,* 119–127.

Waller, G., Cordery, H., Corstorphine, E., Hinrichsen, H., Lawson, R., Mountford, V., & Russell, K. (2007). *Cognitive behavioral therapy for eating disorders: A comprehensive guide.* Cambridge, UK: Cambridge Press.

Walsh, B. (2007). Clinical assessment of self-injury: A practical guide. *Journal of Clinical Psychology, 63,* 1057–1068.

Walsh, B. T., & Cameron, V. L. (2005). *If your adolescent has an eating disorder.* New York: Oxford University Press.

Warfield, J. R. (1999). Behavioral strategies for hospitalized children. In L. Vandecreek, S. Knapp, & T. L. Jackson (Eds.), *Innovations in clinical practice: A sourcebook* (Vol. 17, pp. 169–182). Sarasota, FL: Professional Resource Press.

Waters, V. (1979). *Color us rational.* NY: Institute for Rational Living.

Waters, V. (1980). *Rational stories for children.* NY: Institute for Rational Living.

Webster's ninth new collegiate dictionary. (1991). Springfield, MA: Miriam Webster Publishing.

Webster-Stratton, C. (1986). *Parents and children series: Videocassette program.* Eugene, OR: Castalia.

Weis, R. (2008). *Introduction to abnormal child and adolescent psychology.* Los Angeles: Sage.

Weiss, C., Singer, S., & Feigenbaum, L. (2006). *Too much, too little, just right.* Los Angeles: Western Psychological Services.

Weisz, J. R. (2004). *Psychotherapy for children and adolescents: Evidence-based treatments and case examples.* New York: Cambridge University Press.

Weisz, J. R., Doss, A. J., & Hawley, K. M. (2005). Youth psychotherapy outcome research: A review and critique of the evidence base. *Annual Review of Psychology, 56,* 337–363.

Weisz, J. R., & Jensen, A. L. (2001). Child and adolescent psychotherapy in research and practice contexts: Review of the evidence and suggestions for improving the field. *European Journal of Child and Adolescent Psychiatry, 10,* 12–18.

Weisz, J. R., Jensen-Doss, A., & Hawley, K. M. (2006). Evidence-based youth psychotherapies versus usual clinical care: A meta-analysis of direct comparisons. *American Psychologist, 61,* 671–689.

Weisz, J. R., Southam-Gerow, M. A., Gordis, E. B., & Connor-Smith, J. (2003). Primary and secondary control training for youth depression: Applying the deployment-focused model of treatment development and testing. In A. E. Kazdin & J. R. Weisz (Eds.), *Evidence-based psychotherapies for children and adolescents* (pp. 165–186). New York: Guilford Press.

Weisz, J. R., Thurber, C., Sweeney, L., Proffitt, V. D., & LeGagnoux, G. L. (1997). Brief treatment of mild to moderate child depression using primary and secondary control enhancement training. *Journal of Consulting and Clinical Psychology, 65,* 703–707.

Wells, A. (1997). *Cognitive therapy of anxiety disorders: A practice manual and conceptual guide.* New York: John Wiley.

Wells, K. C., & Albano, A. M. (2005). Parent involvement in CBT treatment of adolescent depression: Experiences in the Treatment for Adolescents with Depression Study (TADS). *Cognitive and Behavioral Practice, 12,* 209–220.

Wells, K. C., & Forehand, R. (1981). Childhood behavior problems in the home. In S. M. Turner, K. S. Calhoun, & H. E. Adams (Eds.), *Handbook of clinical behavior therapy* (pp. 527–567). New York: Wiley.

Wenzel, A., Brown, C. K., & Beck, A. T. (2008). *Cognitive therapy for suicidal individuals: Scientific and clinical applications.* Washington, DC: APA Books.

Wessely, S., Bryant, R. A., Greenberg, N., Earnshaw, M., Sharpley, J., & Hughes, J. H. (2008). Does psychoeducation help prevent post traumatic psychological distress? *Psychiatry: Interpersonal and Biological Processes, 71,* 287–302.

Westen, D. (1996). *Psychology: Mind, brain, and culture.* New York: John Wiley.

Wexler, D. B. (1991). *The PRISM workbook: A program for innovative self-management.* New York: W. W. Norton.

Wiener, D. J. (1994). *Rehearsals for growth.* New York: W. W. Norton.

Wilens, T. E. (2008). *Straight talk about psychiatric medications for kids* (3rd ed.). New York: Guilford.

Wills, F. (2009). *Beck's cognitive therapy.* London: Routledge.

Wilson, G. T. (1981). Behavioral concepts and treatments of neuroses: Comments on marks. *Behavioral Psychotherapy, 9,* 155–166.

Wolraich, M. L., Feurer, I. D., Hannah, J. N., Baumgaertel, A., & Pinnock, T. Y. (1998). Obtaining systematic teacher reports of disruptive behavior disorders utilizing the DSM-IV. *Journal of Abnormal Child Psychology, 26,* 141–152.

Wolraich, M. L., Lambert, W., Doffing, M. A., Bickman, L., Simmons, T., & Worley, K. (2003). Psychometric properties of the Vanderbilt AHDH Diagnostic Parent Rating Scale in a referred population. *Journal of Pediatric Psychology, 28,* 559–568.

Wright, J. H. (2007). Combined cognitive-behavior therapy and pharmacotherapy. *Journal of Cognitive Psychotherapy, 21,* 3–6.

Wright, J. H., Basco, M. R., & Thase, M. E. (2006). *Learning cognitive-behavior therapy: An illustrated guide.* Washington, DC: American Psychiatric Association.

Wurtzel, E. (1994). *Prozac nation.* New York: Houghton Mifflin.

Yamamoto, J., Silva, J. A., Ferrari, M., & Nukariya, K. (1997). Culture and psychopathology. In G. Johnson-Powell, J. Yamamoto, G. E. Wyatt, & W. Arroyo (Eds.), *Transcultural child development: Psychological assessment and treatment* (pp. 34–57). New York: Wiley.

Young, J. E. (1990). *Cognitive therapy for personality disorders: A schema-focused approach.* Sarasota, FL: Professional Resource Exchange.

Young, J. E. (1994). *Cognitive therapy for personality disorders: A schema-focused approach* (Rev. ed.). Sarasota, FL: Professional Resource Exchange.

Young, J. E., & Beck, A. T. (1980). *Cognitive therapy scale.* Unpublished manuscript. Philadelphia, PA: University of Pennsylvania.

Young, P. R., Grant, P., & DeRubeis, R. J. (2003). Some lessons from group supervision of cognitive therapy for depression. *Cognitive and Behavioural Practice, 10,* 30–40.

Youngstrom, E., Loeber, R., & Stouthamer-Loeber, M. (2000). Patterns and correlates of agreement between parent, teacher, and male adolescent ratings of internalizing and externalizing problems. *Journal of Consulting and Clinical Psychology, 68,* 1038–1050.

Zeckhausen, D. (2008). *Full mouse, empty mouse: A tale of food and feelings.* Washington, DC: Magination Press.

Zeman, J., Cassano, M., Perry-Parrish, C., & Stegall, S. (2006). Emotion regulation in children and adolescents. *Developmental and Behavioral Pediatrics, 27,* 155–168.

Zinbarg, R. E. (2000). Comment on "Role of emotion in cognitive behavior therapy": Some quibbles, a call for greater attention to motivation for change, and implications of adopting a hierarchical model of emotion. *Clinical Psychology: Science and Practice, 7,* 394–399.

Index